# Regulatory Writing:
# An Overview

Edited by Lisa DeTora

ISBN: 978-0-9977697-5-3

Every precaution is taken to ensure accuracy of content; however,
the publisher cannot accept responsibility for the correctness of the
information supplied. At the time of publication, all Internet references
(URLs) in this book were valid. These references are subject to change
without notice.

RAPS Global Headquarters
5635 Fishers Lane, Suite 550
Rockville, MD 20852
USA

RAPS.org

# Foreword

This book concentrates on the writerly aspects of regulatory documentation and is intended to help the novice and to provide a refresher for more seasoned professionals. We collected advice and observations from professional experts working in industry, as consultants, at professional agencies, in contract research organizations and in academia. Their expertise spans all areas of regulatory writing, from chemistry, manufacturing and controls to clinical protocols to publications. Many of these experts emphasize not only the characteristics of high-quality writing but also the ethical and scientific benefits that accrue from keeping such practices in mind throughout research and development.

Regulatory documentation is difficult to do well. A complex field of endeavor, regulatory writing requires knowledge about research, legal requirements, guidance for industry and the basic ethics of drug, vaccine, biologic and device development. Most conceptualizations of regulatory writing limit themselves to full-time experts in medical or clinical documentation. However, nonclinical and CMC writing also are important specialization areas, even though these frequently are learned as adjuncts to regulatory or research professions. Any contributor to regulatory documents must have a basic understanding of such writing, but high-level mastery is rare. An understanding of writing is not enough, nor is subject matter expertise or knowledge of regulations. The best regulatory authors and editors successfully balance content, regulations and writing, information that is constantly changing. Thus, best practice requires continual adjustments and revisions.

Audience needs, like reviewers' concerns, may be easy to overlook under the pressure of deadlines and regulations. Reviewers must be able to find essential information quickly and easily. Teams who compose documentation must demonstrate adequate knowledge about the research area, clinical realities and the development process. Finally, reviewers must be able to locate and understand the benefit to risk analyses for products intended for clinical investigation or use. Thus, readers need authors who appreciate the usefulness of the text and supportive data and clearly articulate findings and data, especially regarding benefits and risks. Regulatory writers must build credible, accurate and helpful stories for their readers. This is one reason mastery of the field is difficult.

Of course, this volume is only a starting point, intended to help set the stage for effective writing, using guidelines to aid in the construction of helpful, complete and concise documentation. The authors have cited relevant guidelines, guidance for industry, publication guides and collaborative efforts to streamline, harmonize and advance the production of high quality regulatory documentation. It has been my privilege to work with this highly talented and professional group. I often have felt humbled by their knowledge, poise under pressure and kind collaboration. We all earnestly hope this volume helps its readers to find their way in this challenging professional landscape.

Lisa DeTora
Assistant Professor, Writing and Composition, Hofstra University, and Guest Faculty, Medical Humanities, Hofstra Northwell Medical School

# Contents

## Section 3: Integrated and Interdisciplinary Documentation

## Section 4: Special Topics

# An Overview of Medical and Regulatory Writing

*By Danny A. Benau, MSOD, PhD*

The evolution of regulatory documentation authoring, submission and review has its roots in the 1980s. That decade marked a time of major change in the way drugs were approved, which occurred alongside advances in document and authoring technology. In the US, legislative Code of Federal Regulations (CFR) actions marked the beginning of significant developments in marketing application requirements that led to the current International Council on Harmonisation (ICH) environment. The rise of better authoring technology included changing from dedicated word processors to networked personal computers, the shift from hard copy submissions to electronic submissions, and changes in the way drug candidate reviews are performed and funded.

I began my career as a regulatory medical writer at a pivotal juncture in the field. In 1991, I answered an advertisement posted by Wyeth-Ayerst Research Inc. on the Prodigy® online service requesting people with doctorates in clinical or life sciences who had published journal articles. At the time, I had been doing postdoctoral work in biology at the University of Pennsylvania and did not know finding employment from an online service was unusual. Being a basic sciences researcher, I had little knowledge of clinical research or medical writing. For example, I was unaware drug development document harmonization was an issue or ICH had begun work that would change my career track before I even started in the industry and would change the face of regulatory writing worldwide.

My first task as a medical writer was to edit Summary Basis of Approval (SBA) documents to be incorporated into New Drug Applications (NDAs) to the US Food and Drug Administration (FDA). At that time, the SBA could be submitted with the NDA and was developed collaboratively with FDA reviewers as part of the drug approval process.[1] Even though I had never heard these terms, working on these documents essentially defined me as a regulatory medical writer from the start.

Many people have entered the regulatory writing profession since then and more recent entrants take for granted what were major changes at the time. The following narrative describes the 1980s' regulatory writing environment and documents some of the key changes and their effects on the regulatory writing landscape.

## Regulatory Medical Writing Defined

Although no single official definition of medical writing in general or regulatory medical writing specifically exists, the easiest subset definitions are by audience. As such, medical writing could be defined as writing for any person, group or organization interested in medical information. That audience would include international and national governmental organizations, medical practitioners at the academic and clinical levels, basic and applied researchers, manufacturers of medical products and products that support them, healthcare payers, insurers, many other professionally interested parties and importantly, if not always, adequately acknowledged, patients. One problem in defining medical writing as texts containing any type of health information is that individuals writing about anything even vaguely medical could call themselves medical writers. Therefore, various organizations involved in medical writing have their own definitions as shown in **Table 1-1**.

There are many other definitions as well.[2–4]

I define medical writers as those who produce text, tables, graphics and output in other media that describe medical (primarily clinical) topics for use in documents such as reports, marketing applications and product labeling directed at regulatory personnel, clinical or medical professionals and general audiences. For me, these topics do not include basic animal research, general science topics or philosophical topics other than those related to the ethics of medicine and the dissemination of medical information. A brief general list of documents produced by medical writers includes clinical study reports (CSRs), abstracts, journal articles, regulatory summaries, investigator brochures, package inserts, monographs, slide decks, sales training materials and white papers. In practice, medical writing is divided into various areas: regulatory writing, or documentation produced in the context of research and development to support marketing applications; promotional writing about and advertising marketed products; educational writing, including continuing medical education and other types of training; and peer-reviewed publications. Many different specialist roles exist under the general umbrella 'medical writer.'

Documents commonly composed by medical writers include:

- clinical study documents
  o clinical protocols, protocols, protocol amendments
  o CSRs, clinical evaluation reports (CERs)
  o Investigator Brochures (IBs)
- marketing authorization and application documents
  o investigational new drug applications (INDs)
  o annual reports, IND annual reports, safety reports
  o New Drug Applications (NDAs—same term for US and Japan), Biologics Licensing Agreement (BLA), Marketing Authorization Application (MAA)
  o submissions, Common Technical Document (CTD), electronic Common Technical Document (eCTD), summary documents
  o regulatory responses, background packages and slide decks
- white papers (also can be from companies) and a variety of miscellaneous documents
- publications
  o abstracts, posters, white papers, manuscripts, slide decks
  o publication planning
- promotional materials
- training materials, medical congress materials
- product labeling

## Writing Process Before ICH

Most histories of regulatory agencies and regulatory affairs record changes in laws such as the CFR in the US or Eudralex from the European Commission (EC), methods of regulatory filings, FDA and other agencies' guidance documents and other regulatory actions. An online search using "history of regulatory affairs" and a country or region's name will bring up multiple sources of such information. Few such histories, however, seem to record the everyday work of the regulatory medical writers tasked with implementing those actions and changes.

When I began my career in 1991, the names of many regulatory documents had not been standardized, and what is now called the CSR was called the "Fully Integrated Statistical and Clinical Report" in the FDA guidance and held various names at different companies.[5] What we now refer to as CSRs could differ in format between therapeutic area groups even within a company. In the author's experience and confirmed by other writers, these variations could be significant.

As is now common, regulatory and medical writers could be organized into specialist departments and/or treated as part of a clinical development team organized by therapeutic area. Writers could, and still may, be part of reporting structures in regulatory affairs, clinical development or medical affairs. In addition to writers, most departments required a complement of support staff including word processing operators (especially before the use of personal computers became common) medical editors, technical editors (as electronic submissions became routine) and administrative support. Other than remote meeting technology advances, the project process probably has not changed much. What have evolved dramatically are the methods by which these documents are created.

In the 1980s and early '90s, unlike current practice, there were no standardized templates. For study reports, a shell could be created by removing text from a previous

**Table 1-1. Medical Writer Definitions**

| Organization | Definition of Medical Writer(s) |
|---|---|
| University of the Sciences Biomedical Writing Program | ...writers who take clinical data that they have either created or received and convert these into information and knowledge for transmission to appropriate audiences; medical writers must be part of the checks and balances on the transmission of information and knowledge on therapies and medical issues.[a] |
| American Medical Writers Association (AMWA) | ...medical communicators who gather, organize, and present information on medicine and health in a manner appropriate to target audiences.[b] |
| Bio-Medicine | ...a specialized writer ... generally not one of the scientists or doctors who performed the research. A medical writer is anyone engaged in communication in the medical or allied professions and sciences.[c] |
| Academic Invest | ...responsible for creating medical documents that provide accurate details about medical information and products. Medical writers must combine their knowledge of science with their understanding of research and writing to present information at the right level for their target audience.[d] |
| Nursing School Degrees | ...write for foundations, associations, hospitals, healthcare systems, pharmaceutical companies, managed care organizations, or websites...content, newsletters, public relations materials, marketing materials, proposals, grants, training manuals, internet content, and of course proofreading or editing these materials.[e] |

a. *University of the Sciences Biomedical Writing; Benau D. Message from the Director. USciences website. http://www.gradschool.usciences.edu/biomedical-writing/message-director. Accessed 14 December 2016.*
b. *American Medical Writers Association. About Medical Communications. AMWA website. http://www.amwa.org/about_med_communications. Accessed 14 December 2016.*
c. *Bio-Medicine. Medical Writing. Bio-Medicine website. http://www.bio-medicine.org/medicine-definition/Medical_writing/. Accessed 14 December 2016.*
d. *Academic Invest. How to Become a Medical Writer. Academic Invest website. http://www.academicinvest.com/science-careers/biology-careers/how-to-become-a-medical-writer. Accessed 14 December 2016.*
e. *Nursing School Degrees. Medical writer/medical editor. Nursing-School-Degrees website. http://www.nursing-school-degrees.com/Nursing-Careers/medical-writer.html. Accessed 14 December 2016.*

CSR, especially if the current document was part of a series, or was created partly from previous headings plus sections from the clinical trial protocol. The sections for which there were no established text or displays usually contained blank tables and suggested subheadings. Once the shell was approved, the document was set for authoring.

As a next step, the information technology department would deliver a hand truck stacked with cartons of computer output printed on continuous-feed green bar paper.[6] The output consisted of summary tables, individual reports and line listings. The writer's task was to transcribe the relevant data from the green bar output into the appropriate parts of the approved document shell. Text was added to describe the data and highlight important elements in the tables. Additional subheadings might be added to provide clarity. Once the data were transcribed and the text produced, a biostatistician was tasked with proofreading the numbers, and the clinical research associate would check the descriptive text and provide commentary on the clinical observations drafted. These steps alone could take several weeks. Once these primary authors were satisfied with the draft, it could be distributed to the reviewers.

A meeting between authors and reviewers marked a midpoint in document creation and finalization. Comments from reviewers, in those days done by hand on hard copies, were collected and compared. One of the writer's main tasks was to reconcile conflicting comments. The statistician might be required to rerun an analysis or run a new one, and the CRA might be asked to verify investigator reports or ambiguities between the case report forms (CRFs) and the database, but in my experience and the experience of many of my contemporaries, the main task of reconciliation and coordination of the other authors' input fell to the writer. Once review comments were addressed, the document was circulated for sign off. This may have been done at a meeting in order to get as many of the signatories in the same place simultaneously, or the document might be sent from signer to signer. Frequently, final comments might need to be addressed at meetings, during or after document circulation, but eventually sign off was accomplished. However, no document was considered complete until it was "issued," meaning all parts of the document were present and certified to be submitted to regulatory authorities, with copies going to select reviewers and the company archive.

At this point, another major job would fall to the medical writer. Required attachments and appendices for CSRs and NDAs would need to be assembled, and the writer might be tasked with assembly or could supervise administrative assistants or other staff. For some submission documents, this also might include annotating text to allow the reviewer to locate key information. Pages that were added would be numbered by hand using stamps, stickers or typewriters. Internal supplemental quality control (QC) efforts then would take place, and these were far more time-consuming and encompassed many more elements than current document QC using automated data generation.

Consider that an NDA (under 21 CFR 314.50 (h)) required an archival copy, six reviewing copies—one each for the chemistry manufacturing and controls, nonclinical pharmacology and toxicology, human pharmacokinetics and bioavailability, microbiology, clinical and statistical reviewers; aside from the required copies, there also might be some extra documentation depending on the therapeutic area review group. Aside from the content QC, which was transcribed by hand from various hard copies, each page had to be reviewed for the correct page number, correct printing and legibility. It should not be surprising that the physical QC of an NDA took several days to a couple of weeks and might require one or more 18-wheel trucks to transport to FDA.

Starting in the mid-1990s, the idea of standardizing the TOC for various documents to streamline creation and review was taken a step farther with the concept of "structured writing" by using document templates, style guides or other means of creating standard document organization.[7] The streamlining process shortly would take a giant leap forward as the ICH guidelines began gaining acceptance.

## The Technological Evolution's Impact on Regulatory Writing

Until the late 1980s, in many organizations, writers would submit handwritten text to word processing personnel. Standalone, dedicated word processing hardware and software combinations came into use, such as the Wang® text processing systems, Honeywell's Infowriter®, Digital Equipment Corporation's™ Decwriter®, or IBM's™ Displaywriter®. These systems frequently were a combination of cathode ray tube (CRT) screen, central processing unit, floppy disk drive that took eight-inch diameter disks, and printer—frequently a "daisy wheel" printer that offered interchangeable print wheels with different fonts.[8]

By the early 1990s, the dedicated, standalone word processor had been replaced by the personal computer (PC) using a wide area network system such as Novell

Corporation's NetWare.[9] The most popular word processing software for PCs was WordPerfect™ (WP) and, after teaming up with software developer Borland®, its WordPerfect suite, which included WP, a drawing/slide show application—WordPerfect Presentations™ and Borland's spreadsheet package QuattroPro.™ The most popular WP feature was its "reveal codes" capability, which allowed the writer to see the actual format codes in a separate onscreen box, and, in versions after WP 5.1, actually to manipulate the codes from that box.

Given regulatory documents' complexity, the word processing system's electronic capabilities became increasingly important not only to word processing but also to other functions. For example, recalculating statistical subgroups could take days or weeks. From personal experience, we found the WP's electronic capabilities and the output capabilities of SAS,™ the industry standard for statistical software, could import tabular information directly into a WP document as comma-separated value files. This meant not having to spend time retyping data into the text or checking for typing errors. In addition, we found macros could be used with the SAS software to create Windows™ metafiles that permitted the direct incorporation of graphs instead of having an art department create graphs requiring validation. The time it took to review tables and graphs went from hours to minutes.[10,11]

While SAS remains an industry standard as of this writing, a critical change in the word processing software standard occurred in the mid-1990s. In 1994, Novell™ Corporation bought WordPerfect Corporation and integrated WordPerfect's email client and other networking software, calling the entire suite GroupWise™ instead of WordPerfect Office.[12] Shortly after that, Novell, after a change of administration, began to try and sell WordPerfect Office while keeping the email client and other network components.[13] By the time Corel Corporation bought the WordPerfect Office suite in 1996, the pharmaceutical industry's word processing standard was Microsoft Corporation's® MS Office. Much of the electronic automation developed for the WP system had to be redone to accommodate the new industry standard.

Once PC use became common in the late 1980s, the creation and storage of electronic documents gave rise to the need for different forms of document management.[14] It is tempting to keep the document working copy on the PC's hard drive. The common practice was to save working documents to the network servers, which were backed up routinely, which could lead to problems if IT kept strict storage limits. These limits could lead to computer crashes and document corruption during lengthy projects such as NDAs. Even though the IT model dictated that writers delete older versions of documents to stay within the storage limit, this material might be recalled as the large NDA documents progressed. Litigation, audits and review also could require companies to maintain interim versions of essential and regulated documents.

Network storage limit problems lessened with the advent of the specialized electronic document management system (EDMS). An EDMS has several advantages over network storage, especially version control that allows automated version numbering, differential numbering of minor changes and major changes, and better access control to documents in the system. An FDA-compliant EDMS also creates audit trails that allow internal and external regulators to see document access and changes made over time. In the mid-1990s, using an EDMS became even more crucial in complying with FDA regulations stemming from 21 CFR Part 11, which required version control and audit trails.[15]

An important EDMS feature is the ability to render the document in multiple electronic formats such as portable document format[16] (PDF), required by several regulatory agencies. In a 2003 draft guidance, FDA reported a preference for electronically navigable PDF files for text sections but included the use of SAS transport files, standard generalized markup language, chemical composition (MOL) files, and extensible markup language (XML) files for datasets.[17] Current FDA guidance specifies XML for complex submission documents, PDF for reports and other text files and acceptable electronic formats for statistical datasets.[18] In the 21st century, specialized EDMS-compatible publishing software use has become standard to maintain the integrity of filings, aid review and permit timelines to bring needed products to the market more quickly.

## Drug Approval Evolution

Regulatory writing is bound intimately to regulatory document submission and review methods, and the change from hard copy to fully electronic submissions was accompanied by fragmentation of the authoring role. During the hard copy era, producing a document like a CSR usually was assigned to a single writer. As EDMSs and submission publishing software came into use, reusing parts of documents became easier. Items like patient adverse event narratives, protocols, tables and other components that could be used in multiple documents must be written with strict attention to structure and format. The goal always has been to create documents that read consistently even if they comprise combinations of previously written and electronically stored subdocuments.

The 1980s, especially the latter half, marked a time of major change in the ways drugs were approved, and those changes, with document and authoring technology advances, significantly affected regulatory medical writing. Some were changes to the CFR, others were related to the rise of better authoring technology, including the previously discussed move from dedicated word processors to networked personal computers, the beginning of the idea of migrating hard-copy submissions to electronic submissions and the way drug candidate reviews were performed and funded.

A key 1980s event leading to changes to FDA's NDA regulatory review was the protest group AIDS Coalition to Unleash Power's (ACT-UP) push to speed review of AIDS drugs, end the use of placebo-controlled clinical trials of AIDS drugs, immediately approve promising AIDS medications and conduct an AIDS education campaign.[19] On 11 October 1988, ACT-UP members blockaded the entrance to FDA's Rockville, MD headquarters. By the end of November that year, amendments to 21 CFR Part 312 on investigational new drug applications were implemented to allow expedited reviews of proposed therapies for life-threatening or severely debilitating diseases.[20]

Although expedited IND criteria should have helped, the application review time for a drug to be prescribed for human use was slow. In 1987, review and approval times for new drugs or new indications for already marketed drugs averaged 22 months, which did not improve over the next two years.[21] In 1989, an experimental study division of FDA's Center for Drug Evaluation and Research (CDER) known as the Pilot Drug Division was founded.[22] Pilot Drug's mission was to try and create improved processes and develop new methods to speed the pace of FDA review.[23] Pilot Drug established four principles of review: flatten management oversight to allow reviewers to take more responsibility, conduct research to improve review processes, take an interactive approach with the drug sponsor to reduce formal question and answer exchanges, and start the review at the IND stage rather than the end of Phase 3. Additional meetings between FDA and sponsors were added as well, including an "NDA Day" when the application was given to FDA for review.[24] One critical outcome of these principles was "label-driven drug development," in which clinical trial protocols are designed based on the proposed drug label.[25] The latter two principles remain in general use.[26,27] Another event was the release of *Guideline for the Format and Content of the Clinical and Statistical Sections of an Application* in July 1988,[28] formalizing the NDA filing and CSR presentation order (21 CFR 314.50(d)(5) and (6)), including the integrated summary of effectiveness (ISE) and integrated summary of safety (ISS).[29]

By 1991, despite these efforts, the mean new drug entity review time had increased to 23 months.[30] Outside reviews of FDA procedures included separate committees and commissions chaired by Louis Lasagna, of the Sackler School of Biomedical Sciences, Vice President Daniel Quayle, Charles C. Edwards of the Scripps Clinic and Research Foundation, and the Institute of Medicine. Findings of these outside reviews led to changes in FDA project rating systems, accelerated approval recommendations, expanded use of contracted reviewers, and revision of FDA's Advisory Committee handbook.[31,32]

In 1992, the US Congress, following advice from FDA and the Pharmaceutical Research and Manufacturers Association (PhRMA) regarding slow review times for critically needed drugs, passed the *Prescription Drug User Fee Act* (*PDUFA*), which scheduled fees to expedite FDA reviews.[33] The *PDUFA* fees were to be used to "augment the resources" of FDA in reviewing drugs for human use.[34] This broad guideline for *PDUFA* funds' use proved successful both in funding temporary review help and upgrading FDA's electronic infrastructure. These benefits were spelled out more clearly when *PDUFA* was renewed in 1997 as part of the *Food and Drug Administration Modernization Act* (*FDAMA*),[35] in 2002 as part of the *Public Health Security and Bioterrorism Preparedness and Response Act,*[36] in 2007 as part of the *Food and Drug Administration Amendments Act* (*FDAAA*),[37,38] and in 2012 as part of the *Food and Drug Administration Safety and Innovation Act* (*FDASIA*).[39,40] **Table 1-2** summarizes *PDUFA* and its changes during subsequent five-year reauthorizations.

In the late 1980s, submission guidelines changed in Europe as well. In 1986, the European Commission (EC) established format guides for the MAA[41] in the form of Notice to Applicants (NtA) Volume 2 (NtA2), which were revised in 1989 and again in 1998 as the format changed ultimately to the CTD.[42] These moves toward review and approval globalization were noted and encouraged.[43] Guidelines for submissions in Japan also were changing and being updated at about the same time.[44] These changes set the stage for the globalization of drug evaluation and approval through the formation of the International Conference on Harmonisation (ICH, as of October 2015 renamed the International Council on Harmonisation).

## ICH and the Evolution of Harmonized Submissions

ICH was founded in 1990 after the World Health Organization International Conference of Drug Regulatory Authorities held in 1989.[45] The founding ICH members were the US, EU and Japan:[46]

- US: FDA and Pharmaceutical Research and Manufacturers Association (PhRMA)

- EU: European Commission (EC) and the European Federation of Pharmaceutical Industries and Associations (EFPIA)
- Japan: Ministry of Health, Labour and Welfare (MHLW) along with the Pharmaceuticals and Medical Devices Agency (PMDA) and the Japan Pharmaceutical Manufacturers Association (JPMA)

The original idea behind ICH was a global standard format for applications to regulatory agencies that would improve review quality and time for approval, an important long-term goal for industry and agencies alike.[47–49] Negotiations among the ICH members included attention to each entity's legal and regulatory requirements in addition to the proposed improvements to the document and process. The call for a CTD came from industry in 1995, the proposed content and feasibility plan presented to the ICH Steering Committee in 1996, guidelines finalized in 2000 and accepted by ICH regulatory members in 2001.[50]

ICH currently produces and updates guidelines for the creation of documents in four general areas:[51]

1. quality, defining the format for best practices in the chemistry and manufacturing processes of medicines
2. efficacy, defining best practices for clinical trials and trial data documentation
3. safety, defining best practices for evaluating risk and mitigating safety issues
4. multidisciplinary, defining best practices across other areas, such as safety data encoding from medical terminology and marketing authorization submissions through the CTD

Although detailing all of ICH's activities is beyond the scope of this chapter, the organization has had a profound effect on regulatory writing and regulatory submissions. For example, the ICH E3 guideline on the format and content of CSRs revolutionized clinical study reporting.[52] These changes took time.

The EC updated the NtA2 in 2001 to switch to the CTD and issued a question-and-answer document to recommend when the components of an MAA should be changed from the 1998 NtA2 format to the CTD.[53] In 2006, the EC released a NtA incorporating an extensive guideline to CTD format and content including a mapping table comparing changes from the 1998 NtA2 across all five modules.[54] This map reveals some interesting relationships between the 1998 format and the CTD. For example, CTD Sections 2.3—Quality Summary, 2.4—Nonclinical Overview and 2.5—Clinical Overview map directly to the Expert Reports in the 1998 Nt2A Sections

**Table 1-2. Summary of the *Prescription Drug User Fee Act* (*PDUFA*) and its Reauthorizations**

| Year | PDUFA Number[a] | Name (Abbreviation) | Synopsis |
|------|------------------|---------------------|----------|
| 1992 | | *Prescription Drug User Fee Act* (*PDUFA*) | Established the user fee for the purpose of "augmenting the resources of the Food and Drug Administration that are devoted to the process for the review of human drug applications and the assurance of drug safety"[c] |
| 1997 | II | *Food and Drug Administration Modernization Act* (*FDAMA*) | "reauthorized for an additional 5 years, with certain technical improvements; and carried out by the Food and Drug Administration with new commitments to implement more ambitious and comprehensive improvements in regulatory processes…including–strengthening and improving the review and monitoring of drug safety; considering greater interaction between the agency and sponsors during the review of drugs and biologics intended to treat serious diseases and life-threatening diseases; and developing principles for improving first-cycle reviews"[d] |
| 2002 | III | | Review 90% of NDAs/BLAs within six months; review 90% of resubmitted Class 1 efficacy supplements within six months (FY[b] 2003), four months (FY 2005), three months (FY 2006), two months (FY 2007); review resubmitted Class 2 efficacy supplements within six months and manufacturing supplements within six months (FY 2003–2007); establish priority review[e] |
| 2007 | IV | *Food and Drug Administration Amendments Act* (*FDAAA*) | Required the development of a postmarket safety assessment system, later named Sentinel, to follow risks for drugs and biologics. Also reauthorized with *PDUFA* was the *Medical Device User Fee Act* (*MDUFA*), expanded use of fees for improvement of electronic infrastructure, expanded work for Good Review Practice (GRP) and was done in parallel with the *Best Pharmaceuticals for Children Act* and *Pediatric Research Equity Act*.[f,g] |
| 2013 | V | *Food and Drug Administration Safety and Innovation Act* (*FDASIA*) | Implement and refine Sentinel, risk evaluation and mitigation strategies (REMS) integration and enhanced benefit:risk review, implement enhanced communication plan and upgrade information technology and informatics.[h,i] |

a. *PDUFA needs to be reauthorized every five years.*
b. *FY: Fiscal Year*
c. *Prescription Drug User Fee Act (PDUFA) of 1992. FDA website. http://www.fda.gov/RegulatoryInformation/Legislation/SignificantAmendmentstotheFDCAct/ucm147983.htm. Accessed 14 December 2016.*
d. *Prescription Drug Amendments of 1992; Prescription Drug User Fee Act of 1992. FDA website. http://www.fda.gov/RegulatoryInformation/Legislation/SignificantAmendmentstotheFDCAct/PrescriptionDrugAmendmentsof1992PrescriptionDrugUserFeeActof1992/default.htm. Accessed 14 December 2016.*
e. *PDUFA Legislation and Background: PDUFA III. FDA website. http://www.fda.gov/ForIndustry/UserFees/PrescriptionDrugUserFee/ucm118814.htm. Accessed 14 December 2016.*
f. *PDUFA Legislation and Background: PDUFA IV. FDA website. http://www.fda.gov/ForIndustry/UserFees/PrescriptionDrugUserFee/ucm145390.htm. Accessed 14 December 2016.*
g. *Food and Drug Administration Amendments Act (FDAAA) of 2007. FDA website. http://www.fda.gov/RegulatoryInformation/Legislation/SignificantAmendmentstotheFDCAct/FoodandDrugAdministrationAmendmentsActof2007/default.htm. Accessed 14 December 2016.*
h. *PDUFA V: Fiscal Years 2013–2017. FDA website. http://www.fda.gov/ForIndustry/UserFees/PrescriptionDrugUserFee/ucm272170.htm. Accessed 14 December 2016.*
i. *Sentinel Program Interim Assessment (FY 15). FDA website. http://www.fda.gov/downloads/ForIndustry/UserFees/PrescriptionDrugUserFee/UCM464043.pdf. Accessed 14 December 2016.*

IC1, IC2 and IC3. In 2008, the EC published its revised overall CTD format review including the 2008 version of the instructions for Module 1; earlier instructions for the Introduction (2006), instructions for Module 2 (2003), and Modules 3, 4 and 5 (2004) also were inlcuded.[55] Effective 1 January 2016, all MAA submissions must be in the electronic (eCTD) format.[56,57]

The NDA evolution from hard-copy submission to eCTD took a more technological route. As mentioned previously, a number of steps were taken in the late 1980s and early 1990s to accelerate the NDA review process. Among those were the 1988 NDA TOC, the institution of meetings between FDA and sponsors at defined points in the drug development process, such as at the end of Phase 2 and on the submission of the NDA itself ("NDA Day"), therapeutic classifications and the use of computers as review tools by submitting a computer-assisted NDA (CANDA) along with the paper submission.[58] The CANDA was not a standardized format. Each company submitting a CANDA provided database access, reviewing software that might be off the shelf or customized, and might even include the loan of hardware.[59,60]

Although CANDAs clearly were an improvement over hard copies, the lack of standardized formats limited their usefulness. FDA published a draft guidance for industry in the *Federal Register* (*FR*) giving instructions for the submission of complete NDAs in electronic formats (63 FR 17185; April 1998) (or eNDAs), followed by a final guidance published in January 1999.[61] This guidance gave specific instructions on file formats for statistical datasets and for text, including fonts, page margins, hypertext linking and bookmarks, and instructions for electronic signatures.[62] The 1999 guidance was withdrawn in 2006 after FDA began transitioning to the eCTD.[63]

The effort to create the eNDA paralleled ICH's development of the CTD. As noted, the EC required use of the CTD starting in 2003; FDA released a full eCTD specification in 2003 including TOC, file placement and file formats.[64] One of the noteworthy technological changes that could affect regulatory writers was the use of XML as the final file format for document storage. Some companies switched to XML-based authoring tools. In other cases, the XML output is through the passage of the text file into rendition servers as was done with PDF text files in the eNDA specification.

Like the EU implementation of the CTD, in the US, legal requirements needed to be met. When the 1988 NDA specifications are compared with CTD Section 2.7, the Clinical Summary, requires the same content for the application summary as described in the 1988 NDA. One point of confusion in transition to the CTD/eCTD was whether the Clinical Summary satisfied the requirement for an ISE and ISS. In 2006, CDER's associate director for medical policy presented FDA's position, indicating[65] ISE and ISS were intended to be a detailed analysis of the topics to be included in 5.3.5.3 Reports of Analyses of Data from More than One Study.[66]

The evolution to mandatory electronic submissions to FDA and the other ICH countries is almost complete; all NDAs, BLAs, etc. will need to be filed electronically by 15 May 2017 and most INDs by 15 May 2018.[67] Electronic MAA submissions in eCTD format in the EU became mandatory in October 2016.[68] The mandate in Japan for eCTD submissions currently is set for April 2022.[69]

One of the many advantages of the move to electronic submissions is the submission system itself. The way to file an eCTD is through an electronic gateway established by the regulatory agency; regulatory submissions travel over wires, not roads. The ability to accomplish this also has evolved over the years. The earliest submission methods involved the use of optical media, i.e., CDs and DVDs. The ability to transmit a submission

directly to the regulatory agency became available only once electronic transmission systems gained sufficient band width to allow transit of files this size within a reasonable time with appropriate security.[70]

## Conclusions

Regulatory writing is best defined by primary audience, regulatory reviewers and types of documents created for that audience. The evolution to the current state of regulatory writing projects, technology and review has its roots in the late 1980s establishment of acceptable document formats, the growth of PCs and WANs and the concept of regulatory submission globalization. The 1990s saw these systems' maturation into electronic word processing, EDMSs, electronic publishing, the transition from hard-copy submissions to the eCTD, and the change in application delivery from trucks loaded with paper to electronic files transmitted through Internet gateways. The regulatory writer's role has expanded from simple document creator to regulatory information planner and communicator. The field is still evolving.

**References**

1. *Medical Technology Assessment Directory: A Pilot Reference to Organizations, Assessments, and Information Resources.* Goodman C, ed. Institute of Medicine (US) Council on Health Care Technology. Washington (DC): National Academies Press (US) 1988. Food and Drug Administration Center for Drugs and Biologics. NCBI website. http://www.ncbi.nlm.nih.gov/books/NBK218390/. Accessed 16 December 2016.
2. Sharma S. "How to become a competent medical writer." *Perspect Clin Res.* 2010 Jan-Mar; 1(1): 33–37.
3. Wager E. "What medical writing means to me." *Mens Sana Monogr.* 2007 Jan-Dec; 5(1): 169–178.
4. Lunsford MJ. "The regulatory medical writer: more than a writer, an expert." *Write Stuff.* 2009; 18 (1): 9–10.
5. *Guideline for the Format for the Clinical and Statistical Sections of an Application.* FDA website. http://www.fda.gov/downloads/Drugs/.../Guidances/UCM071665.pdf. Accessed 16 December 2016.
6. Green Bar Paper Information. http://www.pdp8.net/images/green-bar.shtml. Accessed 16 December 2016.
7. Lander S. "Structured document generation-a cornerstone of document management." *Drug Info J.* 1998; 32: 757–760.
8. Kunde B. A Brief History of Word Processing (Through 1986). Stanford University website. http://web.stanford.edu/~bkunde/fb-press/articles/wdprhist.html. Accessed 16 December 2016.
9. Novell, Inc. History. Funding Universe website. http://www.fundinguniverse.com/company-histories/novell-inc-history/. Accessed 16 December 2016.
10. Benau D, DiPrimeo D. Incorporation of SAS-Generated Graphics into Word Processing Documents. Paper presented at: Drug Information Association, Medical Writing Meeting; March 1995, Philadelphia PA.
11. DiPrimeo D, Benau D. Interactions Between SAS-Generated Data and Word Processing Programs. Presented at: PhilaSUG (Philadelphia SAS Users Group); February 1997, Radnor PA.
12. Morettini P. The Rise and Fall of Novell. http://www.pjmconsult.com/index.php/2011/05/rise-and-fall-of-novell.html. Accessed 16 December 2016.

13. Scott MG. A History Lesson Please. In: Forum, Special Topics, News and Views [internet]. WordPerfect Universe; 2004 Jan 28, 11:27 AM.

14. Dobbs JH. "An overview of document management and document processing." *Drug Info J.* 1993; 27. 417–423.

15. Part 11, Electronic Records; Electronic Signatures—Scope and Application. FDA. website. http://www.fda.gov/RegulatoryInformation/Guidances/ucm125067.htm. Accessed 16 December 2016.

16. PDF. Three letters that changed the world. Adobe Systems Incorporate website. https://acrobat.adobe.com/us/en/why-adobe/about-adobe-pdf.html. Accessed 16 December 2016.

17. *Guidance for Industry—Providing Regulatory Submissions in Electronic Format—General Considerations* (January 1999). FDA website. http://www.fda.gov/downloads/Drugs/GuidanceComplianceRegulatoryInformation/Guidances/UCM072390.pdf. Accessed 16 December 2016.

18. *Guidance for Industry—Providing Regulatory Submissions in Electronic Format—Human Pharmaceutical Product Applications and Related Submissions Using the eCTD Specifications.* FDA website. http://www.fda.gov/regulatoryinformation/guidances/ucm126959.htm#_Toc111368377. Accessed 16 December 2016.

19. King H. U.S. AIDS Coalition to Unleash Power (Act Up) demands access to drugs 1987–89. Global Nonviolent Action Database. http://nvdatabase.swarthmore.edu/content/us-aids-coalition-unleash-power-act-demands-access-drugs-1987-89. Accessed July 28, 2016.

20. HIV/AIDS Historical Time Line 1981–1990. FDA website. http://www.fda.gov/ForPatients/Illness/HIVAIDS/History/ucm151074.htm. Accessed 16 December 2016.

21. Spivey RN, Lasagna L, Trimble AG. "New indications for already-approved drugs: time trends for the new drug application review phase." *Clin Pharmacol Ther.* 1987; 41 (4):368–370.

22. Doblin R. "Chapter 3, The Rise and Fall of FDA's Pilot Drug Evaluation Staff. *Regulation of the Medical Use of Psychedelics and Marijuana.* Santa Cruz, CA: Multidisciplinary Association for Psychedelic Studies; 2001, http://www.maps.org/research-archive/dissertation/chapter3.pdf. Accessed 16 December 2016.

23. Ibid, p. 142.

24. Ibid, pp. 151–65.

25. Ibid, p. 163.

26. *Guidance for Industry—Formal Meetings Between the FDA and Sponsors or Applicants.* FDA website. http://www.fda.gov/downloads/Drugs/.../Guidances/ucm153222.pdf. Accessed 16 December 2016.

27. *Draft Guidance for Industry and Review Staff—Target Product Profile—A Strategic Development Process Tool.* FDA website. http://www.fda.gov/downloads/drugs/guidancecomplianceregulatoryinformation/guidances/ucm080593.pdf. Accessed 16 December 2016.

28. Op cit 5.

29. Ibid.

30. DiMasi JA, Kaitin KI, Fernandez-Carol C, Lasagna L." New indications for already-approved drugs: an analysis of regulatory review times." *J Clin Pharmacol.* 1991; 31 (3):205–215.

31. Schulman SR, Hewitt P, Manocchia M. "Studies and inquiries into the FDA regulatory process: an historical review." *Drug Info J.* 1995; 29: 385–413.

32. Kessler DA. "Remarks—1991 Annual DIA Meeting." *Drug Info J.* 1991; 29: 465–470.

33. Woodcock J, Junod S. PDUFA Lays the Foundation: Launching Into the Era of User Fee Acts. FDA website. http://www.fda.gov/AboutFDA/WhatWeDo/History/Overviews/ucm305697.htm#16. Accessed 16 December 2016.

34. *Prescription Drug User Fee Act (PDUFA)* of 1992. FDA website. http://www.fda.gov/RegulatoryInformation/Legislation/SignificantAmendmentstotheFDCAct/ucm147983.htm. Accessed 14 December 2016.

35. *Prescription Drug Amendments* of 1992; *Prescription Drug User Fee Act* of 1992. FDA website. http://www.fda.gov/RegulatoryInformation/Legislation/SignificantAmendmentstotheFDCAct/PrescriptionDrugAmendmentsof1992PrescriptionDrugUserFeeActof1992/default.htm. Accessed 14 December 2016.

36. PDUFA Legislation and Background: PDUFA III. FDA website. http://www.fda.gov/ForIndustry/UserFees/PrescriptionDrugUserFee/ucm118814.htm. Accessed 14 December 2016.

37. PDUFA Legislation and Background: PDUFA IV. FDA website. http://www.fda.gov/ForIndustry/UserFees/PrescriptionDrugUserFee/ucm145390.htm. Accessed 14 December 2016.

38. *Food and Drug Administration Amendments Act (FDAAA)* of 2007. FDA website. http://www.fda.gov/RegulatoryInformation/Legislation/SignificantAmendmentstotheFDCAct/FoodandDrugAdministrationAmendmentsActof2007/default.htm. Accessed 14 December 2016.

39. PDUFA V: Fiscal Years 2013–2017. FDA website. http://www.fda.gov/ForIndustry/UserFees/PrescriptionDrugUserFee/ucm272170.htm. Accessed 14 December 2016.

40. Sentinel Program Interim Assessment (FY 15). FDA website. http://www.fda.gov/downloads/ForIndustry/UserFees/PrescriptionDrugUserFee/UCM464043.pdf. Accessed 14 December 2016.

41. *EudraLex—Volume 2—Pharmaceutical legislation notice to applicants and regulatory guidelines medicinal products for human use.* EC website. http://ec.europa.eu/health/documents/eudralex/vol-2/index_en.htm. Accessed 16 December 2016.

42. *EudraLex—Volume 2B—Medicinal products for human use—Presentation and content of the dossier* (1998). IKev (TR) website. http://www.ikev.org/docs/eu/intr2ben.pdf. Accessed 16 December 2016.

43. Jones K. "Toward internationalization of the pharmaceutical industry." 1993; *Drug Info J.*; 347–354.

44. Hayakawa T. "New drug approval process in Japan." *Curr Opin in Biotech.*1999: 10; 307-311.

45. History. ICH website. http://www.ich.org/about/history.html. Accessed 16 December 2016.

46. Ibid.

47. Vision, ICH website. http://www.ich.org/about/vision.html. Accessed 16 December 2016.

48. Worden DE. "The drive toward regulatory harmonization: what is harmonization and how will it impact the global development of new drugs." *Drug Info J.* 1995: 29; 1663S–1679S.

49. Dumitriu H. "The industry view of international standardization of regulatory dossiers." *Drug Info. J.* 1995: 29; 1121–1123.

50. Molson J. "The common technical document: the changing face of the new drug application." *Nature Reviews Drug Disc.* 2003; 2: 71–74.

51. ICH Guidelines. ICH website. http://www.ich.org/products/guidelines.html. Accessed 16 December 2016.

52. *Structure and Content of Clinical Study Reports E3.* ICH website. http://www.ich.org/products/guidelines/efficacy/efficacy-single/article/structure-and-content-of-clinical-study-reports.html. Accessed 16 December 2016.

53. Questions and answers, rules governing medicinal products in the European Union, volume 2, notice to applicants volume 2B, presentation and content of the dossier, common technical document (CTD). Enterprise Directorate General. EC website. http://ec.europa.eu/health/files/eudralex/vol-2/b/ctd-qa_jan_2003_en.pdf. Accessed 16 December, 2016.

54. *EudraLex—Volume 2B—Medicinal products for human use, Presentation and content of the dossier—Common Technical Document (CTD)*. (2008). pp26-29. EC website. http://ec.europa.eu/health/files/eudralex/vol-2/b/update_200805/ctd_05-2008_en.pdf. Accessed 30 December 2016.

55. *EudraLex—Volume 2B—Medicinal products for human use, Presentation and content of the dossier—Common Technical Document (CTD)*. (2008). EC website. http://ec.europa.eu/health/files/eudralex/vol-2/b/update_200805/ctd_05-2008_en.pdf. Accessed 16 December 2016.

56. Op cit 41.

57. Electronic application form release notes. EMA website. http://esubmission.ema.europa.eu/eaf/eaf_1.20.2/eAF-Release-Notes-MAAH_1.20.0.2.pdf. Accessed 16 December 2016.

58. Kaitin KI, Walsh HL. "Are initiatives to speed the new drug approval process working?" *Drug Info. J.* 1992; 26:341-349.

59. Ibid.

60. Accomando WP. "What should a CANDA look like?" *Drug Info. J.* 1993; 27:407-411.

61. *Guidance for Industry—Providing Regulatory Submissions in Electronic Format—General Considerations*. FDA website. http://www.fda.gov/downloads/Drugs/GuidanceComplianceRegulatoryInformation/Guidances/UCM072390.pdf. Accessed 16 December 2016.

62. Ibid.

63. Gensinger GM. Electronic submissions and the electronic common technical document. http://www.fda.gov/downloads/Drugs/NewsEvents/UCM275455.pdf. Accessed 16 December 2016.

64. *Guidance for Industry—M2 eCTD: Electronic Common Technical Document Specification*. FDA website. http://www.fda.gov/downloads/Drugs/GuidanceComplianceRegulatoryInformation/Guidances/UCM073240.pdf. Accessed 16 December 2016.

65. Temple R. CTD—ISS/ISE introduction and summary of issues. http://www.fda.gov/downloads/AboutFDA/CentersOffices/CDER/ucm120175.pdf. Accessed 16 December 2016.

66. Op cit 64.

67. *Providing Regulatory Submissions in Electronic Format—Certain Human Pharmaceutical Product Applications and Related Submissions Using the eCTD Specifications—Guidance for Industry*. FDA website. http://www.fda.gov/downloads/Drugs/GuidanceComplianceRegulatoryInformation/Guidances/UCM333969.pdf. Accessed 16 December 2016.

68. Use of XML delivery file for submissions via eSubmission Gateway/Web Client—statement of intent on the next step of the phased implementation. EMA website. http://esubmission.ema.europa.eu/gateway/XML%20delivery%20file%20for%20all%20submissions%20via%20Gateway%20and%20Web%20Client%20-%20Statement%20of%20Intent.pdf. Accessed 16 December 2016.

69. Mistry R. Japan and eCTD: What We Know. 29 March 2016. http://theectdsummit.com/japan-and-ectd-what-we-know/. Accessed 16 December 2016.

70. Electronic Submissions Gateway. FDA website. http://www.fda.gov/ForIndustry/ElectronicSubmissionsGateway/. Accessed 16 December 2016.

### Author

Danny A. Benau, MSOD, PhD is an associate professor of biomedical writing and director of biomedical writing programs at the University of the Sciences in Philadelphia. Previously, he worked as a freelance regulatory writer, medical writing project leader (Sanofi) and principal scientific writer (Wyeth-Ayerst Research). His experience includes participation in 14 NDAs and numerous CSRs, IND updates, responses to regulatory authorities and other documents. He holds a PhD in biology from Boston University and a Master of Organizational Dynamics from the University of Pennsylvania.

### Acknowledgements

I would like to acknowledge my mentors from Wyeth who taught me how to be an effective medical writer: Christina Rogers, Diane Petrovich, Victoria Seidenberger, and Betty Kuhnert, and also my systems thinking mentors from Penn who taught me how to use holistic approaches in creating processes: John Pourdehnad and Lawrence Starr. In addition, I would like to acknowledge the many colleagues over the years with who shared knowledge, ideas, and beer with me.

# 2

# Good Documentation Practices

*By Joanne Rupprecht, Esq., RAC (US, Global)*

## Overview of Good Documentation Practices

The goal of ensuring the safety, efficacy and quality of medical devices, drugs and vaccines is not exclusive to regulatory bodies such as the US Food and Drug Administration (FDA). Healthcare organizations share in that goal and must strive to meet it in an increasingly competitive industry.

Documentation is often the first and sometimes the only impression a regulator receives of a research group or organization. A robust documentation system serves as the foundation from which a healthy compliance program can be built and, once in place, will remain a source of important first impressions during audits and inspections. The documents themselves, individually and collectively, represent the face of a company's operations.

Although Good Documentation Practices (GDPs) are essential in any professional setting, they are critical in regulated medical device, pharmaceutical, vaccine and biologic product environments. In general, GDPs include all written activities, processes, studies and results associated with product development, approval, mainte-nance and improvement. Good documentation serves as evidence of product development decisions and provides a basis of reference for all activities required throughout the product's lifetime. Given the dynamics associated with

product development and the time it may take to realize commercialization, good documentation allows consistent information transfer among parties and functional groups and FDA.

A good documentation system also allows regulatory agencies to conduct a complete and efficient review of marketing applications and other communications nec-essary for approval of safe and effective products. Ideally, GDPs help regulators understand a product's history, assess its studies' adequacy, verify the integrity of data generated and, hence, approve the appropriateness of its intended use, and most importantly, confirm the validity of claims about the product's safety, efficacy and quality.

### Organizations Must Use Judgement

Not everything a successful organization should do to maintain GDPs is mandated by FDA or other regula-tory bodies. Almost every FDA guidance document or defined regulatory standard contains elements of GDPs, and each stage of product development has its own nuances as to how documentation should be approached. Although FDA's guidance documents do not establish legally enforceable responsibilities, and their influence is limited to the agency's current thinking on a topic, these recommendations should be applied when possible, and supplemented with existing available statutory require-ments. It also is advisable for an organization, if operating more globally, to consult the expectations of Health Canada, the International Council on Harmonization (ICH) and the World Health Organization (WHO).

Being well-versed in FDA regulations and international equivalents is only the first step in creating a healthy compliance profile for an organization, producing the documentation required throughout product development, maintaining a robust quality system and meeting regulatory requirements. For an organization to be successful in reaching these objectives, documentation must be thorough, accurate and consistent.

GDPs apply to:

- procedures (e.g., standard operating procedures (SOPs))
- documentation during product development (e.g., Product Master Files)
- documentation for purposes of product clearances, approvals and licenses (e.g., 510(k) s, Premarket Approval applications (PMAs), Product License Applications (PLAs) and Biologics Licence Applications (BLAs))
- pharmacovigilance and medical device reporting documentation
- the assembly of justification files to support an organization's decision-making process and conclusions reached

While emphasis often is placed on postmarket documentation, GDPs should be applied from the product's conception. From prototype through clinical trials and up to postmarket surveillance, GDPs should be developed, implemented and maintained. Included in what is considered postmarket documentation are medical information communications, promotional materials and user operation manuals. The contents of this documentation should differ from the labeling submitted to FDA during product approval, and should not stray from the approved indications or safety and efficacy claims. Especially for promotional materials, supporting documentation should be kept on file to defend against any FDA allegations of marketing a misbranded or adulterated product.

This chapter explores the components of GDPs. The reasons for these practices are explained and, while this discussion is not exhaustive, the best efforts have been made to provide a thorough understanding of the principles and concepts necessary to develop, maintain or improve an existing documentation system. FDA expectations and industry best practices will continue to evolve, which underscores the importance of monitoring internal systems regularly and implementing value-added changes at any time. One test for whether updates are required is to answer the question, "can you explain

how this (i.e., the subject matter of the document) all works?" It is not unreasonable for an auditor to expect a document user to be able to explain the contents or their relevance to business operations. If a document, as written, cannot translate information to the reader to allow informed decisions to be made, reworking the document is advisable.

## Goals of Documentation

It is best to start organizing documentation with the end purpose in mind. Documentation is essential for effective and efficient operations and serves the following purposes:

- making internal processes and procedures clear and consistent
- assisting in personnel training and cross-training
- creating a reference for conducting evaluations
- creating standards upon which continual improvements can be built
- tracking product changes and the reasoning behind them
- centralizing important concepts related to business development
- creating a foundation for risk assessments and quality systems' maintenance
- incorporating global regulatory considerations, as necessary
- allowing internal and external product knowledge transfer
- complying with FDA quality and regulatory expectations
- supporting product approval applications
- assisting in putting the product into, and maintaining it in commercial distribution

## Documenting Procedures Are Essential to Good Practices

With increasing emphasis being put on Quality Management Systems (QMS) and risk management during FDA inspections and audits, an organization must pay careful attention to its SOP documentation and how SOPs are applied in generating additional documentation. Even if an organization produces clear, concise, consistent, accurate, thorough and unambiguous documentation, any deficiency in executing or adhering to the specifications, procedures and recordkeeping requirements can create obstacles to creating, implementing and maintaining a healthy compliance profile. More dangerous than not creating a solid documentation system is not adhering to the SOPs, validated specifications or other work instructions referenced within the system. The documents containing validated product specifications are most important, since any deviation could compromise a product's quality, and potentially could pose a danger to consumers.

Procedures established to maintain quality operations are of little value if not followed, and when such documentation is not followed, it by default is creating a trail of noncompliance FDA would view unfavorably. If an organization has no intention of adhering to the documentation, it may be better not to have it.

An organization must understand its documentation system's goals, define its components, review its requirements, implement its execution, train for incorporating it into organizational culture, and maintain both it and its results on a periodic basis.

### *Consistency: An Essential GDP Component*

When developing a documentation system, a primary goal is avoiding conflicting provisions, ambiguous statements, incompatible requirements and unattainable compliance goals, as well as remembering the reading audience. Any one of the harmful practices listed above can undermine a documentation system's consistency. Consistency is important among related documents, FDA requirements and agency documents, so readers can find the information they need to perform their job functions properly and play the roles they have been assigned to ensure product quality and realize regulatory compliance.

A documentation system often involves many cross-functional groups, sometimes with overlapping areas of responsibility. Depending on the evolution of these groups and their respective responsibilities, an organization may develop documents with similar business goals that lay out diverging execution pathways. Internal communication is key when documenting roles, responsibilities and expectations, so every contributor understands his or her respective role.

When it comes to documentation, generalities—i.e., a lack of specificity and detail—can result in unanticipated vulnerabilities for an organization due to readers' subjective interpretations. The best way to avoid this pitfall is to choose the best words to reach the desired outcome and clearly delineate processes and relationships. Achieving consistency involves carefully defining the terms used, abbreviations employed and unifying individual writing styles. In addition, focusing on the documentation's goal and understanding the targeted audience should be taken into consideration.

## The Importance of Transparency and Disclosure in the Regulatory Process

A culture of honesty and openness is an essential component of GDPs and achieving a healthy compliance profile. That, in addition to an organization's willingness to communicate, can open the door to more efficient product review processes, audits, inspections and compliance dispute resolution efforts.

FDA emphasizes the importance of data integrity during inspections, particularly current Good Manufacturing Process (CGMP) inspections.[1] Every regulated environment, regardless of its operations, should be concerned with not only the integrity of the data it produces but also the documentation that speaks to the processes and procedures used in obtaining the data.

In recent years, FDA and industry have been encouraged to become more open and transparent in their communications, and steady progress has been made. In 2009, FDA's commissioner launched the agency's Transparency Initiative, creating a task force intended to increase trust between FDA and industry members, and the agency and the public.[2]

In 2010, the first of three phases was put into place, a web-based resource called FDA Basics,[3] providing the public with basic information about the agency, closely followed by the release of a transparency report meant to present further disclosures about FDA's workings.[4] In 2011, another transparency report was released focusing even more on increasing FDA operations' and decision-making transparency.[5]

The ultimate goal of these efforts to increase transparency remain:

- establishing a collaborative environment between FDA and industry
- improving public trust about healthcare product regulation
- speeding up the process to get necessary medical devices, drugs and vaccines into the hands of patients who need them, without compromising safety

Additionally and importantly, documentation transparency can pave the way to meaningful dialogue, and meaningful dialogue is important to create constructive relationships among those responsible for bringing a safe and effective product to market. On a larger scale, increased transparency and the dialogue it often generates can aid in collaborations across industry, as well as among industry and government and academic research partners.

An organization must consider and make decisions carefully about what content should be both captured in, and omitted from, its documentation. Transparency does not mean making inappropriate disclosures or releasing otherwise confidential information. Internal planning and clear upper management direction are necessary, so an organization's documents remain meaningful, relevant and applicable to its actual operations, without exposing it to unnecessary scrutiny. Helpful questions to consider when putting documentation in place include:

- Is the terminology used consistently throughout the documentation system?
- Does the language cater to the intended reader's level?
- Is the document easy to read and follow?
- Do the processes and/or procedures identified lead the user to desired result efficiently?
- Is the document's information compliant with regulatory expectations?
- Will the document's contents and relevance be easy to explain during inspection?
- Are the reasons information is included or omitted from the document justifiable to FDA or any other regulatory body?

### FDA GDP Expectations

FDA has not produced a GDP regulation for inclusion in the Code of Federal Regulations (CFR) yet. The absence of formal regulatory direction on this subject places the burden on organizations to review codes, regulations and other requirements to identify appropriate documentation practices for various activities, especially during a product's foundational research and development stages.

While emphasis often is on postmarket documentation, GDPs should be developed, implemented and maintained from the initiation of research and throughout the development process. With today's electronic records, organizations should pay special attention to creating document inventory lists so they are readily available to users and FDA upon request. An electronically based documentation system should include copies of historic documents and a robust change control process. Connecting the documentation and any changes to it with the training program would be optimal. The more coordinated these good documentation system elements are, the smoother the transition between product development phases and across different functional groups. The consistent capture of specifications, procedures, records and data, and this information's accessibility are key to successful operations and a healthy regulatory compliance profile.

### International Harmonization Standards

For more than 25 years, the International Council on Harmonisation (ICH) has been instrumental in the global initiative to standardize pharmaceutical product development and regulation. Membership includes the US, EU and Japan, Canada and Switzerland.[2] ICH took on the task of identifying regulatory similarities, mitigating regulatory differences, facilitating collaborations, improving communications and advancing the coordination of pharmaceutical product requirements for development and approval processes among countries. In realizing its vision, ICH has taken the lead on preventing duplication of efforts, reducing product development timelines, streamlining product approvals and contributing to the protection of human health.

One of ICH's most important initiatives has been the creation and implementation of the Common Technical Document (CTD) for the assembly of all the quality, safety and efficacy information for regulatory reviews in each member region. By consolidating the documentation necessary for a product to be reviewed properly and approved efficiently, regulatory authorities, industry sponsors and the public all have benefitted.

## Identifying Documentation Guidelines and Resources

### ICH Guidelines

The following guidance documents and resources may be useful in meeting the expectations of FDA and other member countries:

- *E3: Guideline for Industry Structure and Content of Clinical Study Reports* (PDF—240KB)
  This guideline is helpful in developing a complete, unambiguous and organized clinical report.
- *E6: Good Clinical Practice: Consolidated Guidance* (PDF—261 KB)
  This guideline outlines member countries' unified standard (GCP) for documenting, recording and reporting human clinical trials and ensuring data integrity.
- *Q9: Quality Risk Management* (PDF—113KB)
  Again, while there is no specific GDP CFR, many other references are contained within the requirements of Good Clinical Practice (GCP), GMP and Good Laboratory Practice (GLP) that can be utilized when putting an effective GDP system into place. Other available resources include but are not limited to:
- Capture Source Data (ICH GCP E6 1.52)
- Maintain Adequate Records (21 CFR 812.120 [a])
- Requirements for Data Integrity
  - §211.68 (requiring that "backup data are exact and complete" and "secure from alteration, inadvertent erasures, or loss")
  - §212.110(b) (requiring data to be "stored to prevent deterioration or loss")
  - §§211.100 and 211.160 (requiring certain activities to be "documented at the time of performance" and laboratory controls to be "scientifically sound")

- o §211.180 (requiring records to be retained as "original records," "true copies" or other "accurate reproductions of the original records")
- o §§211.188, 211.194 and 212.60(g) (requiring "complete information," "complete data derived from all tests," "complete record of all data," and "complete records of all tests performed")
- Electronic Signature and Record-Keeping Requirements (21 CFR Part 11)
- *Design Control Guidance for Medical Device Manufacturers* (March 1997) (http://www.fda.gov/downloads/MedicalDevices/DeviceRegulationandGuidance/GuidanceDocuments/ucm070642.pdf )
- *Guidance for Industry: Computerized Systems Used in Clinical Investigations* (May 2007) (http://www.fda.gov/OHRMS/DOCKETS/98fr/04d-0440-gdl0002.pdf)
- *Quality System Information for Certain Premarket Application Reviews; Guidance for Industry and FDA Staff* (3 February 2003) http://www.fda.gov/downloads/MedicalDevices/DeviceRegulationandGuidance/GuidanceDocuments/ucm070899.pd
- *Guidance for Industry: Q7A Good Manufacturing Practice Guidance for Active Pharmaceutical Ingredients* (August 2001) http://www.fda.gov/ICECI/ComplianceManuals/CompliancePolicyGuidanceManual/ucm200364.htm
- *Guidance for Industry: Quality Systems Approach to Pharmaceutical CGMP Regulations* (September 2006) http://www.fda.gov/downloads/Drugs/GuidanceComplianceRegulatoryInformation/Guidances/UCM070337.pdf
- *Guidance for Industry: CGMP for Phase 1 Investigational Drugs* (July 2008) http://www.fda.gov/downloads/Drugs/GuidanceComplianceRegulatoryInformation/Guidances/UCM070273.pdf
- *Guidance for Industry: Q10 Pharmaceutical Quality System* (April 2009) http://www.fda.gov/downloads/Drugs/GuidanceComplianceRegulatoryInformation/Guidances/UCM073517.pdf
- *Guidance for Industry: Process Validation: General Principles and Practices* (January 2011) http://www.fda.gov/downloads/Drugs/GuidanceComplianceRegulatoryInformation/Guidances/UCM070336.pdf
- *Guidance for Industry: Current Good Tissue Practice (CGTP) and Additional Requirements for Manufacturers of Human Cells, Tissues, and Cellular and Tissue-Based Products (HCT/Ps)* (December 2011) http://www.fda.gov/downloads/BiologicsBloodVaccines/GuidanceComplianceRegulatoryInformation/Guidances/Tissue/UCM285223.pdf
- ISO 9001—2008; Clause 4.2; Documentation Requirements
- *Guide to GMP for Medicinal Products Part 1*, "Chapter 4 Documentation: PIC/S PE 009-8 (Part I)"

## Using Form FDA 483 Observations to Create a Good Documentation System

Form FDA 483 is issued to firm management at the conclusion of an inspection when an investigator has observed any condition he or she believes may constitute violations of the *Food, Drug, and Cosmetic Act* (*FD&C Act*) and related acts.[4] Often, the deficiencies cited include the lack of GDPs, i.e., design controls, clinical studies, certificates of analysis/conformance, calibrations or validations, postmarket studies and pharmacovigilance or complaint handling.

The most constructive way to approach a Form 483 observation is to consider each deficiency cited as a lesson from which to learn, and an opportunity to take corrective action and improve operational processes and procedures.

When creating documentation, the questions of what, when, why and how should be addressed and a format created to memorialize the outcome of documented processes or procedures. When completing forms or documenting a process or procedure's results, each required element should be addressed and every blank filled with either the appropriate answer or, if not applicable, N/A. During inspections, FDA will not assume a blank space means a requirement was N/A; it will presume the requirement was not given proper consideration or was overlooked during the process or procedure. During pre-inspections, any use of "not applicable" should be scrutinized carefully and blank spaces eliminated.

Some of the most recent Form FDA 483 findings can be found on FDA's website and are made available to the public through the Office of Regulatory Affairs (ORA) *Freedom of Information Act* (*FOIA*) reading room.[5] The lessons learned, preferably at the expense of other organizations, are invaluable and include the following documentation-related observations organizations should take the time to review, understand and avoid proactively. Some sample findings from the FOIA reading room are:

- Organization failed to maintain complete data from all laboratory tests conducted to ensure compliance with established product specifications and internal quality standards.
- Laboratory records did not contain all raw data generated during each test for active pharmaceutical ingredient (API) batches.
- A sample failed the purity specification limit, but the failure was not documented.
- Sample preparation information was not documented, and quality control records used to support the Drug Master File and batch disposition decisions did not include all testing results.
- None of the explanations justifies the failure to maintain complete records, neither do they support the practice of substituting repeat tests for failed results.
- Address how the organization intends to ensure the reliability and completeness of all records of analytical data generated.
- Specify the measures implemented to ensure oversight of documentation procedures, including the electronic data generated.
- The organization failed to prevent unauthorized access or changes to data and to provide adequate controls to prevent data omission; no passwords are required to log into the databases, credentials are unverified, and there is no electronic or procedural control to prevent data manipulation.
- Software lacks an audit trail feature to document all activities related to the analysis performed; staff cannot demonstrate records include complete and unaltered data or verify there have been no alterations or deletions.
- The organization has no raw data for the test limits reported on the Certificates of Analyses (COAs); release of these batches was approved without data to support that release specifications were met.
- Provide details of the systemic actions taken to prevent recurrence of the cited fundamental deficiencies in laboratory data integrity and COA authenticity.
- Provide a clear and thorough procedure for the retention of the raw data for all laboratory instrumentation and equipment.
- The organization failed to ensure equipment is cleaned in a reproducible and effective manner to prevent contamination of a material that would alter API quality.

- The organization failed to ensure APIs are produced according to preapproved instructions and that batch production records include complete information pertaining to the production of each batch; calculations were erroneous and Batch Production Records (BPRs) do not include or describe calculations to adjust the amounts of starting materials appropriately to be used for a given batch size.
- FDA inspection revealed serious documentation practices and reported missing raw data, which compromised the quality and accountability of APIs in the supply chain.
- Provide a comprehensive evaluation of the extent of records' deletion and destruction, a risk assessment regarding the potential impact on product quality, and a comprehensive corrective and preventive action plan.
- Ensure sustainable compliance with CGMP, including the basic capability to prevent data manipulation and destruction or deletion of records. The lack of reliability and accuracy of data generated by the organization's laboratory is a serious CGMP deficiency that raises concerns with all data generated by the organization.
- Provide the corrective action plan describing the organization's commitment, procedures, actions and controls to ensure data integrity, which should include the corrective actions implemented to ensure all managers, supervisors and quality unit personnel are trained properly in detecting lack of data integrity and manipulation.
- Provide documentation of the specific training offered to all employees regarding the importance of following CGMP and ensuring all required tests are performed.
- The organization is responsible for having controls to prevent data omissions, as well as recording any changes made to existing data, which should include the date of change, identity of person who made the change and an explanation or reason for the change.[6]

What investigators see during an inspection is limited, and documentation is the natural target. Because 483 observations are the result of an inspector's subjective interpretation of *FD&C Act* provisions, foreseeing an inspection's results or preventing issuance of a Form 483 is not always possible, regardless of an organization's best efforts.

# Internal Requirements for a Robust GDP System

As the saying goes, "the first school is one's own home." A culture of compliance begins with demonstrated support from the organization's highest management levels. An environment that fosters open communications allows cross-functional collaborations, rewards good behavior, corrects bad behavior and provides employees with training opportunities to understand FDA's expectations associated with their responsibilities, providing the foundation from which all good practices can stem.

Upper management communication about the importance of complying with FDA requirements should be clear and reflected in their actions. Those expectations should be integrated into the documentation practices at every level of the organization.

Nothing is more dangerous to an organization's success than simply the appearance of GDPs. Short-term profits from cutting corners can be lost quickly by the expense of corrective actions, including the loss of a good public reputation and FDA good will.

## Consider All Applicable Documentation

The documents that should be considered in regulated healthcare environments include but are not limited to:

- research and development
  - conception plans
  - prototype designs
  - specification requirements
  - clinical study protocols
  - Investigator's Brochures
  - Investigational Review Board (IRB) and investigator communications
  - informed consent forms
  - Case Report Forms (CRFs)
  - investigator clinical study reports
  - sponsor narratives
- commercialization
  - FDA presubmission communications
  - supportive documentation for regulatory submissions
  - manufacturing standard operating procedures (SOPs)
  - validation and stability reports
  - batch records
  - COAs
  - labeling justifications and finalization
  - regulatory submissions
- postmarket
  - market and launch documentation
  - proof of compliance with good practices and ISO requirements

- pharmacovigilance reports
- periodic safety updates
- medical information communications
- annual reports
- supplemental filings
- benefit-risk evaluation reports
- serious adverse reaction reports
- postmarket study requirements
- advertising and promotional materials and references

## Good Practices for Signatures, Change Control, Validation and Dating

If records are kept electronically, the system must be validated and backed up, and access should be limited to maintain control over any changes. Under GDPs, only the most current document may be used for any given purpose, and change control is a must. Each document should be assigned an internal control number, and revisions should be tracked. Originators, reviewers and approvers all should be identified and have appropriate qualifications to support their respective decisions.

Documentation should be dated in real time and never pre- or post-dated. Any retrospective additions, modifications or deletions should be signed and dated; having these changes witnessed should be considered.

The time an organization should retain any given documentation can vary, so care should be taken before destroying any records. Documents often require signatures. No document should be signed unless it is understood and the contents are supported.

An organization's documents can be pivotal in a product liability or personal injury case, and it is possible they will be demanded during court proceedings. Likewise, any person within an organization responsible for that documentation also may be called into court. The credibility of a witness or a product's quality can be influenced greatly by implementing GDPs. In today's increasingly litigious environment, all documentation should be viewed through the lens of "could this document be explained, justified or defended in a court of law?"

## Consider Basic Principles

Points to consider in developing GDPs include:

- Look at the consequences of including or omitting information:
  - If information is not documented, it does not exist; retrospective documentation is not recommended.
  - Overkill in reporting minor details or repeating information may impede transparency.

- o Templates are a good start, but customization is crucial and should be specific to each organization, as well as to each internal group within an organization.
  - o Do not make reviewers look too hard to verify the organization's compliance.
- Make required actions and expectations attainable:
  - o Avoid requiring actions that existing personnel cannot support.
  - o Budgetary constraints may exist that limit implementation of the ideal system.
  - o If current operations do not allow for compliance with stated requirements, do not document them as requirements.
- Implement robust change control procedures to capture all changes made to documentation and review periodically:
  - o Corrections to hand-written documentation should be made with a single line, signed and dated.
  - o White out should never be used for corrections. (ICH GCP 4.9.3)
  - o The reason(s) for any documentation corrections or changes should be stated.
- Remain current on quality and regulatory rules and regulations, and update documentation as needed:
  - o Document compliance clearly and reference supporting guidelines and resources used.
  - o If applicable, justification for any necessary noncompliance as a result of business decisions or changes in rules, regulations or policies should be documented.
- Write clearly, using consistent practices and language:
  - o Stick to technical writing basics; this is not creative writing.
  - o Use established words, references and acronyms.
  - o Avoid discrepancies within and between documents. While many groups may contribute to a document, finalization should be centralized within the quality, regulatory, medical writing and labelling group.
  - o Adopt appropriate style for each document. Bench science, manufacturing and regulatory affairs writing styles differ and should be used as appropriate.
  - o Avoid the use of arrows and "ditto" marks.
- Maintain control of contents and records:

- o ALCOA—documentation should be attributable, legible, contemporaneous, original and accurate.
- o Verify what is documented to the extent practicable.
- o In the event of an audit or inspection, the information trail should be clear and complete; where it may lead, or where it may fail to lead, should be anticipated and defensible.
- o Do not destroy records and keep them as accessible as possible for internal use while protecting them from public access.

## Recordkeeping and Best Practices

Understandably, organizations are focused on getting product out the door, but good documentation improves processes and, ultimately, the bottom line. An organization's quality system is based on its documentation system. Even with the best intentions, individual differences in execution or interpretation can result in inconsistencies and compromise product quality. That is why it is best to implement a GDP system at the earliest stages, to minimize subjective interpretation.

Good documentation is an important investment that may not bring immediate returns but provides important protection against internal inconsistencies, adverse regulatory actions and legal liabilities. The human resources required to respond to an FDA 483 warrant the upfront investment in a documentation system that will mitigate communication, performance and recordkeeping failures. Any findings of deficiencies are on the public record, available to competitors and customers alike.

Any documentation system should contain clear, consistent and focused documents, including SOPS and training materials. Inconsistencies or ambiguities can have devastating effects on an organization's operations. Thus, documents should be reviewed periodically and reconciled with each other to minimize confusion among users. Determine which are specific to the organization's operations, and customize policies and procedures accordingly. For example, processes and procedures not currently in place, even if they once were, should not be documented.

Change control will ensure all users are using the most up-to-date version of a document, and an organized change control procedure should be developed and followed. A document change control system is intended to capture changes made to existing documentation and provide a means of tracking these changes and communicating them throughout an organization.

If an organization's operations deal with both medical devices and pharmaceuticals, documentation for each product type should be kept separately. Likewise, specific provisions may be necessary in documents related to an organization's pharmaceutical products if they are DEA-controlled substances, biologics, generics, etc.

Once the documentation system is in place, it should not be neglected or abandoned. Changes should be considered on a regular basis, following schedules mandated in regulations or in conjunction with other appropriate events. In the event of an audit, the trail of the changes made, the dates of those changes and the parties responsible for them should be identifiable easily, and support for those changes should be kept on file accordingly. Documenting the obvious can make short work of inspections.

Training is vital to success, but such training is only as good as the documentation on which it is based. High-quality documents are the basis for high-quality training. In smaller organization without a dedicated technical writer, consultants specializing in GDPs are available.

Good documentation not only supports and advances an organization's quality system, but safeguards public health and can enhance employee retention. When everyone in an organization understands what is expected, product quality will be ensured and the customer experience will be enhanced.

**References**

1. FDA Transparency Initiative. FDA website. http://www.fda.gov/AboutFDA/Transparency/TransparencyInitiative/default.htm. Accessed 18 December 2016.
2. Ibid.
3. FDA Basics. FDA website. http://www.fda.gov/AboutFDA/Transparency/Basics/ucm2021108.htm. Accessed 18 December 2016.
4. Op cit 1.
5. Ibid.
4. FDA Form 483 Frequently Asked Questions. FD website. http://www.fda.gov/ICECI/Inspections/ucm256377.htm. Accessed 18 December 2016.
5. ORA FOIA Reading Room. FDA website, http://www.fda.gov/AboutFDA/CentersOffices/OfficeofGlobalRegulatoryOperationsandPolicy/ORA/ORAElectronicReadingRoom/default.htm. Accessed 18 December 2016.
6. Ibid.

**Author**

Joanne Rupprecht, Esq., RAC (US, Global) is director of legal and regulatory affairs at Aytu BioScience Inc. responsible for the domestic and international regulatory compliance of pharmaceutical products (NDAs, BLAs, INDs), federal and state licensing and international import/export requirements. Previously, she worked for Abbott Laboratories in diagnostic medical device product development, regulatory affairs and medical writing, responsible for the clearance of eight 510(k)s for Class II medical devices and involved in PMA (Class III) and BLA product regulatory matters.

# 3

# General Considerations for Quality Regulatory Writing

*By E. Mitchell Seymour, PhD, RAC (US)*

Regulatory writing combines language, science or engineering, medicine and law to create communications that advance corporate sponsors' medical, scientific and manufacturing objectives. In biopharmaceutical, vaccine and device development, regulatory writing's principal goal is to produce documents for submission to health authorities that:

- are scientifically and editorially accurate
- reflect regulatory strategy and corporate goals
- are compliant with applicable regulations and guidelines
- are clearly worded concerning key messages

Regulatory documents often have multiple authors across several subject matter areas; this reality complicates a team's ability to write with a consistent voice. Writing should be concise, simple, objective, balanced and nonpromotional. Well-designed documents provide information the audience can understand and interpret easily. This chapter discusses barriers to effective communication, regulatory audience uniqueness, and approaches to address these challenges. It also focuses on particularly important strategies for regulatory deliverables and their typical audiences.

## Barriers to Effective Communication

Effective regulatory communication requires an appreciation of both readers (or recipients) and writers (or senders). In regulatory writing, the sender's role is to communicate the key medical, scientific and quality messages clearly and faithfully while also explaining complex data. Recipients of regulatory documents are health authority reviewers (FDA, EMA, etc.), physician investigators, study coordinators, IRB members, pharmacists and insurance providers, among others. Regulatory writers must remain aware of these recipients' diverse backgrounds and needs. The sections below discuss barriers to effective communication with this varied audience.

Poor communication can have some real and costly regulatory consequences. With a health authority like FDA, some of these consequences can include:[1]

- Health authority misunderstands the submission's purpose or content and, therefore, cannot complete its review or give the sponsor a timely answer.
- Submission content does not support its intention or key messages.
- Health authority questions the submission's content because it raises more issues than it answers. Content is not matched or mapped carefully to key messages.

- Health authority refuses to review because the submission is so poorly written.
- Due to poor formatting, reviewers cannot find information and spend more time searching for relevant sections and information than reviewing them.

Sloppy submissions can contribute to a negative impression of the submission and the sponsor.

Text that is too dense or written mainly in the passive voice is challenging to read, comprehend and assess. Inconsistent information can raise questions that delay or confound a regulatory decision. Fortunately, these challenging issues can be addressed.

Authors can limit these problems in regulatory documentation by considering the following:
- organized document layout:
  - o use headings and subheadings to clarify content organization
  - o be consistent in document formatting
- information accessibility:
  - o use a hyperlinked table of contents for documents more than four pages long
  - o use captions for figures and tables, and hyperlinks for content that is not on the same page
- supportive content for intended claims:
  - o map content to support specific conclusions and key scientific messages
- information flow:
  - o maintain a logical flow of details to support conclusions and improve comprehension

## Regulatory Audience Needs

Regulatory audiences include scientists, clinicians, pharmacists or engineers. Given the breadth of therapeutic areas and investigative products, ample background material may be needed in addition to novel results and findings for high-level summaries as well as detailed reports. Reviewers may be rushed and overworked and may not speak English as their first language. Furthermore, job training may have been brief, and agency turnover may be high. As a regulatory writer, this uniquely diverse audience is especially challenging, and the consequences of poor communication have an operational impact.

Regulatory audiences often perform tasks after reading the content, like writing review documents or deliverables for their peers. Effective regulatory writing helps the regulatory reviewer complete these tasks. In the case of a heath authority, reviewers have to read, understand and then present the information to a third party (colleagues, regulatory project manager, division or Advisory Panel) for decisions. They present the information both verbally and in writing. These tasks are performed under deadlines and with many competing priorities. FDA defines Good Reviewer Practices,[2] and the regulatory professional should become familiar with the review templates and guidelines of the audience.

The reviewer may need to "cut and paste" the content into a health authority review document and then add interpretations and conclusions. The reviewers must locate and understand information well enough to either defend or critique the sender's approaches and data. The reviewer's deliverable is shared with others who may need to repurpose this content across many documents. Therefore, miscommunication can be magnified as the review process progresses, and miscommunication can impact the submission and program's perception.

Writing in a reviewer-friendly format helps reviewers create required deliverables, meet their internal review metrics and faithfully communicate the intended key messages to the regulatory review team.

## Formatting Is Important

Formatting is key to cognition and perception. If a page is formatted badly, with text of varying size and positions on the page, the mind will not understand it as readily—this can raise more questions about the material. If a page is well laid out, has lots of white space and is concise and easy to read, the reader will get less distracted and have greater comprehension. Therefore, a style guide should establish the key parameters for document format.

### Traditional Versus Inverted Pyramid Writing Styles

The traditional style starts with a foundation of background information and gradually builds to a conclusion in a pyramid style using the following structure:
- problem statement
- background information
- methodology
- results
- conclusions

Therefore, the most important "takeaway" information is at the end of the document or section. In the fields of biomedicine and engineering, manuscripts and study reports often follow this writing style.

Reviewers of regulatory submissions (such as the subsections of Module 2 of a CTD) typically scan the text, so it is important to state the main points at the beginning. The inverted pyramid style starts with the most important information at the beginning of a section and begins with two to three bullet points highlighting important takeaway messages. The general structure of the inverted pyramid is:

- high-level summary presenting the conclusions, often in a bulleted format
- high-level background information
- technical details and data with hyperlinks to related content or study reports
- restate conclusions

Summarizing data at the beginning of each section forces the author to:

- know and understand the data well enough to summarize it concisely
- structure the section to support those conclusions
- agree on key messages
- focus the section on supporting messages in an organized fashion

These data summaries at the start of each section benefit the reviewer by facilitating:

- focus on data that support or refute conclusions
- repeating information in different formats promotes long-term memory
- engaging curiosity, encouraging active reading; the brain will try to find connections and the supporting data

Writing in the inverted pyramid style takes practice, as it is atypical to most forms of biomedical communication. Nevertheless, it is common in regulatory writing.

## Design is Important for Comprehension

Graphic design principles can apply to text and document formatting, which is especially helpful in regulatory documents. These principles can help the reader navigate text dense with novel information. Consistent page structure is useful. Order, consistency and simplicity constitute elegance in design, as they reduce the reader's work. They also assist regulatory reviewers who must cut and paste the information into their review deliverable. Make their jobs easier.

A pleasant appearance, coupled with visual interest, can draw the reader through the text and reduce the reading effort. Using tables, figures and graphs provides visual interest and can help clarify complex messages.[3,4] Visually, readers also search for "differences." Bulleted or numbered lists and bolded text exploit this advantage and can reveal the key messages. Also, not all spaces need to be filled. White space can frame the message. Appropriate use of white space, a ragged right margin and bulleted or numbered lists all help to make messages stand out.

## Details Vary by Document and Development Stage

One regulatory writing challenge is deciding what content is shared and what is unique among documents. This decision is guided primarily by the document's purpose.

The Common Technical Document (CTD) format for health authority submissions is divided into five modules and is defined by the International Council on Harmonisation.[5] The CTD often is described as a pyramidal structure, or even as a Greek temple;[6] the latter is the author's preferred visualization. The foundation of the pyramid (or temple columns) is Module 3 (Quality), Module 4 (Safety and Nonclinical) and Module 5 (Efficacy and Clinical). Clinical study reports (in Module 5) are highly detailed, as are GLP nonclinical study reports (in Module 4). The study reports in Modules 4 and 5 contain individual subject and animal data points, statistial approaches and results, and tables and figures summarizing the findings by group or cohort. Module 3 content is highly granular and defined by ICH.

Module 2 content (Summaries and Overviews) is positioned higher in the CTD pyramid or temple and requires a higher level of content and data summaries (not to be confused with and ISS or ISE). These integrated documents are critical for regulatory reviewers, and their content is repurposed across many review deliverables. Other documents like the Investigator's Brochure (IB) and the Target Product Profile also may take select content from Module 2 documents, but streamlining is required to ensure these smaller documents are as succinct and readable as possible.

Modules 4 and 5 content composition typically is guided more clearly by ICH and health authority guidelines, while Module 2's content approach and style can vary. Although Module 4 and 5 study reports are very detailed and formulaic, there is more subjectivity and artistry involved in authoring Module 2 content. Compared to Modules 4 and 5, the documents are smaller, and the writing should be streamlined and organized around key messages. Regulatory review and decisions rely very heavily on Module 2 content, including the creation of agency documents like FDA's Summary Basis of Approval. Module 2 typically is authored by the most senior medical writers in close association with regulatory personnel and subject matter leads. What these documents lack in size, they make up for with clear impact on regulatory review, opinion and outcome.

Throughout the development plan, regulatory document's content will change as new information and data are revealed. While some content grows (like the findings of new and ongoing clinical trials), others can be streamlined. The IB is a prime example of this evolving content.

In earlier clinical studies of an investigational new chemical or molecular entity, the IB will contain a considerable amount of nonclinical data. Over time, clinical trial completion should expand the IB clinical sections. Ideally, the regulatory writers will be allowed to reduce and streamline the nonclinical content gradually, to the level that would be contained in an approved drug label. However, this practice and discipline vary by company. If an IB's goal is effective communication to clinical investigators, this is not accomplished by a 300+ page document.

## Reader-Friendly Writing Aids Comprehension

### *Trim the Fat*

Brevity is challenging for many technical content writers, particularly for subject matter experts with little regulatory writing training. Writing simply and concisely requires deep knowledge of the material as well as editorial expertise. Writers and editors often are key to focusing the content effectively.

Streamlining refines text to allow intended conclusions and scientific messages to stand out clearly. Removing excess words, using active voice and language simplicity and brevity all contribute to clear communication. Less usually is better. Writers should try to avoid nominalizations, complicated phrases, redundant expressions and jargon.

Another streamlining method employs bulleted lists. Large blocks of text form "brick walls" that visually obscure information and create reader fatigue.[7] Large content blocks are particularly troubling for text containing numbers and units. Using discrete, visually demarcated lines can bring the most important points into sharp focus.

## Improve Readability

Experts generally advise targeting a 6th- to 8th-grade reading level for most documents. Regulatory language often is composed at a post-graduate level (Grade 18–21). However, this approach does not foster or facilitate better communication, even for an audience with advanced education. The more complicated a document, the harder it is to read because complexity distracts readers at all educational levels. A 10th-grade reading level presents a good compromise; it makes the author think about the material and digest it to frame it at a more basic level. Writing at this level forces the author to provide adequate context and work harder on the document's flow. An easy-to-read text engrosses the reader, facilitates understanding and comprehension and leads readers to the intended conclusions.

To facilitate readability, use:
- many small paragraphs
- up to four levels of headings and subheadings to define segments
- lots of white space
- 12-point font for text and 10-point for tables
- 1.15 spacing between lines
- bulleted lists
- short sentences
- limited jargon

Regulatory documents should be written to inform rather than impress. Active voice should be used whenever possible. Likewise, writers should use simple, declarative sentences most frequently, varying sentence structure as needed to maintain reader interest.

## Plain Language is Both a Law and a Goal

The Plain Writing Act of 2010[8] (described in detail on plainlanguage.gov[9] and fda.gov) requires clear language in documents written by the US government, including FDA:[10]

> "Writing in plain language is not unprofessional. It's not "dumbing down" the message or "talking down" to the audience. When you write clearly and get to the point without using unnecessary words or technical jargon, you get your message across more quickly and increase the chance the information will be understood and used."

Thus, the *Plain Language Act* states documents such as FDA guidances should be understandable by the broader public. FDA also favors receiving content written in plain language. Sponsors can read the act and use the same approach. Plain language also assists reviewers for whom English is not the first language, which represents a significant portion of FDA's workforce.

## Edit for Both Content and Focus

All documents should be reviewed before submission to a health authority. The sponsor must focus each submission clearly around salient points and include only the data and discussion necessary to support those points.

For regulatory deliverables, authors, reviewers and editors should consider:
- Does the document present one clear, consistent representation or narrative of the data?
- Are the safety information and risks disclosed and discussed adequately? Is adequate information included to support safety conclusions?
- Is all information and terminology consistent?
- Are previous discussions with FDA addressed and consistent with all prior meeting minutes?

Editing for grammar, style and syntax is important; however, the technical content must be verified as well. If information from source documents is pulled into submissions, a quality assurance (QA) audit back to the source documents should be completed before verifying the final submission to ensure accurate publishing.

## Teamwork for Success

Expectations and team roles should be clarified early, ideally by a partnership of executive- or director-level leadership, subject matter experts, writers and editors. Writers and editors should not change scientific concepts or conclusions. However, team members should understand formatting and grammatical corrections do not change meaning even if the page looks different.[11] Rapport-building and communication are critical to promote this understanding.

All regulatory submission section conclusions and contents should connect to other dossier sections. The authors should ensure no individual disciplines' contributions contradict other submission sections. One or more team members could be charged with assessing the inter-document alliance of conclusions and key messages.

## Summary

In regulatory writing, it is imperative to communicate simply and efficiently. With this goal in mind, authors, reviewers and subject matter experts should consider the following principles:[12]

- Provide organization and navigation tools. Logical flow is essential to understanding information, and a table of contents, tables and figures are essential to finding information.
- Focus on the key messages. Too many details may obscure conclusions.
- Be concise. Summarize and streamline information to focus on relevant points.
- Be clear. Use short, simple sentences to convey complex messages well. Use bulleted lists throughout.
- Ensure accuracy. Check the facts with a dedicated review, separate from macro- and micro-editing tasks.

**References**

1. Brown-Tuttle M. *IND Submissions: A Primer*. Barnett International. 2009.
2. FDA.gov. Good Review Practices (GRPs). FDA website. http://www.fda.gov/Drugs/GuidanceComplianceRegulatoryInformation/ucm118777.htm. Accessed 13 December 2016.
3. Op cit 1.
4. White A. *The Elements of Graphic Design. Space, Unity, Page Architecture, and Type*. New York, NY: Allworth Press; 2002.
5. International Council on Harmonisation. *M4: The Common Technical Document*. ICH website. http://www.ich.org/products/ctd.html. Accessed 13 December 2016.
6. Katz N. "Effective eCTD Writing - Five Essential Competencies." Global Forum. 2011;3(2):1-5.
7. Wood LF. "Regulatory Writing Tips." In: Wood LF, Foote M, eds. *Targeted Regulatory Writing Tips* 2009:27-32.
8. 111th US Congress. Plain Writing Act of 2010. Vol Public Law 111–274—13 October 2010.
9. The Plain Language Action and Information Network (PLAIN). Plain Language: It's the law.
10. FDA.gov. Plain Language Principles. FDA website. http://www.fda.gov/AboutFDA/PlainLanguage/ucm331958.htm. Accessed 13 December 2016.
11. Op cit 7.
12. Op cit 1.

**Author**

E. Michell Seymour, PhD, RAC (US), through his company R&D Advisors, provides regulatory outsourcing services for industry and academia. His experience includes regulatory writing and regulatory submissions, FDA meeting preparation and engagement, regulatory strategy, regulatory intelligence and regulatory due diligence. Seymour also is an adjunct clinical professor at the University of Michigan College of Pharmacy and adjunct faculty in San Diego State University's graduate regulatory science program. He is an active member of the American Medical Writers Association. Seymour holds a PhD in biochemical and molecular nutrition from Michigan State University and the an RAC (US).

# 4

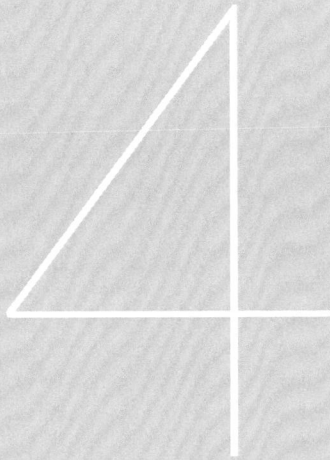

# Guidance Documents: Beyond the Code of Federal Regulations

*By Lisa DeTora, Robin Martin, Jenny Boyar and Jenny Grodberg*

## Introduction

The "regulatory" in regulatory writing generally refers to the fact that such documentation is prepared to address requirements laid out in government regulations and laws. In the US, all government regulations are housed in the Code of Federal Regulations (CFR); 21 CFR governs the Food and Drug Administration (FDA).[1] Similarly, regions, such as the EU, and individual countries also have laws and regulations that must be followed, and the measures to prove compliance for medicinal products, devices, vaccines, biologics, and combination products must be documented. Thus, professionals engaged in producing regulatory documents should have a general understanding of the format and content of the individual documents under preparation and the laws and regulations governing their submission. This understanding should be predicated on a first-hand familiarity with regulations, the regulatory authority's intent and more user-friendly guides for specific documents.

The health authorities or agencies responsible for regulating medicinal products, devices, vaccines, biologics, and combination products also provide extensive guidance for industry to explains current views on how best to engage in the research and/or manufacturing processes that must be documented, validated, and presented for review. Consolidated, harmonized guidelines are provided and regularly updated by the International Council for Harmonisation for Technical Requirements for Pharmaceuticals for Human Use (ICH), and have been adopted by the US FDA. Many guidelines include advice regarding the scientific and technical aspects of research, development and manufacturing, while others describe documentation or the technical aspects of submissions.

### The Federal Register and the Code of Federal Regulations

The history of formal regulation of food, drugs and cosmetics in the US began during the 19th century with the formation of the US Pharmacopeia in 1820, while the genesis of FDA is often recognized as 1862, when then-President Abraham Lincoln appointed Charles Wetherill to head a Bureau of Chemistry in the US Department of Agriculture.[2] This Bureau of Chemistry went through several reorganizations, expanding the scope of its work over time. Two acts commonly viewed as the beginning of the modern FDA are the 1902 *Biologics Control Act*[3] and the *Federal Food and Drugs Act* of 1906.[4] In 1927, the Food Drug and Insecticide Administration, which became FDA in 1930, was formed under the Bureau of Chemistry to house regulatory functions.[5] Of note, biologics and drug products, currently regulated by FDA,[6] have been regulated by different offices and agencies over time.[7]

The origins of the *Federal Register* date to the 1930s when, as Richard J. McKinney notes, an ever-increasing number of federal agencies made it difficult to locate regulations, which, until then, had been published piecemeal, often in pamphlet form, by various government offices and branches.[8] The need for a general repository was recognized, and legislation was introduced. The *Federal Register Act* of 1935 established the Federal Register as a comprehensive publication to contain:

- all rules and regulations promulgated by government agencies;
- all Presidential proclamations and executive orders;
- any other documents that the President determines has general applicability and legal effect; and
- any other documents as may be required by an Act of Congress.[9]

In addition, notices of meetings, agency collection activities and applications and policy statements may be published in the *Federal Register*.[10] The *Federal Register—The Daily Journal of the US Government* may be found at: https://www.federalregister.gov.[11] It is updated daily with notices of rules, proposed rules, meetings and other significant publications.

Historically, to address the lack of a central, organized repository for all previously published regulations, the *Federal Register* addressed some concerns about the proliferation of regulations and offices; but still, its daily publication format presented certain challenges for those seeking to locate and follow regulations. The Code of Federal Regulations (CFR), modeled on the existing US Code (USC), was initiated in 1937, shortly after passage of the *Federal Register Act*, as a means of collecting all existing regulations in a central repository. The CFR hard copy is updated annually in sections,[12] and an electronic version is available at: http://www.ecfr.gov.[13]

Individual chapters in this book address specific sections of 21 CFR that pertain to regulatory documentation. For example, 21 CFR Parts 300–369 detail regulations pertaining to drugs intended for human use, and Parts 600–680.3 present regulations that pertain to biological products.[14] Additional sections of relevance include Good Laboratory Practice (21 CFR Part 58),[15] combination products (21 CFR Part 4),[16] and the protection of human subjects (21 CFR Part 50).[17] These topics are discussed in further detail by DeTora,[18] Shen[19] and Jennings[20] in this book. Also of potential interest is 45 CFR Public Welfare, which includes the regulations that apply to the US Department of Health and Human Services.[21]

### Limitations as Writing Guidance

21 CFR presents the basic requirements that must be met to ensure specific marketed products' purity, safety, effectiveness and potency. Implementation of these regulations is flexible to accommodate the differences among various products and product types currently regulated, as well as the medical conditions they are intended to diagnose, treat or prevent. At the same time, the open-ended nature of these rules can present challenges to the writer who seeks guidance on acceptable submission formats or best documentation practices. For example, 21 CFR part 58 includes a list of the minimum required information to be included in a nonclinical study report;[22] however, the specific items listed provide little to no guidance regarding how the information should be formatted or the level of detail necessary for health authorities to locate and review findings. Although the measures specified in 21 CFR Part 50 provide more specific guidance for authors regarding the information required for informed consent documents,[23] in general, 21 CFR is limited to serving only as a useful starting point for documentation because it allows for flexibility by design.[24]

For regulatory professionals and others who draft documentation for health authorities, 21 CFR is a useful starting point but not the final stop for obtaining vital information regarding applicable regulations. For example, many development programs are conducted internationally or domestically, with the intent to market a product in more than one country or region. In those situations, all applicable international regulations must be considered. The pertinent sections of the EU Directive,[25] for example, present legal requirements for the registration of medicinal products, vaccines, biologics and devices, including in vitro medical devices (IVDs). In addition, the European Medicines Agency (EMA) provides guidance and links for anyone seeking to learn more about EU requirements and recommended best practices.[26] Additional information on the required legal framework for these submissions is available at: http://ec.europa.eu/health/human-use/legal-framework_en.[27] While there are differences between US, EU and other countries' requirements and recommendations, ICH's word has been pivotal in bridging these differences and standardizing respective governmental submission requirements.

### Guidance for Industry

As noted by Rupprecht,[28] regulatory professionals and the authors of regulatory documents must seek out additional guidance documents, such as those provided by FDA's Center for Drug Evaluation and Research (CDER)[29] and Center for Biologics Evaluation and Research (CBER)[30] as well as international groups such as ICH, whose work,

**Table 4-1. FDA Guidances for Vaccines and Related Biological Products**[a]

| Title | Date of Publication |
|---|---|
| *Providing Submissions in Electronic Format—Postmarketing Safety Reports for Vaccines* | August 2015 |
| *General Principles for the Development of Vaccines to Protect Against Global Infectious Diseases* | December 2011 |
| *Clinical Considerations for Therapeutic Cancer Vaccines* | October 2011 |
| *Characterization and Qualification of Cell Substrates and Other Biological Materials Used in the Production of Viral Vaccines for Infectious Disease Indications* | February 2010 |
| *Guidance for Industry: Considerations for Plasmid DNA Vaccines for Infectious Disease Indications* | November 2007 |
| *Guidance for Industry: Toxicity Grading Scale for Healthy Adult and Adolescent Volunteers Enrolled in Preventive Vaccine Clinical Trials* | September 2007 |
| *Clinical Data Needed to Support the Licensure of Pandemic Influenza Vaccines* | May 2007 |
| *Clinical Data Needed to Support the Licensure of Seasonal Inactivated Influenza Vaccines* | May 2007 |
| *Development of Preventive HIV Vaccines for Use in Pediatric Populations* | May 2006 |
| *Considerations for Developmental Toxicity Studies for Preventive and Therapeutic Vaccines for Infectious Disease Indications* | February 2006 |
| *FDA Review of Vaccine Labeling Requirements for Warnings, Use Instructions, and Precautionary Information* | October 2004 |
| *Postmarketing Safety Reporting for Human Drug and Biological Products Including Vaccines (Draft)* | March 2001 |
| *Content and Format of Chemistry, Manufacturing and Controls Information and Establishment Description Information for a Vaccine or Related Product* | January 1999 |
| *How to Complete the Vaccine Adverse Event Reporting System Form (VAERS-1)* | September 1998 |
| *Evaluation of Combination Vaccines for Preventable Diseases: Production, Testing and Clinical Studies* | April 1997 |

a.   *Biologics Guidances. FDA website. http://www.fda.gov/BiologicsBloodVaccines/GuidanceComplianceRegulatoryInformation/Guidances/default.htm. Accessed 24 January 2017.*

**Table 4-2. Overview of Center for Drug Evaluation and Research Guidance for Regulatory Writers**[a]

| Title | Description | Date of Publication |
|---|---|---|
| *Formatting, Assembling and Submitting New Drug and Antibiotic Applications* | Provides guidelines for formatting and assembling new drug and antibiotic applications for FDA approval | February 1987 |
| *Content and Format of INDs for Phase 1 Studies of Drugs, Including Well-Characterized, Therapeutic, Biotechnology-Derived Products* | Clarifies when sponsors should submit final, quality-assured toxicology reports and/or update the agency on any changes in findings since submission of non-quality-assured reports or reports based on non-quality-assured data | October 2000 |
| *Exocrine Pancreatic Insufficiency Drug Products–Submitting New Drug Applications* | Assists manufacturers of exocrine pancreatic insufficiency drug products in preparing and submitting new drug applications | April 2006 |
| *Investigational New Drug Applications (INDs) for Minimally Manipulated, Unrelated Allogeneic Placental/Umbilical Cord Blood Intended for Hematopoietic Reconstitution for Specified Indications* | Outlines the minimum information that should be included in an IND for the hematopoietic progenitor cells, cord | June 2011 |
| *Investigational New Drug Applications (INDs)- Determining Whether Human Research Studies Can Be Conducted Without an IND* | Assists clinical investigators, sponsors, sponsor-investigators and IRBs in determining whether research studies involving human subjects must be conducted under an IND, as described in 21 CFR Part 312 | September 2013 |

a.   *Search for FDA Guidance documents. FDA website. http://www.fda.gov/RegulatoryInformation/Guidances/. Accessed 27 January 2017.*

**Table 4-3 Recently Published FDA Guidance for Regulatory Writers[a]**

| Title | Description | Date of Publication |
|---|---|---|
| *Providing Regulatory Submissions in Electronic Format—Submission of Manufacturing Establishment Information* | Discusses the requirements and implementation of the *Federal Food, Drug, and Cosmetic Act* regarding valid electronic submissions of manufacturing establishment information | December 2016 (draft) |
| *Clinical Pharmacology Section of Labeling for Human Prescription Drug and Biological Products—Content and Format* | Assists in preparing the Clinical Pharmacology section of prescription drug labeling to meet regulatory requirements and ensure appropriate consistency in the format and content of this section for all prescription drugs approved by FDA | December 2016 |
| *Providing Postmarketing Periodic Safety Reports in the ICH E2C(R2) Format (Periodic Benefit-Risk Evaluation Report)* | Describes the conditions under which, and submission procedures by which, applicants can use an alternative reporting format instead of the US periodic adverse drug experience report, US periodic adverse experience report or ICH E2C Periodic Safety Update Report, to satisfy the periodic postmarketing safety reporting requirements in §§ 314.80(c)(2) and 600.80(c)(2) (21 CFR 314.80(c)(2) and 600.80(c)(2)) | November 2016 |
| *Collection of Race and Ethnicity Data in Clinical Trials* | Provides FDA expectations for and recommendations on using a standardized approach for collecting and reporting race and ethnicity data in submissions for clinical trials for FDA-regulated medical products in the US and abroad | October 2016 |
| *ANDA Submissions—Prior Approval Supplements Under GDUFA* | Explains how the *Generic Drug User Fee Act* of 2012 (*GDUFA*) relates to prior approval supplement (PAS) submissions, describes the performance metric goals outlined in the *GDUFA* commitment letter FDA has agreed to meet, and clarifies how FDA will handle certain PAS amendments | October 2016 |

a.    *Search for FDA Guidance Documents. FDA website. http://www.fda.gov/RegulatoryInformation/Guidances/. Accessed 24 January 2017.*

**Table 4-4. Regulatory Requirements for Medical Devices**

| Title | Description | Where Applicable |
|---|---|---|
| *21 CFR 800-1299 Food, Drug, and Cosmetic Act* | **Law:** One of the primary overarching laws for products regulated by FDA; amended in 1976 by the *Medical Device Amendments*, at which time FDA began regulating medical devices | US |
| 21 CFR 801 Labeling<br>21 CFR 803 Medical Device Reporting<br>21 CFR 807 Establishment Registration, Medical Device Listing and Premarket Notification 510(k)<br>21 CFR 812 Investigational Device Exemption (IDE)<br>21 CFR 814 Premarket Approval (PMA)<br>21 CFR 820 Quality System Regulation (QS)/Good Manufacturing Practices (GMP) | **Regulation:** Basic regulatory requirements for US medical device commercial distribution | US |
| EN/ISO 13485 Medical Devices—Quality Management Systems—Requirements for Regulatory Purposes | **Standard:** Internationally agreed upon standard that includes quality management system (QMS) requirements specific to medical device development | US (elective), Canada, EU and numerous global countries |
| EN/ISO 14971 Medical Devices—Application of Risk Management to Medical Devices | **Standard:** Internationally agreed upon standard that includes risk management process requirements and procedures specific to medical device development | US (elective), Canada, EU and numerous global countries |
| EN/ISO 14155 Clinical Investigation of Medical Devices for Human Subjects—Good Clinical Practice (GCPs) | **Standard:** Internationally agreed upon standard that includes Good Clinical Practice (GCP) requirements specific to medical device clinical investigations | US (elective), Canada, EU and numerous global countries. Portions recognized by FDA |

as noted by Benau,[31] has been adopted in many regions and countries. These guidelines can help form the basis for internal standard operating procedures (SOPs) and other strategic documents to streamline the regulatory submission process for medical products.[32] Guidance for industry can clarify requirements or to provide additional detail not practicable for inclusion in laws or regulations. While this is helpful, it also presents additional challenges for authors, writers and regulatory professionals.

The number of guidelines that apply to any given product, regardless of which FDA division regulates it, is likely to be high. For example, **Table 4-1** presents FDA guidance for industry documents on topics related to vaccines and biologics products, excluding ICH guidelines. The number of similar guidelines for drug products is too prohibitive to list here but can be located on FDA's website (www. fda.gov). **Tables 4-2** and **4-3** present additional resources available to industry that may help regulatory document authors. Keeping up with regulatory changes, additions and recommendations, necessitates a significant expenditure of time and effort as well as special regulatory expertise.

## Regulatory Framework—Medical Devices

In the medical device setting, certain key differences impact regulatory submissions.[33] "Standards" are documents issued by domestic and international third-party agencies such as the World Health Organization (WHO), the Clinical & Laboratory Standards Institute (CLSI), the International Organization for Standardization (ISO) and other groups whose mission is to standardize processes related to the development or testing of specific products. Regulatory authorities often adopt these standards as best practices or as requirements on which they will base their clearances, approvals, permits or registrations.

**Table 4-4** provides an overview of various widely-accepted regulatory requirements for medical devices. This is not an all-inclusive list but is intended to show the relationships between laws, regulations, and standards in this setting.

## ICH Guidelines

FDA[34] and EMA,[35] like many other regulatory authorities globally,[36] accept the ICH guidelines.[37] Increasingly, companies and other medical product sponsors have taken a more universal and global approach to writing, engaging in collaborations such as the American and European Medical Writers Associations' Clarity and Openness Reporting—E3 (CORE) reference for Clinical Study Reports (CSRs).[38] In addition, nonprofit organizations, such as TransCelerate, in their respective missions, incorporate fostering collaborations to provide guidance on many topics, including but not limited to protocols, study reports and data tracking tools.[39] Additional guidance available from such organizations sheds light on good practices, specifies the contents and suggests formats that should be considered for various regulatory documentation types, including marketing applications and clinical study reports.

ICH began publishing its guidance in the 1990s.[40] As Benau notes elsewhere in this book,[41] ICH guidelines result from numerous collaborative efforts among government agencies and professional societies in the US, the EU and Japan, including:

- the European Commission[42]
- the European Federation of Pharmaceutical Industries and Associations[43]
- the Ministry of Health, Labour and Welfare of Japan[44]
- US FDA[45]
- Pharmaceutical Research and Manufacturers of America[46]

Although ICH began its work with drug products and pharmaceutical substances, the scope of the ICH guidelines has since expanded. For example, ICH has published several guidelines that include information about biologically-derived products such as ICH S6,[47] which guidelines specifically detail preclinical safety testing requirements for biotechnology-derived pharmaceuticals (see **Tables 4-5–4-8**). ICH Guidelines generally do not apply to medical devices.

Documentation is only a small part of the ICH guidelines, which also define and discuss basic principles for research, employing "good practices"[48] in clinical research (ICH Good Clinical Practice E6)[49] and drug substance manufacturing (quality guidelines) as well as documentation.[50] In addition, ICH guidelines describe Clinical Technical Document (CTD; ICH M4)[51] specifications and suggested formatting for clinical study reports (ICH E3),[52] clinical development plans (ICH E8),[53] clinical trial protocols (ICH E6)[54] and the Investigator's Brochure (ICH E6). In general, ICH guidelines fall into three major categories: quality, i.e., chemistry, manufacturing and controls; safety, i.e., pre- and nonclinical studies; and efficacy, i.e., clinical trials.[55] Multidisciplinary guidelines handle areas of crossover between quality, safety and efficacy guidelines, particularly for clinical development programs and the CTD format for regulatory filings[56] (see **Tables 4-5–4-8**). ICH guidelines undergo regular evaluation, updates and revisions,[57] such as increased attention to vaccines and biologics.[58] Robinett has published an excellent resource that suggests various options for generating Biologics Licensing Applications (BLAs) in the ICH CTD format.[59]

**Table 4-5. Overview of ICH Quality Guidelines[a]**

| Title | Description | Date of Publication in *Federal Register* |
|---|---|---|
| Q1(A–F) Stability | Provides recommendations for Climatic Zones I and II stability testing, with Zones III and IV considered in revised document | 21 November 2003– 6 June 2006 |
| Q2 Analytical Validation | Identifies necessary parameters for analytical methods and analytical procedures' validation | 19 May 1997 |
| Q3(A–D) Impurities | Addresses impurities' chemistry and safety, with specifications and defined thresholds for reporting, identification and qualification | June 2008 |
| Q4(A–B) Pharmacopoeias | Provides framework to set drug requirement specifications and recommends pharmacopoeial texts to ensure consistency among authorities and across regions | 21 February 2008 (B) |
| Q5(A–E) Quality of Biotechnological Products | Provides general framework for viral safety testing and evaluation of biotechnology products | 24 September 1998 |
| Q6(A–B) Specifications | Establishes a single set of global specifications for new drug substances and drug products | 29 December 2000 |
| Q7 Good Manufacturing Practice | Provides Good Manufacturing Practice guidance for active pharmaceutical ingredients under an appropriate quality management system | 25 September 2001 |
| Q8 Pharmaceutical Development | Suggests guidelines for the content of Section 3.2.P2 (Pharmaceutical Development), which provides a comprehensive understanding of the product and its manufacturing for reviewers and inspectors | November 2009 |
| Q9 Quality Risk Management | Provides quality risk management principles and tools applicable to all pharmaceutical quality aspects | 2 June 2006 |
| Q10 Pharmaceutical Quality System | Describes an effective quality management system model that can be implemented throughout different product lifecycle stages | 8 April 2009 |
| Q11 Development and Manufacture of Drug Substances | Describes approaches to understanding and developing a drug substance's manufacturing process | 20 November 2012 |
| Q12 Lifecycle Management | Suggests a framework to facilitate efficient postapproval chemistry, manufacturing and controls changes across a product lifecycle | September 2014 (ICH steering committee endorsement) |

a.  *ICH quality guidelines. ICH website. http://www.ich.org/products/guidelines/quality/article/quality-guidelines.html. Accessed 24 January 2017.*

When drafting text and formatting figures and tables intended for regulatory submission, published regulations and guidelines should be followed to the best of a writer's ability. However, as discussed by Rupprecht, developing and enforcing true Good Documentation Practices requires writers or other contributing regulatory professionals to read and interpret such requirements carefully.[60] In other words, knowing a single set of requirements is not enough. Many of this book's authors present detailed discussions of 21 CFR documentation requirements as they pertain to specific medical products, additional guidelines and general principles of high-quality documentation.

Following is a high-level overview on using ICH guidelines that can be adapted for using regulations as well. More detailed advice for working with specific regulations can be found in RAPS' *Fundamentals of Regulatory Affairs* series.[61]

# Overview of ICH Guidelines for Regulatory Documentation
## Quality Guidelines

ICH has published 12 major quality guidelines for industry (see Table 4-5).[62] These guidance documents cover the areas of chemistry, manufacturing, and controls for drug substances, including stability, the development and scale up of active substances, and lifecycle management. Most ICH quality guidelines are intended to provide advice on best practices for vital initial development of pharmaceutical products; Good Manufacturing Practices (GMPs) for marketed products were considered sufficiently well aligned by the 1990s, and little additional harmonization was needed.[63]

GMPs for active pharmaceutical ingredients is discussed in ICH Q7. The history of this GMP guideline differed somewhat from that of many ICH guidelines, specifically because global GMPs for pharmaceutical

**Table 4-6. Overview of ICH Safety Guidelines[a]**

| Title | Description | Date of Publication in *Federal Register* |
|---|---|---|
| S1(A–C) Carcinogenicity Studies | Defines appropriate conditions for conducting carcinogenicity studies involving animals, especially mice and rats, and provides guidelines for evaluating pharmaceuticals' carcinogenetic potential | 1 March 1996, 23 February 1998, 4 December 1997, 17 September 2008 (R2) |
| S2 Genotoxicity Studies | Provides guidelines for genotoxicity tests and evaluating results, to predict human risks optimally | 7 June 2012 |
| S3(A–B) Toxicokinetics and Pharmacokinetics | Provides guidelines for integrating pharmacokinetics into toxicity testing and developing toxicokinetic test strategies | 1 March 1995 |
| S4 Toxicity Testing | Provides guidelines for repeat-dose toxicity testing in animals | 25 June 1999 |
| S5 Reproductive Toxicology | Provides guidelines for reproductive toxicity tests, particularly extrapolating results of human exposure; includes male fertility addendum | 5 April 1996 (Addendum) |
| S6 Biotechnological Products | Includes preclinical biotechnology-derived pharmaceutical safety testing requirements | 18 May 2012 (Addendum) |
| S7(A–B) Pharmacology Studies | Provides a definition and general principles and recommendations for safety pharmacology studies | 13 July 2001 20 October 2005 |
| S8 Immunotoxicology Studies | Provides nonclinical testing recommendations to identify potentially immunotoxic compounds and guidance on weight-of-evidence decision making for immunotoxicity testing | 13 April 2006 |
| S9 Nonclinical Evaluation for Anticancer Pharmaceuticals | Provides information to assist in designing nonclinical studies for anticancer pharmaceutical development | 8 March 2010 |
| S10 Photosafety Evaluation | Provides international standards for harmonized photosafety assessments to support pharmaceutical clinical trials and marketing authorizations | 26 March 2015 |
| S11 Nonclinical | Proposed to recommend standards for nonclinical juvenile animal testing conditions to support pediatric clinical trials | November 2014 (ICH steering committee endorsement) |

a.    *ICH Safety Guidelines. ICH website. http://www.ich.org/products/guidelines/safety/article/safety-guidelines.html. Accessed 24 January 2017.*

ingredients had been harmonized earlier.[64] Thus, the ICH moved to harmonize the development and manufacture of active pharmaceutical ingredients (APIs). ICH Q7 was developed in consultation with global members outside the usual ICH community (see www.ich.org).[65] A 1998 problem statement, available on the ICH quality page, provides the rationale for developing GMPs for APIs.[66] It is worthy to note current GMP guidelines, or CGMPs, are discussed elsewhere in this book.[67]

For marketing applications in the CTD format, the ICH M4Q(R1) guidelines specifies the contents of Module 2.3, the Quality Overall Summary and Module 3, which contains detailed quality information.[68] As noted by Aslam, integrated quality documentation describes the chemistry, manufacturing and controls applicable to pharmaceutical products.[69] While this documentation often is much more formulaic when compared with nonclinical and clinical data, regional regulatory differences and product lifecycle management activities present

specific quality documentation challenges. In fact, quality documentation generally is the least "common" type of CTD information.

Notably, the manufacture of biologics and vaccines compared to small molecules and new chemical entities may differ substantially, which can affect documentation. ICH Q11 discusses the development and manufacture of both chemical and biotechnological/biological entities.[70] Manufacturing differences are only one important regulatory consideration,[71] as lifecycle management activities of vaccine and biologics products may differ from those for drug products, necessitating distinct documentation.[72]

## Safety Guidelines

ICH safety guidelines cover nonclinical investigations of new pharmaceutical, biologic and vaccine products. Nonclinical research is intended to reassure investigators that clinical evaluation is warranted based on results in animal models. Nonclinical investigations include studies

**Table 4-7. Overview of ICH Efficacy Guidelines[a]**

| Title | Description | Date of Publication in *Federal Register* |
|---|---|---|
| E1 Clinical Safety for Drugs Used in Long-Term Treatment | Provides recommendations for population exposure for drugs intended for long-term treatment of non-life-threatening conditions | 1 March 1995 |
| E2(A–F) Pharmacovigilance | Provides guidance for clinical safety reporting and aids in pharmacovigilance activities to prepare for the early postmarketing period, ensuring drug safety and risk reports | 1 March 1995–23 August 2011 |
| E3 Clinical Study Reports | Describes a single core clinical study report's structure, format and content that is integrated, clear and acceptable across all ICH regions | 17 July 1996 |
| E4 Dose-Response Studies | Provides recommendations for study design and conduct to assess the relationship between drug doses, blood concentration, clinical responses in a new drug's clinical development and identifying a starting dose | 9 November 1994 |
| E5 Ethnic Factors | Provides recommendations for a framework to evaluate ethnic factors' role in a drug's efficacy and safety, and includes the use of bridging studies to extrapolate clinical data across disparate regions | 10 June 1998 |
| E6 Good Clinical Practice | Provides a unified standard for clinical trial conduct, design, monitoring, reporting and archiving and presents investigators, monitors, sponsors, IRB and all other participants responsibilities and expectations | 9 May 1997 |
| E7 Clinical Trials in Geriatric Population | Provides recommendations for special considerations in clinical trial design and conduct for medicines with significant projected use in elderly populations | 2 August 1994 |
| E8 General Considerations for Clinical Trials | Establishes general scientific principles for the conduct, performance, safety and control of clinical trials across a wide range of subjects | 17 December 1997 |
| E9 Statistical Principles for Clinical Trials | Describes clinical trial statistical and analysis considerations and principles, especially in trials used to demonstrate drug effectiveness | 16 September 1998 |
| E10 Choice of Control Group in Clinical Trials | Considers clinical trial control group choice, with emphasis on the participant selection ethical and inferential implications and minimizing bias | 14 May 2001 |
| E11 Clinical Trials in Pediatric Population | Provides recommendations for special clinical trial design safety, efficacy and ethical issues for medicines with significant projected use in pediatric populations | 12 April 2000 |
| E12 Clinical Evaluation by Therapeutic Category | Provides established principles for endpoints and trial designs specific to evaluating new antihypertensive drugs | 9 August 2000 |
| E14 Clinical Evaluation of QT | Provides recommendations for clinical trial design, conduct, analysis and interpretation for non-antiarrhythmic drugs, with emphasis on their potential to delay cardiac repolarization | 1 March 1995 |
| E15 Definitions in Pharmacogenetics/Pharmacogenomics | Ensures consistent use of terminology by providing key pharmacogenomic and pharmacogenetic term definitions, including genomic biomarkers, pharmacogenomics, pharmacogenetics and genomic data and sampling categories | 8 April 2008 |
| E16 Qualifications of Genomic Biomarkers | Provides recommendations for the biomarker qualification regulatory submission applications' context, structure and format to ensure consistency | 11 August 2011 |
| E17 Multi-Regional Clinical Trials | Describes general multi-regional clinical trial planning and design principles across populations and ethnicities. | 8 November 2016 |
| E18 Genomic Sampling | Describes principles for the unbiased management, collection, storage and use of genomic samples and data | 2 August 2016 |

a.    *Efficacy guidelines. ICH website. http://www.ich.org/products/guidelines/efficacy/article/efficacy-guidelines.html. Accessed 24 January 2017.*

in cell culture, in vitro environments, ex vivo environments and animal models. These studies are undertaken to ensure novel drug, vaccine and biologic products (or combination product components) are not brought into the clinic until adequate evidence justifies the expectation that any benefit from its use will outweigh its potential risks. Thus, nonclinical guidelines outline the desired parameters and requirements for studies to identify potential safety concerns such as teratogenicity, toxicity or carcinogenicity[73] (see **Table 4-6**).

ICH has published 11 major safety guidelines for industry.[74] Most ICH safety guidelines provide information about appropriate study design and conduct as well as documentation. A recent development is identifying methods to evaluate the potential for prolonging the QT interval, a common cause of drug withdrawals.[75] A specialized guideline, ICH S6, limits its guidance to special considerations for biotechnology-derived products (or biologicals).[76] Other specialized safety guidelines address dermatology products and oncology products (ICH S9[77] and ICH S10[78]). The multidisciplinary guideline ICH M3[79] discusses required nonclinical safety studies for proceeding to human clinical trials.

ICH M4S(R1) details the contents of CTD Module 2.4, the Nonclinical Overview, Section 2.6, the Nonclinical Written and Tabulated summaries and Module 4.[80] This integrated nonclinical documentation should describe study rationales and the data supporting the benefit-risk ratio to justify proceeding from in vitro studies to animal models to human subjects. Unlike the more formulaic Quality Summary, the Nonclinical Overview and Nonclinical Written Summaries present numerous authoring challenges because a consistent story must be built across various scientific specialities and bridge clinical research results in such a way as to achieve product approval. Seymour's discussion of good regulatory writing provides additional guidance.[81]

Although Good Laboratory Practice (GLP) is not discussed in a dedicated ICH guideline, researchers, writers and regulatory professionals should review and understand GLPs and the applicable regulations in various regions. GLPs generally are enforceable by law and are codified in the US in 21 CFR Part 58.[82] Researchers should consult local GLP regulations and those in other regions where the investigational product is intended to be marketed.[83]

### Efficacy Guidelines

The 18 ICH efficacy guidelines were designed to assist researchers with clinical study design, conduct, data collection, analysis and reporting (**Table 4-7**). Specialized guidelines provide information regarding pediatric trials

(E11),[84] products intended for use in geriatric populations (E7)[85] and multi-regional trials (E17).[86] Statistical analysis (ICH E9)[87] and data management also are discussed in specific guidance documents, as is the clinical study report (E3).[88] Additional guidelines present information regarding control group selection (ICH E10)[89] and genomic biomarker qualification for drug product evaluation (E16).[90] The ICH efficacy guidelines are intended to ensure proper, ethical conduct and reporting of drugs, biologics, vaccines and other medicinal products' clinical trial results.

ICH finalized the initial Good Clinical Practice (GCP) Guideline (ICH E6) in 1996.[91] Although none of the original principles for ethical study conduct detailed therein have changed, ICH E6 was updated via an 'integrated addendum' to modernize information regarding electronic data collection, analysis and reporting.[92] As with the ICH GMP guidelines, it is important to supplement the ICH GCP guidance by following all applicable GCP regulations and laws.

ICH guidelines provide information regarding several documents, including the clinical trial protocol, informed consent forms, Investigator's Brochure, statistical analysis plan and clinical study report, which are discussed in individual chapters within this book.

ICH M4E presents the contents and organization of Module 2.5 (Clinical Overview), Section 2.7 (Clinical Written and Tabulated Summaries) and Module 5.[93] Integrated clinical documentation should describe the rationale for the studies conducted and data that support the a product's benefit-risk profile for clinical use. As with nonclinical documentation, the Clinical Overview and Written Summaries requires the author to compose a consistent story across functional areas, including a convincing discussion of a product's expected benefit-risk ratio in the target population. Seymour's discussion of good regulatory writing in Chapter 3 may provide additional insights.[94]

In general, study conduct considerations, whether for special populations, therapeutic areas or types of delivery (e.g., parenteral), should be identified appropriately in each document.

### Multidisciplinary Guidelines

Eight ICH multidisciplinary guidelines have been published (**Table 4-8**). These include the MedDRA dictionary (ICH M1),[95] which is intended to be used for clinical studies. ICH M3[96] identifies safety evaluations for pharmaceutical products and describes an integrated approach to presenting safety and efficacy (nonclinical and clinical) information.

The most well-recognized multidisciplinary guidelines describe CTD content, format and electronic submission.[97] Integrated documentation is discussed

**Table 4-8 Overview of ICH Multidisciplinary Guidelines[a]**

| Title | Description | Date of Publication in *Federal Register* |
|---|---|---|
| *M1 MedDRA Terminology* | Defines terms and serves as the medical dictionary to be used for regulatory activities | Not specified |
| *M2 Electronic Standards for the Transfer of Regulatory Information (ESTRI)* | Provides general guidance for electronically transferring regulatory information | Not specified |
| *M3 Nonclinical Safety Studies for the Conduct of Human Clinical Trials and Marketing Authorization for Pharmaceuticals* | Harmonizes the types of nonclinical studies needed to justify clinical trials and marketing authorizations | Not specified |
| *M4 Common Technical Document* | Specifies the Common Technical Document format and contents to be used for harmonized marketing applications | Not specified |
| *M5 Data Elements and Standards for Drug Dictionaries* | Identifies the specific data elements for standardizing medicinal product identifiers and related terminology, and, in particular, product information to facilitate the electronic exchange of Individual Case Safety Reports | Not specified |
| *M6 Virus and Gene Therapy Vector Shedding and Transmission* | Provides recommendations to industry and regulators on nonclinical and clinical studies and guidance on using analytical assays for the detection and characterization of shed virus | Not specified |
| *M7 Assessment and Control of DNA Reactive (Mutagenic) Impurities in Pharmaceuticals to Limit Potential Carcinogenic Risk* | Offers guidance on Structure Activity Relationship analyses for genotoxicity and intends to resolve questions such as whether impurities with similar alerts that potentially have similar mechanisms of action should not be combined in calculating a Threshold of Toxicological Concern | 28 May 2015 |
| *M8 Electronic Common Technical Document* | Details the technical specifications for electronic delivery of the Common Technical Document | Not specified |

*Multidisciplinary Guidelines. ICH website. http://www.ich.org/products/guidelines/multidisciplinary/article/multidisciplinary-guidelines.html. Accessed 25 January 2017.*

elsewhere in this book, and the CTD sections addressing quality, safety and efficacy are specified in **Table 4-8**. ICH M4 also outlines region-specific CTD contents.[98]

## Working With Guidelines

As noted above, many health authorities and government agencies worldwide have adopted the ICH guidelines. These guidelines should be used in connection with local regulations and other forms of guidance in creating internal SOPs and regulatory document templates.

### Consider Other Good Practice Guidelines

Good practice implies ethical and transparent conduct, consistent with commonly-accepted guidelines like the Declaration of Helsinki[99] or the PhRMA Code.[100] As noted above, ICH guidances on GMP (ICH Q7) and GCP (ICH E6) are not enough. Thus regulatory professionals must work with other experts in clinical and nonclinical research and manufacturing, to identify the appropriate professional codes and regulations to be

referenced and cited in regulatory documentation, SOPs and templates.

For example, in the US, 21 CFR describes required GLPs, including required elements for nonclinical study reports in Title 58, Good Laboratory Practice for Nonclinical Laboratory Studies. 21 CFR, Title 58, Subpart J, Section 58.185 specifies report requirements for nonclinical studies.[101] GLP standards have been published by the Organisation for Economic Co-operation and Development (OECD).[102] EMA's GLP standards appear in EU Directives 2004/9/EC[103] and 2004/10/EC.[104] FDA also is a source of information about cGMPS for drug products, medical devices and biological products. See 21 CFR Title 211.[105]

GCPs are described in ICH E6.[106] FDA provides a list of applicable regulations, specifically FDA Regulations Relating to Good Clinical Practice and Clinical Trials.[107] See **Table 4-5** for a listing of some guidelines applicable to specialized medical product areas.

As noted by Rupprecht in Chapter 2, GDocP presents special challenges because no centralized guidance exists.[108] Thus, writers and other professionals must familiarize themselves with many different guidance documents. Good documentation practice, while not regulated, is strongly suggested; a familiarity with its principles can aid regulatory writers.[109]

Good practice guidelines should be reviewed and considered at all product development stages. Teams designing and implementing SOPs and templates should refer to the most commonly-used and current GMP, GCP and GLP guidelines specific to the region in which studies are performed and products are intended to be marketed.[110]

### Seek Out Professional Society Guidelines

As noted above and throughout this book, country-, region- and therapeutic area-specific guidelines exist for many different purposes. For example, when drafting clinical trial protocols and reports, guidance such as the PhRMA Code,[111] the SPIRIT Checklist[112] and various works on the EQUATOR network[113] may be helpful to ensure that appropriate data are collected to meet reporting requirements. Clinical trial protocols also should be authored with an eye to clinical trials.gov[114] and EudraCT[115] registration and data posting requirements.

Rare disease investigations may lack prior precedents; therefore, reviewing professional society guidelines, published literature and practice guidelines may be useful. Silverstein presents special considerations regarding rare disease development program documentation in Chapter 24.[116]

### Update SOPs as Guidelines and Codes Change

SOPs and document templates necessarily lag behind updates to regulations and guidance for industry; however, regular SOP and template review and updates are necessary. Teams should consider the impact of new guidelines broadly and develop guidelines, policies and templates that meet their scientific and regulatory needs.[117]

For example, as described by Shen in Chapter 23,[118] FDA clarification of combination product guidance resulted in a greater impact on these products than anticipated initially. It may not be sufficient to simply plug new information into these documents; carefully reviewing all guidelines may be necessary to ensure SOPs and templates address new regulations, codes and guidance specific to these products.

## Conclusion

Regulations form the foundation of the guidance industry should use to ensure research, manufacturing and documentation properly support clinical and laboratory investigations. Codes and regulations alone are not enough, however, which has led to a proliferation of guidance documents. Researchers, manufacturers, writers and regulatory professionals must be familiar with general guidance, such as the ICH guidelines, especially when working in global environments, and consider local guidance documents as well. Finally, regulatory submissions should meet good practice standards, including but not limited to consistent ethical conduct.

### References

1. US Code of Federal Regulations. Title 21. Food and Drugs. Electronic Code of Federal Regulations website. http://www.ecfr.gov/cgi-bin/text-idx?SID=3ee286332416f-26a91d9e6d786a604ab&mc=true&tpl=/ecfrbrowse/Title21/21tab_02.tpl. Accessed 25 January 2017.
2. Significant Dates in US Food and Drug Law History. FDA website. http://www.fda.gov/AboutFDA/WhatWeDo/History/Milestones/ucm128305.htm. Accessed 25 January 2017.
3. *Biologics Control Act* of 1902. US Pharmacopeia website. http://www.usp.org/sites/default/files/fda-exhibit/legislation/1902.html. Accessed 25 January 2017.
4. *Federal Food and Drugs Act* of 1906. FDA website. http://www.fda.gov/RegulatoryInformation/Legislation/ucm148690.htm. Accessed 25 January 2017.
5. Op cit 2.
6. Center for Biologics Evaluation and Research. FDA website. http://www.fda.gov/BiologicsBloodVaccines/default.htm. Accessed 25 January 2017.
7. Op cit 2.
8. McKinney RJ. A Research Guide to the Federal Register and the Code of Federal Regulations. Rev 2016. Originally published in *Law Library Lights* 2002; 46(1): 10-15. Law Librarians' Society of Washington DC website. http://www.llsdc.org/fr-cfr-research-guide#H-CFR. Accessed 25 January 2017.
9. Ibid.
10. Ibid.
11. Federal Register website. https://www.federalregister.gov. Accessed 25 January 2017.
12. Op cit 8.
13. Op cit 1.
14. 21 CFR 300–399. GPO website. https://www.gpo.gov/fdsys/granule/CFR-2009-title21-vol5/CFR-2009-title21-vol5-part300. Accessed 25 January 2016; 21 CFR 600–799. GPO website. https://www.gpo.gov/fdsys/granule/CFR-2014-title21-vol7/CFR-2014-title21-vol7-part600. Accessed 25 January 2017.
15. 21 CFR Part 58. ECFR website. http://www.ecfr.gov/cgi-bin/text-idx?SID=849857ae5df56681465173b31b1bbb-6f&mc=true&tpl=/ecfrbrowse/Title21/21cfr58_main_02.tpl. Accessed 25 January 2017.
16. 21 CFR Part 4. ECFR website. http://www.ecfr.gov/cgi-bin/text-idx?SID=849857ae5df56681465173b31b1bbb-6f&mc=true&tpl=/ecfrbrowse/Title21/21cfr58_main_02.tpl. Accessed 25 January 2017.
17. 21 CFR Part 50. ECFR website. Available at: http://www.ecfr.gov/cgi-bin/text-idx?SID=849857ae5df56681465173b31b1bbb-6f&mc=true&tpl=/ecfrbrowse/Title21/21cfr50_main_02.tpl. Accessed 25 January 2017.
18. DeTora L. Chapter 13 Integrated Nonclinical Documentation. *Regulatory Writing: An Overview*. Regulatory Affairs Professionals Society. Rockville, MD. ©2017.
19. Shen J. Chapter 23 Combination Products. *Regulatory Writing: An Overview*. Regulatory Affairs Professionals Society. Rockville, MD. ©2017.
20. Grodberg J. Chapter 9 Informed Consent. *Regulatory Writing: An Overview*. Regulatory Affairs Professionals Society. Rockville, MD. ©2017.

21. 45 CFR. ECFR website. http://www.ecfr.gov/cgi-bin/text-idx?tpl=/ecfrbrowse/Title45/45tab_02.tpl. Accessed 25 January 2017.

22. Op cit 15.

23. Op cit 20.

24. Op cit 17.

25. Directive 2001/83/EC of the European Parliament and of the Commission of 6 November 2001 on the Community Code relating to medicinal products for human use. Eur-Lex website. Directive 2001/83/EC. http://eur-lex.europa.eu/LexUriServ/LexUriServ.do?uri=OJ:L:2001:311:0067:0128:en:PDF. Accessed 1 February 2017.

26. EMA website. http://www.ema.europa.eu. Accessed 25 January 2017.

27. Legal Framework Governing Medicinal Products for Use in the EU. EC website. http://ec.europa.eu/health/human-use/legal-framework_en. Accessed 25 January 2017.

28. Rupprecht J. Chapter 2 Good Documentation Practice. *Regulatory Writing: An Overview*. Regulatory Affairs Professionals Society. Rockville, MD. ©2017.

29. Guidances (Drugs). CDER website. http://www.fda.gov/Drugs/%20GuidanceComplianceRegulatoryInformation/Guidances/default.htm. Accessed 25 January 2017.

30. Biologics Guidances. CBER website. http://www.fda.gov/BiologicsBloodVaccines/GuidanceComplianceRegulatoryInformation/Guidances/default.htm. Accessed 25 January 2017.

31. Benau D. Chapter 1 An Overview of Medical and Regulatory Writing. *Regulatory Writing: An Overview*. Regulatory Affairs Professionals Society. Rockville, MD. ©2017.

32. Aslam M. Chapter 6 Developing SOPs, Planning and Strategy Documents. *Regulatory Writing: An Overview*. Regulatory Affairs Professionals Society. Rockville, MD. ©2017.

33. Op cit 19.

34. FDA website. http://www.fda.gov. Accessed 25 January 2017.

35. Human Medicines: Regulatory Information. EMA website. http://www.ema.europa.eu/ema/index.jsp?curl=pages/regulation/landing/human_medicines_regulatory.jsp&mid. Accessed 25 January 2017.

36. Op cit 31.

37. International Council on Harmonisation website. http://www.ich.org/home.html. Accessed 25 January 2017.

38. Hamilton S, Bernstein AB, Blakey G, et al. Developing the Clarity and Openness in Reporting: E3-based (CORE) Reference user manual for creation of clinical study reports in the era of clinical trial transparency. *Research Integrity and Peer Review* (2016) 1;4: DOI 10.1186/s41073-016-0009-4.

39. TransCelerate website. http://www.transceleratebiopharmainc.com. Accessed 25 January 2017.

40. Op cit 37.

41. Op cit 31. Section on Aims of Regulatory Documentation.

42. European Commission website. http://ec.europa.eu/index_en.htm. Accessed 25 January 2017.

43. European Federation of Pharmaceutical Industries and Associations website. http://www.efpia.eu. Accessed 25 January 2017.

44. Japan Ministry of Health, Labour, and Welfare. http://www.mhlw.go.jp/english/. Accessed 25 January 2-17.

45. Op cit 34.

46. PhRMA website. http://www.phrma.org. Accessed 25 January 2017,

47. *Preclinical Safety Evaluation of Biotechnology-Derived Pharmaceuticals S6(R1)*. ICH website. http://www.ich.org/fileadmin/Public_Web_Site/ICH_Products/Guidelines/Safety/S6_R1/Step4/S6_R1_Guideline.pdf. Accessed 25 January 2017.

48. Op cit 28.

49. *Guideline for Good Clinical Practice E6(R1)*. ICH website. http://www.ich.org/fileadmin/Public_Web_Site/ICH_Products/Guidelines/Efficacy/E6/E6_R1_Guideline.pdf. Accessed 25 January 2017.

50. Quality Guidelines. ICH website. http://www.ich.org/products/guidelines/quality/article/quality-guidelines.html. Accessed 25 January 2017.

51. *M4: The Common Technical Document*. ICH website. http://www.ich.org/products/ctd.html. Accessed 25 January 2017.

52. *Structure and Content of Clinical Study Reports E3*. ICH website. http://www.ich.org/fileadmin/Public_Web_Site/ICH_Products/Guidelines/Efficacy/E3/E3_Guideline.pdf. Accessed 25 January 2017.

53. General Considerations for Clinical Trials E8. ICH website. http://www.ich.org/fileadmin/Public_Web_Site/ICH_Products/Guidelines/Efficacy/E8/Step4/E8_Guideline.pdf. Accessed 25 January 2017.

54. Op cit 49.

55. Op cit 37.

56. Multidisciplinary Guidelines. ICH website. http://www.ich.org/products/guidelines/multidisciplinary/article/multidisciplinary-guidelines.html. Accessed 25 January 2017.

57. ICH History. ICH website. http://www.ich.org/about/history.html. Accessed 25 January 2017.

58. *Quality of Biotechnological Products: Stability Testing of Biotechnological/Biological Products Q5C*. ICH website. http://www.ich.org/fileadmin/Public_Web_Site/ICH_Products/Guidelines/Quality/Q5C/Step4/Q5C_Guideline.pdf. Accessed 25 January 2017.

59. Robinett RSR. The Biologics License Application (BLA) in Common Technical Document (CTD) Format. *Vaccine Development and Manufacturing*. First edition. New York: Wiley, 2015.

60. Op cit 28.

61. *Fundamentals of US Regulatory Affairs, Ninth Edition*. Regulatory Affairs Professionals Society. Rockville, MD. ©2015.

62. Quality Guidelines. ICH website. http://www.ich.org/products/guidelines/quality/article/quality-guidelines.html. Accessed 25 January 2017.

63. Concept paper: Q7: Good Manufacturing Practices for Pharmaceutical Ingredients. ICH website. http://www.ich.org/fileadmin/Public_Web_Site/ICH_Products/Guidelines/Quality/Q7/Concept_papers/Q7_Concept_Paper.pdf. Accessed 25 January 2016.

64. Ibid.

65. Ibid.

66. Concept paper; Q7: Good Manufacturing Practices for Pharmaceutical Ingredients ICH website. http://www.ich.org/fileadmin/Public_Web_Site/ICH_Products/Guidelines/Quality/Q7/Concept_papers/Q7_Concept_Paper.pdf. Accessed 1 February 2017.

67. Aslam M. Chapter 12 Integrated CMC Documentation. *Regulatory Writing: An Overview*. Regulatory Affairs Professionals Society. Rockville, MD. ©2017.

68. The Common Technical Document for the Registration of Pharmaceuticals for Human Use: Quality—M4Q(R1); Quality Overall Summary of Module 2, Module 3: Quality. ICH website. http://www.ich.org/fileadmin/Public_Web_Site/ICH_Products/CTD/M4_R1_Quality/M4Q__R1_.pdf. Accessed 26 January 2017.

69. Op cit 67.

70. Development and Manufacture of Drug Substances (Chemical Entities and Biotechnological/Biological Entities) Q11. ICH website. http://www.ich.org/fileadmin/Public_Web_Site/ICH_Products/Guidelines/Quality/Q11/Q11_Step_4.pdf. Accessed 26 January 2017.

71. DeTora L. Chapter 21 Vaccines and Biologics. *Regulatory Writing: An Overview*. Regulatory Affairs Professionals Society. Rockville, MD. ©2017.

72. Ramchnadani M. Chapter 22 Biosimilars. *Regulatory Writing: An Overview*. Regulatory Affairs Professionals Society. Rockville, MD. ©2017.

73. *Guidance on Nonclinical Safety Studies for the Conduct of Human Clinical Trials and marketing authorization for Pharmaceuticals (M3(R2)).* ICH website. http://www.ich.org/fileadmin/Public_Web_Site/ICH_Products/Guidelines/Multidisciplinary/M3_R2/Step4/M3_R2__Guideline.pdf. Accessed 26 January 2017.

74. Safety Guidelines. ICH website. http://www.ich.org/products/guidelines/safety/article/safety-guidelines.html. Accessed 26 January 2017.

75. *The Non-Clinical Evaluation of the Potential for Delayed Ventricular Repolarization (QT Interval Prolongation) by Human Pharmaceuticals S7B.* ICH website. http://www.ich.org/fileadmin/Public_Web_Site/ICH_Products/Guidelines/Safety/S7B/Step4/S7B_Guideline.pdf. Accessed 26 January 2017.

76. *Preclinical Safety Evaluation of Biotechnology-Derived Pharmaceuticals S6(R1).* ICH website. http://www.ich.org/fileadmin/Public_Web_Site/ICH_Products/Guidelines/Safety/S6_R1/Step4/S6_R1_Guideline.pdf. Accessed 26 January 2017.

77. *Nonclinical Evaluation for Anticancer Pharmaceuticals S9.* ICH website. http://www.ich.org/fileadmin/Public_Web_Site/ICH_Products/Guidelines/Safety/S9/Step4/S9_Step4_Guideline.pdf. Accessed 26 January 2017.

78. *Photosafety Evaluation of Pharmaceuticals S10.* ICH website. http://www.ich.org/fileadmin/Public_Web_Site/ICH_Products/Guidelines/Safety/S10/S10_Step_4.pdf. Accessed 26 January 2017.

79. Op cit 72.

80. *The Common Technical Document for the Registration of Pharmaceuticals for Human Use: Safety—M4S(R2); Nonclinical Overview and Nonclinical Summaries of Module 2, Organisation of Module 4.* ICH website. http://www.ich.org/fileadmin/Public_Web_Site/ICH_Products/CTD/M4__R2__Safety/M4S_R2_.pdf. Accessed 26 January 2017.

81. Seymour EM. Chapter 3 General Considerations for Quality Regulatory Writing. *Regulatory Writing: An Overview*. Regulatory Affairs Professionals Society. Rockville, MD. ©2017.

82. Op cit 15.

83. Good laboratory practice compliance. EMA website. http://www.ema.europa.eu/ema/index.jsp?curl=pages/regulation/general/general_content_000158.jsp. Accessed 26 January 2017.

84. *Clinical Investigation of Medicinal Products in the Pediatric Population E11.* ICH website. http://www.ich.org/fileadmin/Public_Web_Site/ICH_Products/Guidelines/Efficacy/E11/Step4/E11_Guideline.pdf. Accessed 26 January 2017.

85. *Studies in Support of Special Populations: Geriatrics E7.* ICH website. http://www.ich.org/fileadmin/Public_Web_Site/ICH_Products/Guidelines/Efficacy/E7/Step4/E7_Guideline.pdf. Accessed 26 January 2017.

86. *General Principles for Planning and Design of Multi-Regional Clinical Trails E17.* ICH website. http://www.ich.org/fileadmin/Public_Web_Site/ICH_Products/Guidelines/Efficacy/E17/E17_Step2.pdf. Accessed 26 January 2017.

87. *Statistical Principles for Clinical Trials E9.* ICH website. http://www.ich.org/fileadmin/Public_Web_Site/ICH_Products/Guidelines/Efficacy/E9/Step4/E9_Guideline.pdf. Accessed 26 January 2017.

88. *Structure and Content of Clinical Study Reports E3.* ICH website. http://www.ich.org/fileadmin/Public_Web_Site/ICH_Products/Guidelines/Efficacy/E3/E3_Guideline.pdf. Accessed 26 January 2017.

89. *Choice of Control Group and Related Issues in Clinical Trials E10.* ICH website. http://www.ich.org/fileadmin/Public_Web_Site/ICH_Products/Guidelines/Efficacy/E10/Step4/E10_Guideline.pdf. Accessed 26 January 2017.

90. *Biomarkers Related to Drug of Biotechnology Product Development: Context, Structure and Format of Qualification Submissions E16.* ICH website. http://www.ich.org/fileadmin/Public_Web_Site/ICH_Products/Guidelines/Efficacy/E16/Step4/E16_Step_4.pdf. Accessed 26 January 2017.

91. Op cit 49.

92. *Integrated Addendum to ICH E6(R1): Guideline for Good Clinical Practice E6(R2).* ICH website. http://www.ich.org/fileadmin/Public_Web_Site/ICH_Products/Guidelines/Efficacy/E6/E6_R2__Step_4.pdf. Accessed 26 January 2017.

93. *Revision of M4E Guideline on Enhancing the Format and Structure of Benefit-Risk Information in ICH Efficacy—M4E(R2).* ICH website. http://www.ich.org/fileadmin/Public_Web_Site/ICH_Products/CTD/M4E_R2_Efficacy/M4E_R2__Step_4.pdf. Accessed 26 January 2017.

94. Op cit 81.

95. M1 MedDRA. ICH website. http://www.ich.org/products/meddra.html. Accessed 1 February 2017.

96. Op cit 73.

97. M4: The Common Technical Document page. ICH website. http://www.ich.org/products/ctd.html. Accessed 26 January 2017.

98. Organisation of the Common Technical Document for the Registration of Pharmaceuicals for Human Use M4. ICH website. http://www.ich.org/fileadmin/Public_Web_Site/ICH_Products/CTD/M4_R4_Organisation/M4_R4__Granularity_Document.pdf. Accessed 1 February 2017.

99. *WMA Declaration of Helsinki—Ethical Principles for Medical Research Involving Human Subjects.* WMA website. http://www.wma.net/en/30publications/10policies/b3/. Accessed 26 January 2017.

100. Code on Interactions With Health Care Professionals. PhRMA website. http://www.phrma.org/codes-and-guidelines/code-on-interactions-with-health-care-professionals. Accessed 26 January 2017.

101. Op cit 15.

102. OECD Series on Principles of Good Laboratory Practice (GLP) and Compliance Monitoring. OECD website. http://www.oecd.org/chemicalsafety/testing/oecdseriesonprinciplesofgoodlaboratorypracticeglpandcompliancemonitoring.htm. Accessed 26 January 2017.

103. Op cit 83.

104. Ibid.

105. 21 CFR 211 Current Good Manufacturing Practice for Finished Pharmaceuticals. GPO website. http://www.ecfr.gov/cgi-bin/text-idx?SID=269fd3be61d5fcf4d5585b81f6c9e308&mc=true&tpl=/ecfrbrowse/Title21/21cfr211_main_02.tpl Accessed 26 January 2017.

106. Op cit 49.

107. FDA Regulations Relating to Good Clinical Practice and Clinical Trials. FDA website. http://www.fda.gov/ScienceResearch/SpecialTopics/RunningClinicalTrials/ucm114928.htm. Accessed 26 January 2017.

108. Op cit 28.

109. Battisti WP, Wager E, Baltzer L, Bridges D, Cairns A, Carswell CI, et al. Good Publication Practice for Communicating Company-Sponsored Medical Research: GPP3. *Ann Intern Med.* 2015;163:461-464; doi:10.7326/M15-0288

110. Op cit 32.

111. Op cit 100.

112. The SPIRIT Statement. SPIRIT website. http://www.spirit-statement.org/spirit-statement/. Accessed 26 January 2017.

113. Enhancing the QUAlity and Transparency Of health Research, EQUATOR Network. http://www.equator-network.org/. Accessed 26 January 2017.
114. ClinicalTrials.gov. NIH website. https://clinicaltrials.gov. Accessed 26 January 2017.
115. EudraCT website. https://eudract.ema.europa.eu/. Accessed 26 January 2017.
116. Silverstein B. Chapter 24 Rare Diseases. *Regulatory Writing: An Overview*. Regulatory Affairs Professionals Society. Rockville, MD. ©2017.
117. Op cit 32.
118. Op cit 19.

## Authors

Jenny Boyar is a medical writer at a contract research organization. The recipient of a Fulbright English Teaching Assistantship, she has published both collaboratively and independently in a variety of medical, psychology and literary resources, including *Psychology of Women Quarterly* and *New Directions in Aging Research: Health and Cognition*. She has taught writing and literature courses at both the University of Rochester and its School of Medicine and Dentistry and worked as a research assistant at the Nova Southeastern University College of Pharmacy. She holds a PhD in English from the University of Rochester.

Lisa DeTora is an assistant professor of writing studies at Hofstra University and a guest lecturer in humanities at the Hofstra Northwell School of Medicine. She began her career in medical writing at Merck and Co. Inc. and was a co-author of the company's internal guidances to comply with ICH E3 and M4. Her subsequent work experience has included regulatory writing and publication management in various therapeutic areas.

Jennifer Grodberg, PhD, RAC (US), is vice president, regulatory affairs for VenatoRx Pharmaceuticals Inc. She has more than 23 years of experience in the pharmaceutical industry, including almost 13 years in regulatory. Her experience spans the pre-IND enabling phase through NDA submission, including FDA inspections and Advisory Committee Meetings, and has interacted with Health Canada and EU regulatory authorities. Previously, Grodberg served on Harvard Medical School's Department of Medicine faculty. She holds a PhD in microbiology and has earned the RAC. She is a Fellow of the American Medical Writers Association and past-president of AMWA's Pacific Southwest Chapter.

Robin Martin is co-founder of Kinetic Compliance Solutions, LLC and a regulatory consultant with 10 years of industry experience, with eight in regulatory. She has worked with a variety of medical devices (US FDA Class I – III) and has extensive global submission experience (CE Mark, Brazil, China, Japan, Russia and rest of world). Previously, she held a variety of regulatory roles at GE Healthcare and a small device company on IDEs, PMAs and 510(k)s. Martin has a background in biomedical engineering and holds an MBA from Marquette University.

# 5

# Medical Device Submission Considerations Beyond the US, Canada and EU

*By Robin Martin, MBA, RAC*

## Introduction

Markets outside the US, Canada and the EU can be important for a medical device manufacturer's business strategy. Aligning the regulatory submission strategy with anticipated business needs is an important aspect of ensuring the business team a regulatory professional supports can obtain success in its market strategy.

To do this, it is important to understand common components of each global submission and whether there are dependencies on the Quality System, internal design/development activities or external regulatory processes.

Because the regulatory paths in the US, Canada and the EU are well established, this chapter focuses on medical device submission considerations outside those markets. However, the general considerations can be leveraged for all markets.

## General Considerations

### Consistency and Writing for the Audience

Regulatory personnel often are close to the technology with which they work. An external regulator must be able to pick up a submission and understand the product, sometimes with no prior familiarity of the technology. Visuals of the technology, such as photographs, drawings or videos, can be extremely helpful in explaining the technology to someone not familiar with it.

Information presented should be consistent and clear, so it does not lead to additional questions. Key documents, such as labeling, risk management and verification/validation summary reports, should specify the named product being registered consistently.

### Level of Registration Detail

Although it can be time consuming, ensuring the product team and regulatory professional understand the regulations and the 'why' behind what is included in submissions and dossiers can be very important in understanding the level of detail to provide. Registrations should be structured to ensure enough detail is given to understand the product, but not so much that small and insignificant product changes trigger the need for lengthy re-registrations.

### Technical Understanding

For regulatory professionals, having a technical understanding of the product being designed and eventually submitted presents clear benefits. One benefit is the ability to communicate with development teams as to when regulators may have technical concerns (for example, design attributes raising new or changed risks).

Another is the ability to respond quickly to regulators' questions without having to rely heavily on other team members' responses.

## Regional Requirements

### Site License

Certain countries require each manufacturing or design location to maintain a separate site license. Many times, these site licenses must be in place prior to the sites registering the medical devices they manufacture.

### Quality System Requirements

A number of countries require separate quality system or Good Manufacturing Practice (GMP) audits. Typically, these audits apply to sites physically manufacturing medical devices. When multiple physical manufacturers are involved, the final assembly location likely will be a target for these audits. These countries do not accept US Food and Drug Administration (FDA) or Notified Body inspection reports or International Standards Organization (ISO) 13485 Certificates; instead, they require their own certified agencies to conduct these audits. If the design owner and physical manufacturer differ, it is important to identify, by country, which site is subject to these audits. With some health authorities, such as Brazil's ANVISA, medical device registration cannot occur until the GMP audit is complete, and the audit wait list can be up to two years for a new site. These requirements may change with further implementation and acceptance of the Medical Device Single Audit Program (MDSAP), but today, the impact of separate audits on registration timing needs to be considered.

### Type or Product-Specific Testing Requirements

In addition to separate site audits, and depending on device classification and target country, a new product registration can trigger local in-country or on-site product testing. Typically, this includes evaluations of labeling, standards test reports, design history file documents and even physical device testing. Consideration of whether required physical testing is destructive can assist product teams in planning.

### In-Country Presence

Many times, countries require a local representative to be named in a submission package. This could be a distributor or separate entity, depending on a company's strategy, and the local entity could be responsible for postmarket activities or registration, or simply be a contact point for governmental agencies. Therefore, manufacturers may need to elect a representative in global countries targeted for registration.

### Approval Requirements

It is common for target countries to require evidence for approval by the country named on the product label as part of its own submission package. For example, an EU Declaration of Conformity or 510(k) clearance letter may be required by global target countries prior to registration.

When a product is not manufactured in the country of registration, a Free Sales Certificate (FSC) often is required from the manufacturer named on the label (country on the product's label). If the product's labeled manufacturer is in the US, the Free Sales Certificate, known as a Certificate to Foreign Government (CFG), can be obtained by the manufacturer from FDA. For products under recall, a CFG cannot be obtained. Sometimes, a regulatory strategy will include CE Marking or other Global Harmonization Task Force (GHTF) country approval prior to FDA clearance or approval. In these cases, it may be permissible to use an FSC from a GHTF country instead of the country of origin. This should be evaluated for each global target country.

These requirements create important dependencies that dictate timing in target markets, and the regulatory professional can assist the product team in understanding them.

### Country-Specific Documentation and Requirements

Unfortunately, medical device submission harmonization has not been widely adopted, though certain countries are moving toward accepting GHTF's Summary Technical Documentation (STED) format. As such, when products are 'going global,' they will need to be tested against multiple versions of a required standard, or have country-specific product labels or data formatted slightly differently. For example, it is important to understand the required translations (labels, user manuals or instructions and/or user interfaces). Another example is the scenario requiring multiple versions of the same standard for registration.

In addition to differing language and standards requirements, certain countries simply require a greater level of general documentation detail. For example, a country may require a technical file with photographs of each component and accessory.

Understanding these as product development design inputs can save time, as they can be completed in parallel with design efforts. The regulatory professional should ensure the engineering and development teams understand these requirements and then can assist in gathering information that typically is not part of design work. This can be particularly difficult with devices that have a long development cycle, where changing regulations can have an impact, but this knowledge and communication can save key target country registration time.

## Conclusion

Understanding target market inputs for global registrations in advance allows appropriate planning and assists in streamlining registrations. The regulatory professional working on global product launches needs to communicate with product teams and in-country representatives to achieve a successful global product launch.

**Author**

Robin Martin is co-founder of Kinetic Compliance Solutions, LLC and a regulatory consultant with 10 years of industry experience, with eight in regulatory. She has worked with a variety of medical devices (US FDA Class I – III) and has extensive global submission experience (CE mark, Brazil, China, Japan, Russia and rest of world). Previously, she held a variety of regulatory roles at GE Healthcare and a small device company on IDEs, PMAs and 510(k)s. She has a background in biomedical engineering and holds an MBA from Marquette University.

6

# Developing SOPs, Planning and Strategy Documents

*By Mariam Aslam*

## Introduction

Regulatory is a profession that acts on rules and regulations to ensure products are in compliance with existing laws and best practices. It is imperative for regulatory professionals to understand and execute regulatory activities efficiently and 'get it right first time.' Each regulatory professional will have a unique approach to his or her work method. For an independent consultant, the approach should be aligned with the client's requirements and goals. Regulatory professionals working for a company must consider the business' needs and best practices. Companies can sometimes have a variable approach in planning and preparing submission documents. Although every submission package may vary in content, this variable method leads to irregularity not only from one submission package to another but also from one regulatory professional to another within the same company.

How can regulatory professionals avoid irregularities and ensure regularity when preparing regulatory documents? One solution is to have standard operating procedures (SOPs) in place. SOPs are comprehensive, written guidelines to achieve consistency in accomplishing specific tasks. How does this process work? The first step is to develop the SOPs. A number of points should be considered when developing and planning an SOP, such as the SOP's purpose, who will be assigned to prepare it, who will read or use it and who is responsible for any specific

task as well as the appropriate format under the company's business rules. Before writing SOPs, companies need to establish why they are needed and who will be responsible for seeing they are followed. At this stage, it also is worth considering SOP authors and reviewers. These points are described in more detail later in this chapter.

Developing effective SOPs ensures consistency and good organization in executing regulatory activities. An SOP should capture the reader's attention from start to finish, at which point the reader should have fully understood it and know how to follow the procedure. The SOP should ensure the main points and tasks are written clearly and can be followed efficiently. An important aspect in developing an SOP is to determine the reviewer(s) and approver(s) of the final version. This requires careful consideration, since too many assessors can result in delays and an inefficient process.

It is prudent to have an SOP for SOP preparation and management. This is useful for preparing company SOPs and provides guidance on achieving consistent format and version numbering and the review and approval process, as well as periodic SOP review and updating.

SOPs can be integral to preparing planning and strategy documents (PSDs). Regulatory professionals should take advantage of PSDs that are in place because they are essential to successfully communicating the correct regulatory path for preparing and submitting regulatory documentation to support medicines' pre- and postapproval requirements. When embarking on a new regulatory activity, regulatory professionals can prepare PSDs that will enable them to consult all concerned company departments responsible for implementing postapproval regulatory change. Prior to any decision-making process, PSDs will be valuable tools to ensure timelines are met. PSDs should be documented and referenced and, if possible, signed off by all relevant functions collaborating in the regulatory process.

Before discussing how to develop SOPs and PSDs, following are their definitions.

## What are SOPs?

An SOP is a set of complete, written guiding principles to help execute tasks and/or projects consistently. They are procedures within an organization that also can be specific to each function or department. In the regulatory profession, SOPs are beneficial for executing regulatory activities that require a consistent and efficient approach. In addition to being a set of instructions, SOPs also serve as a guidance and reminder for those routine regulatory tasks that sometimes can become habits and carry a risk of becoming inconsistent. Other important reasons for SOPs are to ensure efficient communication and to ensure duties are performed to a high quality and in compliance with rules and regulations.

### How to Develop Effective SOPs

Before a regulatory professional prepares an SOP, a number of vital points need to be addressed. These points range from the reason for the SOP to identifying its title, format, content, audience, reviewer and approver. The SOP reader needs to be engaged from start to finish. Therefore, making an SOP effective requires careful planning and consideration to prevent the reader from falling asleep before reaching the main content. When developing an effective SOP, communication with peers who are collaborating is imperative. This will be most essential at the draft stage, before final approval and the effective date.

### What are PSDs?

PSDs are reports for strategic analysis of regulatory project-related responsibilities. They are a form of communicating, decision making, assessing, managing risks and documenting simple to complex regulatory strategies that may or may not impact other organizational functions. They are key to successful communication for selecting the correct regulatory path during both medicines' pre- and postapproval phases. Prior to any decision-making process, PSDs will be a valuable tool for forecasting timelines.

### How to Develop PSDs

Before a regulatory professional prepares PSDs, a number of vital points need to be addressed, such as the documents' purpose, content, author, audience, reviewer and approver.

A PSD template should be prepared and made available to the regulatory professional planning and recommending the best regulatory submission path. When developing PSDs, highlight and discuss all possible scenarios. For example, the proposed strategy should consider any risks that need to be assessed and managed, regulatory requirements, current legislation compliance, collaborators who will impact planning and strategy and timelines to address.

PSDs should be shared with all concerned company departments and used as an opportunity to challenge any factors that may impact the proposed submission strategy. Regulatory professionals must be flexible and review all possible scenarios to avoid delays and further questions from regulatory agencies when developing PSDs.

Signed and dated copies of PSD reports are recommended. Following is a discussion of preparing PSDs for regulatory submissions.

## PSDs for Regulatory Submissions

As a reminder, PSDs are reports for strategic analysis of regulatory project-related responsibilities. PSDs can be prepared and formatted in accordance with regulatory submission requirements. A basic PSD template should be in place and adapted for each regulatory submission. It is advisable to have an SOP linked to the PSD template and work instructions (WI) on how to adapt the template in accordance with the submission requirements. The SOP's purpose should be 'Preparing Planning and Strategy Documents for Regulatory Submissions.' Such documents are helpful for organization, communication, documentation and establishing the submission requirements.

Conducting Regulatory Intelligence (RI) is an important action in preparing PSDs. RI should include data collection, data analysis, risk assessment, regulatory strategy preparation, communication and application submission or delivery. Once data have been collated, they should be analyzed and summarized in the PSDs. Risks should also be highlighted and measures to be taken to manage them. For example, if possible at each step of the proposed regulatory strategy, determine where delays and deficiencies in the review of the dossier may be likely to arise. After the PSDs have been prepared, they should be shared with all parties that are concerned with the submission. In summary, before preparing a regulatory submission, determine what needs to done and prepare the PSDs and submission deliverables. PSDs should be

**Figure 6-1. Example Template Guide to Preparing Planning and Strategy Document for Regulatory Submission**

| Document Title:<br>[e.g., Planning and Strategy Documents for Regulatory Submission]<br><br>Document Reference: | Print Date: |
|---|---|
| Prepared By:<br>[Author's Name] | Date Prepared: |
| Reviewed By:<br>[Reviewer's Name] | Date Reviewed: |
| Approved By:<br>[Approver's Name] | Date Approved: |

**Introduction:** (A regulatory strategy is a summary and data analysis for maintaining a product's legal lifecycle management. RI should be implemented to prepare a strategy, i.e., collating and analyzing regulatory information available in the public domain.)

**Purpose:** (This note for guidance is to ensure the regulatory professional can advise a realistic and achievable strategy to support the objectives to maintain a product's legal lifecycle. The aim also is to assess and manage any potential risks in meeting deadlines.)

**Procedure:** (When a new project is undertaken, the objectives' purpose must be understood and a timeline to achieve the project's goals identified. A regulatory strategy document should be prepared using the templates in Appendices 1 and 2. To facilitate completing these templates, RI should gather product history, current SmPC, pending submissions, current regulations and guidelines from websites such as Eudralex, EMA, NCA. If necessary, the regulatory agency query inbox should be checked, e.g., for initial consultation and/or confirmation of variation proposal change code, grouping of variations. A copy of the strategy should be retained for review and agreement with the relevant business functions, e.g., marketing, quality and manufacturing.)

| Appendix 1 | |
|---|---|
| **Regulatory Strategy Document** | |
| Date | DD Month YYYY |
| Version number | 01.1 |
| Product name | As registered on the SmPC |
| License number(s) and country(s) of registration | e.g., PL 00000/0000<br><br>Registered in the UK |
| Product background | e.g., reason for update/variation |
| Justification for submission | For variations, provide background, justify variation change(s) and propose postapproval commitments, if applicable.<br>Points to be included in cover letter and application form. |
| Identification of submission and corresponding submission type(s) | Example<br>**Submission:**<br>MAA, renewal, grouping/single variation, labeling and leaflet Article 61(3) application<br>**For variations:**<br>**Procedure Type(s):**<br>IA$_{IN}$, IA, IB, II<br>**EU Variation Change Code(s):**<br>A.z, B.III.a.1, C.1.z, C.1.4*(Refer to the following pages for the number of variations)<br>*(For grouping of variations, assess the number of variations and present in a table using the template in Appendix 2) |
| Grouping of variations | **Highest procedure type:**<br>Type II<br>**Is preapproval required from the Competent Authority?**<br>Yes/No<br>**If yes, has this been achieved?**<br>Yes/No<br>N.B., for grouping of variations, it is imperative to include wording that one change is a consequence of another |

**Figure 6-1. Example Template Guide to Preparing Planning and Strategy Document for Regulatory Submission (cont'd.)**

| | |
|---|---|
| Total fees and payment method, if applicable | **Total fees:**<br>(confirm payment method with Competent Authority website and any additional documentation required in submission) |
| Variation conditions to be fulfilled and documentation checklist (Delete this row if not applicable to submission.) | Copy and paste conditions and documentation from relevant change code(s). Confirm with relevant function, such as manufacturing, that conditions have been fulfilled and documentation is available. State 'confirmed' after each condition and 'available' after each type of documentation listed. For example:<br>**Change code:**<br>B.III.1 a 2—Updated certificate from an already approved manufacturer<br>**Conditions to be fulfilled:**<br>1. The finished product release and end of shelf life specifications remains the same. **(confirmed)**<br>5. The active substance is not sterile. **(confirmed)**<br>**Documentation:**<br>1. Copy of the current (updated) Ph. Eur. Certificate of Suitability. **(available; refer to Module 3R)**<br>3. Amendments of the relevant sections of the dossier (presented in EU-CTD format). **(available; refer to Module 1 and Module 3.2.S and 3R)**<br>**Documentation to accompany variation package:**<br>(Example)<br>Cover letter<br>Application form<br>EU guidelines change code<br>CTD TOCs (M1, M2, M3 and M5)<br>Proof of payment<br>Preclinical/Clinical/Quality Overview<br>Literature references |
| Timeframes | **Preparation of submission package:**<br>(include start date; date sent for review; completion date)<br>**Launch date:**<br>e.g., proposed date to market the product with the approved changes<br>**Implementation date for variation(s):**<br>e.g., within six months of approval date for Type IB and II.<br>For Type IAIN, MHRA requires 'immediate notification' within two weeks of the change being implemented. Type IA changes should be implemented before notifying the agency, ensuring the application is submitted within 12 months.<br>**Preapproval from Competent Authority:**<br>(include date request sent; date preapproval accepted)<br>**Competent Authority review timeframe:** e.g., MHRA will take up to 30 days to process Type IA applications.<br>MHRA will take 30, 90 or 120 days to assess a Type II application depending on the urgency or complexity of the changes, excluding time taken to answer questions. |
| Risk assessment | This list is not exhaustive. The main risks in not meeting launch dates are as follows:<br>1. Incomplete submission, such as insufficient data, resulting in Request for Further Information (RFI)/questions from the assessor.<br>2. Incorrect variation procedure type and change code resulting in nonacceptance<br>3. Error in implementation date for Type IA and Type $IA_{IN}$ resulting in nonacceptance<br>4. Error in fee submission<br>5. Submission package not valid in accordance with e-CTD and NeeS format<br>6. Grouping of variations submitted to the MHRA has not been preapproved.<br>7. Preapproval notification of grouping of variations has not been included in the submission package.<br>8. Relevant pages from the guidelines have not been attached.<br>9. Boxes have not been ticked in relevant pages from the guidelines. |

**Figure 6-1. Example Template Guide to Preparing Planning and Strategy Document for Regulatory Submission (cont'd.)**

| | |
|---|---|
| Risk management | 1. Confirm correct change code with Competent Authority, if necessary.<br>2. Ensure all conditions have been fulfilled, and documentation is available.<br>3. For variation grouping, it is imperative to include wording that one change is a consequence of another in the cover letter and application form.<br>4. For variation Type IA, ensure the implementation date is within 12 months of submission to the Competent Authority.<br>5. For variation Type $IA_{IN}$, ensure the implementation date is within two weeks of submission to the Competent Authority.<br>6. Quality check all supporting documentation.<br>7. Thoroughly check that the prepared submission package is complete; all boxes in the pages from the guidelines are ticked, application form is complete and proof of payment is included.<br>8. Check to ensure all hyperlinks and book markings in the submission package are functioning.<br>9. Execute a submission validation report.<br>10. Obtain a secondary quality check of the prepared submission package. |

| Appendix 2 | |
|---|---|
| **Tabulation and Analysis of the Number of Variations** | |
| **Total Number of Variations:** N (N x Type IB; N x Type II) | |
| **Highest Type Procedure:** Type IB/II | |
| **Amends to MA** (list all changes affecting the license) | **Comments** |
| e.g., proposed text for Section 4.4, 4.8, 6.6 of SmPC to align with an updated CCDS | For each change, classify according to EU variation guidelines. Include change code and procedure type. For example, C.I.4, Type II |

**Revision History**

| Revision | Date Effective | Description of Change | Reason for Change |
|---|---|---|---|
| 1.0 | | First issue | Not applicable or first issue |
| 2.0 | | | |
| 3.0 | | | |

documented and referenced to each regulatory submission. If possible, they should be signed off by all relevant functions collaborating on the project.

**Table 6-1** and the sidebar provide a sample template guide for preparing PSDs for postapproval submissions.

## SOPs for Content, Review, Approval, Quality Control and Quality Assurance

### Content of SOPs

A generic template should be available to format all SOPs consistently (see **Figure 6-2**). In addition, an SOP should be available for managing SOP preparation, outlining format, content, version control, review, approval, relevant training, maintenance and archiving.

Content should include at minimum:

a. Title
The SOP's title should be relevant to the procedure's purpose. When considering the title, the SOP reader always should be considered. The title must alert readers immediately of the SOP's topic. For example, a regulatory professional planning to author an SOP for regulatory dossier preparation and submission may suggest the title 'Preparation and Submission of Regulatory Dossiers.'

b. Version
The SOP should include a version number to indicate its revision history.

c. Reviewer(s) and Approver(s) Names
A reviewer will assess the SOP's content to ensure it is accurate. An approver will agree to the content. Often, the reviewer and approver are the same. A list of the SOP reviewers and approvers, with signatures and dates, will indicate the document is effective for use.

d. Table of Contents
This is essential to navigate to each SOP section. In an electronic SOP, hyperlinks can be applied to the table of contents for quick navigation to each section.

e. Purpose
The SOP's purpose should be a brief paragraph or sentence to explain the reason for the SOP.

**Figure 6-2. Example SOP Template**

| Document No.<br>[ID] | SOP Title: | | Print Date: |
|---|---|---|---|
| Version No.<br>1.0 | Prepared By:<br>[Author's Name] | | Date Prepared: |
| Effective Date: | Reviewed By:<br>[Reviewer's Name] | | Date Reviewed: |
| | Approved By:<br>[Approver's Name] | | Date Approved: |

**Table of Contents:**
[List title of each section in the SOP and the page number where it is located]
**Purpose:**
[The purpose of this SOP is to ...]
**Scope:**
[This SOP applies to all employees within function...]
**Procedure:**
1.0 [First Step]
    1.1 [Who is responsible for the first step of the process and what do they need to do?]
    1.2 [Who is responsible for the first step of the process and what do they need to do?]
2.0 [Second Step]
    2.1 [Who is responsible for the second step of the process and what do they need to do?]
    2.2 [Who is responsible for the second step of the process and what do they need to do?]
3.0 [Third step]
    3.1 [Who is responsible for the third step of the process and what do they need to do?]
4.0 [Fourth step]
    4.1 [Who is responsible for the third step of the process and what do they need to do?]

**Responsibilities**

| Role | Responsibility |
|---|---|
| Author | [List author responsibilities<br>e.g., creates and updates SOP<br>Responsible for review and approval process<br>Training delegates in using the SOP] |
| Reviewer | [List reviewer responsibilities<br>e.g., review SOP for accuracy<br>Ensures the SOP is in line with current practices and regulations] |
| Approver | [List approver responsibilities<br>e.g., confirm accuracy of SOP and that it meets current regulations and requirements] |
| Responsible Person 1 | [List responsibilities of actions] |
| Responsible Person 2 | [List responsibilities of actions] |
| Responsible Person 3 | [List responsibilities of actions] |
| Responsible Person 4 | [List responsibilities of actions] |

**References**
[List all documents, procedures and work instructions that must be read with the SOP]

**Abbreviations**

| Abbreviation | Full Text |
|---|---|
| SOP | Standard Operating Procedure |
| WI | Work instruction |

**Revision History**

| Revision | Date Effective | Description of Change | Reason for Change |
|---|---|---|---|
| 1.0 | | First issue | Not applicable or first issue |
| 2.0 | | | |
| 3.0 | | | |

**Figure 6-3. Example Template Flow Diagram**

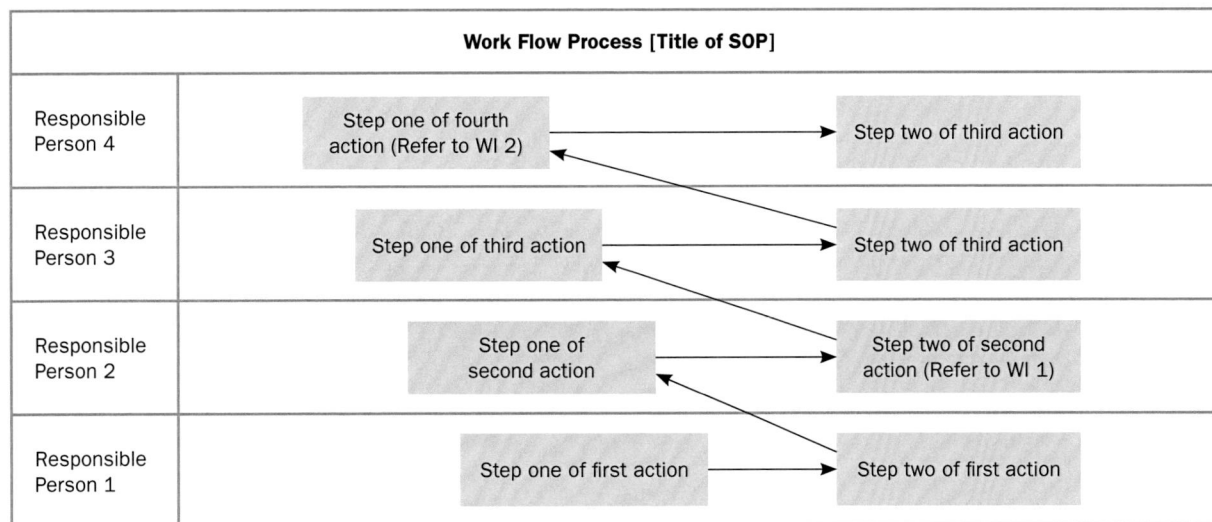

| Work Flow Process [Title of SOP] | | |
|---|---|---|
| Responsible Person 4 | Step one of fourth action (Refer to WI 2) | Step two of third action |
| Responsible Person 3 | Step one of third action | Step two of third action |
| Responsible Person 2 | Step one of second action | Step two of second action (Refer to WI 1) |
| Responsible Person 1 | Step one of first action | Step two of first action |

f.  Scope
The SOP's purpose also can be included in this section, which also can describe how the SOP is used. Include standards, regulatory requirements, roles and responsibilities in this section.

g.  Procedure
This section will provide step-by-step guidance on how to execute the SOP. It also can reference personnel who are responsible for each procedure step.

h.  Responsibilities
This section lists each individual's role and responsibility for the preparation, review and approval of the SOP and indicates which departmental functions will implement the SOP.

i.  References
Where appropriate, this section will list procedures and documents that should be read in conjunction with the SOP.

j.  Abbreviations
If any texts are used more than once in the SOP, abbreviations can be used, e.g., work instructions can be abbreviated to WI. The abbreviations section should list and define all acronyms.

k.  Revision History
This section details the number of times the SOP has been authored, version dates, reasons for updates and a description of the current version's changes. It also is practical for history tracking and version control during an audit.

l.  Review Frequency

The frequency of SOP review can be referenced. If no immediate updates are required due to business activity and regulation changes, SOPs generally are reviewed annually in accordance with business practice and rules.

m.  Flow Diagram and Work Instruction
A flow diagram can summarize key points and can contain links to navigate to other SOP sections. Nonetheless, a flow diagram can be either too detailed and complex or too concise and simple. The flow diagram's detail will be subject to the SOP's content and purpose. A WI, which is a more-detailed document on how to execute a specific task, also can be referenced as an additional document that needs to be read with the SOP.

Figures **6-2, 6-3** and **6-4** contain example templates for SOP format and content, flow diagram and WI.

## SOP Review, Approval, QC and QA

After an SOP has been authored, the reviewer and approver need to understand the procedures associated with their review and approval tasks. An SOP should be available for SOP review and approval. This should contain a checklist of responsibilities for the reviewer and approver to use as a reference. The reviewer also will be completing QC checks, while the reviewer will give the final QA check.

**Figure 6-4. Example Template of Work Instruction**

| Document No.<br>[ID] | WI Title: | | Print Date: |
|---|---|---|---|
| Version No.<br>1.0 | Prepared By:<br>[Author's Name] | | Date Prepared: |
| Effective Date: | Reviewed By:<br>[Reviewer's Name] | | Date Reviewed: |
| | Approved By:<br>[Approver's Name] | | Date Approved: |

**Table of Contents:** [List title of each WI section and the page number where it is located]
**Purpose:** [The purpose of this WI is to …(Provide reference to relevant SOP, as appropriate)]
**Procedure:**
1.0 [First step of WI]
1.1 [Part I of WI]
1.2 [Part II of WI]
2.0 [Second step of WI]
3.0 [Third step of WI]

**References**
[List all documents and procedures that must be read with the WI]

**Abbreviations**

| Abbreviation | Full Text |
|---|---|
| SOP | Standard Operating Procedure |
| WI | Work instruction |

**Revision History**

| Revision | Date Effective | Description of Change | Reason for Change |
|---|---|---|---|
| 1.0 | | First issue | Not applicable or first issue |
| 2.0 | | | |
| 3.0 | | | |

## Reviewer Role

The reviewer has two main responsibilities: assessing the SOP's accuracy and its compliance with current business practices and regulations. In addition to accuracy, the reviewer should check the SOP's application. Ideally, the reviewer will be a person involved in the process who can provide valuable input. When the reviewer receives the draft SOP, all supporting data and references also must be available to complete the review. It is advisable for the reviewer to meet with the author to discuss any required updates, so both parties can align on the final version before it is sent to the approver.

Following is a QC checklist the reviewer, at minimum, should be assessing:

1.  content alignment to generic SOP format
2.  grammar and spelling
3.  data correctness
4.  references
5.  SOP meets regulatory requirements

## Approver Role

The approver's primary role is to confirm the review has been completed to ensure the SOP is accurate and in line with current requirements and regulations. The approver should represent the department function that will implement the SOP. If required, the approver should liaise with the author to confirm the SOP's relevance and data are correct before final approval.

A QA checklist for the approver should confirm, at minimum:

1.  content alignment to generic SOP format
2.  grammar and spelling
3.  data correctness
4.  references
5.  the process meets regulatory requirements

## Regional Differences

From a global perspective, what regional differences should be considered: e.g., language, culture and law of the land? Many international companies use global SOPs as references to be translated to meet local procedures.

Companies need to determine whether global SOPs impact local procedures. Processes must be in place to decide whether global SOPs need to be implemented regionally. Roles and responsibilities must be defined to implement local SOPs.

During the review and approval process, one person per country should review and approve the local procedures. The regional reviewer and approver will be acting for any other personnel/functions involved in the process.

## Summary

- SOPs are beneficial for executing regulatory activities that require a consistent and efficient approach.
- PSDs are reports for strategic analysis of regulatory project-related responsibilities. They help communication, decision making, assessing and managing risks and documenting of simple to complex regulatory strategies that may or may not impact other functions within an organization.
- SOPs can be integral to PSDs.
- PSD templates should be prepared and made available to regulatory professionals involved in planning and recommending the best path for regulatory agency submissions.
- When developing an effective SOP, communication with collaborating peers is imperative.

**Author**

Mariam Aslam is a senior consultant at PAREXEL Consulting and a qualified chemist with eight years of laboratory and more than 10 years of regulatory experience. She has worked in postapproval marketing authorizations and has an excellent understanding of regulations, guidelines and implementing them within a pharmaceutical or healthcare organization to ensure compliance. She also has pharmacovigilance experience as a deputy QPPV, interviewed in an MHRA pharmacovigilance inspection, attended EMA Eudravigilance training and gained qualified reporter status.

# 7

# Future Directions for Regulatory Writing

*By Steve Carr and Helle Gawrylewski*

Information is a key asset in any organization. Google, for example, is a master at managing information and extracting value from it. The Google Books Library Project has an ultimate goal of working with "publishers and libraries to create a comprehensive, searchable, virtual card catalog of all books in all languages that helps users discover new books and publishers discover new readers."[1] Regulatory professionals can do something similar with the information in our corporate and regulatory documents. The drug development enterprise is an evidence-generating machine, but falls short by not using standardization or common understanding to make these large amounts of information usable to their full extent. As high value is placed on a product, like a new drug or device, assigning such value to the information contained in regulatory documents should be considered. A lot could be learned from the marketing world on forward thinking about content management and content presentation to various audiences.

## Written Content as Data

Thinking about content as data may be a culture change in many organizations. How can written content be considered as data? And how can written content be managed as data is managed? In essence, a document can be thought of as a compilation of searchable data elements. While this mindset may be anathema to the purist writer or document reviewer, it could allow an organization to extract more value out of existing content, freeing writers and other professionals to write important new content, rather than re-hashing material that could be used "as is." This culture change would require writers to develop material for a project, not a specific document. For example, a writer summarizing a pivotal Phase 3 study's efficacy results for a clinical study report (CSR) also could think, "how could this content be used in other downstream documents like a Module 5 integrated summary of efficacy or Module 2 summary of clinical efficacy, or even a clinical overview?" Likewise, reviewers would have to accept the content "as is," and not succumb to the temptation to edit at will. Thus, strategic content would be available for use in a number of venues, ensuring consistency and accuracy.

## Structured Content Management

To get to this new state and mindset, an organization would need to embrace the concept of structured content management (SCM). SCM tenets are modular authoring, metadata and re-use. The idea is writers produce "modules" that could be stored in a library, available for use within documents as needed. To make this process work, metadata, or data about the data or content, are assigned to enable searches and re-use. A simple example is re-purposing protocol or study report elements to populate the document's synopsis. Word's bookmarking functionality can be used to assign metadata (i.e., a name) to a text element like the subject population description, and the cross-referencing tool then can be used to pull that text element into the synopsis. Of course, writers may need to make some adjustments to the document's body to support this re-use, such as including brief summary statements at the beginning of various sections or limiting the number of words. Once the synopsis is populated in this way, no additional writing would be needed, only minimal review and quality control checks. Further, the writer would need to update only the document's body after reviews, because the synopsis would be populated automatically.

Similarly, information could be populated across documents. For example, a CSR's methods section should be in the protocol; it would be most efficient to use those modules verbatim. The potential for content re-use is even greater when considering the last two to three months before a submission target date, when the final, pivotal Phase 3 studies are being completed and other submission documents are being written and finalized. Approved modular content in a pivotal CSR could be re-used in downstream submission documents, reducing the need to worry about consistency, re-review or quality control checks. Similar applications could be envisioned for worldwide labeling or chemistry, manufacturing and controls submission content and dossier maintenance. Labeling and submission data elements, for plain language summaries, could be prepared in parallel, in multiple languages. Key sections of these documents also could be used for health authorities, public release, or in plain language for documents for participants.

Many teams, Institutional Review Boards and investigational sites likely have encountered complex and lengthy Investigator's Brochures (IBs) that are difficult to navigate. SCM could help improve an IB's usability, by adopting a "highlights" section, much like a product label in the new format to "provide immediate access to the information to which practitioners most commonly refer and regard as most important."[2] A highlights cover page for each IB could employ boxes, multiple columns, bolding, italics and other formatting to emphasize key information for the reader. Writing the IB in a modular fashion would allow this key content to be repurposed, redisplayed and reformatted to provide a format likely to be more user-friendly than the typical IB summary.

SCM also would allow a writer to pull information into documents from authoritative data sources in the organization, or push information to data repositories outside the organization. For example, basic protocol study information like compound name, protocol number and protocol title could be pulled to a title page from a master data hub, rather than re-typed. Protocol and study result elements from the CSR also could be pushed to a public registry like ClinicalTrials.gov for disclosure purposes. Since disclosure requirements only will increase, SCM could save a great deal of rework.

## Automated Redaction, Translation and Big Data Summaries

The move toward greater transparency with trial data is good for patients, caregivers and companies. Initiatives like the Yale Open Data Access Project[3] and the new Policy 0070 in Europe[4,5] require organizations to provide redacted, anonymized documents for public consumption. Yet, manually reviewing and redacting personally identifiable information and company commercial information in clinical documents are laborious. Organizations are working on ways to use machine reading to auto-redact this type of information. These approaches include the concept of machine "learning" whereby the redaction algorithm is refined and improved based on review of the machine redactions. An automated approach to redaction and anonymization would be a big efficiency gain for any organization.

The innovation target is to move routine summary activities to an automated function and allow the use and re-use of well formulated text and concepts. This innovation is needed particularly in the area of translation, since the global demand for understandable native language study documents and results is increasing. Free software like Moses, a statistical machine translation system that can be used to train statistical models of text translation for any language pair, is a promising option. All that is needed is a collection of translated texts (parallel corpus or translation memory). Moses is supported primarily by the EU and is open source. Machine writing and translation also is possible at this time with natural language processing capabilities. News stories and financial reports already are being summarized daily for smartphone consumption.

Another promising option that could be applied to the medical writing landscape is machine summarization of information in big data repositories. Using real-world evidence and actual treatment experiences to inform efficacy and safety assessments has been discussed for a number of years, but still is evolving.

With the renewed focus on payers and patients, using existing data, while tempting, also is challenging. Some health authorities have granted approvals based on rigorous noninterventional studies and accepted such clinical evidence for regulatory decision making. As the FDA Center for Devices and Radiological Health notes: "harvesting, validating, organizing, and disseminating information in these data warehouses, when appropriate, can potentially enhance the quality and effectiveness of regulatory decision making."[6] The approaches already used to address the public health situation with Alzheimer's will impact other disease areas: better use of observational studies and real-world data; patient involvement and wearable monitors; collaborations among industry groups and researchers to aggregate data; transparency and data sharing; even social media and patient self-reporting. All these data sources need to be accessible, analyzable and capable of creating value and impacting public health. Making the analytics accessible and useful is another opportunity to generate machine summaries conveying results in a human readable way. Machine-directed analytics and natural language summaries already enable synthesis of large volumes of data. Making sense of the large data volumes generated from patient wearables or monitoring tools requires analysis and summary before the knowledge becomes useful and applicable in novel ways.

## Conclusion

In conclusion, we all can acknowledge that the biopharmaceutical industry, like many industries, often is slow to change. The industry is highly regulated, which contributes to some inertia, but other factors also are important. Structured content and machine-driven summaries will free writers to be scientist-writers and strategists and to write important new content rather than languishing in a world of endless manual re-working of old content like assembly line compilers. New ways of thinking and technology can be harnessed to improve the writing process and products, and continue to meet evolving regulatory requirements. Generating new knowledge and treatments to further public health requires new ways of approaching problems, such as SCM. Thinking beyond the current world of individual documents in PDF format, it is possible to imagine other platforms like tablets, smartphones or some future electronic device could provide content to investigators in a mobile and accessible way.

These are the future challenges.

**References**

1. https://www.google.com/googlebooks/library/. Accessed 1 January 2017.
2. *Guidance for Industry: Labeling for Human Prescription Drug and Biological Products —Implementing the PLR Content and Format Requirements* (2013). FDA website. http://www.fda.gov/downloads/drugs/guidancecomplianceregulatoryinformation/guidances/ucm075082.pdf. Accessed 1 January 2017.
3. Yale Open Data Access (YODA) Project. Yale University website. http://yoda.yale.edu/. Accessed 1 January 2017.
4. European Medicines Agency policy on publication of clinical data for medicinal products for human use (Policy 0070), EMA/240810/2013, 2 October 2014. EMA website. http://www.ema.europa.eu/docs/en_GB/document_library/Other/2014/10/WC500174796.pdf. Accessed 1 January 2017.
5. External guidance on the implementation of the European Medicines Agency policy on the publication of clinical data for medicinal products for human use, EMA/90915/2016, 2 March 2016. EMA website. http://www.ema.europa.eu/docs/en_GB/document_library/Regulatory_and_procedural_guideline/2016/03/WC500202621.pdf. Accessed 1 January 2017.
6. US Food and Drug Administration, Center for Devices and Radiological Health, Regulatory Science Priorities (FY2016). FDA website. http://www.fda.gov/downloads/MedicalDevices/ScienceandResearch/UCM467552.pdf. Accessed 1 January 2017.

Note: The opinions expressed in this chapter are those of the authors and not necessarily those of the company or institution that employs them.

**Authors**

Steve Carr is a director, medical writing at Janssen Research & Development LLC. He has more than 25 years of experience in the pharmaceutical industry, with experience in basic research, regulatory affairs and medical writing, and has authored a number of scientific publications. He is interested in innovation in the medical writing space.

Helle M Gawrylewski, MA, is a senior director in medical writing at Janssen Research & Development LLC, with more than 40 years of work promoting medical writing and translation as professions in the pharmaceutical industry and being a force for change in professional organizations like DIA, CDISC, AMWA and RAPS.

**Acknowledgements**

The authors thank Frank Meloni, PhD; Diane Klatzman, RN, BSN; Carl Jameson, MS; Paul Sokol, PhD; and Joe Lallier, MS, MBA, RAC of Janssen Research and Development, LLC for their review and suggestions for improvement of this chapter.

# 8

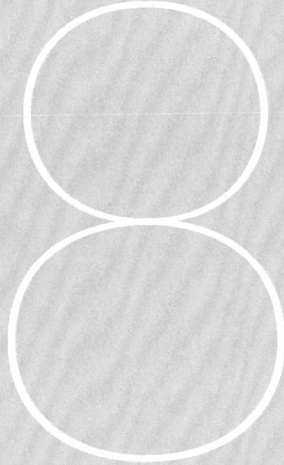

## Clinical Protocols

*By Sharanya Ramasubramanian*

A study protocol is a regulated document required to conduct nonclinical, clinical, epidemiological or public health research. More simply, the protocol is the planned blueprint to conduct a research study. The protocol also is a 'living document:' as new information becomes available, the document should be updated as required to maintain transparency and communicate accurate information to the investigators, regulatory authorities, sponsors and others, as needed.

Scientific personnel, physicians, research coordinators and other trial staff will need access to the clinical protocol to conduct the study. In recent years, protocols also have been made available to the public. As there are different stakeholders, the document should be clear and written in simple, easy-to-understand language. The information provided across the protocol should be consistent, because inconsistencies lead to ambiguity, which leads to poor study conduct. To ensure consistency, repetition of information within a protocol should be kept to a minimum.

The fundamental research requirements, study design, therapeutic area of research, statistical design, population availability, the research site, the study phase and research funding organization requirements all should be considered while developing a protocol.

## Ethical Considerations

*The design and performance of each research study involving human subjects must be clearly described and justified in a research protocol—Declaration of Helsinki*

Ethical requirements are in place to ensure clinical research participants' rights and welfare. A number of published codes and guidelines must be followed while conducting research involving human subjects. These include the *Declaration of Helsinki*, the *Nuremberg Code*, the *Belmont Report*, the World Health Organization (WHO) guidelines and the International Council on Harmonisation (ICH) Good Clinical Practice guidance.

The protocol must include details on funding, sponsors, institutional affiliations, potential conflicts of interest, incentives for participants (if provided) and information regarding provisions for treating and/or compensating subjects who are harmed as a consequence of participating in the research study. Depending on the type of research and its purpose, there may be additional study requirements. In the US, at minimum, most clinical studies are required to follow the Common Rule (45 CFR 46) and US Food and Drug Administration (FDA) regulations, if they are regulated by FDA.

An investigator must submit the protocol to the Ethics Committee for review prior to conducting clinical research study at a site. If the Ethics Committee does not exempt the study, Ethics Committee approval is required prior to conducting research. Approval also may be needed from additional committees, such as a radiation committee or scientific review committee, based on the study objectives and planned interventions during the trial. If a study is designed to enroll a vulnerable population, justification must be provided in the protocol to obtain these approvals.

The protocol should be written in compliance with Good Clinical Practice (ICH *Good Clinical Practice E6*) and existing national and international regulations, as applicable, in the region where the clinical research will be conducted and the product is planned to be marketed.

## Sponsor and Funding Agency

The sponsor is the person or organization that initiates a clinical study. A funding agency provides monetary support for the clinical study. Therefore, the funding agency can be different from the sponsor. A protocol document is a required part of the proposal for many funding bodies. The funding agency or sponsor may have specific templates and requirements, which may vary from one agency to another. The protocol submitted with a research proposal should state the research's objective, target subject population availability, justification for choosing the population and how study results may benefit society or science.

The funding agency or sponsor also may have specific requirements, such as how to train research staff, study monitoring frequency, study registration, publications, etc. The clinical study sponsor should understand funding agency requirements prior to finalizing the protocol to ensure ordered study conduct. For instance, NIH requires protocols to be written clearly for an audience that includes both the public and scientists. For NIH intervention studies, the protocol must include data and safety monitoring plans and must be registered at clinicaltrials.gov. Sponsor also may have additional requirements.

## Study Design

A study's scientific integrity depends substantially on the credibility of its design and methodology.[1] The study design must be robust and should answer the research questions. Similarly, the study type, duration and eligible participants all should be chosen with the research question in mind. The clinical research study type can be classified in more than one way:[2]

- Prospective studies enroll participants to track the outcome of interest and address the research study's objective. In this type of study, the outcome of interest is yet to occur.

- Retrospective studies examine prior events, so the data points required for analyses have been collected already.

The study type can be classified into one of the two main categories: observational or interventional studies.

- observational study—the outcome of interest is observed without introducing any intervention
- interventional study—an intervention is introduced to all participants or set of participants (With increased clinical trial complexity, there are five different phases of studies: Phase 0, Phase 1, Phase 2, Phase 3 and Phase 4.)

For Randomized Control Trials (RCTs), considerations and steps to minimize bias between the control and intervention arm must be specified.

A clinical study can have multiple endpoints. These may be primary, secondary and/or exploratory; definitions of each should be provided in the protocol. A statistical plan should account for each endpoint analysis.

For successful clinical trial enrollment and completion, the sponsor should have an in-depth understanding of the availability of the population,[3] which may depend on the geographic location, facilities available at a clinical research site, or the condition of interest, among other factors.

The protocol's methodology section explains how the clinical study should be conducted. Every effort must be taken to protect the research subject's privacy and safety. In this era of modern technology, with increasing use of mobile applications in clinical studies, potential privacy issues must be considered when writing the procedures to collect samples or data from research participants. Per Bioresearch Monitoring (BIMO) metrics, in Fiscal 2015, some of the most common and significant clinical investigator violations reported were protocol violations, failure to follow the investigational plan and inadequate safety reporting.[4] To minimize unintentional violations, it is imperative to consider any limitations on the participants or the investigators in conducting the study procedures. An early discussion with trial investigators may help identify these limitations. A poorly written methodology section may cause unintentional investigator violations or deviations.

## Regulatory Agency

The protocol should reflect the regional health authority's regulatory requirements where the study will be conducted and also where an investigational product is intended to be registered and marketed. International multi-site studies should follow ICH E6 and any additional local and national regulatory requirements for each individual study sites. Based on the study type, the sponsor may be required to inform the regulatory agency of the plan to conduct the study. In the US, an Investigational New Drug (IND) must be submitted prior to conducting clinical research with drug or biologics or an IDE prior to conducting significant risk device study.

It is recommended the sponsor consult the national regulatory agency to determine whether any support is available for the protocol development process. For example, the European Medicines Agency (EMA) offers protocol assistance for orphan medicinal products. In the US, FDA offers Special Protocol Assessment (SPA) for specific Phase 3 trials.

## Safety Considerations

The risk to clinical trial participants should be in proportion to the expected benefits. Participant safety should be foremost in clinical research conduct. The sponsor is responsible for taking every possible measure to reduce participants' risks.

The protocol or Investigator's Brochure must provide a list of anticipated adverse events[5] and their definitions based on the investigational product's expected mechanism of action or other known characteristics. Adverse effects expected based on study procedures should be noted in the protocol. For example, the sponsor must specify expected safety events in the study documents, including information on expected severity and specificity. Investigators may rely on these definitions when assessing the likely relationship of adverse effects to any test articles or study procedures. Investigators are responsible for reading and understanding these potential risks and conducting the clinical study according to the protocol. The safety events listed in the study documents, such as the Investigator's Brochure, are intended to help investigators classify the events.

The protocol specifies the timeline for the investigator to report safety events to the sponsor and appropriate Ethics Committees per their requirements. The sponsor also may require to report the study results to the regulatory agency per the timeline specified in the protocol. Thus, the sponsor must be aware of the local regulatory agency's reporting requirements. For example, FDA requires a sponsor to report all Suspected Unexpected Serious Adverse Reactions (SUSARs) within 15 working days from the time sponsor is aware of the event occurrence, and to further report any SUSAR, to all the study investigators.

In addition, the sponsor may be required to provide the safety events report to an Independent Monitoring Committee (IDMC). An IDMC's role and the frequency with which it should meet must be provided either in the protocol or in the IDMC charter.

As adverse event attribution and classification by investigators may be subjective, the study sponsor also may request an independent Clinical Events Committee (CEC) to review selected safety events. This is not a regulatory requirement; however, regulatory agencies accept CEC reports within the context of safety reporting. If an independent CEC is used, it should be included in the protocol, and the CEC member composition and events to be classified should be provided in a CEC charter.

## Statistical Analysis Plan

Depending on the intended trial's size and development stage, a statistical analysis may be executed to determine the number of study participants to be enrolled to perform the endpoint analyses.[6] The analysis helps evaluate the feasibility of meeting the enrollment numbers needed to address the research's aims and the likely timeline required to meet that goal. The enrollment target number may determine the number of sites required to participate in a research study. The protocol must include the target number of participants and an explanation of how the sample size was determined.

The protocol's statistical section should provide a detailed description of the data analysis methods and when the analysis will be performed, including planned interim and final analyses. The methods to handle missing data and minimize bias during trial conduct also should be specified. ICH's *Statistical Principles of Clinical Trials E9* provides in-depth guidance for late-phase clinical trials. In many cases, late-stage clinical trials may require a separate data analysis plan.

## Protocol Templates

Various commercial and noncommercial templates are available to aid protocol development. Templates can enhance consistency, minimize amendments and, thereby, save preparation time and money. Templates also can facilitate site and research staff efforts to understand and implement the protocol.

While protocol templates should meet current regulations, novel protocol writing approaches may be encouraged to enhance study design. Several efforts underway may help sponsors create an electronic protocol template or a protocol:[7]

- Standard Protocol Items: Recommendation for Interventional Trials (SPIRIT)
- An international initiative to provide guidance to sponsors that includes a protocol template and easy-to-use checklist. The protocol items currently are available in English, Chinese, Korean and Spanish.

**Table 8-1. Protocol Outline**

| Protocol Element | Description |
|---|---|
| Title page | • Title<br>• Version number<br>• Date of protocol version<br>• Regulatory sponsor information<br>• CRO/ARO information, if applicable<br>• Funding entity<br>• Trial registration number(s) (e.g., EudraCT, clinicaltrials.gov) |
| Statement of Compliance | • Statement study will be carried out per ethical regulations |
| Protocol Agreement | • Investigator will conduct study in compliance with protocol approved by Ethics Committee (EC) and applicable regulations<br>• Statement that no deviations without prior approval from sponsor and IRB/EC unless it is an emergency<br>• Investigator signature |
| List of Abbreviations | • Expanded for abbreviations used in the protocol |
| Background and Rationale | • Relevant scientific information on prior preclinical and clinical studies<br>• Rationale for the current study |
| Study Design | • Single center/multi-center<br>• Prospective/retrospective<br>• Study duration |
| Study Endpoints | • Description of the primary endpoint(s); secondary and exploratory endpoints, if any, should be listed |
| Study Enrollment and Withdrawal | • Participant eligibility criteria<br>• Plan to enroll study population and/or the justification to include a vulnerable population (if applicable)<br>• Sample size and the anticipated accrual timeline<br>• Reasons for withdrawal or to terminate participation in the trial |
| Investigation IP/Device | • Details of the investigational product and planned procedures<br>• Accountability of the product administered during the study<br>• Agent shipping and retrieval processes<br>• Product formulation, packaging and labeling<br>• Product preparation, administration, storage and handling |
| Procedures Schedule | • Study-specific procedures<br>• Standard of care study procedures to be performed during the enrollment period (if applicable)<br>• Procedures during screening, after study enrollment, follow-up and final study visit<br>• Details of the data, sample and specimens that will be collected, including handling, storage and shipment<br>• Study flowchart or table<br>• Concomitant medications or treatments required or not allowed during study |
| Safety | • Definitions of Adverse Event, Serious Adverse Event and SUSAR as well as adverse events of special interest (if applicable)<br>• Method for determining the relationship between adverse events and test products, with definitions<br>• Procedure and timelines for reporting safety events<br>• Expected events with severity and specificity (if applicable or known)<br>• Pregnancy reporting<br>• Reporting to Independent monitoring or safety reporting committee<br>• Routine monitoring plan<br>• Use of IDMC/CEC and the plan |
| Statistical Considerations | • Statistical analysis plan or reference to a separate document<br>• Planned interim analyses and final analysis and timing<br>• Randomization procedure and the method to break the study blind in emergencies |
| Ethical Considerations | • Ethics Committee review and approval<br>• Any application submitted to regulatory agency to conduct the study<br>• Methods to obtain and document informed consent |

- NIH and the FDA Joint Leadership Council (JLC) has developed a protocol template for clinical studies in later phases.
- The National Cancer Institute (NCI) recommends using its protocol template when conducting research in collaboration with it.
- Transcelerate developed a standardized template in collaboration with industry partners.

In addition to these, the study collaborators and IRBs may recommend using their own templates. **Table 8-1** outlines the essential elements required in the protocol. Repetition of protocol information can lead to inconsistency and errors.

## Amendments

The protocol must be amended when new information becomes available that necessitates changes in the study design and methodology. It is best to avoid multiple protocol amendments if possible.

When changes are made, it is important to track the versions. The protocol's version date and version number should be included in the document to track:

- the modified versions released for the study
- the versions approved by the Ethics Committee and regulatory agency
- the current version of the document the investigator is required to follow

Any amendment to the protocol must be approved by the local Ethics Committee or IRB prior to implementation and, if required, submitted to the regulatory agency. The re-training requirement for research staff must be evaluated when the protocol is amended to ensure proper study conduct.

## Registration and Publishing

The *Declaration of Helsinki* suggests all clinical trials be published to benefit society by sharing information.

Legislation, regulatory agencies, the funding sponsor and scientific journals may require the researcher to register the study in an online database before any participants are enrolled. National registries were created to increase transparency, provide a platform for knowledge sharing in the research community and allow the public to learn about information on research studies open to participants.

In the US, clinicaltrails.gov was created to provide summarized protocol information and completed study results. All applicable clinical trials are required to be registered and their main results posted in clinicaltrials.gov as per the *Food and Drug Administration Amendments Act* (*FDAAA*) Section 801. The definition for each section is provided in the portal that facilitates sponsors' submissions.

Most international journals mandate protocol submission with authors' scientific papers as part of the peer-review process. Protocols may also be published in scientific journals as standalone documents. The *British Medical Journal* provides guidance for publishing protocols, and the SPIRIT guidelines also can assist researchers seeking to publish protocols.[8]

## Conclusion

The protocol is a vital document that plays a key role in successful study conduct. The protocol should communicate the research's plan and purpose effectively. It is best practice to begin drafting a protocol as soon as the sponsor has a hypothesis, with the protocol evolving as more information about the investigational product, study target population, safety profile, study conduct, regulatory requirements and other key elements of a trial are gathered.

### References

1. Recommended format for a research protocol. WHO website. http://www.who.int/rpc/research_ethics/format_rp/en/. Accessed 5 January 2017.
2. Project Goals (29 Augusr 2016). National EMSC Data Analysis Center (NEDARC) website. http://www.nedarc.org/statisticalhelp/projectDesign.html. Accessed 5 January 2017.
3. Karp BI, Nussenblatt RB. *Writing a Protocol, Principles and Practice of Clinical Research* (2012). pp. 483–487.
4. Food and Drug Administration (FDA) Bioresearch Monitoring (BIMO) Metrics –FY'15 (PDF document) Retrived from FDA website: http://www.fda.gov/ScienceResearch/SpecialTopics/RunningClinicalTrials/ucm261409.htm
5. Op cit 3.
6. Ibid.
7. Groves T. How to Write and Publish a Study Protocol (web course) 07May2015. BMJ Publishing website. http://learning.bmj.com/learning/rtop/course-intro/.html?courseId=10053116&locale=en_GB. Accessed 5 January 2017.
8. Op cit 4.

**Author**

Sharanya Ramasubramanian has in-depth knowledge and a passion for clinical research with several years of combined hands-on experience at Dana-Farber/Harvard Cancer Center and Stanford University. She has assumed various roles in clinical research operations and conduct of wide range of research studies from initiation to close-out Ramasubramanian hold a Master's in bioscience regulatory affairs from The Johns Hopkins University.

**Acknowledgment**

I dedicate my writing to my family, especially to my husband. I thank my friends and colleagues who have not only provided me numerous opportunities to enhance my knowledge in this field but also helped me learn alongside and grow. Last but not least, I would like to thank RAPS for allowing me to take part in this effort.

# 9

# Informed Consent Form Preparation
# The Whys, Whats, Whos, Wheres, Whens and Hows

*By Jenny Grodberg, PhD, RAC (US)*

*I will apply dietetic measures for the benefit of the sick according to my ability and judgement; I will keep them from harm and injustice.*—Hippocratic Oath

## The Whys

Over 2,400 years ago, Hippocrates established high ethical standards for physician conduct. These principles have echoed in numerous medical teachings throughout the centuries: physician Sun Simiao's physician's code of conduct, the 7th century Oath of Asaf from a Hebrew medical manuscript and the ethical code of conduct published by the English physician Thomas Percival in 1803.[1] Despite this universal doctrine for physicians to preserve life and protect the patients' interests, the era of human medical research unfortunately all too often has seen a disregard of these principles to advance medicine "for the greater good." These studies often involved marginalized members of society unable to make a voluntary and informed choice to participate (**Table 9-1**).

Public awareness of these events triggered federal and global responses to protect human subjects involved in all types of research. The *Nuremberg Code*, established in 1948 in response to Nazi wartime medical crimes, made voluntary consent mandatory for any clinical research.[2] In 1964, the World Medical Association issued the *Declaration of Helsinki*, which developed the 10 principles first stated in the *Nuremberg Code* and tied

them to the *Declaration of Geneva* (1948), a statement of physicians' ethical duties, including medical research involving human subjects and research on human biomaterials and data.[3] The US, with the *National Research Act* of 1974, established the National Commission for the Protection of Human Subjects of Biomedical and Behavioral Research, which, in response to public concern over the Tuskegee study, published the *Belmont Report* in 1979.[4] The *Belmont Report* summarizes three basic ethical principles of human biomedical research that underpin all clinical studies conducted in the US: 1) respect for persons, 2) beneficence and 3) justice. (In 1983, Beauchamp and Childress, in their textbook on the principles of biomedical ethics, added a fourth principle—that of non-maleficence.[5]) A key tenant of the respect for persons is "subjects, to the degree that they are capable, be given the opportunity to choose what shall or shall not happen to them." In other words…informed consent.

The *Belmont Report*, in large part, is the basis for US regulations governing human subject protections, including informed consent. National Institutes of Health (NIH)-sponsored studies refer to the regulations found in the Code of Federal Regulations (CFR) Chapter 45, Part 46 (45 CFR 46).[6] Informed consent requirements for clinical studies conducted under the US Food and Drug Administration's (FDA) jurisdiction are described in 21 CFR 50.[7] Of note, federal regulations instruct the

**Table 9-1. Selected Historical Events in Human Experimentation**

| Date(s) | Event |
|---|---|
| 1932–72 | Tuskegee study examining the long-term effects of syphilis in 400 African American males, mostly poor sharecroppers, unaware they were infected and denied treatment[a] |
| 1940s | Experiments involving plutonium injection of human research subjects and secret radiation experiments; indigent patients and mentally retarded children were deceived about the nature of these treatments[b] |
| 1940s | Psychotic patients at Illinois State Hospital given malaria to test a cure; institutionalized orphans and mentally retarded individuals were used to test a dysentery vaccine and developed dangerously high fevers, showing the vaccine did not work[c] |
| 1948 | Concentration camp prisoners used by Nazis for experimentation; prisoners usually died as a result of the experiments[d] |
| 1960s | Mentally retarded children infected with hepatitis virus at a state school by researchers looking for a cure[e] |
| 1963 | Elderly patients in a New York hospital injected with viable cancer cells; patients were told their immune response was being tested[f] |

a.  *US Public Health Service Syphilis Study at Tuskegee. Centers for Disease Control and Prevention website. https://www.cdc.gov/tuskegee/timeline.htm. Accessed 16 January 2017.*
b.  *Ibid.*
c.  *Miller FG. "The Stateville Penitentiary Malaria Experiments: A Case Study in Retrospective." Ethical Assessment Perspectives in Biology and Medicine. 2013:56(4):548–567.*
d.  *Op cit a.*
e.  *Krans B. Pain, Suffering and the History of Human Experimentation. Healthline News Website. http://www.healthline.com/health-news/strange-the-sordid-history-of-human-experimentation-101213#1. Accessed 1 January 2017.*
f.  *1962: Dr. Chester Southam injected live cancer cells into 22 elderly patients. Alliance for Human Research Protection website. http://ahrp.org/1962-dr-chester-southam-injected-live-cancer-cells-into-22-elderly-patients-at-jewish-chronic-disease-hospital-in-brooklyn/. Accessed 1 January 2017.*

documentation of informed consent by means of a written consent form, thereby providing the regulatory writer a template for preparing an informed consent form (ICF).

Many states also have implemented informed consent legislation. California guidelines, for example, mirror the federal requirements defined in 45 CFR 46, plus requirements outlined in California's *Protection of Human Subjects in Medical Experimentation Act* and "California Health and Safety Code."[8] By September 2013, 30 states had enacted informed consent laws. Facets of these laws frequently include ICF content requirements.

Both FDA and the International Council on Harmonisation (ICH) have issued guidances to aid in ICF development: FDA's *Informed Consent Information Sheet: Draft Guidance for IRBs, Clinical Investigators, and Sponsors*[9] and ICH's *Guideline for Good Clinical Practice E6(R1)*.[10] Each document describes the current regulatory authority expectations an ICF writer should meet.

These key regulations and guidelines provide the starting point for successful ICF preparation. Their fundamental precept is viewing the consent process as containing three elements: information, comprehension and voluntariness. The specific ICF components and facets to consider to achieve these attributes are described below.

## The Whats

The information provided in the ICF to support a clinical study is divided into two categories: the "essential (or basic) elements" and the "additional elements." Lists of these elements are located in 45 CFR 46.116 and 21 CFR 50.25 and are presented in **Tables 9-2** and **9-3**, respectively. Although not required, the ICF typically contains the additional elements indicated.

This list is reproduced in the aforementioned FDA guidance and is accompanied by excellent descriptions of what text to provide for each item.[11] The regulations do not specify the order in which the information is presented in the ICF, only that it should be included.

ICFs supporting clinical trials that must be registered at ClinicalTrials.gov also are required to include the statement "A description of this clinical trial will be available on http://www.ClinicalTrials.gov, as required by U.S. Law. This Web site will not include information that can identify you. At most, the Web site will include a summary of the results. You can search this Web site at any time."[12] Some funding agencies require all studies be posted on ClinicalTrials.gov even if not meeting the regulatory requirement to do so; pharmaceutical sponsors more often than not post their clinical studies regardless of the regulatory obligation as a means to bring public awareness to their development program. In those instances, the

**Table 9-2. Essential Informed Consent Form Elements**

| Element | Description |
| --- | --- |
| Description of Clinical Investigation | A statement that the study involves research, an explanation of the research's purposes and the expected duration of the subject's participation, a description of the procedures to be followed and identification of any experimental procedures |
| Risks and Discomforts | A description of any reasonably foreseeable subject risks or discomforts |
| Benefits | A description of any benefits to the subject or to others that reasonably may be expected from the research |
| Alternative Procedures or Treatments | A disclosure of appropriate alternative procedures or courses of treatment, if any, that might be advantageous to the subject |
| Confidentiality | A statement describing the extent, if any, to which confidentiality of subject identification records will be maintained, noting the possibility FDA may inspect the records |
| Compensation and Medical Treatment in Event of Injury | For research involving more than minimal risk, an explanation as to whether any compensation and any medical treatments are available if injury occurs and, if so, what they are or where further information may be obtained |
| Contacts | An explanation of whom to contact for answers to pertinent questions about the research and research subjects' rights, and whom to contact in the event of a research-related subject injury |
| Voluntary Participation | A statement that participation is voluntary, refusal to participate will involve no penalty or loss of benefits to which the subject is otherwise entitled, and the subject may discontinue participation at any time without penalty or loss of benefits to which the subject is otherwise entitled |

phrase "as required by U.S. Law" does not apply and can be removed.

The final ICF component is the Statement of Consent or Signature Page. This section contains phrasing that varies somewhat depending on the study but generally runs along the following lines:

You have read (or have had read to you) the above description of this research study. You have been informed of the risks and benefits involved, and all of your questions have been answered to your satisfaction. You understand that your participation in the study is voluntary, and that you are free to withdraw at any time. By signing this form, you voluntarily consent to participate in the research study.

Unless you authorize the use and disclosure of your personal health information, you cannot participate in this research study. If you refuse to give your authorization, your medical care will not be affected.

You will receive a copy of this consent form.

If optional tests are to be performed, check boxes for each item can be included for the participant to tick (yes or no) and initial. For example:

| Optional Procedures—Lumbar puncture | Yes | No | Subject Initials |
| --- | --- | --- | --- |
| You voluntarily agree to participate in the optional CSF sub-study. | | | |

The signature lines are the last components—one for the study subject, the second for a legally authorized representative (to be completed if needed) and the third for the individual obtaining the consent. Each signatory is requested to print his or her name, sign and date the document.

If a clinical trial involves a study partner participating in conjunction with a given study subject, that individual signs a Study Partner Consent form, which may be a separate page of the subject's consent. The study partner also indicates his or her relationship to the study subject.

## The Whos

A truism of all writing is to know the audience. In ICF preparation, at least three "whos" influence ICF design or content: the study participant, the sponsor and the clinical study.

### Who is the study participant?

The characteristics of the intended clinical trial participants influence reading level and comprehension. Per 21 CFR 50.20 and 45 CFR 46.116, the information given to a prospective subject is to be in language "understandable to the potential subject or legally authorized representative." Relevant attributes include:

- age—Are the trial participants adults, adolescents, children?
- education—Is educational level a factor in patient enrollment?

**Table 9-3. Additional Informed Consent Form Elements**

| Element | Description |
|---|---|
| Unforeseeable Risks | A statement that the particular treatment or procedure may involve risks to the subject (or to the embryo or fetus, if the subject is or may become pregnant) that are currently unforeseeable |
| Involuntary Termination of Subject's Participation | Anticipated circumstances under which the subject's participation may be terminated by the investigator without regard to the subject's consent |
| Additional Costs to Subject | Any additional costs to the subject that may result from research participation |
| Consequences of Subject's Decision to Withdraw | The consequences of a subject's decision to withdraw from the research, and procedures for orderly termination of subject participation |
| Number of Subjects | The approximate number of subjects involved in the study |

- special population—Are the study subjects cognitively impaired, dyslexic or limited in some fashion that potentially impacts reading comprehension?
- disease under study—Will consent be provided by a legally authorized representative (LAR) due to the incapacitating nature of the disease? Or can either the participant or LAR sign the ICF?

According to the US Department of Education and the National Institute of Literacy, 14% (32 million) of US adults cannot read at a basic level, with 21% reading below a fifth-grade level.[13] One-third of US adults (77 million) have basic or below basic health literacy.[14] Many Institutional Review Boards (IRBs) suggest writing at anywhere between a sixth- to eighth-grade level; erring on the lower end of that scale to maximize potential readability for a broader adult audience is recommended.

The ICF should be written directly to the reader, as if explaining the facts in person. Informed consent language uses the second person ("you"), not the first person ("I"). Often, the ICF is structured in a question and answer format:

- What will happen to you in this study, and which procedures are standard of care and which are experimental?
- What risks are associated with this study?

Informed "assent" is the agreement of someone not of a legal age to give consent. In the US, that legal age generally is 18 years, but state regulations sometimes allow younger individuals to give consent. Therefore, informed consent laws governing the state in which a clinical study is conducted should be considered. For an individual not of legal consenting age to participate in a clinical study, the regulations require both the pediatric subject's assent and the permission of the parent(s) or LAR. The language used to prepare assent forms varies by the study population's age. Any discomforts and inconveniences the child may experience if agreeing to participate are described in nontechnical terms. An assent form for an adolescent subject can be very similar to that of a standard consent form, or a hybrid of an adult's consent form and a child's (seven- to 11-years old) assent form.

- If you decide you want to be in this research study, this is what will happen to you.
- Sometimes kids don't feel good while being in this study. You might feel these things…

The consenting adult(s) for a pediatric subject sign(s) a "Parent Consent for Child to Act as a Research Subject" form. Here, wording is adjusted to reflect what will happen in the study to "your child."

In some instances, assent forms are created for use in selected adult populations, such as those with Down Syndrome, Alzheimer's disease or other syndromes limiting an individual's ability to comprehend the language used in a standard ICF.

### Who is the sponsor?

Some sponsors or funding sources may require specific wording for selected sections. For example, clinical investigators participating in Alzheimer's disease studies funded by the National Institute of Aging (NIA) are required to obtain a "Certificate of Confidentiality" due to the potentially highly sensitive nature of the data collected on study subjects. NIA requires specific wording describing these additional privacy protections be included in the ICF to assure the prospective participant every effort is being made to keep his or her information confidential. Pharmaceutical industry sponsors also may have standardized wording for shared sections across ICFs. Inquiring about available template content prior to initiating ICF development potentially saves the writer considerable time and effort reinventing what already works (or minimally, what already was reviewed and approved).

### Who is the study for which the ICF is being created?

The "who" here is the scope of the clinical activity the ICF supports. An ICF containing all of the essential elements supports a main clinical study. Some ICFs support an optional, additional clinical question that extends the initial study. This ICF's content would be limited to the study's new facet. Specific medical procedures such as a PET scan also may require a separate ICF. Studies employing a two-step screening process may use an abbreviated ICF first to quickly assess potential eligibility, followed by a full-length ICF after further examination and determination the prospective participant is eligible for the study.

To add to the who's who of ICF options, a short-form ICF may be created to use as an alternative to the long-form supporting the main study in situations where the required ICF elements are presented orally, such as when a subject or the subject's LAR is unable to read (illiteracy, blindness or non-English speaking). The short-form essentially documents the oral presentation of the required ICF elements. Both this short-form and a summary of the oral presentation are submitted for regulatory review and IRB approval.

Once the writer understands who the clinical study or activity is for, he or she will know who the ICF needs to address.

## The Whens

### When should the ICF writer first become involved with the project?

ICF writer involvement should occur early enough in protocol development to learn about the "whos," so the right template(s) can be developed. Standardized template content can be introduced, and the preparation of study-specific content can be initiated while the study design process is ongoing. Every effort should be made to continue interacting with the clinical team throughout protocol development, so no late-breaking changes in study design catch the writer unaware.

### When should the writer update the ICF?

A writer may need to update an ICF as early as after FDA's 30-day review of an Investigational New Drug Application (IND) if the ICF supports the initial clinical study described in the application. FDA may be aware of other safety information for other marketed or investigational drugs in a similar chemical class, for example, and may request the information's inclusion in the ICF as a precaution. The addition of clinical protocol sub-studies or extensions also may trigger the need to revise a current ICF or create an associated ICF. A change in research procedures or new safety information collected during the course of the clinical study or as a result of nonclinical study investigations also require an ICF update. Additionally, feedback from a clinical site's IRB can lead to not only site-specific ICF changes but a global change in the study's ICF template. Clearly, the writer's work truly is never done.

## The Hows

The first step in any ICF preparation is stepping through the Whos described above systematically. This information is collected when the writer meets with the clinical team during protocol development. The second step is assembling the multiple source materials that provide both the content and structure for drafting the ICF. From the content perspective:

- placebo information: chance allergic reactions to any inactive ingredient(s) are potential study risks and should be mentioned
- comparator drug or reference medication package insert (if applicable): the risk profile for the comparator drug is provided since, in a blinded study, the subject could be exposed to one or the other agent
- toxicology summaries: especially for early phase clinical trials where little to no human safety data has been collected, the pivotal nonclinical studies identify the potential safety signals to be monitored during the trial and should be described
- drug safety update report/periodic safety update report: these reports, prepared annually during ongoing clinical development programs or for commercial products, contain the most recent

**Table 9-4. Examples of Lay Language**

| Medical Term | Lay Language Wording |
|---|---|
| Abdomen | Belly (or stomach) |
| Acute | Lasting a short time |
| Catheter | A tube that is inserted into the body to collect or deliver fluid |
| Double Blind | Neither you nor the doctor will know which drug you will be taking |
| Edema | Swelling caused by fluid collecting (in tissue) |
| Participate | Take part |
| Protocol | Study plan |
| Random | By chance, like the flip of a coin |
| Supine | Lying face up (or lying on your back) |

safety information collected and may describe new safety signals warranting inclusion

From the nuts and bolts ICF construction perspective:

- ICF standard operating procedure (SOP) or standard work instruction: sponsors (both pharmaceutical and government) may have specific ICF development processes covering preparation, review and approval
- ICF template: in the absence of an established template, the writer considers:
  o font size and type (recommended 12 point, Times New Roman; larger type size may be appropriate such as for children, the elderly or the visually impaired)
  o use of figures to aid description of a study procedure
  o adding (a) table summarizing activities per study visit
  o company logo
  o page numbering
  o footer with ICF version (and revision date)
- ICF checklist: to facilitate the draft document's development and quality control

The wording used in an ICF should be understandable to the people being asked to participate, i.e., in lay language. Words with one or two syllables are preferable, as well as short sentences and paragraphs. Medical terminology should be avoided as much as possible and defined when used. **Table 9-4** lists a few examples of lay language for terms commonly encountered during ICF preparation.

Many university IRBs or human subject protection offices make lists of suggested lay language available on their websites to use in place of medical terms. These sites also frequently provide links to sample ICFs. These examples can be exceedingly helpful, especially when drafting an ICF for the first time (or even first few times). If possible, obtain "readability feedback" from clinical personnel with experience interacting with the target study population and involved in the consenting process. Other writers experienced in lay language medical writing also are great resources. With practice, the writer will acquire a feel for an ICF's readability.

## Conclusion

The informed consent process is not a single, one-time event, or simply a form to be signed. It is an educational process that begins during the initial exchange of information with a prospective study participant and continues throughout the trial if new information may influence a participant's choice to continue the study. A well-written ICF is central to achieving the overarching objective of ensuring a study participant's rights, safety, dignity and well-being are protected.

**References**

1. Bioethics-Codes/Oaths. Dalhousie University website. http://dal.ca.libguides.com/c.php?g=256990&p=1715964. Accessed 1 January 2017.
2. *Nuremberg Code.* Office of History National Institutes of Health website. https://history.nih.gov/research/downloads/nuremberg.pdf. Accessed 1 January 2017.
3. *Declaration of Helsinki.* World Medical Association website. http://www.wma.net/en/30publications/10policies/b3/index.html. Accessed 1 January 2017.
4. Ethical Principles and Guidelines for the Protection of Human Subjects of Research. US Department of Health & Human Services website. http://www.hhs.gov/ohrp/regulations-and-policy/belmont-report/index.html#xbasic. Accessed 1 January 2017.
5. Beauchamp TL and Childress JF. *Principles of Biomedical Ethics.* New York, NY: Oxford University Press; 1983.
6. Electronic Code of Federal Regulations (eCFR). Government Publishing Office website. http://www.ecfr.gov/cgi-bin/ECFR?page=browse. Accessed 1 January 2017.
7. Ibid.
8. California Informed Consent Guidelines. State of California Department of Justice, Office of the Attorney General website. https://oag.ca.gov/research/consent. Accessed 1 January 2017.
9. *Informed Consent Information Sheet: Draft Guidance for IRBs, Clinical Investigators, and Sponsors.* FDA website. http://www.fda.gov/downloads/regulatoryinformation/guidances/ucm405006.pdf. Accessed 1 January 2017.
10. *Guideline for Good Clinical Practice E6(R1).* ICH website. http://www.ich.org/fileadmin/Public_Web_Site/ICH_Products/Guidelines/Efficacy/E6/E6_R1_Guideline.pdf . Accessed 1 January 2017.
11. Op cit 9.
12. Ibid.
13. Illiteracy Statistics. National Center for Education Statistics. Statistic Brain website. https://nces.ed.gov/fastfacts/display.asp?id=69. Accessed 1 January 2017.
14. Op cit 9.

**Author**

Jennifer Grodberg, PhD, RAC (US), is vice president, regulatory affairs for VenatoRx Pharmaceuticals Inc. She has more than 23 years of experience in the pharmaceutical industry, including almost 13 years in regulatory. Her experience spans the pre-IND enabling phase through NDA submission, including FDA inspections and Advisory Committee Meetings, and has interacted with Health Canada and EU regulatory authorities. Previously, Grodberg served on Harvard Medical School's Department of Medicine faculty. She holds a PhD in microbiology and has earned the RAC. She is a Fellow of the American Medical Writers Association and past-president of AMWA's Pacific Southwest Chapter.

# 10

# Data Analysis Plans

*By Lisa DeTora*

Mark Twain popularized the phrase "there are three kinds of lies: lies, damned lies, and statistics," a quip he attributed (possibly erroneously) to Benjamin Disraeli, and which, as Stephen Jay Gould explained, presents a continuum of worsening falsification of information.[1,2] As Gould notes in "The Median Isn't the Message," a failure to contextualize and interpret statistical data correctly can lead to many different untoward medical consequences. Gould specifically criticizes the medical community's tendency to either ignore statistics entirely or accept them wholesale because statistics, read correctly, can provide helpful, even essential, information.[3]

In the clinical trial setting, statistical analyses are required. The ability of a reader to understand statistical information in connection with a clinical trial can be aided by the quality of the initial planning for data analysis.

## Rationale for Writing a Statistical Analysis Plan

As noted by many regulatory agencies, pre-specified data- or statistical analysis plans (SAPs) may be needed not only for pivotal clinical trials, but also for the integrated analyses that may be required to support marketing applications, as in the US.[4–6] The International Council on Harmonisation's (ICH) *Guideline on Good Clinical Practice E6(R1)*, which specifies parameters for protocols and Investigator's Brochures, also emphasizes the importance of statistical analyses in planning and evaluating clinical trials, as do ICH *Structure and Format of Clinical Study Reports E3* and ICH *Common Technical Document M4E*, which outlines the portions of the CTD Module 2 that summarize and discuss[7–9] clinical data. The ICH *Statistical Principles for Clinical Trials E9* presents considerations for appropriate statistical analysis design and contents recommended for evaluating clinical trial data.[10]

The rationale for an SAP is both regulatory and scientific. That is, a high-quality SAP supports regulatory requirements and also plays an important part in ensuring scientific data can be evaluated properly by health authorities and other audiences. Increasingly, journals will request copies of the SAP to assist in evaluating manuscripts reporting data from pivotal clinical trials.[11] Further, the predefinition of statistical analyses is an indirect indicator of a study's rigor and integrity, especially large-scale Phase 3 clinical trials intended to provide the bulk of the data necessary to support a drug, vaccine, biologic, device or combination product's registration.[12] Although predefinition of all anticipated study data statistical analyses is ideal, careful design and documentation of *post-hoc* analyses also can improve the rigor and enhance the quality of results, particularly for analyses requested by a health authority or other body after initial clinical trial data analysis.

As explained in ICH E9, the choice of specific measures and analytical tests should be left to statistical experts who can determine the best method for evaluating the data collected.[13] Specific SAPs should incorporate and present explicit statistical models and analyses to be used in the study or studies to which the planning document applies. The SAP should include the specific formulae and tests to be used to explain, precisely and accurately, how the analyses will be performed. The analyses chosen should be in line with accepted practices for the planned study type and the therapeutic area as well as any applicable codes and guidelines for industry.

This chapter focuses on producing high-quality SAPs and other statistical planning documents that can be understood by not only the statistician who designed them but also other readers of the analysis plan, the methods it describes and their results. These other SAP readers may include medical writers, medical directors, regulatory professionals and publications professionals. Further, statistical analysis planning should account for activities across the clinical program's lifecycle.[14] Given that the SAP's primary purpose is to specify statistical testing and analysis, high-quality documentation must be accurate, complete and comprehensible. This chapter concentrates on SAPs written and reviewed as separate formal documents, but the general principles described herein also may be helpful for other data analysis planning, as, for example, when the data analyses are specified in a protocol.

## High-Level Overview of ICH E9

As indicated above, the authors of ICH E9 view statistical principles as related to the overall clinical development process as well as marketing applications, other regulatory filings and postmarket reporting. The ICH E9 guidance is divided into seven sections.

1. Introduction
   o   presents the purpose of the guideline and its scope
2. overall clinical development considerations
   o   identifies important considerations for trials in the context of the overall clinical development plan and trial type (confirmatory versus exploratory)
   o   discusses the scope of trials in humans, based on populations and various variables to be assessed in the course of the study
   o   identifies design techniques, such as blinding and randomization, intended to avoid bias

3. trial design considerations
   o   discusses design configurations (parallel group, crossover, factorial), multicenter trials, types of comparisons (superiority, noninferiority, dose-response) and group sequential design
   o   provides guidance on the best methods of reporting sample size calculations and specifies samples should be large enough to address the trial's stated hypotheses
   o   presents advice on data capture in various media, including paper, as well as data processing
4. trial conduct considerations
   o   outlines monitoring considerations, including the role of an independent data monitoring committee, and interim analyses
   o   addresses the possibility for inclusion and exclusion criteria or sample size changes during a study, as well as early stopping
   o   presents considerations regarding accrual rates that may affect statistical analyses
5. data analysis considerations
   o   notes the benefits of pre-specified analyses
   o   identifies the different data analysis sets (per protocol versus all randomized) and their roles in interpreting data
   o   discusses the appropriate handling of missing data and outliers
   o   presents guidance about: transformation of key variables and timing relative to conducting an analysis; estimation, confidence intervals and hypothesis testing; adjustments of significance and confidence levels
   o   considers subgroup analysis, interactions and covariate handling
   o   comments on data integrity and computer software validation
6. safety and tolerability evaluation
   o   discusses elements that should be reported: scope of evaluation; choice of variables and data collection; sets of human subjects evaluated and the presentation of data; statistical evaluations
   o   provides some guidance on integrated summaries such as the Integrated Summary of Safety (ISS) and Integrated Summary of Efficacy (ISE)
7. reporting

**Table 10-1. Guidelines Specifically Referenced in ICH *Statistical Principles for Clinical Trials E9***

| Guideline | Brief explanation |
|---|---|
| E1: *The Extent of Population Exposure to Assess Clinical Safety* | Specifies numbers of patients (or other trial subjects) and the duration of exposure required to support safety for products intended for the long-term treatment of non-life-threatening chronic conditions |
| E2A: *Clinical Safety Data Management: Definitions and Standards for Expedited Reporting* | Defines parameters for expedited safety data reporting of specific adverse event types during clinical trials |
| E2B: *Electronic Transmission of Individual Case Safety Reports* | Defines parameters for the electronic transmission of required case report form elements for regulatory filings |
| E2C: *Periodic Benefit-Risk Evaluation for Marketed Drugs* | Defines parameters for safety update reporting for products approved for marketing, including ongoing benefit-risk analyses |
| E3: *Structure and Content of Clinical Study Reports* | Provides principles for clinical study reporting and a suggested format |
| E4: *Dose-Response Information to Support Drug Registration* | Identifies the study and data types needed to support claims regarding dose responses and blood levels |
| E5: *Ethnic Factors in the Acceptability of Foreign Clinical Data* | Suggests principles to be applied to clinical data evaluation across various populations identified by race or other ethnic factors (either intrinsic or extrinsic to the target patient population) as well as considerations for bridging studies |
| E6: *Good Clinical Practice: Consolidated Guideline* | Defines good practice for clinical research and presents guidance for protocols, protocol amendments, Investigator's Brochures and other essential documents. An addendum currently is under review to add information about electronic systems validations, source document retention and benefit-risk analysis and reporting |
| E7: *Studies in Support of Special Populations: Geriatric* | Identifies principles for clinical trials for products to be used in the elderly |
| E8: *General Considerations for Clinical Trials* | Outlines general considerations for clinical trials in the context of nonclinical studies and the clinical development plan |
| E10: *Choice of Control Group in Clinical Trials* | Presents ethical and scientific principles for selecting appropriate control groups in clinical trials |
| M1: *Standardisation of Medical Terminology for Regulatory Purposes* | Presents the MedDRA dictionary |
| M3: *Non-Clinical Safety Studies for the Conduct of Human Clinical Trials for Pharmaceuticals* | Presents recommendations for nonclinical studies to be conducted prior to introducing a pharmaceutical product into clinical trials |

*Note: The most updated versions are cited. ICH E9 was finalized in 1998. Current ICH guidelines are available at www.ich.org.*

o   refers the reader to ICH E3, which outlines clinical study report function and suggested structure

o   presents focused hints on handling statistical information in reports that expand on advice given in ICH E3[15]

It is worth noting the current version of the ICH E9 guidance was finalized in 1998. Hence, some of the contents focus on practices, such as the use of paper case report forms, which have become increasingly obsolete. Further, the versions, scope and content of many of the ICH guidance documents cross-referenced in ICH E9 since have changed. **Table 10-1** outlines the current state of the ICH guidelines mentioned in ICH E9.[16]

## Statistics Exist in Context

To be of the highest quality, a planned statistical analysis may require knowledge outside the scope of statistics, *per se*. For example, the better the data collection and handling quality, the better the analysis results, independent of the rigor and conduct of the analysis itself. Knowledge about the context within which statistics will be presented and interpreted also is vital to effective data analysis planning. For example, ICH E9 was prepared by drawing on multiple existing guidelines for biostatistical methodology, and notes additional helpful information for statisticians is presented in various ICH guidelines (See **Table 10-1**). The authors of ICH E9 also clearly viewed their statistical principles as meaningfully integrated into an overall process of clinical development from a product's transition into the initial Phase 1 studies and past the clinical development process into postmarketing safety and risk reporting.[17]

The comments below are meant to supplement information in ICH E9. Planning statistical analyses promotes not only effective reporting but also other writing downstream of a clinical study. Several aspects of clinical study and regulatory filing planning may benefit from the advice of a project statistician as may publication planning and data posting.

### Definition of a High-Quality Document

For the purposes of the current discussion, "high-quality" documentation is defined as:

- accurate
- consistent with accepted clinical trial conduct ethical principles
- sufficiently rigorous to meet scientific goals
- consistent with applicable regulatory guidelines, professional practice and Good Clinical Practice
- polished in terms of presentation of both data and text
- sufficient to meet the needs of all anticipated readers

The SAP should outline all applicable analyses clearly and sufficiently for all planned assessments and data sets. It should be easy for the reader to 'map' the parameters discussed in the SAP to both the clinical protocol and any resulting report or other regulatory documentation.

### Data Considerations

An understanding of good data handling practices is essential to providing solid advice about the best approach to clinical trial data statistical analysis; hence, ICH E9 refers to several data management guidelines (See **Table 10-1**). Cleaner data can produce better-quality reporting of results. Therefore, the statistician responsible for writing an SAP should have access to information about planned data handling during the trial as well as an opportunity to provide advice regarding best practices to ensure consistent data collection and coding. If necessary, medical writers can help develop consistently worded queries for data reconciliation as well as fields for data entry or case report forms. Although it may seem counterintuitive to consider the Clinical Study Report (CSR) while writing an SAP, data handling guidelines or database query text, consistent wording can improve the overall database quality and consistency, ease data review and analysis and contribute to high-quality documentation.

Consistency within the clinical database often depends on the ability of those conducting the trial and reviewing the data collected to reconcile verbatim text entries with accepted medical terminology. Standard dictionaries should be used, as recommended by GCP

guidelines.[18] When considering SAP development, knowledge of the most current versions of dictionaries such as MedDRA or, less commonly, WHO-DDE, may be helpful, as may knowledge of the most commonly used dictionary and version within the therapeutic area and at each concerned health authority or agency. Ideally, teams should employ the same version of a dictionary (usually MedDRA) throughout a clinical program.[19] However, it may become necessary to employ different dictionaries or versions, for example, when a clinical development program is conducted over several years, or medical dictionaries are built into new data management software. In such cases, SAP planning allows the team to include measures to account for these changes. In some cases, statisticians may desire to plan analyses to ensure reviewers are able to evaluate statistical analyses' consistency across studies or groups of studies using different dictionaries (or versions of dictionaries). In a setting where a meta-analysis or an integrated analysis is required (as for an ISS or ISE), the ability to ensure data can be combined is even more critical, because inconsistent collection or term definitions can reduce the reliability of subsequent analysis.[20,21]

Statisticians may be able to provide advice about additional aspects of data coding to ensure consistency not only within an individual trial, but also across a clinical development program and between a trial, a program and the medical literature. This latter consideration is important, given the increasing emphasis on disclosing clinical trial results, and advice in the latest version of the *Declaration of Helsinki* that all medical research be published promptly and in such a way as to foster understanding within the medical community.[22]

Finally, statisticians should supervise the development of lists of tables and figures to be programmed to ensure not only all required data presentations are included, but also appropriate formats are used. Planning ahead for data packages and programming is common practice in many organizations conducting clinical trials and analyzing their data. Data package review meetings may allow team members to decide which data outputs should be included in the body of a report, appendices or as attachments. It is vital the data managers and statisticians involved in this planning consider not only the requirements within their areas of expertise but also the needs of future readers of all documents who will report or recount their data. A useful introductory guide for nonexperts is Boe and colleagues' "Introduction to Regulatory Documents in New Drug Applications" (2011).[23]

### Study Reporting Requirements

SAP planning should consider reporting requirements described in all pertinent guidelines, including ICH E3, which outlines the suggested parameters for CSRs. As noted by Ellison and colleagues in Chapter 11 of this book, the ICH E3 guidance was developed as a general set of recommendations for reporting clinical trial data and should be adapted as needed to present individual studies and their data best.[24–25] Adjustments to study report formats and templates should not be made without the input of statistical and data-handling experts, because they have the best understanding of data presentation and the influence of table and figure formats on data interpretation.

For trials intended to generate data that must be reported per study and also combined into integrated summaries, initial planning should include all analyses from the initiation of each study. In cases where table formats must change between types of reports (for example, reports of a single study and reports of more than one study made to fulfill requirements for ISSs and ISEs), it may be beneficial to generate tables in all required formats for individual pivotal studies from an early stage. This practice can afford teams an opportunity to review table formats and headings for problems before reaching the critical timing pathway for a regulatory submission. Information regarding the recommended and required tables for reporting clinical study data CSRs, the ISS, the ISE and applicable sections of CTD Module 2 is available in guidance for industry from ICH (E3 and M4) and FDA.[26–29] Special considerations for devices, vaccines, biologics and combination products should be taken into account as applicable to the product under study.[30–32]

A familiarity with additional documents submitted to regulatory agencies—such as background packages, responses to agency questions and requests, marketing applications (in all formats routinely submitted in the therapeutic area including devices and combination products), and required updates and pharmacovigilance activities—also may be helpful to those who develop SAPs routinely, especially for products that are anticipated to go to market and then are investigated for additional indications, or products undergoing accelerated review. A knowledge of essential lifecycle management activities, such as ongoing benefit-risk reporting, also is important to consider.[33–35]

### Clinical Trial Ethics and Transparency

GCP guidelines, as discussed in ICH E6, emphasize the importance of high-quality statistical analyses in evaluating clinical trial data; however, additional information can fortify and supplement the practices encouraged therein. A brief discussion of the history of ethical concerns leading to current GCP guidelines is presented by Grodberg in Chapter 9 of this volume.[36] Key clinical ethics documents include the *Belmont Report* and the *Declaration of*

*Helsinki*.[37,38] Industry codes, such as the PhRMA code, outline additional considerations, such as prioritizing clinical trial results' dissemination that directly impact clinical practice over more preliminary studies.[39]

Increasingly, discussions of ethical clinical study conduct are emphasizing transparency of trial results for new drug products, devices, vaccines and biologics. One transparency element is the requirement to include information about the study in one or more trial registries during enrollment and to post results in associated databases within a specified period, which varies (from six months following the last study assessment to 12 months following product approval) depending on the product type, its regulatory stage, target patient population and marketing status. For example, clinical study results in children may be required to be posted regardless of product regulatory status or phase of development. In contrast, the results of Phase 1 studies of unlicensed products that do not enter Phase 3 may never be required to be posted in some registries. Specific requirements and timing for including information in trial registries and posting results have been formalized not only in US and EU law, but also by many individual states and countries worldwide. The most commonly used clinical trial databases and results registries, ClinicalTrials.gov and EudraCT, are administered by the US NIH and the European Medicines Agency (EMA), respectively.[40,41]

The EudraCT and Clinicaltials.com data entry parameters differ in several particulars from each other and from accepted table formats described in ICH E3. For example, results databases focus on required entries, most of which must comply with specific character counts. Further, character count limitations vary between databases for several fields, and data presentation, as for patient demographics, also may differ from materials compatible with ICH E3. Of note, results databases are designed for disclosure to and use by the general public, whereas ICH E3 assumes an audience of highly trained clinical and statistical reviewers. Statistical analysis planning, therefore, should include suitable tables for inclusion in both results databases and regulatory documents. Guidelines and checklists for planning purposes are available on the EudraCT and ClinicalTrials.gov webpages.[42–44]

### Common Statistical Practices in the Therapeutic Area

Although the chief purpose of ICH E9 is to outline statistical principles to support reporting requirements for regulatory agencies and health authorities, SAP authors also may benefit from knowledge about common data-handling methods within the therapeutic area or pharmaceutical class as well as analyses commonly requested by medical journals. For instance, FDA has published *Guidance for the Use of Bayesian Statistics in Medical Device Clinical Trials,* to describe specific analyses in use in a specialized product area. Cochrane maintains a trusted database of systematic reviews and reports that provide integrated or meta-analytical information on marketed drug products, vaccines and biologics. Cochrane's chief aim is to inform medical decision making better.[46] By providing information that follows published information's existing parameters, industry sponsors can support the production of systematic reviews indirectly. Given that many systematic review authors also serve as advisors to health authorities and peer reviewers at journals, following accepted practices also can aid the process of interpreting data in settings other than a regulatory submission.

Many industry sponsors routinely publish the results of their clinical trials in keeping with recommendations in the *Declaration of Helsinki.*[47] SAP planning can anticipate the need for specialized data presentations for specific medical journals, which can be found in guidelines such as CONSORT on the EQUATOR network.[48–49] This planning may be especially helpful when publication is intended for a specialty journal. Generating tables, listings and figures that meet regulatory reporting, CTD, trial posting and publication requirements can promote consistency and reduce potential problems that can arise from minor data discrepancies in print.[50]

Consistency in a therapeutic or other specialty area is not limited to statistical analysis. It also is critical for teams to employ language in keeping with accepted definitions and practices. For example, using nonstandard abbreviations on tables and figures may seem logical from a programming perspective, but the tables and figures then might need to be redrawn or tabulated for publication, or even requested for evaluation by a regulatory agency or advisory panel. A good habit when considering table and figure headings is to adhere to language used by the relevant agency or such prominent medical journals as *The New England Journal of Medicine.*[51] Another helpful information source may be trial registries, particularly if several sponsors have registered trials; using others' information as examples may save work. The *AMA Manual of Style* also is a valuable resource.[52] Another consideration for SAP writers is that the same outcome measures may be used in more than one therapeutic area, which may employ slightly different writing conventions.

## Hints for Developing a High-Quality SAP

Collaboration is the key to a high-quality SAP. Although a statistical expert can ensure SAP contents are correct and of the highest quality, consultation with other experts is vital. Therefore, a few practices are recommended during SAP authoring and review. These activities should be considered and incorporated with any existing SOPs or best practices governing clinical studies and regulatory documentation within the organization conducting or sponsoring the clinical trial.

Hints:

1.  Consult with experts in all pertinent areas, even if an SOP does not require this.
    o   Many institutions maintain SOPs specifying the minimum contributors to key study and regulatory documents. However, most also have provisions for adding additional experts as needed. A minimalist approach may seem easier; however, it may lead to problems and cause additional work later. For example, the SAP for a study evaluating biomarkers might benefit from consultation with a scientific biomarker expert.
    o   Various methods can be used to obtain expert input. For example, experts may be consulted during an initial draft stage rather than waiting for an official review cycle. Getting early input can make the official review cycles easier by enabling an author to submit a higher-quality document to reviewers and limiting the need for comment resolution.
    o   Regulatory experts and medical writers may have a helpful perspective. Unlike many other specialists, regulatory and medical writing professionals often have worked in different therapeutic areas (and job functions) at various points in their careers and may be able to provide unique advice regarding the best ways to address the various audiences' needs. Due to their roles, these colleagues also may be more highly aware of language use in various contexts.
2.  If possible, list the SAP in overall regulatory documentation and/or study plans.
    o   If team members are reminded of the draft SAP's existence and the need for review, they will be able to plan their time better.
    o   In addition, mentioning the SAP in a study's tracking sheets or a clinical development plan can help team members remember to consider the need for review if unforeseen changes must be made to ongoing studies. This is an important consideration during certain parts of long-term

clinical studies when a statistician may not be needed during routine meetings.

3. Review carefully.

   o Careful SAP review, like careful review of any document, is essential to ensure its accuracy and integrity. Identifying possible problems, even for seemingly minor issues like abbreviations or table headings, early in the study can save time during the "critical path" activities of data analysis, CSR writing and data posting.

4. Update as needed.

   o The SAP should be in line with the clinical trial protocol; however, SAP updates also should be consistent with the need for statistical analyses. If, for instance, a protocol amendment might result in a change to an existing SAP, and study evaluations are scheduled to be ongoing for several years, it may be sufficient to add a memo to a study file closer to the actual data analysis, when all existing protocol amendments may be addressed in a single SAP update.

Special SAP considerations also include the use of accessible language for all clinical and regulatory team members. Not all team members are statistical experts. A corollary to this idea is SAP review and development also is an ideal time to remind team members that best practice in clinical and regulatory writing is never to use statistical terms in a non-statistical way. For example, the term "significant" always should refer to measures of statistical or clinical significance rather than indicating any perceptible, numeric or noticeable difference.

## Conclusion

Statistical information is at the heart of data interpretation in regulatory contexts. Writing a high-quality SAP can contribute to better data handling and analysis and help teams complete documentation in a timely fashion. Collaboration and an awareness of the context and audience for statistical analyses can contribute to this quality.

### References

1. Lies, Damned Lies, and Statistics. University of York Department of Mathematics. Last updated 19 July 2012. https://www.york.ac.uk/depts/maths/histstat/lies.htm. Accessed 2 January 2017.
2. Gould SJ. "The Median Isn't the Message. In *Bully for Brontosaurus: Reflections in Natural History*. New York: WW Norton, 1991.
3. Ibid.
4. Boe P, Snyder B and Weiss M. "Introduction to Regulatory Documents in New Drug Applications." *AMWA Journal* 2011; 26 (3): 122-124.
5. Robinett RS. *The Biologics License Application in Common Technical Document Format. Vaccine Development and Manufacturing*, 1st ed. EP Wen, R Ellis, and NS Pujar, eds. New York: Wiley, 2015.
6. Myers S, Baron B, Radke-Mitchell L, Rieger M and Miller MA. "Preparing an Integrated Summary of Safety: A Writer's Perspective." *Drug Information Journal* 1998; 32(12): 53-63.
7. ICH *Integrated Addendum to ICH E6(R1): Guideline for Good Clinical Practice E6(R2)* (2016). ICH website. https://www.ich.org/fileadmin/Public_Web_Site/ICH_Products/Guidelines/Efficacy/E6/E6_R2__Addendum_Step2.pdf. Accessed 2 January 2017.
8. ICH *Structure and Content of Clinical Study Reports E3* (1995). ICH website. http://www.ich.org/fileadmin/Public_Web_Site/ICH_Products/Guidelines/Efficacy/E3/E3_Guideline.pdf. Accessed 2 January 2017.
9. ICH *Revision of M4E Guideline on Enhancing the Format and Structure of Benefit-Risk Information in ICH Efficacy M4E(R2)* (2016). ICH website. http://www.ich.org/fileadmin/Public_Web_Site/ICH_Products/CTD/M4E_R2_Efficacy/M4E_R2__Step_4.pdf. Accessed 2 January 2017.
10. ICH Statistical Principles for Clinical Trials E9. ICH website. http://www.ich.org/fileadmin/Public_Web_Site/ICH_Products/Guidelines/Efficacy/E9/Step4/E9_Guideline.pdf. Accessed 2 January 2017.
11. The JAMA network. *Journal of the American Medical Association.* Instructions for authors. Jama website. http://jamanetwork.com/journals/jama/pages/instructions-for-authors. Accessed 2 January 2017.
12. Ibid.
13. Ibid.
14. Ibid.
15. Op cit 8.
16. Op cit 10.
17. Ibid.
18. Op cit 7.
19. ICH *M1 MedDRA* (1997). ICH website. http://www.ich.org/products/meddra.html. Accessed 2 January 2017.
20. *Integrated Summaries of Efficacy and Safety: Guidance for Industry* (1988). FDA website. http://www.fda.gov/downloads/Drugs/GuidanceComplianceRegulatoryInformation/Guidances/ucm079803.pdf. Accessed 2 January 2017.
21. *Integrated Summary of Effectiveness: Guidance for Industry* (2015). FDA website. http://www.fda.gov/downloads/drugs/guidancecomplianceregulatoryinformation/guidances/ucm079803.pdf. Accessed 2 January 2017.
22. *WMA Declaration of Helsinki—Ethical Principles for Medical Research Involving Human Subjects* (2013). WMA website. http://www.wma.net/en/30publications/10policies/b3/. Accessed 2 January 2017.
23. Op cit 4.
24. Op cit 7.
25. Diorio B, Ellison J, Gawrylewski H, Mendlin A and Wagner B. Chapter 11 Clinical Study Reports. *Regulatory Writing: An Overview.* Regulatory Affairs Professionals Society. Rockville, MD. ©2017
26. Op cit 8.
27. Op cit 20.
28. Op cit 21.
29. Op cit 9.
30. Martin R. Chapter 20 Regulatory Framework—Medical Devices. *Regulatory Writing: An Overview.* Regulatory Affairs Professionals Society. Rockville, MD. ©2017
31. DeTora L. "Chapter 21 Biologics and Vaccines." *Regulatory Writing Handbook.* Regulatory Affairs Professionals Society, Rockville, MD, 2017.

32. Shen J. "Chapter 23 Combination Product Design and Development." *Regulatory Writing Handbook*. Regulatory Affairs Professionals Society, Rockville, MD, 2017.

33. Rupprecht J. "Chapter 2 Good Documentation Practices." *Regulatory Writing Handbook*. Regulatory Affairs Professionals Society, Rockville, MD, 2017.

34. Innocent N. "Chapter 18 Responses to Question or Requests for Information." *Regulatory Writing Handbook*. Regulatory Affairs Professionals Society, Rockville, MD, 2017.

35. De la Vega E. "Chapter 19 Dossier Maintenance." *Regulatory Writing Handbook*. Regulatory Affairs Professionals Society, Rockville, MD, 2017.

36. Seymour M. "Chapter 3 High Quality Regulatory Writing." *Regulatory Writing Handbook*. Regulatory Affairs Professionals Society, Rockville, MD, 2017.

37. *The Belmont Report* (1979). The National Commission for the Protection of Human Subjects of Biomedical and Behavioral Research. US Department of Health and Human Services website. http://www.hhs.gov/ohrp/regulations-and-policy/belmont-report/. Accessed 2 January 2017.

38. Op cit 22.

39. PhRMA Principles on Conduct of Clinical Trials (2013). PhRMA website. http://www.phrma.org/codes-and-guidelines/phrma-principles-on-conduct-of-clinical-trials. Accessed 2 January 2017.

40. ClinicalTrials.gov website. www.clinicaltrials.gov. Accessed 2 January 2017.

41. EudraCT website. https://eudract.ema.europa.eu. Accessed 2 January 2017.

42. Op cit 8.

43. Op cit 40.

44. Op cit 41.

45. *Guidance for the Use of Bayesian Statistics in Medical Device Clinical Trials* (February 2010). FDA website. http://www.fda.gov/medicaldevices/deviceregulationandguidance/guidancedocuments/ucm071072.htm. Accessed 2 January 2017.

46. Cochrane website. http://www.cochrane.org. Accessed 2 January 2017.

47. Op cit 22.

48. CONSORT website. http://www.consort-statement.org. Accessed 2 January 2017.

49. EQUATOR Network. CONSORT website. http://www.consort-statement.org/resources/equator. Accessed 2 January 2017.

50. DeTora L, Foster C, Skobe C, Yarker YE and Crawley FP. "Publication planning: promoting an ethics of transparency and integrity in biomedical research." *IJCP* 2015 Sep 1;69(9):915-21.

51. Author Center: New Manuscripts. *New England Journal of Medicine* website. http://www.nejm.org/page/author-center/manuscript-submission. Accessed 2 January 2017.

52. *American Medical Association Style Guide, 10th edition*. AMA website. http://www.amamanualofstyle.com. Accessed 2 January 2017.

## Author

Lisa DeTora is an assistant professor of writing studies at Hofstra University and a guest lecturer in humanities at the Hofstra Northwell School of Medicine. She began her career in medical writing at Merck and Co. Inc. and was a co-author of the company's internal guidances to comply with ICH E3 and M4. Her subsequent work experience has included regulatory writing and publication management in various therapeutic areas.

## Acknowledgements

I thank Stavros Valenti and James O'Malley for their kind review and comments on this chapter. I also thank Jenny Grodberg for her review of the outline.

# 11

# Clinical Study Reports

*By Brooke Diorio, John Ellison, Helle-Mai Gawrylewski, Anna Mendlin and Bertil Wagner*

## Introduction

The clinical study report (CSR) describes a single clinical study's purpose, conduct and results. In many cases, it serves as a fundamental document to support marketing applications for pharmaceutical, biologic and medical device/diagnostic products. As a basic unit of many regulatory submissions, CSRs ultimately may support product labeling. Higher-level summary documents in each regulatory submission place individual studies in the overall context for a particular target indication or formulation. Thus, the CSR should be a comprehensive summary of a particular study without extensive interpretation or extrapolation to allow for future flexibility in interpreting the findings in different contexts (e.g., other indications or formulations).

The primary audience for the CSR includes regulatory reviewers across various health authorities. In addressing these reviewers, the writer should aim for a streamlined presentation that would work in a global format. Efforts should be made to avoid redundancy, to use cross-referencing within the document and to ensure the key messages are presented clearly and concisely. A secondary audience is the general public, since clinical data and reports will be posted publicly in some regions.

Writing a CSR is, first and foremost, a collaborative team effort that requires effective and open communication across functions and organizations. The medical writer's role is essential for successful and timely delivery of a high-quality document. In many cases, the writer may not be an employee of the study sponsor. Regardless of the writer/sponsor relationship, the writer should lead CSR preparation rather than simply follow the team's directions. The writer can serve as the subject matter expert in document preparation, who provides continuity, whenever possible, across multiple documents within the same program or therapeutic area. In addition, many medical writers have backgrounds in science and research and can contribute to study data interpretation. The writer should contribute to the team's CSR timeline planning based on an evaluation of the study's complexity and the steps required to publish the document and complete the necessary quality checks.

This chapter describes the goals and the process of CSR preparation based on existing regulatory guidelines and industry practice. Potential issues and planning strategies a medical writer can use in working with the project team also are discussed.

## General Guidance

A CSR should be prepared in accordance with the International Council on Harmonisation's (ICH) *Guidance for Structure and Content of CSRs E3*, *Guidance for Good Clinical Practice E6* and other organization's guidances outlined in **Table 11-1**. As guidelines are

**Table 11-1. Guidance Documents for CSRs**

| Reference | Website Address |
|---|---|
| ICH *Structure and Content of Clinical Study Reports E3* (1995) | http://www.ich.org/fileadmin/Public_Web_Site/ICH_Products/Guidelines/Efficacy/E3/E3_Guideline.pdf |
| ICH *Guideline for Good Clinical Practice E6 (R1)* (1996) | http://www.ich.org/fileadmin/Public_Web_Site/ICH_Products/Guidelines/Efficacy/E6/E6_R1_Guideline.pdf |
| ICH *Structure and Content of Clinical Study Reports: Questions and Answers E3(R1)* (2012) | http://www.ich.org/fileadmin/Public_Web_Site/ICH_Products/Guidelines/Efficacy/E3/E3_QAs_R1_Step4.pdf |
| FDA *Guidance for Industry: Submission of Abbreviated Reports and Synopses in Support of Marketing Applications* (1999) | http://www.fda.gov/downloads/Drugs/.../Guidances/ucm072053.pdf |
| CORE (*Clarity and Openness in Reporting: E-3 based*) (2016) | http://www.core-reference.org/ |

revised, and new ones emerge, medical writers must keep up to date and maintain a good working knowledge of study reporting requirements.

## Definitions
### General Terms

A number of general industry terms are used across the pharmaceutical sector when referencing a CSR. A summary of the most common terms is provided in **Table 11-2**.

### CSR Types

The CSR types acceptable to most health authorities (i.e., full, abbreviated or synoptic reports) are described in the ICH E3 guidance and in the US Food and Drug Administration's (FDA) *Guidance for Industry: Submission of Abbreviated Reports and Synopses in Support of Marketing Applications* (**Table 11-1**). To determine which type of CSR should be produced for a given study, the CSR team should consider a number of factors including, but not limited to: the clinical development stage, the study type, the study's importance in supporting a submission and team resource availability. For an early development bioequivalence-food effect study, it may be sufficient to write a synoptic CSR. If the CSR is for a pivotal registration study, a full report will be essential for obtaining health authority approval.

## Key Source Materials

Items needed to prepare a CSR include a sponsor's template (if applicable), final protocol and statistical analysis plan (SAP). Topline results and associated clinical input can provide insight into which data are considered most relevant and can also provide key scientific messages that the team would like to convey in the final CSR.

Other source information needed for CSR preparation may include:

- EudraCT number
- National Clinical Trial (NCT) number (ClinicalTrials.gov identifier)
- other clinical registry numbers
- Principal or Coordinating Investigator name, address, and affiliation
- contract research organizations and/or central clinical laboratories names and addresses
- Data Safety Monitoring Board chairperson name
- Steering Committee Chairperson name
- list of investigators and Institutional Ethics Committees (IECs) or Investigational Review Boards (IRBs)
- batch numbers and expiration information for study drug(s)
- protocol deviation listings and summaries and criteria leading to determination of which (major) deviations will be included in the summary tables
- any changes to planned analyses
- any significant Good Clinical Practice issues
- Council for International Organizations of Medical Sciences CIOMS forms
- data listings and programmed outputs
- publications based on the study

## CSR Planning/Kick-off Meeting

Before preparing a CSR, it is best practice to hold a planning/kick-off meeting with all contributors to ensure alignment on key processes, issue mitigation strategies and agreed timelines. The goal of the medical writer or document author at this stage is to establish the role of document owner. The writer should lead the planning in collaboration with other contributors, solicit input from all functions involved, help the team evaluate potential report preparation issues and facilitate communication. This should ensure a much smoother CSR preparation process. CSR planning and kick-off meetings can be conducted separately or combined. Kick-off meetings for more than one report also may be combined if appropriate, as when several documents are being prepared for an upcoming submission. If the CSR is being prepared by a medical writer from outside the institution sponsoring the

**Table 11-2. Common Terminology for CSRs**

| Term | Definition |
|---|---|
| CIOMS Forms | Council for International Organizations of Medical Sciences forms are used to report suspect adverse reactions and typically are provided by an organization's safety or pharmacovigilance groups. CIOMS form information may be used to augment case information not found in the sponsor's clinical database to complete a patient narrative. |
| Clinical Trial | A research investigation involving human subjects; designed to answer specific questions about a biomedical intervention's (drug, treatment, device) safety and efficacy or new ways of using a known drug, treatment or device. |
| Commercially Confidential Information | Any information contained in a clinical report submitted to a health authority by the applicant that is not in the public domain or publicly available and where disclosure may undermine the applicant's legitimate economic interest. |
| Database Lock (DBL or Data Lock) | Action taken to prevent further changes to a clinical trial database. Locking a database occurs only after review, query resolution and a determination the database is ready for analysis. |
| EudraCT Number | EudraCT is the European clinical trials database. Any study being conducted in Europe should be assigned a EudraCT number. |
| Health Authority | Government body having the power to regulate product approval, distribution, marketing and usage. The ICH GCP definition includes the authorities that review submitted clinical data and those that conduct inspections. These bodies are sometimes referred to as Competent Authorities or regulatory agencies. |
| Independent Ethics Committee (IEC)/ Independent Review Board (IRB) | An independent body (a review board or a committee, institutional, regional, national or supranational) constituted of medical/scientific professionals and non-scientific members, who ensure the protection of the rights, safety and well-being of human subjects involved in a trial and provide public assurance of that protection by, among other things, reviewing and approving/providing favorable opinion on the trial protocol, the suitability of the investigator(s), facilities, methods and material to be used in obtaining and documenting informed consent of the trial subjects. |
| National Clinical Trial (NCT) Number | A unique identification code given to each clinical study registered on ClinicalTrials.gov. |
| Outputs (i.e., TFLs/TLGs) | The tables, listings and figures/graphs produced by statisticians and/or programmers; these generally summarize study data and analyses. |
| Principal/Coordinating Investigator | An individual under whose immediate direction the test article is administered or dispensed to a subject; in an investigation conducted by a team, the responsible leader of that team. |
| Protected Personal Data or Protected Personal Information | Any information relating to an identified or identifiable person, directly or indirectly, in particular by reference to an identification number or to one or more factors specific to their physical, physiological, mental, economic, cultural or social identity (adapted from Article 2(a) of Regulation (EC) No 45/2001). |
| Protocol | A document that describes a trial's objective(s), design, methodology, statistical considerations and organization. The protocol usually also gives the trial's background and rationale, but these could be provided in other protocol-referenced documents. Throughout the ICH GCP guideline, the term "protocol" refers to protocols and protocol amendments. |
| Statistical Analysis Plan (SAP) | A more technical and detailed elaboration of the principal features of the analyses described in the protocol, including detailed procedures for executing the statistical analysis of the primary and secondary endpoints and other data. |
| Topline Results | A summary of the study's most important results, usually prepared by statisticians in collaboration with project physicians. |

study, expectations for roles and responsibilities should be established in a contract.

## Timing

The kick-off meeting can occur any time after protocol finalization and prior to CSR preparation; however, the kick-off meeting typically occurs approximately one to two months before database lock (DBL). This ensures any issues that may affect the DBL or dataset and output preparation can be discussed prior to their completion.

## Key Agenda Items

Items that could be discussed at the kick-off meeting include:

**Figure 11-1. Flowchart for Developing CSRs**

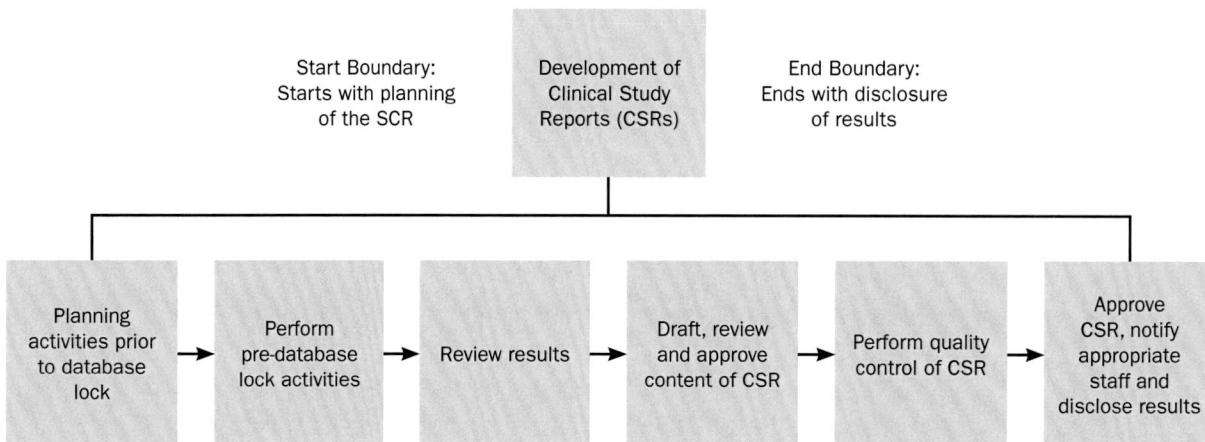

- CSR timelines
- resources
- coauthor, reviewer, approver/signatories and other team members' roles and responsibilities, as appropriate
- report type (see section above for report types)
- narratives (see narrative section below)
- source documentation availability, such as the SAP, topline results, data outputs or other external deliverables to support CSR preparation
- appendices, including which are appropriate for inclusion, what will be in each appendix and who will be responsible for obtaining those documents
- identification of potential issues specific to the study in question—These may include design complexity, similarity to other studies in the program and the need to maintain consistent presentation, how the CSR may fit into the submission strategy and the need to address any recently received regulatory comments from health authorities that might be applicable to the study (e.g., additional safety presentations). Issue mitigation plans also should be discussed.
- post-finalization redaction and anonymization of the CSR text, if appropriate—This should include subject-level information presentation in the results section and the need to avoid the discussion of rare diseases, pregnancies or other information that inadvertently could lead to the re-identification of a subject (see CSR Disclosure section below for details on CSR results' redaction and disclosure.

Other discussion topics may include document review processes and tools, as well as contributors' access and training to appropriate software, sponsor repositories or internal shared sites.

## Timelines
### General Considerations

Timelines should be agreed upon with contributors and reviewers before writing the CSR begins. Many companies or sponsors may have timeline standards or benchmarks in place, which are a good starting point for developing the specific CSR timeline. Often, the timeline is based on program needs, such as overall team resource prioritization, health authority submission timing, study complexity and clinical data availability. If there is a partnership agreement between organizations for a product co-development, this also can add complexity and should be factored into the timeline.

When planning the date for the CSR's approval and final placement in the sponsor's document repository with no additional changes, the team should take the European Medicines Agency (EMA) requirement into consideration for a CSR to be submitted no later than one year after study completion (or the date of last observation for last subject) for trials in adults and six months for pediatric trials.

### Key Milestones

**Figure 11-1** provides an overall schematic of the CSR development process. CSR activities can start as soon as the final protocol is available.

The timing of each CSR preparation step will depend on the amount of time available and the requirements of the team preparing the document; however, most key milestones will remain the same. Sufficient time must be allocated to each draft's preparation, team review, quality control (QC) review and publishing. Starting at the kick-off/planning stage and throughout document preparation, the medical writer needs to keep the team aware of the required QC and publishing time, which generally is not as well known or understood except by experts or those with prior CSR experience. Prior to DBL, the team should confirm resources and timelines, review table mockups, prepare and QC the CSR shell and review programmed narrative output and related discussions.

Activities following DBL include results review; drafting, reviewing and approving CSR content; QC review; and publishing, final approval, notifying appropriate staff and disclosing results. Once the CSR content is considered final, QC should be performed by an independent party. Of note, the disclosure of primary endpoint results to a trial registry or in a publication may occur when final data and topline results are available and may not always be the last step in the process.

## CSR Appendices
### ICH Requirements

ICH E3 provides details regarding CSR appendices; however, both FDA and the EMA have their own specific guidelines (based on ICH E3) that also should be taken into consideration. Following publication of the 2012 ICH E3 Questions and Answers document, certain appendices, e.g., sample consent forms, investigator CVs, listings of batch numbers per subject and Ethics Committee approvals, no longer need to be included with the CSR.

From a reviewer's perspective, any information needed to understand the study should be included, and other information should be available upon request. Non-standard appendices (e.g., patient-reported outcomes (PRO) reports, pharmacogenomic reports, adjudication packages, ECGs) too large to be included should be listed below the List of Appendices under an Additional Information heading.

Key appendices are:
- Protocol and Amendments (ICH E3 16.1.1): only the latest amended version of the global protocol should be included. Country-specific protocol amendments should be summarized in text only, unless the amendment implements a significant change, as determined by the clinical team, in which case it should be included.
- Sample Case Report Form(s) (ICH E3 16.1.2): copies of all sample case report forms or other data collection instruments used to obtain the data should be included.

- List of IECs or IRBs and Consent Forms (ICH E3 16.1.3)
- List and Description of Investigators and Sites (ICH E3 16.1.4): text descriptions of investigators and sites should match the database. For the List of Key Individuals, other important study participants whose participation materially affected the study's conduct or outcome should be included.
- Signature of sponsor's Responsible Medical Officer and the Principal or Coordinating Investigator(s) (ICH E3 16.1.5): the Principal or Coordinating Investigator's signature is to attest the CSR describes the study's conduct and results accurately.
- Randomization Scheme (ICH E3 16.1.7)
- Audit Certificates and Reports (if available) (ICH E3 16.1.8)
- Documentation of Statistical Methods (ICH E3 16.1.9): derived from the SAP. It also may contain bioanalytical quality and/or statistical summaries. Data Management Charter and Data Management Committee meeting minutes, if applicable, also can be included in this appendix.
- Documentation of Interlaboratory Standardization Methods or Quality Assurance Methods if Used (ICH E3 16.1.10): this appendix may be used to describe standardization methods for unusual, technically complex or specialized tests where validation may be necessary. Information on converting measurement units or normalizing raw laboratory data across laboratories should be included, if appropriate. If a central laboratory was used for biological sample analysis, this may be omitted.
- Publications Based on Study (ICH E3 16.1.11): a list of key publications (full manuscripts published in peer reviewed journals) based on the study.
- Important Publications Referenced in the Report (ICH E3 16.1.12): copies of all published literature referenced in the report should be verified and reviewed but not provided. If the CSR is part of a submission, corresponding literature will be referenced in the associated summary documents and submitted in Module 5.4.
- Subject Listings (ICH E3 16.2.1–16.2.8): will be included to address subject data, i.e., listings of discontinued subjects, protocol deviations, subjects excluded from the efficacy analysis, demographic data, compliance and/or drug concentration data, individual efficacy response

data, adverse events and individual laboratory measurements. Extremely long listings or those that may not be useful to the reviewer may be included elsewhere in the submission with the electronic datasets if permitted by the relevant health authority.

Note that appendix numbering may differ depending on sponsor-specific templates or guidelines.

## Narratives

### Planning Strategies (Subject Selection and Scope Principles)

The narrative writing process and narrative(s) location, in the body of the report or appended, may be very sponsor-specific. The narrative selection process also may be sponsor- or product-specific. Of note, health authority buy-in may be required regarding the narrative types to be included, especially for registration studies. Narratives typically are required for subjects who have died, had serious adverse events or discontinued study treatment due to adverse events. However, depending on the program, narratives also may be required for adverse events of special interest, or other events defined by the sponsor or health authority.

All narratives should be written in accordance with recommendations in ICH E3, which states narratives should describe "the nature and intensity of event, the clinical course leading up to event, with an indication of timing relevant to test drug/investigational product administration, relevant laboratory measurements, whether the drug was stopped, and when; countermeasures; postmortem findings; investigator's opinion on causality; and sponsor's opinion on causality, if appropriate." ICH also recommends the following information be included in narratives: subject identifier; subject age and sex; subject's general condition, if appropriate; disease being treated (unless it is the same for all patients) with illness duration (of current episode); relevant concomitant/previous illnesses with occurrence/duration details; relevant dosage details of concomitant/previous medication; test drug/investigational product administered; drug dose, if this varied among subjects; and length of administration.

Narrative writing activities may be initiated prior to DBL using draft safety data, if necessary. Portions of the narrative, such as tabular or other identifiable information, may be programmed. Programming also may be useful for generating a list of subjects for which narratives will be required. A study clinician and statistician should provide advance input into the design of the narratives, including which parts of the narrative could be programmed. When programming is not possible, a by-subject data output or subject profile can support narrative writing. CIOMS reports can be used to supplement information from the clinical database to write narratives of deaths and serious adverse events. If information is inconsistent between CIOMS and the clinical database, the clinical database is considered the verified source.

Narrative presentation in text should be limited to accommodate disclosure and privacy considerations (see Disclosure of CSRs below).

### Writing Conventions

The American Medical Association (AMA) manual of style is considered standard, and medical writers should be familiar with its contents; however, it also is important to consider any sponsor-specific standards to ensure consistency across an institution's CSRs. In fact, some companies may have program-specific style guides or writing conventions. If no style guide is available, rely on the AMA style.

## Process for Writing/Reviewing a CSR

As with many regulatory documents, CSRs typically are prepared in stages, starting with an outline or shell document, followed by a first draft, second draft and a final draft. In preparing a CSR, medical writers often will use sponsor-specific templates as well as checklists to ensure all necessary information is collected and facilitate CSR review.

### CSR Shell Preparation

Ideally, a CSR shell should be prepared using a template developed in accordance with ICH guidance (see **Table 11-1**), keeping in mind "flexibility is inherent in its use," as indicated in the 2012 ICH E3 Questions and Answers document. Shell preparation can begin as soon as the final protocol and SAP are available and should include the introduction and methods, preliminary table placement and organization of results. Information easily referenced in the protocol or SAP should not be repeated in the CSR unless critical to understanding the study design. Some information, such as key inclusion and exclusion criteria, can be summarized rather than repeated in full. The medical writer also may propose an overall logical organization of the results and tables, ensuring consistency with formatting and content guidance specific to the sponsor. In some cases, in consultation with the clinical and statistical programming teams, draft data outputs may be included in the shell to facilitate discussion of the output design and applicability to each section.

The CSR shell should be distributed to the designated reviewers, and a review meeting may be conducted, if necessary, to finalize non-data dependent sections of the CSR and to confirm table placement and general report organization. When distributing the document, the medical writer should instruct each reviewing function or department (e.g., clinical, pharmacology, biostatistics, regulatory) to focus its review on document sections most relevant to that department's expertise rather than commenting on style and grammar. Comments on the CSR shell should be incorporated, as appropriate, and the approved shell may be placed on hold until final data become available. Approved sections of the shell may be "greyed out" to discourage the team from revisiting text in subsequent review stages.

Note, while the shell is being prepared, the medical writer may begin collecting and organizing the appropriate CSR appendices. Communication and tracking tools provided by the study sponsor or developed by the medical writer can be used to facilitate appendices' coordination and collection.

### Results Review

When final results are available, a team meeting should be scheduled to review the results of preplanned analyses. Common review meeting objectives are to assess results and conclusions to be included in the CSR (i.e., agree on an interpretation of the results) and develop key messages that may be repeated elsewhere in the marketing application. Other topics may include confirming table and figure placement based on the significance of results and planning for additional *ad hoc* analyses, if needed.

### CSR Preparation

Throughout the process, it is important to remember CSR writing is a team effort. Following team alignment on study results, a full draft of the CSR may be written based on discussion and agreements and in collaboration with co-authors as needed. Additional collaboration meetings may be held to address specific draft document aspects. The medical writer should ensure all contributions are incorporated, as appropriate.

The CSR synopsis may be prepared at this stage if time allows; however, it may be prudent to wait for a later draft to allow teams to focus on the CSR's body. Through the use of word processing tools such as cross-referencing and bookmarks, it may be possible to auto-populate the synopsis with text taken directly from the CSR body (e.g., methods, results). When ready, the medical writer may send the first full draft CSR for review, specifying the review timeline. As mentioned above, providing specific instructions to reviewers to focus on areas of expertise rather than commenting on all areas of the document is highly recommended to reduce reviewer burden and expedite the process.

Following review of the first draft, the medical writer should incorporate consolidated comments and ensure all agreed upon changes are reflected accurately and completely prior to making the second draft available to reviewers. If needed, the medical writer can organize and facilitate a review meeting to discuss any outstanding issues and consolidate comments across functions. Additional statistical analyses or re-analyses may be considered along with subsequent incorporation or replacement of original outputs in the CSR. Any input that may be required from additional reviewers (including external experts, the Principal or Coordinating Investigator) should be coordinated by each respective function before providing consolidated, reconciled comments to the medical writer.

If Principal or Coordinating Investigator review of the CSR is required, the second or pre-final draft version may be sent to the investigators. It is important to communicate to the Principal or Coordinating Investigator the review's purpose is to attest the CSR describes the conduct and results of the study accurately rather than provide comments on data presentation and interpretation.

When the final CSR is ready, the medical writer will send it to team members for content approval (as determined at the CSR kick-off meeting). At this stage, the goal is to send the document only to individuals with approval rights according to the sponsor's policy rather than conduct another larger scale team review. Following approval, it is recommended the CSR be sent for final QC review by an independent reviewer. Ideally, QC steps should occur throughout the CSR development process, so quality is built into the product rather than added at the end. The medical writer may need to consult with team members or functional area approvers if the QC review leads to significant changes to the CSR's content. The medical writer should address all QC findings and initiate technical formatting and publishing processes as directed by the sponsor.

A signature by the sponsor's Responsible Medical Officer establishes the CSR finalization date. It should be noted, in some regions (e.g., the EU), a signature from the Principal or Coordinating Investigator also may be required.

### Finalization and Notification

Document finalization should allow efficient publishing and electronic or hardcopy submissions that conform to standard formats and regulatory expectations. Clinical study reports contain many different parts, and the individual files should be managed through an electronic system that contains all document components and ancillary administrative documents. The medical writer may use checklists and tracking tools to ensure the appropriate file organization is communicated to technical personnel responsible for CSR assembly. During the CSR publishing process, the medical writer should ensure appropriate CSR technical finalization is performed (e.g., bookmark and hyperlink placement and submission readiness), and all necessary components are included prior to issuing final document approval. After issuing and archiving the published CSR, the medical writer should ensure appropriate parties are notified to meet regulatory and sponsor requirements. Using standardized communication lists is helpful.

## Disclosure of CSRs

Public disclosure of information from clinical reports, such as CSRs, is a rapidly evolving area and has the potential to enhance the understanding of disease and treatment understanding, facilitate data mining and linkage, increase trust in the clinical development process and reduce the likelihood of redundant studies.[1] In 2013, the Pharmaceutical Research and Manufacturers of America (PhRMA) and the European Federation of Pharmaceutical Industries (EfPIA) published principles for responsible data sharing.[2] Registration and disclosure of clinical study results also are required by many health authorities (EU Policy 0070 and freedom of information requirements elsewhere) and professional journals. The EMA is leading the effort to provide broad access to clinical data and clinical reports from several marketing applications have been posted on their website.[3] Current regulations in many countries specify that information from clinical studies be redacted before public disclosure to ensure the privacy of study subjects and others who may be identified individually from clinical study documents. Further, document redaction serves to protect study sponsors from exposing commercially confidential information or protected personal data or information publicly. The redaction process is more difficult because various countries have inconsistent transparency criteria. In the EU, clinical reports submitted in a marketing authorization application are required to be anonymized, not redacted, including the Serious Adverse Event data listings and patient safety narratives. However, it is important to follow local and regional privacy laws. Efforts to harmonize redaction and anonymization methods have been initiated by Transcelerate BioPharma, a non-profit organization comprising many of the world's leading biopharmaceutical companies.[4]

In general, direct identifiers (subject identification number, name, address, telephone number, facsimile number, email address and sensitive data) are redacted (masked) or anonymized (resynthesized text).

Quasi-identifiers (e.g., sex, date of birth or age, geographic location, race, ethnicity, height, weight, event dates, profession, socioeconomic status, number of pregnancies, number of children, high-level diagnoses or procedures, marital status, criminal history) may be de-identified if the available information has a high potential to lead to the re-identification of an individual, e.g., small studies (few subjects or single site) or a small target population (rare diseases). The medical writer should prepare CSRs with care to ensure this type of information is displayed minimally, if at all, to ensure subsequent document redaction or anonymization can be conducted more efficiently. For this reason, commercially sensitive information, such as clinical development strategy or interactions with health authorities, should be omitted, if possible. Also, other associated documents, such as individual by-subject by visit data listings, figures and tables with individual subject data, full subject narratives and corresponding forms, should be contained as separate CSR elements to facilitate their removal or redaction, except in the EU under Policy 0070. The redaction process is conducted best in a pre-defined manner, guided by standard operating procedures, to ensure high-quality deliverables meeting regulatory and sponsor needs.

## Multiple CSRs From a Single Study

In general, it is desirable to generate a single CSR for each study to ensure uniform reporting standards and avoid confusion. However, studies with different reporting periods, containing interim analyses or requiring safety updates, may require multiple CSRs. The medical writer should discuss the appropriate reporting format (synoptic, abbreviated, or full CSR) with the team. Programmed outputs for studies requiring multiple CSRs should contain unique identifiers for each reporting interval (e.g., each reporting interval's tables should have different names). Appendices included in the first CSR for a given study should not be included in subsequent CSRs if they have not changed. A statement to this effect also may be included in the report's list of appendices section. Each CSR can be managed through an overall virtual folder structure to ensure components can be retrieved and submitted easily.

## CSR Errata, Addenda, or Revisions

Changes to an issued, final CSR may be needed to correct errors, add important data or respond to health authority requests.. The medical writer should consult with regulatory and quality management staff and other relevant sponsor representatives to determine whether an erratum, addendum or revision is appropriate. In certain instances, confirmation with applicable health authorities also may be necessary. An erratum generally is a smaller document that describes the error(s) and provides corrected text, tables and figures. It usually is generated when the scope of changes is small, and no changes are made to the conclusions. An addendum may be required when new information needs to be added for the same reporting interval to an already issued CSR, and the changes are too extensive for an erratum, but the overall CSR conclusions have not changed. An example is an additional data analysis in response to a health authority request for information. As such, the addendum may require a separate publishing effort if many new files need to be included. As with the erratum, if the CSR is submitted to a health authority, the addendum should be included in the submission.

The decision to revise an existing CSR must not be taken lightly, as it involves additional writing, review, QC and republishing of very large documents. An issued CSR may require modification for a number of reasons (e.g., health authority request, additional analyses, or substantial errors) that impact the overall conclusions of the study. All CSR errata, addenda and revisions must be approved in accordance with regulatory and sponsor guidelines and undergo applicable document QC processes to ensure conformity with regulatory and sponsor standards.

## Summary

As fundamental regulatory submission documents, CSRs must be organized carefully and written in a way to minimize development time, allow the sponsor to convey clear messages to health authorities and facilitate regulatory review and market clearance. By providing leadership and technical expertise, the medical writer plays an important role in planning and developing high-quality CSRs.

Note: The opinions expressed in this chapter are those of the authors and not necessarily those of the companies or institutions who employ them.

**References**
1. Committee on Strategies for Responsible Sharing of Clinical Trial Data; Board on Health Sciences Policy; Institute of Medicine. Sharing clinical trial data: maximizing benefits, minimizing risk. The National Academies Press website. http://www.nap.edu/catalog.php?record_id=18998. Accessed 4 January 2017.
2. Pharmaceutical Research and Manufacturers of America (PhRMA) and the European Federation of Pharmaceutical Industries and Associations (EfPIA). Principles for Responsible Clinical Trial Data Sharing. http://phrma-docs.phrma.org/sites/default/files/pdf/PhRMAPrinciplesForResponsibleClinicalTrialDataSharing.pdf. Accessed 4 January 2017.
3. The European Medicines Agency. Online access to clinical data for medicinal products for human use. https://clinicaldata.ema.europa.eu/web/cdp/home. Accessed 21 January 2017.
4. Transcelerate BioPharma. Clinical data transparency. http://www.transceleratebiopharmainc.com/initiatives/clinical-data-transparency/. Accessed 21 January 2017.

**Authors**
Brooke Diorio is a principal medical writing scientist at Janssen research & Development LLC. She has almost 10 years of experience in medical writing and regulatory affairs and also has authored several scientific publications in peer reviewed journals. Diorio holds a PhD in molecular biology from the University of Melbourne, Australia, and was a post-doctoral fellow at the National Institutes of Health.

John Ellison is a principal medical writing scientist at Janssen Research & Development LLC. He has more than 15 years of experience in scientific publishing and medical writing. Ellison is a Certified Medical Publication Professional (CMPP) and has authored several publications. He holds an MS from the University of Michigan.

Helle M Gawrylewski, MA, is a senior director in medical writing at Janssen Research & Development LLC, with more than 40 years of work promoting medical writing and translation as professions in the pharmaceutical industry and being a force for change in professional organizations like DIA, CDISC, AMWA and RAPS.

Anna Mendlin is an associate director in regulatory medical writing at Janssen Research & Development LLC, with 17 years of medical writing experience. Mendlin holds a PhD in neuroscience from Princeton University.

Bertil Wagner, PharmD, is an associate director in regulatory medical writing at Janssen Research & Development LLC. He has more than 25 years of experience in scientific research and writing in academia and pharmaceutical industry.

**Acknowledgements**
The authors thank Frank Meloni, PhD; Diane Klatzman, RN, BSN; Carl Jameson, MS; Paul Sokol, PhD; and Joe Lallier, MS, MBA, RAC of Janssen Research and Development, LLC for their review and suggestions for improvement of this chapter.

# 12

# Integrated CMC Documentation

*By Mariam Aslam*

## Introduction

Quality documentation reports chemistry, manufacturing and controls (CMC) information about pharmaceutical products, including the drug substance and any excipients they include. CMC data are important requirements for drug registrations worldwide. In Common Technical Document (CTD) format, quality information is presented in Module 2.3 Quality Overall Summary and Module 3 Quality, chemical-pharmaceutical and biological information for active chemical substances and biological medicinal products. The CTD format is used for the Marketing Authorisation Application (MAA) registration dossier in the EU, or a New Drug Application (NDA) in the US, as well as marketing applications for other regions or countries. It is imperative that CMC data, and all data, achieve the highest standard and integrity.

During the drug development stage, a New Chemical Entity (NCE) or a New Molecular Entity's (NME) chemistry and its potential therapeutic effects are identified, and a drug substance is manufactured. Drug substance manufacture, control and stability are investigated in accordance with the final anticipated markets' current regulations and guidelines. Once the drug substance is developed, it is researched further as a drug formulation. As research continues, the final drug product's pharmaceutical form, excipients, drug formulation, manufacturing process and quality also are determined.

This is known as drug product pharmaceutical development. Pharmaceutical development's objective is to create a manufacturing process and quality product that will produce a drug product consistently for its intended use. The drug substance's chemistry is studied to investigate whether its physical, chemical, biological or microbiological characteristics will have any effect on the drug product's manufacture and function. The drug substance's quality characteristics are controlled within suitable limits to ensure the drug product's required quality. Excipients also may be chosen to develop the drug product during manufacture. The excipient's function will influence the overall drug product manufacture, quality and the proposed indication.

The drug formulation then is investigated further to identify and control critical physical, chemical, biological or microbiological characteristics that will contribute to the drug product's quality. Manufacturing process development will include investigating the choice of the process and defining any parameters that need to be controlled (e.g., temperature, quality control testing) to produce a quality drug product. Another critical element to be considered during pharmaceutical development is the container closure system. The drug product's chemistry and intended use will impact the final commercial packaging presentation. Factors such as dosage form compatibility with immediate packaging materials, storage

**Table 12-1. Example Template of Section 3.2.P.3 Manufacture and 3.2.P.3.1 Manufacturer(s)\***

| Site Name and Address | Manufacturing Activity or Responsibility |
|---|---|
| Company Name and Address | Drug product manufacturer<br>Intermediate manufacturer<br>Quality control<br>Stability testing<br>Microbiology testing<br>Batch release<br>Assembler<br>Distributor |
| Company name and address | Drug product manufacturer<br>Intermediate manufacturer<br>Quality control<br>Stability testing<br>Microbiology testing<br>Batch release<br>Assembler<br>Distributor |
| Company name and address | Drug product manufacturer<br>Intermediate manufacturer<br>Quality Control<br>Stability testing<br>Microbiology testing<br>Batch release<br>Assembler<br>Distributor |

*\* (Include name, address, and responsibility of each manufacturer, including contractors, and each production site or facility involved in manufacturing and testing. In column 'Manufacturing activity/responsibility', delete site activity that is not relevant.)*

conditions (e.g., protection from sunlight and moisture) will need to be considered. The proposed commercially packed drug product is studied further to establish the shelf life from time of manufacture. Stability studies identify any drug product quality changes over time under various conditions, such as temperature and humidity. Depending on where the drug product will be marketed, regional environmental stability condition differences are applied during stability studies.

In accordance with ICH guidelines and consistent with the drug development process, medicinal products' quality documentation should consist of two parts: drug substance and drug product. Drug product documentation also contains data for any intermediates and excipients used in the product's manufacture. Generally, quality documentation follows a fairly strict format and does not require very much story building or explanation. The major challenges associated with quality documentation include ensuring accuracy and adapting CTD sections to accommodate information required by different markets or regions.

## Quality Documentation Formatting and Content

Quality documentation structure is explained systematically in the International Council on Harmonisation's (ICH) *The Common Technical Document for the Registration of Pharmaceuticals for Human use: quality M4Q(R1).* The drug substance's quality dossier is CTD Section 3.2.S Drug Substance, and the drug product's is Section 3.2.P Drug Product. Although CTD structure and format are internationally harmonised, regional requirements may vary, depending on the quality documentation's content. Ideally, a regulatory professional can seek regulatory agency advice on the quality dossier's content. To achieve this successfully, regulatory professionals should establish a good rapport with the assessors. Reading and understanding relevant guidelines will help with content requirements. Companies may wish to adopt a basic CTD template from the ICH guidelines that can be adapted to each market's requirements. The quality dossier sections likely to impact regional content differences are manufacture, specifications, analytical procedures, batch analyses and stability.

The list of all manufacturers involved in the supply chain from manufacture, quality control testing, batch release, assembler and distributor are likely to vary from one market to another. This will depend on the market and a company's decision to supply from multiple sources for commercial reasons. Therefore, for CTD Sections 3.2.S.2.1 and 3.2.P.3.1 Manufacturer(s), the regulatory professional may consider correlating the list of manufacturers with their related supply chain activities to aid in necessary modifications for each market. **Figure 12-1** includes a sample template for Section 3.2.P.3.1.

This point also may be applied to Sections 3.2.S.4.1 and 3.2.S.5.1 Specification. There may be regional differences in drug component testing and specification limits and, as a consequence, the analytical procedures and batch analyses sections will vary for the impacted markets. For the batch analyses section, regulatory agencies may accept either tabulated data or a copy of the certificate of analysis. Tabulating large amounts of batch analyses data introduces the risk of typographical errors. If including tabulated batch analyses is mandatory, it is recommended a copy of the certificate of analysis be included, which will be beneficial for future reference if the assessor or another regulatory professional question the tabulated data at a later stage.

Stability study data also will vary from region to region, in part because the stability protocol's environmental conditions are subject to climate zones. For example, a drug marketed in the UK normally would have long-term stability data under conditions 25°C/60% or 30°C/65%

RH, while the same product marketed in Malaysia will be tested at 30°C/75% RH. The regulatory professional will benefit from a CTD template that includes all climate zone conditions and can be modified for each market where the drug product is to be registered.

When a regulatory professional starts authoring a quality dossier, the content should be considered carefully to avoid unnecessary repetition of text. Authoring an easy-to-read dossier with relevant content requires a regulatory professional who has the appropriate knowledge and skills.

## Points to Consider When Preparing Quality Documentation

'Keep it simple' is a prudent strategy to ensure the quality documentation contains all the required data, limited to relevant points, and does not raise questions from the regulatory agency. Regulatory professionals may be tempted to write reams of information or provide too little information in the dossier, strategies thought to prevent further information requests by the agency. In fact, the agency assessor has an invitation to probe further if data are irrelevant or missing, which may lead to additional requests for information and explanations and, in turn, delay the dossier's evaluation.

Thus, the regulatory professional must use skilled judgement in utilizing company data, the CTD and other relevant guidelines when preparing the content of each quality section.

For example, when preparing the section description of manufacturing process and process controls, the data obtained from the manufacturing site should not be copied word for word. The data from the site may include internal information to demonstrate compliance with Good Manufacturing Practice (GMP); however, this information is not required in the CTD's manufacturing process section. It is sufficient to include only the steps involved in drug substance and drug product manufacture. Typically, the manufacturing process description will include quantities and/or volumes of ingredients, operating conditions (e.g., heated for 20 minutes at 20°C) and details of any in-process controls.

The analytical procedures section is an example of where details often are not represented adequately. The regulatory professional must write the analytical procedures, so they can be repeated by the regulatory agency, if necessary. For chromatography procedures, ensure chromatographic conditions such as column type, detector conditions and oven temperature are included. However, analytical procedures that are compendial, e.g., *European Pharmacopoeia* (*Eur.Ph.*) and *United States Pharmacopoeia* (*USP*), should not be repeated in the quality dossier.

Instead, simply reference the pharmacopeia from which the analytical method is drawn.

Referencing data to its particular section is best practice for avoiding repetition and unnecessary amendments during variation. Sections should contain only the data relevant to the stated topic, and cross-references should be provided if necessary. Regulatory professionals sometimes include the shelf-life specification in Section 3.2.P.8.1 Stability Summary and Conclusion; however, the shelf-life specification should be provided in 3.2.P.5.1. Regulatory professionals may not remember to update Section 3.2.P.8.1 if changes are required to the shelf-life specification in 3.2.P.5.1, which creates the possibility of inconsistencies. Also, if changes are required to Section 3.2.P.8.1, the current shelf-life data may be out of date (or need to be updated), which may cause unnecessary work and awkwardness for the company. To avoid this scenario, the 3.2.P.5.1 shelf-life specification should be cross-referenced to Section 3.2.P.8.1.

Avoiding unnecessary updates to all quality dossier sections is also aligned with the above points. Too much detail can be a risk, requiring costly and time-consuming variations if details change. For example, when equipment is declared in Section 3.2.S.2.2 and 3.2.P.3.3 Description of Manufacturing Process and Process Controls, avoid providing serial numbers and manufacturer names unless required explicitly by an agency or health authority. Such information usually is irrelevant and can be costly to amend in the dossier if the equipment manufacturer or serial numbers change. It is both pragmatic and acceptable to state only the equipment type and size, e.g., 100 L stainless steel vat.

## Regional Information

Depending on where the medicine is marketed, additional regional information may be required per local legislation. The quality documentation should reference this data in Section 3.2.R Regional Information of CTD Module 3. Examples of regional information are the drug product process validation scheme, data relating to drug products containing or using materials of animal and/or human origin and the European Certificate of Suitability of monographs of the *European Pharmacopoeia* (CEP) for a drug substance.

## Lifecycle Management

Another challenge of preparing quality documentation is postmarketing data lifecycle management, and ensuring any changes are updated and authorized by the regulatory agency in a timely manner. If at all possible, regulatory professionals should avoid submitting too many postmarketing variations. Following the tips listed above will minimize the need for variations and permit the regulatory professional to dedicate time to necessary changes such as manufacturing site transfer. During a drug product manufacturing site transfer, the quality dossier will be required. In theory, if the quality documentation has been authored correctly, registered and maintained postapproval, the only variation will be to the manufacture section.

**Recommended Reading**
- ICH, *The Common Technical Document for the Registration of Pharmaceuticals for Human use: quality M4Q(R1)*
- ICH, *The Common Technical Document for the Registration of Pharmaceuticals for Human use: Pharmaceutical Development Q8(R2)*
- ICH, *The Common Technical Document for the Registration of Pharmaceuticals for Human use: Stability Testing of New Drug Substances and Products Q1A(R2)*

- World Health Organization, WHO Technical Report Series, No. 953 (2009), *Annex 2 Stability testing of active pharmaceutical ingredients and finished pharmaceutical products*
- *The Rules Governing Medicinal Products in the European Union, Volume 2B, Notice to Applicants, Medicinal products for human use*

**Author**
Mariam Aslam is a senior consultant at PAREXEL Consulting and a qualified chemist with eight years of laboratory and more than 10 years of regulatory experience. She has worked in postapproval marketing authorizations and has an excellent understanding of regulations, guidelines and implementing them within a pharmaceutical or healthcare organization to ensure compliance. She also has pharmacovigilance experience as a deputy QPPV, interviewed in an MHRA pharmacovigilance inspection, attended EMA Eudravigilance training and gained qualified reporter status.

# 13

# Integrated Nonclinical Documentation

*By Lisa DeTora*

Ethical questions about the appropriate use of animals in research far predate the current century. For example, H.G. Wells' 1896 science fiction classic, *The Island of Dr. Moreau*,[1] examines the collision between appropriate and ethical models of scientific inquiry to address well-defined questions and the callous use of nonhuman creatures to satisfy idle curiosity. This story demonstrates what critic Wayne Booth[2] might consider "the ethics of fiction," using storytelling to deliver a message about appropriate research conduct and the use of animals.

Today, animal research is highly regulated, and the use of animals to support trials in humans must be conducted and documented following appropriate laws, guidelines and codes.

## General Considerations for High Quality Nonclinical Documentation

All regulatory documentation should be of high quality.[3] For the purposes of this discussion, high-quality nonclinical documentation should be:

- scientifically accurate
- concise
- complete
- consistent with all applicable regulatory standards
- formatted correctly

In addition, high-quality regulatory documentation should meet the needs of readers who must evaluate the design, conduct and results of scientific studies and use that information to make judgments about the appropriateness of the use of medicinal products in humans.

Pre- or nonclinical studies generally are undertaken to evaluate a pharmaceutical, vaccine or biologic product's effects and preliminary safety profile prior to initiating clinical trials and also may be conducted to support later-stage clinical trials. These nonclinical studies may include *in vitro* evaluations and characterization, such as *ex vivo* studies and investigations using cell cultures or human or animal tissues. Studies in animal models generally are conducted first in rodents and begun only after adequate evidence has been collected to warrant more in-depth nonclinical safety and efficacy evaluation.[4] Nonclinical research also may include assay development and studies of biomarkers deemed necessary to conduct the types of studies described above or to justify and establish clinical trial evaluations.

The US Food and Drug Administration (FDA) publishes and updates guidance documents for nonclinical testing on a regular basis (see **Table 13-1**). In addition, the International Council on Harmonisation (ICH) routinely publishes, reviews and updates guidance documents describing safety evaluations of medicinal products for human use.[5] The ICH guidelines are widely recognized

**Table 13-1. US FDA Nonclinical Testing Guidance Documents**[a]

| Title | Type | Date |
|---|---|---|
| Guidance for Industry: Carcinogenicity Study Protocol Submissions | Final | May 2002 |
| Guidance for Industry: Q&A: Content and Format of INDs for Phase 1 Studies of Drugs, Including Well-Characterized, Therapeutic, Biotechnology-Derived Products | Final | October 2000 |
| Guidance for Industry: Developing Medical Imaging Drug and Biological Products—Part 1: Conducting Safety Assessments | Final | June 2004 |
| Guidance for Industry: Estimating the Maximum Safe Starting Dose in Initial Clinical Trials for Therapeutics in Adult Healthy Volunteers | Final | July 2005 |
| Guidance for Industry, Investigators, and Reviewers: Exploratory IND Studies | Final | January 2006 |
| Guidance for Industry: Immunotoxicology Evaluation of Investigational New Drugs | Final | October 2002 |
| Investigational Enzyme Replacement Therapy Products: Nonclinical Assessment | Draft | May 2015 |
| Nonclinical Evaluation of Endocrine-Related Drug Toxicity: Guidance for Industry | Final | September 2015 |
| Guidance for Industry: Nonclinical Evaluation of Late Radiation Toxicity of Therapeutic Radiopharmaceuticals | Final | November 2011 |
| Nonclinical Pharmacology/Toxicology Development of Topical Drugs Intended to Prevent the Transmission of Sexually Transmitted Diseases (STD) and/or for the Development of Drugs Intended to Act as Vaginal Contraceptives | Final | July 2015 |
| Guidance for Industry: Nonclinical Safety Evaluation of Drug or Biologic Combinations | Final | March 2006 |
| Guidance for Industry: Nonclinical Safety Evaluation of Pediatric Drug Products | Final | February 2006 |
| Nonclinical Safety Evaluation of Reformulated Drug Products and Products Intended for Administration by an Alternate Route: Guidance for Industry and Review Staff | Final | October 2015 |
| Guidance for Industry: Nonclinical Studies for the Safety Evaluation of Pharmaceutical Excipients | Final | May 2005 |
| Osteoporosis: Nonclinical Evaluation of Drugs Intended for Treatment: Draft Guidance for Industry | Draft | June 2016 |
| Guidance for Industry and Review Staff: Recommended Approaches to Integration of Genetic Toxicology Study Results | Final | January 2006 |
| Guidance for Industry: Reproductive and Developmental Toxicities—Integrating Study Results to Assess Concerns | Final | September 2011 |
| Safety Testing of Drug Metabolites: Guidance for Industry | Final | November 2016 |
| Guidance for Industry: Single Dose Acute Toxicity Testing for Pharmaceuticals | Final | August 1996 |
| Guidance for Industry: Statistical Aspects of the Design, Analysis, and Interpretation of Chronic Rodent Carcinogenicity Studies of Pharmaceuticals | Draft | May 2001 |
| Testicular Toxicity: Evaluation During Drug Development: Guidance for Industry | Draft | July 2015 |

a   FDA Guidance for Industry. Nonclinical Search. FDA website. http://www.fda.gov/RegulatoryInformation/Guidances/default.htm. Accessed 9 January 2017.

as standards for nonclinical program design and implementation. A table of ICH safety guidance documents is presented elsewhere in this book.[6]

As noted in the ICH *Guidance on Nonclinical Safety Studies for the Conduct of Human Clinical Trials and Marketing Authorization for Pharmaceuticals M3(R2)* (2009),[7] pharmaceutical development is performed in a stepwise fashion to evaluate the efficacy and safety profile of an agent. This process includes evaluations in both animal models and the clinic in order to provide the best characterization of a product's expected safety and to justify studies and routine use in humans. Thus, the documentation of nonclinical information, particularly

integrated discussions of nonclinical data, should be undertaken within the context of planned or ongoing clinical trials and intended use. A further consideration for producing high-quality nonclinical documentation is the need to balance expected benefits and risks at all stages of product development. The pharmaceutical development process currently emphasizes an approach to risk management that requires increased attention to integrated information and analysis of relative benefits versus potential harms,[8] such as adverse effects, that reasonably can be expected in the target population with widespread clinical use.[9] While benefit-risk analysis recording and reporting are necessary, a best practice approach to all forms of documentation considers the risk management context and the need to balance expected effects and safety profiles.

Since nonclinical studies should establish the likely action and preliminary safety profile or answer questions about the safety or tolerability of the product or one of its parts or excipients relative to its possible benefits, ICH provides guidance for specific types of safety investigations, the order in which they should be conducted and what constitutes a core testing battery.[10] For example, ICH M3 indicates nonclinical safety evaluations should characterize the toxic effects of a drug with respect to:

- target organs—the organs or systems most likely to be impacted by the product or its metabolism
- dose dependence—whether such effects appear to be proportional to increasing or decreasing doses or dose intervals
- relationship to exposure—how undesired effects may be related to systemic or local exposure
- potential reversibility—whether unintended effects resolve with medical intervention, cessation of treatment or spontaneously[11]

High-quality nonclinical study documentation should address each of these concerns and integrate these findings into a larger discussion of the expected benefits and risks of a given product in clinical use, whether such use is in trials or medical practice.

A recent FDA guidance, *Safety Testing of Drug Metabolites: Guidance for Industry*, indicates safety testing of drug metabolites should be considered, as needed to support claims and scientific findings, specifically regarding the product's tolerability and harms profile in the clinic. The guidance notes it is not usual practice to evaluate all known metabolites of drug products in nonclinical studies; however, it is important to understand their potential impact in certain circumstances. For example, in animal models where metabolite formation differs from that anticipated or known to occur in humans, adequate data should be available to support a discussion of these differences and their scientific and clinical significance.[12]

ICH M3 also indicates any serious adverse events that occur after administering a product in nonclinical trials should be examined carefully, because such events may influence the decision to proceed to clinical studies.[13] This decision must be taken in the context of intended use. For instance, the acceptable safety and tolerability parameters for products intended for the long-term treatment of non-fatal conditions may differ markedly from those for the short-term, acute treatment of immediately life-threatening conditions. Authors of nonclinical documents should be familiar with the treatment paradigms for patients with the target conditions and/or solicit opinions from medically-qualified persons.

## Nonclinical Study Reports

Nonclinical study reports are an important source of information needed to produce high-quality integrated documentation. Nonclinical study reports present the results of studies individually and are used to support a medicinal product's development and registration. In the Common Technical Document (CTD) format, nonclinical reports appear in Module 4, and support the data presented in Module 2.[14]

Nonclinical report formats may vary. Although ICH does not provide a report format for nonclinical studies, individual countries often provide guidance. A minimum format to meet Good Laboratory Practices (GLP) is specified in US 21 CFR 58, Subpart J (58.158).[15]

### Brief Overview of Nonclinical Study Report Formats

Results of individual studies or closely related groups of studies must be presented in nonclinical reports and included in Module 4 of filings in the CTD format.[16] Minimum content for such reports for US regulatory filings is included in 21 CFR 58, Subpart J (58.158) and summarized below:[17]

- name and address of the facility performing the study
- initiation and completion dates
- objectives and procedures from the approved protocol
- changes to the original protocol
- statistical methods
- test and control articles identified by name, chemical abstracts number or code number, strength, purity and composition or other appropriate characteristics
- test and control articles' stability of the test and control articles under the conditions of administration
- methods used
- description of the test system used, including the number of animals, their sex, body weight range, source of supply, species, strain and sub-strain and age, and procedure used for identification
- dosage, dosage regimen, route of administration and duration
- any circumstance that could have affected data quality or integrity
- names of the study director, other scientists or professionals and all supervisory personnel

- transformations, calculations, or operations performed on the data, a summary and analysis of the data, and conclusions drawn from the analysis
- signed and dated reports of each individual scientist or other professional involved in the study
- location(s) where all specimens, raw data and the final report are to be stored
- statement prepared and signed by the quality assurance unit as described in 58.35(b)(7).

Nonclinical study reports typically are prepared by the contract research organization (CRO) responsible for conducting the study and provided to the sponsor.[18] The guidance in 21 CFR 58 lists the basic information necessary to confirm the location of the nonclinical study, who performed it, the study conduct methods and data analysis, study results and measures for assuring quality assurance and record retention. Literature references or scientific background to justify the research are not required. However if references appear, they must be managed appropriately to prevent problems in assembling filings that may require the inclusion of .pdf references.[19]

### Readiness for Electronic Publishing

Many more new chemical entities, biologics and vaccine components or products enter nonclinical studies than progress to clinical development. This reflects the nature of scientific inquiry and also presents special challenges for the documentation of nonclinical studies in formal regulatory filings such as Investigational New Drug Applications (INDs) and New Drug Applications (NDAs). Dozens of nonclinical reports may need to be submitted to regulatory authorities. Therefore, as soon as it becomes clear nonclinical study reports will be included in an IND, Investigational Medicinal Product Dossier (IMPD) or any other type of regulatory filing, they should be reviewed for readiness to include in electronic publishing systems.

A potential stumbling block for including clinical study reports seamlessly in regulatory submissions is excessive published literature citations. In some situations, copies of references will be required to be provided in a regulatory submission. Therefore, and in keeping with good practice in report writing, nonclinical reports should cite only those references critical to scientific understanding. For example, references cited in a background or discussion section of a nonclinical study report may be of limited value in interpreting results or supporting study conduct. Early assessment of nonclinical reports can prevent delays in regulatory filings. Identifying a consistent set of "core" references may be helpful to both the sponsor and the CRO by allowing the scientists writing reports

to concentrate on reporting data rather than developing background information. As each nonclinical study report should be a standalone document, it generally also is recommended to omit references to guidelines, codes and additional study reports.

### Nonclinical Study Report Style Guides

Establishing a standard style guide can enhance the ability of regulatory professionals and nonclinical scientists to ensure consistency in nonclinical study reports. A guide for nonclinical study reports might specify formal requirements such as minimum font sizes, suggested table layouts, preferred methods for recording units of measure, the number and type of literature references to be included and accepted product nomenclature.

Standard report templates for nonclinical studies may seem helpful; however, given the broad scope of nonclinical investigations,, the effort involved in developing, review and management of different templates should be considered in relation to the numbers of such studies. Of note, the FDA provides templates for the following food additive toxicology reports:

- Subchronic Toxicity Study in Rodents
- Subchronic Toxicity Study in Dogs
- Genetic Toxicity Study: In Vitro Bacterial Reverse Mutation (Ames) Test
- Genetic Toxicity Study: In Vitro Mouse Lymphoma Thymidine Kinase Gene Mutation Assay
- Genetic Toxicity Study: Mammalian Erythrocyte Micronucleus Test
- Genetic Toxicity Study: In Vitro Mammalian Chromosomal Aberration Test
- Chronic Toxicity Study With an In Utero Phase
- Chronic (1 Year) Dog Toxicity Study Template
- Two-Generation Reproduction Toxicity Study[23]

Although these templates were not designed specifically for reporting nonclinical data to support the use or investigation of medicinal products, they may be useful as models.

If reports are completed by agencies or colleagues in different countries, attention should be paid to translations and abbreviations. For example, the standard abbreviation for "intravenous" varies globally. It is not always necessary to regularize usage and abbreviations across all nonclinical reports; however, the use should be clear within each report.

To aid in the production of nonclinical written and tabulated summaries, standard table formats or report templates could be based on ICH M4S guidance, to ensure necessary data is easily found in nonclinical study reports.

## Integrated Discussions of Nonclinical Data

Integrated discussions of nonclinical study information appear in various regulated documents including:

- background packages to support regulatory authority meetings[24]
- Investigator's Brochures (IBs)[25]
- introductory statements in clinical protocols and study reports[26]
- written and tabulated summaries in CTD format for submissions such as INDs and marketing applications, such as NDAs or Biologics License Applications (BLAs) and IMPDs[27]
- answers to questions posed by a health authority or regulatory body[28]
- product labeling[29]

Individual chapters in this book review the clinical protocol,[30] IB[31] and background regulatory authority meeting packages,[32] so this discussion provides detail on presenting nonclinical safety information in the CTD[33] format and general advice for creating integrated discussions of nonclinical research. Of note, the CTD format is generally used for NDAs and is recommended to be employed in IND[34] or IMPD[35] documentation.

Those interested in the details of nonclinical study conduct should consult the ICH safety guidelines,[36,37] Regulatory professionals and writers should bear in mind local regulatory bodies, such as FDA, publish guidance regarding GLP legal requirements and current thinking regarding the best way to fulfil the requirements outlined by ICH and in 21 CFR.[38]

## CTD Safety Structure

ICH M4S[39] specifies the format and contents for the Nonclinical Overview and Written and Tabulated Summaries presented in Module 2, sections 2.4 and 2.6, and the structure for including nonclinical study reports in Module 4. The contents of the Nonclinical Overview and the Written and Tabulated Summaries should be presented in a specific order, reflecting the stepwise nature of pharmaceutical development. For example, *in vitro* studies should be presented prior to *in vivo* studies, and studies of pharmacology and metabolism should precede specialized or repeat-dose toxicity studies. Similarly, acute (or short-term use) studies are provided before sub-chronic and chronic dose studies, and animal studies are presented in a predefined order.

## Nonclinical Overview

### Format

ICH[40] recommends the Nonclinical Overview be 30 pages or less in length and critically discuss the expected effects and likely safety profile of the investigational product. Safety profiles for excipients, known impurities and identified metabolites also should be considered, keeping in mind the differences between findings in humans and animal models (if known). GLP assessments, a consideration of nonclinical findings against the chemical and other quality characteristics of the product, and known impurities should be discussed. Finally, findings should be presented in the context of appropriate published literature, ideally from studies considered relevant to the medicinal product, dose form, dose and model studied.

In general, the audience for the Nonclinical Overview includes reviewers from all scientific disciplines at a health authority or other reviewing body and, therefore, the text should be written for a non-specialist reader. The nonspecialist reader of some portions of a Nonclinical Overview is likely to be a specialist in one or more scientific or clinical area; therefore, the discussion should be aimed at an audience similar to that of a general scientific or medical journal like *Science, Nature* or *The Lancet* rather than specialists in pharmacology or genotoxicity.

ICH M4S specifies the order of appearance of specific information and analyses in the Nonclinical Overview:

1. overview of nonclinical testing strategy
2. pharmacology
3. pharmacokinetics
4. toxicology
5. integrated overview and conclusions
6. list of literature references[41]

### Special Considerations

The Nonclinical Overview is perhaps the most complex and scientifically varied regulatory document because of both the different studies included and the need to guide clinical decision making. For example, the conclusion of an IND should use the NOAEL to justify the clinical starting dose considered safe, based on the maximum recommended starting dose. A determination as to whether the proposed therapeutic clinical dose is supported by the nonclinical data should be included. In an NDA, it may be more appropriate to discuss nonclinical findings against available clinical study information.

ICH M4S indicates the Nonclinical Overview should present an evaluation of the program, the relevance of the studies and animal models selected and the relationships between nonclinical study findings and product chemistry, impurities, metabolites (if applicable), excipients and

**Table 13-2. Content Areas of the Three Nonclinical Written Summaries**

| Pharmacology | Pharmacokinetics | Toxicology |
|---|---|---|
| Brief Summary | Brief Summary | Brief Summary |
| Primary Pharmacodynamics | Methods of Analysis | Single-Dose Toxicity |
| Secondary Pharmacodynamics | Absorption | Repeat-Dose Toxicity |
| Safety Pharmacology | Distribution | Genotoxicity |
| Pharmacodynamic Drug Interactions | Metabolism | Carcinogenicity |
| Discussion and Conclusions | Excretion | Reproductive and Developmental Toxicity |
| | Pharmacokinetic Drug Interactions | Studies in Juvenile Animals |
| | Other Pharmacokinetic Studies | Local Tolerance |
| | Discussion and Conclusions | Other Toxicity Studies |
| | | Discussion and Conclusions |

expected clinical study outcomes. In addition, the product's toxicity profile should be discussed in the context of pharmacodynamics, toxic signs, causes of death, genotoxicity and carcinogenic potential, and their implications for use its in the clinic.[42] Metabolites should be considered in each of these discussions as appropriate, based on the product's specific characteristics in humans and animal models.[43] Discussion should include an overview of any nonclinical studies undertaken to answer or clarify specific questions. Authors should consider the numbers and types of animals used, mode of administration, dose, duration, exposure and expected effects in humans. ICH M4S also specifies the integrated overview should be clear and recommends presenting a high-level human pharmaceutical (or other product) characterization that ends with logical, well-reasoned conclusions supported by the available data.[44]

Of note, although specific study data and reports may be cross-referenced to the Nonclinical Overview using the ICH M4S-specified format (table number and study or report number),[45] it may be preferable to cross-reference to information in the Nonclinical Written and Tabulated Summaries (CTD Section 2.6). The Nonclinical Overview should not repeat details that appear in the written or tabulated summaries.

## Nonclinical Written and Tabulated Summaries

The Nonclinical Overview should be written after CTD Section 2.6: the pharmacology, pharmacokinetics and toxicology written and tabulated summaries (Table 2). ICH M4S recommends the total page length for the three written summaries not exceed 100–150 pages.[46] Pages should be allocated depending on the number and types of studies performed and their relative importance to the clinical development stage and in the context of the overall regulatory filing aims.

Like the Nonclinical Overview, the nonclinical written summaries should address a broad scientific audience. Each nonclinical written summary should begin with a brief presentation of the relevant nonclinical findings and end with a critically-written discussion and conclusions. Ideally, these critically written sections will be the basis for the Nonclinical Overview. Of note, while the brief pharmacology and pharmacokinetic summaries are recommended not to exceed two to three pages, ICH M4S suggests the brief toxicology summary may be up to six pages.[47] Although this suggestion is not an official requirement, it does provide indirect guidance regarding the relative importance of specific data within the written summaries and possibly the Nonclinical Overview.

ICH M4S specified the order for presenting nonclinical data,[48] in keeping with the stepwise research approach described in ICH M3.[49] As mentioned above, *in vitro* studies should precede *in vivo* studies. In the pharmacokinetics and toxicology written and tabulated summaries, specific studies should be presented in order by:

- species: first rodents, ordered as mouse, rat, hamster and other rodents; followed by additional mammals, ordered as rabbit, dog, non-human primate and any other mammals (except rodent species, which are listed earlier); followed by any other animals
- route: intended route for human use, oral, intravenous, intramuscular, intraperitoneal, subcutaneous, inhalation, topical or other
- duration: shortest to longest[50]

To facilitate review, the use of tables and figures is recommended. For example, a table of toxicology studies presenting study type and duration, route of administration, species and specific compound administered is recommended for inclusion in CTD Module 2, Section 2.6.6.1.[51] It may be useful throughout each written summary to present tables and figures to support the conclusions and discussion.

Tabulated summary formats are provided in an appendix to ICH M4S; however, authors should adapt these as needed to enhance reader understanding or for conciseness or clarity. For example, although some tables specify a column for GLP status, such a column may not be necessary if all such studies were GLP compliant. A best practice is to consult, if possible, with the health authority.

## Authoring Integrated Discussions

As noted above, integrated nonclinical data discussions appear in several types of documents, from IBs to NDAs, and take many forms. Nevertheless, the same general principles apply to ensuring these discussions effectively meet the needs of their intended audiences.

### Building a Narrative to Meet Audience Needs

Nonclinical documentation should build a coherent, consistent scientific story that bridges into the clinical development narrative, following the general principles in ICH M3,[52] ICH M4S[53] and ICH M4E.[54] It should be easy for a reviewer to understand the relationship of the nonclinical work undertaken and choices such as outcome measures/interventions or adverse events of special interest in clinical trials.

The specific measures used to ensure GLP adherence should be represented accurately, especially in filings that span countries or regions or include GLP and non-GLP studies. GLP requirements are among the most stringent good practice guidelines for industry,[55] making it important to articulate the relationships between studies following GLP and others that provide related or ancillary data. Authors should ensure that both the full scientific story makes sense in the context of GLP and the GLP information makes sense in the context of the scientific story, keeping in mind not every nonclinical study may have been required to meet the same GLP standards. If documentation is submitted to more than one regulatory body, authors should specify how GLP requirements were met for each applicable agency, country or region, either in the integrated documentation or by cross-referencing to applicable study reports.

Any nonclinical information in product labeling, integrated documentation, and the IB should present a similar narrative in keeping with any published product information.

### Adapting Text as Needed During Lifecycle Management

While it is tempting to write a base document such as the Nonclinical Overview and then plug the same text into the integrated discussion sections of additional documents (such as an IB), readers may be better served if authors consider the primary audience for each document separately. The scope of information required in an IB, for example, may fall somewhere between that provided in a Nonclinical Overview and the accompanying written summaries in an IND. A skilled writer may augment the former with tables and figures from the latter. In contrast, a background package should be designed to ask or address specific questions and may require distinct text. Channeling final scientific or medical review and sign off through an expert who understands the needs of the target audience (regulators or physicians) may help authors and their managers to prepare suitable text. If nonclinical data appear in clinical documents like protocols or IBs, consultation with a professional medical writer also may benefit authors, reviewers and readers.

### The Need for Collaboration

Nonclinical programs cover specialized studies designed to answer particular questions about a product's pharmacology, pharmacokinetics and toxicology and its excipients, metabolites and impurities. Although clinical (efficacy) and CMC (quality) documentation can be written by relatively few experts, nonclinical documentation may require collaboration from specialists in pharmacology, toxicology, biomarkers and other areas, often with input from clinical pharmacology, CMC, and clinical research colleagues. For these authors, an open mind and a willingness to communicate and compromise are critical to the successful completion of high-quality nonclinical documentation that meets the its audience's needs.

Obstacles to effective collaboration among large teams of scientists can include varying nomenclature, laboratory shorthand and other convenience practices, such as the use of nonstandard abbreviations to accommodate computer programs' limitations. In some situations, personal preferences can become a material impediment to producing high-quality documentation. Early planning and ongoing communication can prevent many potential missteps.

### The Regulatory Professional

Regulatory professionals generally have a good understanding of audience needs for regulatory filings and background packages[56] and should initiate planning meetings for the interdisciplinary authoring groups responsible for nonclinical documentation as early as possible. Nonclinical colleagues may have little or no prior experience with regulatory documentation, making the regulatory professional's role even more critical in these cases. Meeting early and often is a key to meeting requirements in a timely fashion.

An initial kick-off meeting may be conducted to review regulatory requirements, templates and style guides for specific documents; training needs may be identified at that time, if necessary. As noted above, nonclinical study reports may need to be reviewed for submission-readiness; a regulatory professional should guide and advise this process. In addition, the regulatory professional can guide the team in selecting necessary internal advisors, such as clinicians, whose insights may aid the team in producing high-quality research.

## Product Nomenclature

Integrated discussions must use the correct name for the material tested in nonclinical studies in compliance with health authority expectations. If the health authority mandates the use of a generic product name, that name should be spelled and abbreviated consistently throughout all integrated discussions. However, product nomenclature extends beyond generic names. A drug substance versus a drug product should be easily identifiable to any integrated documentation reader. In some nonclinical programs, racemic mixtures are tested against one racemate; authors should ensure such materials always are named consistently and differentiated. Similarly, different dose forms, formulations and dosages should be named clearly and used consistently, following accepted naming conventions.

CMC and regulatory colleagues can help ensure appropriate naming conventions for drug products, drug substances, excipients and metabolites are applied consistently across submission sections.

## Style Guides

Although the difference between abbreviating "intravenous" as "i.v." versus "IV" versus "iv" may seem small, when all variations appear in a single document, this may detract from a reviewer's perception of the reported research's quality.

Style guides for nonclinical documentation may address style issues like abbreviations and nomenclature, as well as more substantive concerns such as standard table and figure layouts. Style guides may serve as a repository for agreements regarding specialized vocabulary, such as terms pertaining to disease states, or descriptions of statistical analyses. The phrasing of claims and hypotheses or adverse events of special interest, and other product-specific language may be gathered in the style guide to ensure consistency within integrated documentation or even across a development program. Ideally, such a style guide would be developed by a regulatory professional and/or a professional medical writer for use in all CTD Module 2 subsections.

If research is undertaken at sites in different countries, a specific version of English should be chosen, and its rules, including standard abbreviations, should be followed in integrated discussions. Generally, for FDA filings, Standard American English is recommended and is accepted at many other agencies worldwide, including the European Medicines Agency (EMA).

There is no requirement that text in the written summaries or the Nonclinical Overview correspond exactly to the nonclinical study reports. Therefore, it is recommended the Module 2 text generally be consistent with regard to style, abbreviations and product nomenclature, even if this means making adjustments from individual study reports' text.

## Templates and SOPS

Templates for integrated discussions may be based on guidelines such as ICH M4S[57] or ICH E6,[58] which provides the basic outline of the IB. Of note, ICH M4S specifically requests authors to adapt these suggested formats as needed to enhance scientific information presentations. Since ICH M4S directions stress the author's responsibility to enhance the potential for scientific understanding,[59] caution should be exercised when authoring documents in templates. Although it may seem more rigorous to internal stakeholders to maintain the integrity of standardized templates, unnecessary headings may be confusing to health authority reviewers even if the content is listed as "not applicable."[60] Therefore, SOPs and working instructions for nonclinical documentation authors should be designed to accommodate expected scientific differences.

## References

Electronic submissions of regulatory dossiers may require the inclusion of literature references cited in integrated discussions or individual study reports. To facilitate review and reduce unnecessary work, authoring teams should consider identifying a core group of scientifically relevant references. These references should be reviewed regularly to ensure up-to-date information is included.

Reference management may be facilitated by using electronic tools and repositories. Librarians or information technologists may be able to advise or assist in reference management.

## Training

Most nonclinical expert authors do not receive formal training in regulatory writing. If time and budgets permit, attending a formal workshop in regulatory writing or a professional society meeting such as the American Medical Writer's Association,[61] may be helpful to nonclinical authors.

If available, professional medical writers may be able to provide advice and support; however, the majority of nonclinical authors must rely on the guidance of more-experienced peers or regulatory professionals. Close partnerships between nonclinical scientists and regulatory colleagues can ensure success in the preparation of regulatory documentation.

## Conclusion

Integrated discussions of nonclinical information are necessary to support clinical studies. These documents present vital information to investigators engaged in clinical trials and regulators. The best nonclinical documentation is clear, concise and meets its readers' needs. Thus, attention should be paid to the end user during nonclinical documentation authoring, review and approval.

### References

1. Wells HG. *The Island of Dr. Moreau.* 1896. New York: Stone and Kimball.
2. Booth W. *The Company We Keep: An Ethics of Fiction.* 1989. Los Angeles: U Cal Press.
3. Seymour M. Chapter 3 General Considerations for Quality Regulatory Writing. *Regulatory Writing: An Overview.* Regulatory Affairs Professionals Society. Rockville, MD. ©2017.
4. FDA. *Guidance for Industry: Nonclinical Safety Evaluation of Drug or Biologic Combinations* (2006). FDA website. http://www.fda.gov/OHRMS/DOCKETS/98fr/05d-0004-gdl0002.pdf. Accessed 12 January 2017.
5. ICH Safety Guidelines. ICH website. http://www.ich.org/products/guidelines/safety/article/safety-guidelines.html. Accessed 12 January 2017.
6. DeTora L. Chapter 4 Beyond the Code of Federal Regulations. *Regulatory Writing: An Overview.* Regulatory Affairs Professionals Society. Rockville, MD. ©2017.
7. *Guidance on Nonclinical Safety Studies for the Conduct of Clinical Trials and Marketing Authorization for Pharmaceuticals M3(R2)* (2009) ICH website. http://www.ich.org/fileadmin/Public_Web_Site/ICH_Products/Guidelines/Multidisciplinary/M3_R2/Step4/M3_R2__Guideline.pdf. Accessed 12 January 2017.
8. Nonclinical Overview and Nonclinical Summaries of Module 2; Organisation of Module 4 M4S(R2) (2002). ICH website. http://www.ich.org/fileadmin/Public_Web_Site/ICH_Products/CTD/M4__R2__Safety/M4S_R2_.pdf. Accessed 12 January 2917.
9. Ibid.
10. Op cit 5.
11. Op cit 7.
12. Safety Testing of Nonclinical Metabolites: Guidance for Industry (November 2016). FDA website. http://www.fda.gov/downloads/drugs/guidancecomplianceregulatoryinformation/guidances/ucm079266.pdf. Accessed 12 January 2017.
13. Op cit 7.
14. Op cit 8.
15. 21 CFR 58 Good Laboratory Practice for Nonclinical Laboratory Studies. FDA website. https://www.accessdata.fda.gov/scripts/cdrh/cfdocs/cfcfr/CFRSearch.cfm?CFRPart=58&showFR=1. Accessed 12 January 2017.
16. M4: The Common Technical Document. ICH website. http://www.ich.org/products/ctd.html. Accessed 12 January 2017.
17. Op cit 15.
18. Fiebig D. "The Investigator's Brochure: A Multidisciplinary Document." *Medical Writing*, June 2014. Trilogy Writing website. http://www.trilogywriting.com/publications/investigators-brochure-multidisciplinary-document/. Accessed 12 January 2017.
19. Op cit 3.
20. Ibid.
21. Op cit 18.
22. Op cit 15.
23. *Guidance for Industry: Templates for Reporting Toxicology Data* (March 2004). FDA website. http://www.fda.gov/food/guidanceregulation/guidancedocumentsregulatoryinformation/ingredientsadditivesgraspackaging/ucm094188.htm. Accessed 12 January 2017.
24. Jennings J. Chapter 17 Background Packages. *Regulatory Writing: An Overview.* Regulatory Affairs Professionals Society. Rockville, MD. ©2017.
25. Aslan M. Chapter 15 Investigator's Brochure. *Regulatory Writing: An Overview.* Regulatory Affairs Professionals Society. Rockville, MD. ©2017.
26. Ramasubramian S. Chapter 8 Clinical Protocols. *Regulatory Writing: An Overview.* Regulatory Affairs Professionals Society. Rockville, MD. ©2017.
27. Op cit 6.
28. Innocent N. Chapter 18 Responses to Questions or Requests for Information. *Regulatory Writing: An Overview.* Rockville, MD. Regulatory Affairs Professionals Society. ©2017.
29. O'Brien T. Chapter 16 Product Labeling. *Regulatory Writing: An Overview.* Regulatory Affairs Professionals Society. Rockville, MD. ©2017.
30. Op cit 26.
31. Op cit 25.
32. Op cit 24.
33. Op cit 16.
34. Investigational New Drug Application. FDA website. http://www.fda.gov/drugs/developmentapprovalprocess/howdrugsaredevelopedandapproved/approvalapplications/investigationalnewdrugindapplication/default.htm. Accessed 12 January 2017.
35. IMPD Guidance. EU website. http://www.imp-dossier.eu/imdp_guidance/. Accessed 12 January 2017.
36. Op cit 5.
37. Op cit 6.
38. Op cit 5.
39. Op cit 8.
40. Ibid.
41. Ibid.
42. Ibid.
43. Op cit 12.
44. Op cit 8.
45. Ibid.
46. Ibid.
47. Ibid.
48. Ibid.
49. Op cit 7.
50. Op cit 8.
51. Ibid.
52. Op cit 7.
53. Op cit 8.
54. *Revision of M4E Guideline on Enhancing the Format and Structure of Benefit-Risk Information in ICH Efficacy M4E(R2).* ICH website. http://www.ich.org/fileadmin/Public_Web_Site/ICH_Products/CTD/M4E_R2_Efficacy/M4E_R2__Step_4.pdf. Accessed 12 January 2017.
55. Op cit 15.
56. Op cit 24.
57. OP cit 8.

58.  *Guideline for Good Clinical Practice E6(R1)* (1996). ICH website. http://www.ich.org/fileadmin/Public_Web_Site/ICH_Products/Guidelines/Efficacy/E6/E6_R1_Guideline.pdf. Accessed 12 January 2017.

59.  Op cit 16.

60.  Aslam M. Chapter 6Developing SOPs, Planning and Strategy Documents. *Regulatory Writing: An Overview.* Regulatory Affairs Professionals Society. Rockville, MD. ©2017.

61.  American Medical Writers Association. http://www.amwa.org. Accessed 12 January 2017.

**Author**
Lisa DeTora is an assistant professor of writing studies at Hofstra University and a guest lecturer in humanities at the Hofstra Northwell School of Medicine. She began her career in medical writing at Merck and Co. Inc. and was a co-author of the company's internal guidances to comply with ICH E3 and M4. Her subsequent work experience has included regulatory writing and publication management in various therapeutic areas.

**Acknowledgements**
Thanks to Beth Silverstein for her review. I also thank Jenny Grodberg for her review of the outline.

# 14

# Integrated Clinical Documentation

*By Lisa DeTora and Dan Benau, MSOD, PhD*

## Overview

In this discussion, integrated analyses are defined as comparisons across multiple clinical trials, whether descriptive or based on formal statistical testing. Sponsors provide such integrated clinical documentation at pivotal decision points, such as the End-of-Phase 2,[1] consistent with US Food and Drug Administration (FDA)[2] guidance. FDA has adopted International Council for Harmonisation (ICH) guidelines[3] for the Common Technical Document (CTD);[4,5] however, other international agencies, national and local health authorities and professional societies also provide guidance to aid integrated clinical documentation authors. ICH and health authorities worldwide consider benefit-risk assessments to be the fundamental basis for regulatory decision making.[6] Thus, clinical data integrated analyses and interpretation are critical factors in deciding whether further development or marketing can proceed.

The project team producing integrated clinical documents generally includes clinicians, clinical pharmacology, drug safety, biostatistics and medical writing colleagues as well as experts in risk management and pharmacovigilance. Input or participation from experts in regulatory, biomarkers, genetics, genomics, serology or other scientific areas may be needed, depending on the development program. In addition, consultation with manufacturing, chemistry manufacturing and controls (CMC) and nonclinical toxicology and pharmacology experts will be necessary to build specific discussions in those areas

## General Considerations for Integrated Clinical Documentation

### Goals of Integrated Clinical Data Discussions

A clinical filing should support program initiation, continuation or product registration. Thus, reviewers must be able to evaluate the benefits conferred and risks incurred in the target population. For example, researchers seeking to initiate Phase 3 trials must demonstrate the product's acceptable tolerability and safety profile and sufficient evidence to support a potential to impart benefits with its use. Further, researchers must support clinical dose and dosage form choices.[7] The discussion should cover positive and negative findings and create a clear scientific and medical picture of the investigational product for each indication. Requirements specific to accelerated filings[8] may allow the compression of some development phases; however, researchers then must justify their program design.[9] Documentation also should reflect the development ethical study conduct.[10]

### Consistency With Regulations and Guidelines

Best practice for developing integrated documents includes careful attention to regulations, such as the US

Code of Federal Regulations, Title 21 (21 CFR; Food and Drug Administration[11]) and applicable guidance for industry.[12] Authors and regulatory professionals involved in project oversight should review guidelines and regulations pertinent to their roles and the documentation for which they are responsible. Sources like RAPS' Fundamentals of Regulatory Affairs series[13] provide detailed advice for fulfilling regulations and requirements. In addition, recent publications provide detailed advice for special topics such as biologics[14] or devices.[15]

Given recent developments, such as the release of new Integrated Summary of Effectiveness (ISE) guidance by FDA,[16] it is clear the work of maintaining familiarity with guidance for industry never truly ends. In the current environment, such work should be undertaken by regulatory specialists and those preparing regulatory documentation. These professionals should review the most recent guidance documents in addition to any existing internal SOPs and templates.[17] When guidance lacks information about the placement of specific data in regulatory documents, product development teams might request clarification from the concerned agency or health authority. As noted by Aslam elsewhere in the current volume, SOPs and templates can facilitate authoring and review.[18] SOPs and templates governing the production of specific documents should be updated regularly, in line with updates to guidance for industry.

Data pertaining to a product or disease process may not fit neatly within the formats suggested by guidance. For example, in vaccine development programs, purity and potency (or immunogenicity) as well as efficacy in reducing disease incidence may be reported. While models exist for such cases, innovative science or rare diseases may require individualized adjustments to documentation. Researchers and regulatory professionals may need to adapt templates, or even guidance. As noted by Aslam[19] and Seymour[20] elsewhere in this book, when guidance does not address the placement of specific data in regulatory documentation, product development teams might request clarification from the concerned agency or health authority regarding the best placement to support readability and review. Style guides, if developed, can address how to present specialized information, such as microbiology information required under 21 CFR 314.50, or information about how to adapt and present purity, sterility and potency information for BLA submissions.

## Maintaining Consistency Within a Filing

A regulatory filing must present a consistent, well-supported argument. The filing should build an accurate, logical narrative, and reviewers should be able to locate the rationale for each critical decision and all data

interpretation. Most guidelines suggest repeating information across CTD sections impedes review. Repetition not only increases document size but also increases the possibility of introducing errors and inconsistencies. The CTD guidelines provide guidance for cross-referencing between sections of Module 2 and between Module 2 and Modules 3, 4 and 5.[21] In fact, the CTD guidelines— ICH M4,[22] M4Q (Quality or CMC),[23] M4S (Safety or Nonclinical)[24] and M4E (Efficacy or Clinical)[25]—strongly suggest progressive summarization from reports to tabulated summaries and written summaries, with interpretion in the overviews. Each guideline explicitly states information should be summarized and/or interpreted consistently across Module 2. The overviews, in particular, should provide adequate interpretation to support the rationale for a desired next step.

As noted elsewhere in this book, desired label claims or indications must be supported by information in Module 2.[26] Planning for consistency across Module 2 is critical for complex, multi-authored, multi-indication filings. The clinical, nonclinical and CMC documentation, should build a credible story showing how the product provides a favorable benefit-risk profile in the target patient group. The relationships between findings from Phase 1 through Phase 3 should be clear, as should future plans for research or safety assessments. In multi-indication filings, the relationships between the studies supporting the various indications also should be clear, particularly with regard to any differences in the product's safety and tolerability profile in different populations and any measures necessary to protect patient welfare during clinical use.

## Systematic Approaches to Facilitate Consistency

The consistency of an NDA submission should result from planning long before submission preparation begins, probably from the first IND version. For example, when calculating extent of exposure, how will the team account for withdrawals "at the final visit" when the investigator learns the patient stopped taking treatment shortly before that visit? To prevent long discussions among submission authors to take these into account, handling withdrawals should be specified in the core dossier and all case report forms (CRFs). The same could be true of deciding whether to distinguish a primary reason for patient withdrawal in clinical trials (which must match the number of withdrawals) from all reasons for withdrawal in the CRF (which almost always will be greater than the number of withdrawals). Numerous other examples exist of beginning a development program with the submission format in mind.

**Table 14-1. Documents That May Contain an Integrated Discussion of Clinical Data**

| Document | Brief Explanation |
|---|---|
| Background Packages[a] | Background packages may present brief integrated data intended to provide background for a specific question posed to a health authority. |
| Investigator's Brochures[b] | A brief integrated discussion of benefits and risks based on clinical trials' experience should be included. |
| Clinical Overview | CTD Module 2, Section 2.5 should present an overall critical appraisal of the clinical program and expected benefits and risks in clinical use.[c] |
| Clinical Summary | CTD Section 2.7 should contain a detailed summary of the clinical development program by study and an overall integrated assessment. The Clinical Summary does not always meet US requirement for integrated safety and efficacy discu ssions.[d] |
| Integrated Summary of Efficacy (ISE) | If possible, the ISE should include formal integrated analyses of data across duplicate studies. A new ISE guidance for industry was published in 2015.[e] |
| Integrated Summary of Safety (ISS) | The ISS should present an in-depth consideration of safety outcomes across a clinical development program as well as key safety information, such as exposure data and outcomes to meet requirements for products intended for chronic, long-term use for nonfatal conditions. |
| Safety Update Reports[f] | Various report types are used to provide up-to-date safety information to health authorities. The Development Safety Update Report (DSUR), for example, is used to update INDs and NDAs annually during the reporting period following a specified format.[g] Periodic Safety Update Reports (PSURs) are required in the EU and have slightly different requirements.[h] |
| Answers to Questions Posed by a Health Authority or Regulatory Agency[i] | Like background packages, answers to questions posed by health authorities should present focused integrated information as necessary. |
| Product Labeling[j] | Package inserts intended for prescriber use often contain an overview of therapeutic and adverse effects. |
| Patient Information Documents | Information sheets intended for patient use often contain an overview of therapeutic and adverse effects in plain language. |
| Literature Reviews[k] | Published information that bridges several studies requires an integrated discussion. |

a.    *Chapter 17 Background Packages*
b.    *Chapter 15 Investigator's Brochures*
c.    *ICH M4E Efficacy*
d.    *Ibid.*
e.    *Op cit c.*
f.    *Chapter 11 Clinical Study Reports*
g.    *Guidance for Industry: E2F Development Safety Update Report*
h.    *Guideline on good pharmacovigilance practices (GVP)*
i.    *Chapter 18 Responses to Questions or Requests for Information*
j.    *Chapter 16 Labeling*
k.    *Chapter 28 Literature Reviews*

Ironically, maintaining consistency across CTD Module 2 might result in less consistency among the integrated documentation and earlier protocols or reports. One possible barrier to consistency across an entire project is when the pharmaceutical class nomenclature has changed since IND initiation. It is advisable that subsequent documentation (such as an NDA) conform to the current accepted best practice and nomenclature at the time of the submission. In such situations, authoring teams should find ways to provide a clear picture to regulatory reviewers regarding the evolution of the terminology and the justification for any changes.

## Transparency

Although the informed consent, safety and treatment of human research subjects has been paramount since development of the Nuremburg Code,[27] the rights of clinical research participants and the public to access clinical trial results emerged more recently . Data transparency requirements such as posting trial designs and results in EudraCT[28] or clinicaltrials.gov[29] enhance the need

**Table 14-2. Clinical Overview Goals**

| Basic Goal | Specific Advice |
|---|---|
| Present the strengths and limitations of the development program and study results | • Describe and explain the overall approach to the clinical development of the medicinal product, including critical study design decisions.<br>• Assess the quality of the design and performance of the studies, and include a statement regarding GCP compliance.<br>• Provide a brief overview of the clinical findings, including important limitations (e.g., lack of comparisons with an especially relevant active comparator, or absence of information on some patient populations, on pertinent endpoints, or on use in combination therapy). |
| Analyze the benefits and risks of the medicinal product in its intended use | • Provide an evaluation of benefits and risks based on the conclusions of the relevant clinical studies, including interpretation of how the efficacy and safety findings support the proposed dose and target indication and an evaluation of how prescribing information and other approaches will optimize benefits and manage risks.<br>• Address particular efficacy or safety issues encountered in development, and how they have been evaluated and resolved.<br>• Explore unresolved issues, explain why they should not be considered as barriers to approval, and describe plans to resolve them. |
| Describe how the study results support critical parts of the prescribing information | • Explain the basis for important or unusual aspects of the prescribing information. |

*\* Text is quoted from ICH M4 and recombined here for convenience.*

for meticulous data handling. Regulators must receive documentation consistent with publicly available data, including publications. If data reporting formats, like the CONSORT[30] participant flow diagram, differ from those in other guidelines such as ICH E3,[31] or a results registry reporting template, integrated documentation should refer to and account for any apparent differences in these data presentations.

As discussed in the data analysis chapter, coordinated data efforts can improve overall data reporting[32] and trial design integrity.[33] Expert statisticians have important insights into data handling and should be consulted during such planning. Data consistency also should be maintained for information presented over the course of the clinical development program, for example, in IND and IB updates.

### Lifecycle Management

All clinical documentation, from protocols through safety update reporting, should build a consistent, rigorous picture of the evidence supporting the product's benefit-risk profile. Particular attention should be paid to ensuring consistency and offering adequate explanations for any new findings over time and differences in interpretations in publications authored by academics and views of the manufacturer. Health authority and regulatory body reviewers often are scientists and clinicians and may be familiar with published material. Regulators may consult scientific and clinical advisors who have authored publications in the therapeutic area. Therefore, those preparing integrated clinical trial discussions should engage actively

with current published material. It also may be helpful to provide a brief explanation of terminology at the beginning of each new filing, noting any expected shifts in language if the reviewer consults prior documentation.

Various chapters in this book provide advice regarding general considerations for lifecycle management,[34] Good Documentation Practice[35] and the history of such documentation practices.[36] Advice also is provided on general practices that support high-quality documentation and for specific documents such as the Investigator's Brochure (IB),[37] protocols,[38] background packages,[39] study reports[40] and labeling.[41] These chapters consistently recommend authoring documentation with an eye to its ultimate uses, such as supporting label claims, and stress the importance of setting up study documents, so subsequent documentation may be produced easily.

## Specific Documents

Integrated discussions of clinical trials and their data appear in several different types of regulatory documents (**Table 14-1**). This chapter focuses primarily on integrated discussions of clinical data in the CTD format, the Integrated Summary of Safety (ISS) and ISE. However, many of the principles also may apply to discussions presented in other documents, such as the IB.

FDA has been hesitant to accept the Clinical Summary universally as a replacement for the ISS and ISE described as necessary under 21 CFR 314.50,[42] especially for large-scale clinical development programs including many studies or multiple indications. In fact, as noted by

Benau,[43] FDA has issued specific guidance[44] indicating that the Clinical Summary is not a de facto replacement for the ISS and ISE.

However, teams should make a careful assessment as to whether these document requirements may be fulfilled in certain clinical program types. This is especially important in the context of accelerated filings,[45] rare diseases[46] and annual evaluations of seasonal vaccines, which may contain few studies. In such cases, where comparison of the product under investigation must be undertaken against best practice or published literature, there may be insufficient data to warrant a standalone ISS or ISE, particularly since the ICH M4E guideline suggests the Clinical Summary may be up to 400 pages in length, excluding appendices. Ideally, this decision would be made after consultation with the agency.

## Medical Writer's Role

Medical writers often play an essential role in developing integrated clinical data discussions for many of the documents listed in Table 14-1, and can provide vital expertise and insight in preparing the various integrated discussions required in an NDA, BLA or other regulatory submission. For example, medical writers can establish consistent standards for style and produce focused style guides for individual development teams. Writers assigned to support a program can ensure wording consistency for outcome measures, endpoints and core concepts (such as terminology used to describe a disease state) across studies. In addition, professional medical writers can help teams limit repetition within and across documents.

Template development is another area in which medical writers can contribute to producing high-quality, consistent documentation. Templates for a specific clinical program may include standard text for outcome measures and table formats; these should be developed after consulting with subject matter experts.[47] Regulatory professionals can review draft templates before finalization to ensure all templates, directions for their use and any training developed to ensure adherence to the templates are consistent with current guidelines for content development and eCTD readiness.

Generally, medical writers are responsible for developing drafts, conducting review cycles and making needed revisions to all documents.[48] Medical writers can assist subject matter experts in developing consistent stories within documents and across a filing or filings. The medical writing role may include conducting and scheduling consensus-building meetings to resolve conflicting comments. In addition, medical writers often collect references and appendices for regulatory documents and ensure they are eCTD ready.

## The Common Technical Document

The CTD clinical sections include Module 2, Section 2.5 Clinical Overview, Section 2.7 Clinical Summary and Module 5 Clinical Study Reports. These are described in ICH's Common Technical Document for the Registration of Pharmaceuticals for Human Use: Efficacy M4E. The CTD format may be used for various documents, including INDs and NDAs; however, given that clinical data generally are lacking at the initial IND stage, integrated clinical documentation in the CTD format more commonly is developed within the context of the NDA. Since annual IND updates necessarily are incremental and focus on supporting continued research conduct rather than product marketing, authors should use caution when considering how to adapt existing text for use in the NDA.

FDA currently advises submissions from the IND onward to be made in eCTD format, so the final document is built along the way.[49] This may not be possible for development programs currently underway, but future planning of new programs should take this into consideration. Corrections still may be needed during NDA submission authoring, but the NDA's basic structure should be available and should decrease the final NDA production time. This makes production of the integrated documents a source of reconciliation from older drug development program submissions to the newest ones.

The sections below provide some detail regarding discussions to be presented in the clinical sections of CTD Module 2 and the ISS and ISE. This discussion is intended to provide general advice, primarily for pharmaceuticals. Special considerations for developing content that describes combination products[50] are specified in a later chapter. A substantive chapter on developing a BLA in CTD format was published by Robinett.[51]

### Clinical Overview

The Clinical Overview is intended to provide critical analysis and interpretation regarding the investigational product's benefits and risks to aid regulatory review (See **Tables 14-2** and **14-3**). As noted in **Table 14-2**, development program limitations should be mentioned specifically. If specific data are missing from the application, it is advisable to provide a rationale as to why the data were unavailable and present a plan for obtaining these data or any other measures that justify the investigational product's use in the intended population.

Although Clinical Overview's primary goal is to facilitate clinical review, ICH M4E indicates the overview also should serve as a useful reference for regulatory agency staff in other areas.[52] The Clinical Overview is recommended to be no more than 30 pages in length, depending on its complexity, which is related to the

**Table 14-3. Clinical Overview Text Sections With Brief Explanations[a]**

| Section | Brief Summary of Suggested Contents[b] |
|---|---|
| 2.5.1 Product Development Rationale[c] | • pharmacologic class and target indication<br>• scientific background that supported the indications investigated<br>• clinical development program, ongoing and planned clinical studies<br>• reason to submit the application<br>• plans for foreign clinical data use<br>• concordance or lack thereof with current standard research approaches regarding study design, conduct and analysis<br>• references to pertinent published literature<br>• regulatory guidance and advice and its implementation |
| 2.5.2 Overview of Biopharmaceutics | • critical analysis of any important issues related to bioavailability that might affect the intended formulation's efficacy and/or the safety intended for marketing |
| 2.5.3 Overview of Clinical Pharmacology | • critical analysis of pharmacokinetic (PK), pharmacodynamic (PD) and related in vitro data<br>• pharmacokinetics (PK), e.g.:<br>  o comparative PK in healthy subjects, patients and special populations<br>  o PK related to intrinsic or extrinsic factors<br>  o absorption, distribution, metabolism and excretion<br>  o time-dependent PK changes<br>  o stereochemistry issues<br>  o clinically relevant PK interactions<br>• pharmacodynamics (PD), e.g.:<br>  o mechanism of action (e.g., receptor binding)<br>  o action onset and/or offset<br>  o PK/PD relationships<br>  o PD support for the proposed dose and dosing interval<br>  o clinically relevant PD interactions<br>  o possible genetic differences in response<br>• immunogenicity study, clinical microbiology study or other class-specific PD study result and implication interpretation |
| 2.5.4 Overview of Efficacy | • critical analysis of clinical data pertinent to efficacy in the intended population, including (but not limited to):<br>  o all relevant data, whether positive or negative<br>  o why and how data support the proposed indication and prescribing information<br>  o reasons studies were deemed relevant or irrelevant for evaluation of efficacy<br>  o prematurely terminated studies and their impact |
| 2.5.5 Overview of Safety | • concise safety data critical analysis, noting how results support and justify proposed prescribing information, including (but not limited to):<br>  o pharmacological class adverse effect characteristics<br>  o special approaches to monitoring particular adverse events<br>  o relevant animal toxicology and product quality information<br>  o patient population nature and extent of exposure<br>  o safety database limitations<br>  o common and non-serious adverse events<br>  o serious adverse events and other significant adverse events<br>  o study results' similarities and differences<br>  o differences in rates of adverse events in population subgroups<br>  o relation of adverse events to dose, dose regimen and treatment duration<br>  o long-term safety<br>  o methods to prevent, mitigate, or manage adverse events<br>  o reactions due to overdose and the potential for dependence, rebound phenomena and abuse<br>  o world-wide marketing experience |
| 2.5.6 Benefits and Risk Conclusions | • succinct, integrated and clearly explained benefit-risk assessment of the medicinal product for its intended use |

a. *Contents were adapted from ICH M4E for brevity and general applicability to various types of products. Refer to ICH M4 for a full list of issues that should be considered if applicable.*

b *Ibid.*

c. *Many of the contents required in the Product Development Rationale can be derived from the General Investigational Plan required to be provided in the Investigational New Drug Application (IND) as specified under 21 CFR 312.23 (a)(3).*

**Table 14-4. Summary of New Guidance on Clinical Overview Section 2.5.6 Benefit-Risk Conclusions (Text Sections)**

| Section | Brief Description[a] |
|---|---|
| 2.5.6.1 Therapeutic Context | • disease or condition and intended population<br>• current therapies' benefits and risks |
| 2.5.6.1.1 Disease or Condition | • disease or condition aspects most relevant to the intended population<br>• disease aspects that would be covered by the proposed indication<br>• disease societal or public health implications |
| 2.5.6.1.2 Current Therapies | • therapies used most frequently and/or currently recommended in clinical guidelines<br>• medical need for a new therapy in terms of efficacy, safety, tolerability, convenience and preference (as applicable) |
| 2.5.6.2 Benefits | • medicinal product's favorable effects<br>• benefit's clinical importance<br>• absolute frequency in effect's magnitude in the study population versus the comparator<br>• key benefit's time course and variability<br>• strength, limitation and uncertainties' analyses of the evidence related to each key benefit and their implications |
| 2.5.6.3 Risks | • unfavorable effects, e.g., adverse events, drug interactions, risks identified in nonclinical data and risks to individuals other than the patient<br>• strength, limitation and uncertainties' analyses of evidence related to each key risk and their implications<br>• proposed approach to managing each key risk, including an explanation of why the approach provides reasonable assurance the risk can be managed appropriately |
| 2.5.6.4 Benefit-Risk Assessment | • applicant's benefit-risk assessment conclusion of the medicinal product in all proposed indications<br>• succinct explanation of the reasoning and judgment used in assessing and weighing key benefits and risks<br>• explanation of how any uncertainties affected the interpretation of the evidence and impact on the benefit-risk assessment<br>• impact of the therapeutic context on the assessment<br>• key risk management aspects important in reaching a favorable benefit<br>• risk assessment |

a.    Contents were excerpted from ICH M4E and edited for brevity. Refer to ICH M4 for a full list of issues that should be considered if applicable.

development program's complexity. Since the Clinical Overview should present critical analysis, detailed supportive information should not be included, with one exception: the permitted appendix to the benefits and risks conclusions. A recent update to ICH M4E provides extensive guidance for the benefits and risks conclusions but does not expand the Clinical Overview page count or account for page limitations for the appendix section, which is more commonly a feature of the Clinical Summary (see **Table 14-4**). This circumstance suggests benefit and risk conclusions should be concise and should reference, rather than repeat, information presented elsewhere in the Clinical Overview.

Since the Clinical Overview should focus on a critical presentation of data, authors should concentrate on the analysis and interpretation of study findings across the development program rather than what ICH refers to as "factual presentation." The Clinical Overview discussion should provide a succinct discussion and interpretation of these findings together with any other relevant information, such as pertinent animal data or product

quality issues that may have clinical implications. Data interpretation should differentiate between statistical and clinical significance or the implications for these findings in medical practice. Thus, the Clinical Overview primarily should present the conclusions and implications of data and should not recapitulate the discussion in the Clinical Summary or the individual reports in Module 5.[53] The Clinical Overview is the only dossier location where a "critical evaluation," including what might have been done differently had current knowledge been available at the beginning of the program, is supposed to be given.

The Clinical Overview should cross-reference the factual presentation of information and tabular formats from the Clinical Summary Nonclinical data necessary to support the Clinical Overview's critical discussion might be cross-referenced to the Nonclinical Overview rather than the written and tabulated summaries, although it is permissible to cross-reference these if necessary. If quality information is referenced, a cross reference should be provided to the Quality Overall Summary before CTD Module 3 information. References to reports in Modules

**Table 14-5. Clinical Summary Text Subsections**[a]

| Biopharmaceutic Studies and Associated Analytical Methods | Clinical Pharmacology Studies | Clinical Efficacy | Clinical Safety |
|---|---|---|---|
| Background and Overview Summary of Results of Individual Studies Comparison and Analyses of Results Across Studies | Background and Overview Summary of Results of Individual Studies Comparison and Analyses of Results Across Studies Special Studies | Background and Overview of Clinical Efficacy Summary of Results of Individual Studies Comparison and Analyses of Results Across Studies Analysis of Clinical Information Relevant to Dosing Recommendations Persistence of Efficacy and/or Tolerance Effects | Exposure to the Drug Adverse Events Clinical Laboratory Evaluations Vital Signs, Physical Findings and Other Observations Related to Safety in Special Groups and Situations Postmarketing Data |

a.    *ICH M4E*

4 and 5 should be included in the Clinical Overview only if absolutely necessary. If microbiology information is required under the provisions in 21 CFR 314.50, only critical analysis and conclusions should appear in the Clinical Overview.[54]

Within the Clinical Overview, published literature should be cited, especially with regard to the investigational product's place within a given pharmaceutical class and current best medical practices for the target indication.[55] As the documentation in marketing applications is intended to support label claims, authors should work to ensure adequate consistency between the labeling documents and the Clinical Overview.[56] If information about the investigational product has been published, these publications may be referenced in the Clinical Overview, and the data presented therein generally should be consistent with published information.

### Benefit and Risk Conclusions

An ICH concept paper suggests existing guidance did not guarantee consistent benefit-risk discussions in CTD-formatted dossiers across therapeutic areas and research sponsors.[57] Therefore, the ICH M4E Working Group developed new guidance. to help differentiate the benefit-risk analysis presented in the CTD (see **Table 14-4**) and subsequent analyses and updates as described in ICH E2C.[59] ICH M4E(R2) provides a more granular outline for benefit-risk assessment (see **Table 14-4**) and now permits an appendix of supportive benefit-risk information to be included in the Clinical Overview.

As the CTD Module 2, Section 2.5.6 guidance preamble notes, benefit-risk assessment requires weighing a medicinal product's key benefits, or favorable effects identified during studies, and risks, or unfavorable effects considered potentially important from a clinical and/or public health perspective in frequency and/or severity.

Not all benefits and risks should be considered as "key." Identifying key benefits and risks requires a critical evaluation of all efficacy and safety information. Many different approaches are acceptable for benefit-risk assessment; hence, ICH M4E does not prescribe a specific method or methods. A descriptive approach, explicitly communicating the data interpretation and benefit-risk assessment, generally will be adequate.[60]

### The Clinical Summary

The Clinical Summary is intended to provide clinical data across a development program in both written and tabulated formats. Comparisons and analyses of results across studies in the summaries should focus on factual observations rather than critical interpretation. The Clinical Summary should provide sufficient information to support the critical analysis and conclusions in the Clinical Overview. The Clinical Summary generally should be 50–400 pages in length.[61]

ICH M4E provides guidance regarding the Clinical Summary contents by section (see **Table 14-5**). The divisions in the first three subsections share a general format, requiring a summary of individual studies before data across multiple studies. Data consideration across multiple studies should present logical groupings of studies and data, such as by indications or patient groups, as applicable to the development program. The integrated discussion across studies may take either a descriptive or a formal analytical approach; formal analyses should be supported by statistical analysis planning. Discussions of data across multiple studies should take an approach consistent with an ISS or ISE (if applicable). If one or more ISS and/or ISE is provided in Module 5, the Clinical Summary should contain a summary of the high-level results of each with a cross-reference to the full document in Module 5.

Detail relevant to dosing, dosing intervals and persistence should be provided, as should information regarding adverse events and tolerability measures across the clinical program.[62] The Clinical Summary also includes synopses of individual study reports, which should be compliant with the guidance in both ICH E3[63] and ICH M4E.[64] If microbiology information is required as described in 21 CFR 314.50, it should be included under "special studies" in Clinical Summary Section 2.7.4, per FDA's Guidance for Industry: Microbiology Data for Systemic Antibacterial Drugs—Development, Analysis, and Presentation.[65]

ICH M4E provides templates for specific tables (see **Table 14-6**), which may be edited to facilitate clarity and coreectness.[66] For example, the title may be edited for correctness relative to the clinical development program. Additional tables should be used only if they forward the scientific presentation of data and support the Clinical Overview analysis and conclusions.[67] Of note, extensive data from clinical study reports should not be reproduced in the Clinical Summary but cross-referenced to Module 5.

## Module 5

ICH M4E presents detailed guidance on the order of clinical study reports and a template for the clinical studies table.[68] Ideally, as indicated by Ellison and colleagues, study synopses to be included in Module 2, Section 2.7.6 and the list of clinical studies to be included in Module 5, Table 5.1 should be prepared in tandem with the clinical study report.[69] If microbiology information indicated in 21 CFR 314.50 is required, it should be included in Module 5 under "Other Study Reports."[70]

## Integrated Summaries to Meet 21 CFR 314.50 Requirements

Under 21 CFR 314.50,[71] integrated safety and efficacy summaries are required in marketing applications. These integrated summaries are not the same as the summary information presented in CTD Module 2, specifically the CTD Section 2.7, Clinical Summary, as noted in FDA's 2009 Guidance for Industry: Integrated Summaries of Effectiveness and Safety: Location Within the Common Technical Document (see Box 14-1).[72] A more detailed explanation is provided by Benau in Chapter 1.

Sponsors should evaluate their documentation carefully to ensure all applicable regulations are met for each of the countries and regions to which a CTD filing is submitted.

### Tables of Included and All Studies

A number of NDA sections, including the ISE as described in 21 CFR 314.50, require a table of relevant studies.[73] The table of studies required in the ISS, described in 21 CFR 314.50 (d)(5)(vi), is:[74]

"A table of all investigations pertinent to safety, identified by protocol number and principal investigator, grouped by type (clinical pharmacology, adequate and well-controlled studies, uncontrolled studies, and other studies), and including studies of indications other than those sought in the application…"

Essentially, this is a table of all clinical studies conducted with the treatment candidate no matter what indications are sought. These tables (included studies and all studies) should contain:

**Table 14-6. ICH M4E Table Templates for Clinical Summary Subsections**[a]

| |
|---|
| **2.7.1 Summary of Biopharmaceutic Studies and Associated Analytical Methods**<br>Table 2.7.1.1 Summary of Bioavailability Studies<br>Table 2.7.1.2 Summary of in vitro Dissolution Studies |
| **2.7.2 Summary of Clinical Pharmacology Studies**<br>Table 2.7.2.1 Summary of Drug-Drug Interaction PK Studies |
| **2.7.3 Summary of Clinical Efficacy**<br>Table 2.7.3.1 Description of Clinical Efficacy and Safety Studies<br>Table 2.7.3.2 Results of Efficacy Studies |
| **2.7.4 Summary of Clinical Safety**<br>Table 2.7.4.1 Study Subject Drug Exposure by Mean Daily Dose and Duration of Exposure<br>Table 2.7.4.2 Demographic Profile of Patients in Controlled Trials<br>Table 2.7.4.3 Incidence of Adverse Events in Pooled Placebo and Active Controlled Trial Database<br>Table 2.7.4.4 Incidence of Adverse Events in Individual Studies<br>Table 2.7.4.5 Patient Withdrawals by Study: Controlled Trials<br>Table 2.7.4.6 Listing of Deaths |

a.  *Revision of M4E Guideline on Enhancing the Format and Structure of Benefit-Risk Information in ICH M4E Efficacy M4E(R2)*

**Box 14-1. Differentiating Integrated Summaries From Abbreviated Summaries in CTD Module 2[a]**

The word "summary" in the terms "integrated summary of effectiveness" and "integrated summary of safety" has caused confusion for companies submitting applications in CTD format, as it suggests a reference to the abbreviated overview documents that are placed in Module 2 of an application in the CTD format.

However, the ISE and ISS are not summaries but rather detailed integrated analyses of all relevant data from the clinical study reports that belong in Module 5.2

a.  *Guidance for Industry: Integrated Summaries of Effectiveness and Safety: Location Within the Common Technical Document. FDA website. http://www.fda.gov/downloads/drugs/guidancecomplianceregulatoryinformation/guidances/ucm136174.pdf. Accessed 9 January 2017.*

- protocol number
- study type (controlled, double blind, randomized, etc.)
- completion status (completed, continuing, discontinued)
- full report location (with hyperlinks now that submissions are XML)
- CRFs (again, with electronic navigation aids)
- number of patients on each treatment
- indication studied
- patients' age range
- sex/race distribution
- study drug exposure duration
- study dose range
- dosing frequency

The 1988 guidance on the ISS table of all studies suggests combining all other study tables plus any other relevant study(ies) in the ISS table.[75] Anecdotally, some sponsors have placed the table of all studies in the Clinical Summary, Module 2, Subsection 2.7, as an introduction to the tabular formats of all studies in the various subsections of 2.7. A hyperlink to this from the ISS probably would meet regulatory requirements.

## Integrated Summary of Efficacy

The ISE should present a detailed, factual analysis of data regarding a medicinal product's clinical efficacy, generally for a specific indication or closely-related group of indications.[76] Integrated analyses include close examination of individual study results and, when appropriate, combined quantitative analyses (pooled analyses). An integrated analysis does not replace individual study analyses but is intended to provide a clear understanding of responses across studies, different populations (e.g., demographic, disease-related) and dosing regimens.

Under 21 CFR 314.50 (d)(5)(v),[77] an ISE must contain:

- "Identification of studies fulfilling the statutory requirements for adequate and well-controlled studies showing that the drug has its intended effect
- An integrated summary of the data demonstrating substantial evidence of effectiveness for each claimed indication
- Evidence that supports the dosage and administration section of the labeling, including support for the recommended dosage and dose interval
- Effectiveness data analyzed by sex, age, and racial subgroups, identifying any modifications of dosing for specific subgroups
- Effectiveness data from other subgroups of the population of patients treated, when appropriate, such as patients with renal failure or patients with different levels of severity of the disease"

FDA finalized new ISE guidance in 2016, adopting the Clinical Summary of Efficacy format described in ICH M4E (see **Box 14-2**).[78]

The contents for the ISE as listed in the 2016 FDA guidance are:

- Listing and Brief Results of Individual Studies
- Analysis of Study Designs
- Overall Analysis of Effectiveness Results
- Comparison of Results of Individual Studies
- Pooled Analyses of Data From More Than One Study
- Comparison of Results in Subpopulations
- Analysis of Clinical Information Relevant to Dosing Recommendations
- Time Course of Effect, Persistence of Effect and/or Tolerance, Distribution of Responses
- Exploratory Investigations.[80]

The ISE should present detailed information regarding the medicinal product that forms a basis to support the Clinical Study summary data. The new suggested structure supports its use for this purpose by mirroring the pertinent CTD Module 2 subsection. However, FDA guidance also indicates that the ISE format is flexible so long as it meets the requirements under 21 CFR 314.50. Authoring teams should carefully consider the reviewer who must make an effective assessment of the investigational product.

21 CFR 314.50[80] and the 2016 guidance both indicate that large, multi-indication programs may require

a separate ISE for each indication. Each such ISE should be a complete, standalone document fulfilling all 21 CFR 314.50 criteria. The type of analysis provided for the different indications are not required to be the same. For example, one ISE might contain a formal statistical analysis across studies, while the other contains a descriptive comparison. The ISE should be included in Module 5.[81]

## Integrated Summary of Safety

The regulation under 21 CFR 314.50 (d)(5)(vi) indicates an ISS must contain:

- a table of all investigations pertinent to safety (essentially a table of all clinical studies)
- a table summarizing the extent of exposure to the treatments (could be a hyperlink from Module 2, section 2.7.4.1)
- all available information about the safety of the drug product, including pertinent animal data,
- demonstrated or potential adverse effects of the drug,
- clinically significant drug/drug interactions, and
- other safety considerations, such as data from epidemiological studies of related drugs
- presentation of data by gender, age, race, and any other pertinent subgroups
- description of any statistical analyses not already described
- description of any studies related to abuse of the medicinal product, including a proposal for scheduling under the Controlled Substances Act
- studies related to overdosage and any known antidotes for overdose
- integrated summary of benefits and risks that shows why the benefits of the product under the proposed labelling exceed the risks.[83]

Although little detail is available about the expected ISS format, the recent ISE guidance indicates a move toward the CTD format and an emphasis on different modes of integration: whether by discussion across studies or by formal statistical analysis. The recent ISE guidance might serve as an indirect suggestion that ISS may adopt the CTD Clinical Summary format.

**Box 14-2. FDA Guidance for Industry Text Describing Possible Analyses to Include in the ISE[a]**

The Agency interprets the regulation (21 CFR) to refer not only to a discussion of the major effectiveness studies' results and design, but also to detailed integrated analyses of relevant sources of information concerning effectiveness. Such analyses generally fall into two broad categories:
(1) comparing the individual studies to better understand the overall results (see section III.C.1., Comparison of Results of Individual Studies); and
(2) using the greater power of pooled analyses to gain insight into the nature of the drug's effectiveness in demographic (e.g., age, sex, race, and ethnicity) and other subpopulations, into dose-response, and into onset and duration of effect (see section III.C.2., Pooled Analyses of Data From More Than One Study).

a.    *2015/6 ISE Guidance FDA*

However, since 21 CFR 314.50 indicates periodic safety update reports should be provided in the same format as the ISS,[83] it may be prudent to adopt the format for the DSUR or other required safety reports.[84] Under 21 CFR 314.50, periodic safety updates should occur four months after the initial submission, in a resubmission following receipt of a complete response letter (if applicable), and as requested by FDA. The agency encourages consultation prior to the submission of the first such report.[85] If the approach is unclear, or the applicant also is required to provide a PSUR to the European Medicines Agency (EMA), it may be wise to consult the agency for guidance.

## ISE and ISS Relationship to the Clinical Summary

FDA provides clear guidance differentiating the ISS, ISE and the abbreviated summaries included in CTD Module 2; however, in smaller filings, these requirements may overlap significantly. Sponsors and authoring teams should assess the regulations under 21 CFR 314.50 and available guidance carefully. For small, simple programs or accelerated filings (or other filings based on a single, substantive study), the conditions for 21 CFR 314.50 might be met within the scope of a 400-page Clinical Summary. However, adding discussion to the Clinical Summary also might create complications for other health authorities (or even FDA reviewers seeking such information in Module 5). For larger or more complex filings, meeting all requirements within a 400-page document is less likely. Consultation with the health authority may provide needed clarification. In any case, should one or more ISS or ISE documents be necessary, they should be cross-referenced and linked to the Clinical Summary and/or Clinical Overview as needed.

## Conclusion

Recent guidelines from ICH and FDA emphasize the role of benefit-risk analysis in the evaluation of regulatory documentation. The move toward increasing consistency between the ISE and the CTD Clinical Summary indicates further harmonization with ICH guidelines. In the current dynamic environment of new guidance, consultation with regulatory agencies will gain importance.

### References

1. Guidance for Industry: Formal Meetings Between the FDA and Sponsors or Applicants (May 2009). FDA website. http://www.fda.gov/downloads/Drugs/Guidances/ucm153222.pdf. Accessed 17 January 2017.
2. Integrated Summary of Effectiveness: Guidance for Industry (October 2015). FDA website. http://www.fda.gov/downloads/Drugs/GuidanceComplianceRegulatoryInformation/Guidances/ucm079803.pdf. Accessed 17 January 2017.
3. ICH website. www.ich.org. Accessed 17 January 2017.
4. Organisation of the Common Technical Document for the Registration of Pharmaceuticals for Human Use M4(R4) (15 June 2016). ICH website. http://www.ich.org/fileadmin/Public_Web_Site/ICH_Products/CTD/M4_R4_Organisation/M4_R4__Granularity_Document.pdf. Accessed 17 January 2017.
5. Revision of M4E Guideline on Enhancing the Format and Structure of Benefit-Risk Information in ICH. Efficacy M4E(R2) (15 June 2016). ICH website. http://www.ich.org/fileadmin/Public_Web_Site/ICH_Products/CTD/M4E_R2_Efficacy/M4E_R2__Step_4.pdf. Accessed 17 January 2017.
6. Final Concept Paper M4E(R2) Enhancing the Format and Structure of Benefit-Risk Information in ICH. Efficacy M4E(R1) Guideline (27 March 2015). ICH website. http://www.ich.org/fileadmin/Public_Web_Site/ICH_Products/CTD/M4E_R2_Efficacy/M4E_R2__Final_Concept_Paper_27_March_2015.pdf. Accessed 17 January 2017.
7. Guidance for Industry: End-of-Phase 2A Meetings (September 2009). FDA website. http://www.fda.gov/downloads/drugs/guidancecomplianceregulatoryinformation/guidances/ucm079690.pdf. Accessed 17 January 2017.
8. Rupprecht J. Chapter 26 Accelerated Filings. Regulatory Writing: An Overview. Regulatory Affairs Professionals Society. Rockville, MD. ©2017
9. Guidance for Industry: Expedited Programs for Serious Conditions—Drugs and Biologics (May 2014). FDA website. http://www.fda.gov/downloads/Drugs/Guidances/UCM358301.pdf. FDA website.
10. Op cit 5.
11. Code of Federal Regulations—Title 21—Food and Drugs. FDA website. http://www.fda.gov/MedicalDevices/DeviceRegulationandGuidance/Databases/ucm135680.htm. Accessed 17 January 2017.
12. Op cit 2.
13. Fundamentals of Regulatory Affairs series. Regulatory Affairs Professionals Society. Rockville, MD. RAPS website. http://raps.org/store/#. Accessed 17 January 2017.
14. Robinett RS. The Biologics License Application in Common Technical Document Format. Vaccine Development and Manufacturing, 1st ed. EP Wen, R Ellis, and NS Pujar, eds. New York: Wiley, 2015.
15. Walker RS, Opie J, Whitman S, et al. Writing for Pharmaceutical or Device Companies. EMWA Journal. June 2016. Np.
16. Op cit 2.
17. Aslam M. Chapter 6 Developing SOPs, Planning and Strategy Documents. Regulatory Writing: An Overview. Regulatory Affairs Professionals Society. Rockville, MD. ©2017.
18. Ibid.
19. Aslam M. Chapter 12 Integrated CMC Documentation. Regulatory Writing: An Overview. Regulatory Affairs Professionals Society. Rockville, MD. ©2017.
20. Seymour M. Chapter 3 General Considerations for Quality Regulatory Writing. Regulatory Writing: An Overview. Regulatory Affairs Professionals Society. Rockville, MD. ©2017.
21. CTD page. ICH website. http://www.ich.org/products/ctd.html. Accessed 17 January 2017.
22. Op cit 5.
23. The Common Technical Document for the Registration of Pharmaceuticals for Human Use: Quality—M4Q(R1) (12 September 2002.) ICH website. http://www.ich.org/fileadmin/Public_Web_Site/ICH_Products/CTD/M4_R1_Quality/M4Q__R1_.pdf. Accessed 17 January 2017.
24. The Common Technical Document for the Registration of Pharmaceuticals for Human Use: Safety—M4S(R2) (12 September 2002). ICH website. http://www.ich.org/fileadmin/Public_Web_Site/ICH_Products/CTD/M4__R2__Safety/M4S_R2_.pdf. Accessed 17 January 2017.
25. Op cit 5.
26. O'Brien T. Chapter 16 Product Labeling. Regulatory Writing: An Overview. Regulatory Affairs Professionals Society. Rockville, MD. ©2017.
27. The Nuremburg code. NIH website. https://history.nih.gov/research/downloads/nuremberg.pdf. Accessed 17 January 2017.
28. EudraCT. https://eudract.ema.europa.eu. Accessed 17 January 2017.
29. Clinicaltrials.gov. https://clinicaltrials.gov. Accessed 17 January 2017.
30. Schulz KF, Altman DG, Moher D for The Consort Group. CONSORT 2010 Statement: Updated Guidelines for Reporting Parallel Group Randomized Trials. BMC Medicine 2010, 8:18. Available at: http://www.consort-statement.org/downloads/consort-statement. Accessed 17 January 2017.
31. Structure and Content of Clinical Study Reports E3 (1995). ICH website. http://www.ich.org/fileadmin/Public_Web_Site/ICH_Products/Guidelines/Efficacy/E3/E3_Guideline.pdf. Accessed 17 January 2017.
32. DeTora L. Chapter 10 Statistical Analysis Plans. Regulatory Writing: An Overview. Regulatory Affairs Professionals Society. Rockville, MD. ©2017.
33. DeTora L, Foster C, Skobe C, Yarker YE, Crawley FP. Publication planning: promoting an ethics of transparency and integrity in biomedical research. IJCP 2015 Sep 1;69(9):915-21.
34. De la Vega E. Chapter 19 Dossier Maintenance. Regulatory Writing: An Overview. Regulatory Affairs Professionals Society. Rockville, MD. ©2017.
35. Rupprecht J. Chapter 2 Good Documentation Practice. Regulatory Writing: An Overview. Regulatory Affairs Professionals Society. Rockville, MD. ©2017.
36. Benau D. Chapter 1 An Overview of Medical and Regulatory Writing. Regulatory Writing: An Overview. Regulatory Affairs Professionals Society. Rockville, MD. ©2017.
37. O'Brien T. Chapter 15 Investigators Brochures. Regulatory Writing: An Overview. Regulatory Affairs Professionals Society. Rockville, MD. ©2017.
38. Ramasubramian S. Chapter 8 Clinical Protocols. Regulatory Writing: An Overview. Regulatory Affairs Professionals Society. Rockville, MD. ©2017.
39. Jennings J. Chapter 17 Background Packages. Regulatory Writing: An Overview. Regulatory Affairs Professionals Society. Rockville, MD. ©2017.

40. Diorio B et al. Chapter 11 Clinical Study Reports. Regulatory Writing: An Overview. Regulatory Affairs Professionals Society. Rockville, MD. ©2017.
41. Op cit 26.
42. 21 CFR 314.50 Content and format of an application. FDA website. https://www.accessdata.fda.gov/scripts/cdrh/cfdocs/cfcfr/CFRSearch.cfm?fr=314.50. Accessed 17 January 2017.
43. Op cit 36.
44. Op cit 2.
45. Op cit 8.
46. Silverstein B. Chapter 24 Rare Diseases. Regulatory Writing: An Overview. Regulatory Affairs Professionals Society. Rockville, MD. ©2017.
47. Op cit 17.
48. Op cit 40.
49. Guidance for Industry: Integrated Summaries of Effectiveness and Safety: Location within the Common Technical Document (April 2009). FDA website. http://www.fda.gov/downloads/drugs/guidances/ucm136174.pdf. Accessed 17 January 2017.
50. Shen J. Chapter 23 Combination Product Design and Development. Regulatory Writing: An Overview. Regulatory Affairs Professionals Society. Rockville, MD. ©2017.
51. Op cit 14.
52. Op cit 5.
53. Ibid.
54. Op cit 14.
55. Op cit 5.
56. Op cit 26.
57. Op cit 6.
58. Op cit 5.
59. Periodic Benefit-Risk Evaluation Report (PBRER) E2C(R2) (17 December 2012). ICH website. http://www.ich.org/fileadmin/Public_Web_Site/ICH_Products/Guidelines/Efficacy/E2C/E2C_R2_Step4.pdf. Accessed 17 January 2017.
60. Op cit 5.
61. Ibid.
62. Ibid.
63. Op cit 31.
64. Op cit 5.
65. Op cit 14.
66. Op cit 5.
67. Ibid.
68. Ibid.
69. Op cit 40.
70. Op cit 14.
71. Op cit 42.
72. Op cit 49.
73. Op cit 42.
74. Ibid.
75. Guideline for the Format and Content of the Clinical and Statistical Sections of an Application (July 1988). FDA website. http://www.fda.gov/downloads/Drugs/Guidances/UCM071665.pdf. Accessed 17 January 2017.
76. Op cit 2.
77. Op cit 42.
78. Op cit 2.
79. Ibid.
80. Op cit 42.
81. Op cit 2.
82. Op cit 42.
83. Ibid.
84. Guidance for Industry: E2F Development Safety Update Report (August 2011). FDA website. http://www.fda.gov/downloads/Drugs/GuidanceComplianceRegulatoryInformation/Guidances/UCM073109.pdf. Accessed 17 January 2017.
85. Op cit 1.

**Authors**

Lisa DeTora is an assistant professor of writing studies at Hofstra University and a guest lecturer in humanities at the Hofstra Northwell School of Medicine. She began her career in medical writing at Merck and Co. Inc. and was a co-author of the company's internal guidances to comply with ICH E3 and M4. Her subsequent work experience has included regulatory writing and publication management in various therapeutic areas.

Danny A. Benau, MSOD, PhD is an associate professor of biomedical writing and director of biomedical writing programs at the University of the Sciences in Philadelphia. Previously, he worked as a freelance regulatory writer, medical writing project leader (Sanofi) and principal scientific writer (Wyeth-Ayerst Research). His experience includes participation in 14 NDAs and numerous CSRs, IND updates, responses to regulatory authorities and other documents. He holds a PhD in biology from Boston University and a Master of Organizational Dynamics from the University of Pennsylvania.

# 15

# Investigator's Brochure

*By Tina O'Brien, MS, RAC (US)*

The International Council on Harmonisation (ICH) Good Clinical Practice (GCP) guideline sets forth an international standard for conducting clinical studies involving human subjects. One GCP element is an Investigator's Brochure (IB) provided by the study sponsor to provide key information about the investigational product and investigational method to potential and participating investigators, Institutional Review Boards (IRBs) and Ethics Committees (ECs). The IB functions like a product label, which is discussed later in this chapter. IBs also typically are provided as part of clinical investigation applications, such as Investigational New Drug (IND) and Investigational Device Exemptions (IDE) in the US and Investigational Medicinal Product Dossier (IMPD) and Paediatric Investigation Plan (PIP) submissions in Europe. The IB not only provides key product information related to a clinical study, but also is the predecessor of and basis for final product labeling. The IB should include a concise, objective summary of clinical and nonclinical data sufficient for the study investigators and key decision makers to evaluate the investigation's purpose and method and to ensure study protocol compliance. However, for complex investigations or products, conciseness may not result in brevity. There is no guideline for the IB's length; however, it is desirable to omit non-relevant or non-value-added information. For example, the detailed results of nonclinical safety studies may be less relevant for the clinical investigator when the clinical trial results become available.

If multiple indications are under investigation for a single product, it may be necessary to develop separate IBs for each indication. However, repeating information across two different IBs may result in inconsistencies or errors, especially if the IBs are not updated in tandem. Therefore, clinical development teams should weigh and consider the advantages and disadvantages of multiple versus single IBs. In some cases, especially if a marketed product is under investigation for additional indications, it may be acceptable to use existing product labeling and/ or brochures that contain information relevant to the investigation's scope in lieu of, or as an adjunct to, the study IB. For example, if an investigator is also the study sponsor, and does not have access to the investigational product's relevant technical information, a product brochure and other relevant information should be obtained from the manufacturer to meet the minimum IB information requirements.

## Content Contributors

To ensure the IB provides sufficient technical detail for investigators and agency reviewers, its content should be reviewed and/or coauthored by individuals with the applicable knowledge and experience for the various required content types. For example, nonclinical toxicology

**Table 15-1. Investigator's Brochure Contents Specified in ICH E6, Section 7**

| Section | Description |
| --- | --- |
| Title Page | Provide the name of the sponsor, the product(s) being investigated, study identification and IB release date of the IB. Revision history is optional, but recommended |
| Confidentiality Statement | Optional statement to instruct the audience to consider the IB's content as confidential and for the sole use of key stakeholders (investigation team, IRBs, IECs, etc.) |
| Table of Contents | Two-level table of contents |
| Summary | Brief summary (1–2 pages) discussing the investigational product's significant characteristics and relevant clinical information |
| Introduction | Introduction of the investigational product's chemical/technical details and summary of the study's intent, rationale and method |
| Detailed Product Description | Detailed description of the investigational product, including a summary of physical, chemical and/or pharmaceutical properties relevant to the study, instructions for safe use during the course of the trial, and instructions for storage/handling (as applicable) |
| Nonclinical Studies | Tabular summary of protocol and results of relevant nonclinical studies, including the methodology, results, adverse events and relevance to the subject study<br>Further information on nonclinical pharmacology, pharmacokinetics and product metabolism in animals, and toxicology should be addressed (as applicable) |
| Effects in Humans | Detailed narrative of the known effects of the investigational product's use on humans, including details of other clinical studies and commercial use, safety and efficacy, and known side-effects and adverse events<br>Include summaries of pharmacokinetics and product metabolism in humans, safety and efficacy and marketing experience |
| Summary of Data and Guidance for the Investigator | Summary of the aforementioned nonclinical and clinical data to provide the reader with an overview of the investigational product and to convey possible safety considerations related to the investigation and allow the investigator to assess the study's appropriateness<br>Discuss published reports for related products, as applicable |
| Bibliography | Note: Publications and reports should appear at the end of the section in which they are referenced |
| Appendices | If applicable |

or pharmacology experts may collaborate with clinical pharmacology and clinical research experts on some IB subsections, such as a summary of benefit-risk ratios. Other IB sections, such as product chemistry or toxicology study overviews, may be managed by a single expert author.

If IB authoring is divided by subject matter area, challenges such as merging styles in a cohesive manner while preserving the technical detail, or managing updates from various sources throughout the investigation may emerge. Therefore, in some cases, a medical writer with the appropriate background may be engaged to author or coauthor IB content. In other situations, unity of style and content may be assured by a key reviewer in a responsible area, identified by the development stage. For example, a clinical pharmacologist may fulfill this role for a program in Phase 1, while a medical expert may assume this function when Phase 2 or 3 studies begin.

In any scenario, effective IB development and maintenance management is a key consideration to ensure continued compliance. Identifying a primary author or coordinator at the beginning of the IB development process can be an effective way to direct individual contributions,

set timelines and expectations, as well as clarify author, contributor and reviewer roles and responsibilities.

## Content Development

Once the contributors have been identified, it will be necessary to implement a project plan and/or timeline to ensure clarity on key milestones, deadlines and contributors' roles and responsibilities. Consider who will review the content and at which phase of development. For example, will all contributors (or other parties) need to review the final document? Who will approve the final IB? How will consistency be assured? How will differences of opinion be managed?

It may be helpful to provide templates to contributors to assist in compiling final content into a document and reduce the amount of rework to consolidate style, format and organization. In some settings, required templates and standard operating procedure (SOPs) are available to aid in IB content development, review and approval. Project management also is important in developing IB content. A core team should develop a timeline taking into account key data availability and their relationship to additional regulatory documents, such as an IND. If possible, the plan and timeline should be published in a location accessible by all contributors and other key stakeholders, and meetings should be scheduled throughout the development process to communicate the current status and next milestones and discuss questions or challenges.

## Format and Contents

The IB should be organized and contain the minimum content described in **Table 15-1**. Note that additional information may be necessary, commensurate with the investigational product, nature of the study, patient population and other relevant considerations to achieve the IB's intended use. Relevance in this context refers to material necessary to understand the scientific and clinical implications of administering the product to human subjects enrolled in clinical trials. Also, keep in mind US CFR 21 provides a list of information to be included in the IB; depending on the planned clinical studies' location, additional local regulations may need to be consulted.

The IB's content should focus on the end user, the investigator. Therefore, an IB intended for submission as part of an IND should be consistent with IND subsections but should summarize rather than reproduce them. The language should focus on key investigator concerns in using the intervention in a clinical setting. Attention should be paid to how easily the investigator can use the document. Therefore, the table of contents, table headings and formats should provide information accessible by the investigator. For example: "Outcomes of Studies PQXRT-1652, 1985, 1482, and 1652A" is less helpful than "Toxicology Studies in Animal Models." Conciseness may be served by omitting the product name from subheadings.

In global research settings, it may be necessary to consider translation. (See the Labeling section for a discussion of good practice when writing in a global context.)

## IB Updates

The IB should be considered a living document and be updated as information related to the study or the product changes. Content should be reviewed at least annually or as new information relevant to the study becomes available. In some cases (per GCP guidelines), it may be necessary to notify study investigators and key stakeholders of changes prior to revising the IB. Updated IBs should be provided to study investigators, IRBs, ECs and applicable regulatory authorities.

When updating an IB, the existing one should be reviewed for information that now is incorrect or redundant or has lost relevance based on the development stage. For example, in an IB used to support only Phase 1 studies, detailed information about safety studies in animal models may be important. However, details of these studies may become less important for the clinical investigator after additional large-scale Phase 3 studies are completed.

The IB serves a vital clinical research function because it is the repository for safety, chemistry and prescribing information provided in marketed product labels. Writing a clear and concise IB can aid investigators in conducting a clinical study.

### References

- US Code of Federal Regulations (CFR) Title 21, Section 312.23(a)(5), IND Content and Format, Investigator's brochure.
- 21 CFR Part 312 Investigational New Drug Application, Subpart B Investigational New Drug Application (IND), Section 312.23 IND Content and Format. FDA website. http://www.accessdata.fda.gov/scripts/cdrh/cfdocs/cfcfr/cfr-search.cfm?fr=312.23. Accessed 31 August 2016.
- ICH. *Guideline For Good Clinical Practice* E6(R1). ICH website. http://www.ich.org/products/guidelines/efficacy/efficacy-single/article/good-clinical-practice.html. Accessed 31 August 2016.
- FDA. *Guidance for Institutional Review Boards and Clinical Investigators 1998 Update*. FDA website. http://www.fda.gov/ScienceResearch/SpecialTopics/RunningClinicalTrials/GuidancesInformationSheetsandNotices/ucm113793.htm. Accessed 31 August 2016.
- IMDRF. *Statement regarding Use of ISO 14155:2011 "Clinical investigation of medical devices for human subjects—Good clinical practice."* IMDRF website. http://www.imdrf.org/docs/imdrf/final/procedural/imdrf-proc-150326-statement-iso141552011.pdf. Accessed 31 August 2016.
- ISO 14155:2011 Clinical investigation of medical devices for human subjects—Good clinical practice.

### Additional Reading

Fiebig D. "The investigator's brochure: a multidisciplinary document." *Medical Writing* 23(2): 2014. Trilogy Writing and Consulting website. http://www.trilogywriting.com/wp-content/uploads/2015/02/The-Investigators-Brochure_A-multidisciplinary-document_Douglas-Fiebig_MEW-23-2_Jun-2014.pdf. Accessed 31 August 2016.

### Author

Tina O'Brien, MS, RAC (US) is Director of Regulatory Affairs at Aroa Biosurgery, Ltd. (Auckland, New Zealand). She started her regulatory career with Medtronic Navigation, subsequently working at Covidien and Terumo BCT. She then moved to New Zealand as Senior RA Specialist at Fisher & Paykel Healthcare. O'Brien has presented for AdvaMed and provides pro bono consultation services to new start-up device companies in the Auckland area. She earned the RAC (US) certification and holds an MS from Northeastern University.

# 16

## Labeling

*By Tina O'Brien, MS, RAC (US)*

Medical product labeling is affixed to or accompanies a product to convey key information such as identification, intended use, indications for use, description, dosage, instructions for safe and effective use and benefit-risk information. Labeling provides information essential for prescribing physicians assessing benefits and risks to individual patients and for patients' safety and welfare. As illustrated in **Figure 16-1**, labeling can take many forms and address a variety of audiences.

### Identifying the Audience

When developing medical product labeling, it is important to identify the audience for which the content is intended. Labeling may include not only information relevant for the prescriber and patient; audiences also may include external entities such as regulatory authorities. In addition, product labels may be included in drug compendia (e.g., *Physician's Desk Reference* (US), *Data Sheet Compendium* (UK), etc.). Knowing the target audience also is helpful in determining which labeling pieces are required. **Table 16-1** provides a few examples of the correlation between sample document types and their potential target user profiles.

User profiles generally are identified early in product development, usually within the scope of risk management and indications for use, but can be supplemented throughout development and commercialization. Profiles,

and therefore labeling, may vary based on users' roles and responsibilities within a particular geographic region or organization. Analyzing the intended audience of the labeling, as well as evaluating details such as delivery methods, writing style, and number and types of labeling pieces required for the product, can help ensure content consistency, quality and usefulness.

### Writing for a Nontechnical Audience

Many medical products are administered and/or used by patients or other laypeople and, therefore, it is important to acknowledge, while content may be the same between user profiles, the presentation may be significantly different to accommodate the intended audience's education, literacy and experience. Not only must the content for a nontechnical audience be written to ensure comprehension, but the writer must take into account the conditions and environments in which the medical product is intended to be used. This information also may impact the risk information contained in the labeling, as well as how it is presented.

As most adults read at a level between the eighth- and ninth-grade (Safeer, Keenan, 2005), simple and concise language should be used to communicate only those details relevant to their use profile in sufficient detail to explain the "what" as well as the "why" in common language. Use of common "lay" terminology, appropriate

**Figure 16-1. Labeling Examples**

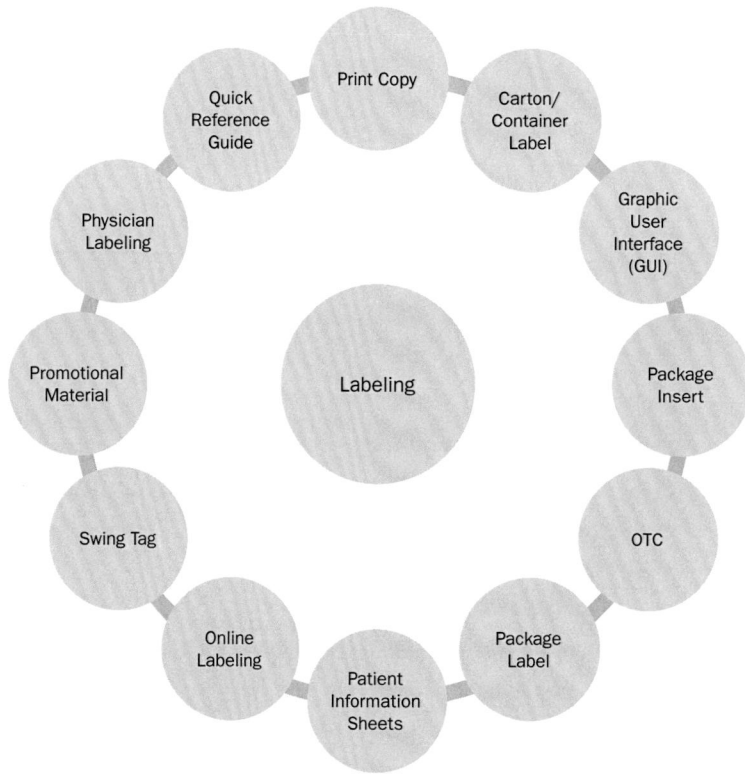

formatting, such as larger fonts, symbols, graphics and illustrations, also may enhance comprehension. Avoid technical terminology and jargon wherever possible. If it is necessary to explain a technically complex topic, provide a simplified explanation of the technical term and the context in which it is used. Seeking draft labeling review by a representative sample of the intended user group during the development process is highly recommended to ensure readers fully understand all information.

## Writing for a Global Audience

After identifying the various product user profiles and types of labeling required, the next step is to consider target regions and/or countries. Many medical products are intended for the global market. Thus, a single piece of product labeling may need to be available in many different languages for use in specific markets. Global writing techniques can be key to effective labeling development and usage.

A good place to start in the globalization of medical product labeling is the use of international or global English guidelines for drafting labeling content, which are available in a variety of publications and online resources. International and global English refer to written content

in which the author has minimized the use of cultural or regional language, colloquialisms, slang and uncommon terminology. These practices are intended to allow non-native English speakers to follow the document easily and to minimize problems among locations where English usage varies, for example, the UK versus the US. Additionally, the use of globalized English facilitates accurate content translation. Regardless of the language in which the content is being drafted, product labeling should be written with suitable verbiage for the user profile(s) that can be translated easily as needed.

Considerations to support global usability and translation include the following:

- Avoid using specific cultural styles of writing, such as metaphors and idioms.
- Ensure all users are considered when developing content.
- Avoid using verbal forms as nouns (for example, using "filing" rather than "marketing application" as a noun) because these usages may not exist in all the languages in scope for translation.
- Avoid the passive voice because it does not exist in all languages.
- Keep sentences as short as possible because longer sentences can be difficult to read and

translate. A general rule is to keep sentences at 24 words or less.

- Avoid complicated grammatical constructions.
- Remove needless words or phrases.
- Be consistent in the content wording and structure. Say the same thing, the same way, every time it is said.
- Use the same word to mean the same thing throughout the document, and use different words to mean different things.
- Avoid the use of ALL CAPS and especially SMALL CAPS because they do not exist in some alphabets.
- Use correct grammatical structures.
- Make sure each bullet in a bulleted list is a complete thought. In English, a bulleted list in the middle of a sentence is usually understandable, but that structure is not always conducive to localization.
- Avoid using more than one meaning for a single term. For example, do not use "service" as a noun and as a verb in the same document.
- Ensure content is not ambiguous. When in doubt, choose the word that has only one meaning in the source and the target languages.
- If appropriate, provide a list of definitions.

## Use of Symbols, Colors and Codes

For some types of medical products (medical devices, IVDs and some biologics), the use of internationally recognized symbols and codes is widely accepted and encouraged to communicate key product information in a global manner. The following standards commonly are applied to medical product labeling:

- ISO 15223-1—Medical devices—Symbols to be used with medical device labels, labeling and information to be supplied—Part 1: General requirements
- ISO 7000—Graphical symbols for use on equipment—Registered symbols
- ISO 3864-1—Graphical symbols—Safety colours and safety signs—Part 1: Design principles for safety signs and safety markings
- ISO 3864-2—Graphical symbols—Safety colours and safety signs—Part 2: Design principles for product safety labels
- ISO 3166-1 Country codes
- ISO 639-1 Language codes

If product labeling uses a custom symbol or identification color, the meaning of the symbol or identification color must be defined in the information provided with the

**Table 16-1. User Profile Examples**

| Document Category | User Profile(s) |
|---|---|
| Carton Label | Persons responsible for product shipping, transport or receipt |
| Instructions for Use | Persons required to prescribe, use or operate the product:<br>• Prescribing physician<br>• Medical professional<br>• Patient<br>• Caregiver<br>• Consumer |
| Technical Manual | Persons required to provide routine product maintenance and service:<br>• Biomedical engineers<br>• Service technicians |

device, such as the instructions for use. Custom symbols also require usability validation, in which the symbols are presented to a representative set of users to confirm the symbol's intent is understood in its intended context.

Note, other country-specific symbols, colors and codes also may be required for product labeling but do not necessarily contribute to the global audience.

## General Content Principles

When developing labeling content, remember the format, content and location of the information should be appropriate for the device and its intended purpose. It is imperative to consult product-specific laws, regulations and guidelines for the target market(s) to develop a comprehensive list of medical product labeling requirements prior to drafting content. It also may be advantageous to develop a series of templates, style guides and internal requirements covering the breadth of medical products and users to ensure a consistent look and feel and capture all content required.

Although specific medical product labeling content may be variable, **Table 16-2** describes some common elements.

## Risk Statements

Risk statements (e.g., warnings, precautions) are intended to inform users of potential personal and/or environmental hazards. This messaging is intended to modify a user's behavior to avoid a hazard resulting in the injury or damage to the person, environment and/or property (including the product in some cases), thus becoming a product risk control measure. The key to developing successful risk statements is combining clear, concise language with globally recognized symbols and colors in

**Table 16-2. Common Labeling Elements**

| Content Category | Description |
| --- | --- |
| Glossary | If a glossary is used, place it after the table of contents to alert readers it is there to help them. Whether or not a glossary is used, definitions should appear in the text. |
| Intended Use | Include the product's intended use statement. |
| Indications for Use | The patient population, condition, use environment, etc., for which the product is indicated for use. |
| Description of the Product | Give a brief description of the device, its chemical/material composition, dosage, appearance, parts, accessories, etc. Graphics often are the simplest and clearest way to describe the product's physical appearance. |
| Contraindications | State when the product should not be used (contraindications). Contraindications are conditions under which the product should not be used because its use risk clearly outweighs any possible benefit. |
| Risk Statements | Include applicable warning, and caution/precaution statements—see Risk Statement section for further guidance. |
| Set-up Instructions (if applicable)<br>• Product Set-up<br>• Patient Use Set-up | Provide clear instructions for product set-up and patient use set-up, as appropriate. Separate instructional documents may be necessary if different tasks are intended to be carried out by different user types.<br>• list of needed set-up materials and tools<br>• unpacking instructions, if appropriate<br>• instructions on proper disposal of packing materials or how to return packaging<br>• directions for where the product should be placed, such as a table top or floor (Also state whether the product should remain in one place after set-up.)<br>• any warnings or safety instructions specifically related to set-up<br>• results of incorrect set-up<br>• numbered set-up instruction steps in logical order<br>• any special preparation required before the product's first use, such as cleaning or disinfecting<br>• whom to contact if there is a problem |
| Use Instructions<br>• Prescription Use<br>• Professional Use<br>• Home Use<br>• OTC | Provide clear instructions for the product's use. The user needs to know what to do, how to do it and when.<br>• provide logically ordered steps for the task and make the user aware of the importance of doing the steps in order<br>• state each task's purpose and expected outcome<br>• tell the user what steps are essential and which are optional<br>• write the content at a reading level sufficient to reach most of the intended user population |
| Cleaning Instructions | Provide clear and complete cleaning instructions, as applicable to the product and its use environment.<br>• list the supplies needed<br>• provide step-by-step procedures<br>• state how often to clean the product<br>• tell the user what cleaning accomplishes<br>• include appropriate warnings and precautions for cleaning agents<br>• describe the results of using improper cleaning solutions or methods<br>• include suggestions for the proper disposal of the suggested cleaning agents, if appropriate |
| Maintenance and Servicing | • Clearly describe which maintenance activities are the user's responsibility.<br>• briefly outline proper maintenance activities, who is responsible, and how often the activity should be done. The lay user then will know what to expect and can take action if proper maintenance is not provided. |
| Storage Instructions | • Clearly describe proper storage conditions.<br>• State the results of improper storage.<br>• Note if extended storage may affect the device, including effect on set-up, check-out, operation and/or maintenance, as applicable. |
| Disposal | When appropriate, identify products with special disposal requirements (e.g., mercury-containing devices, sharps) and explain their safe disposal. Include the manufacturer's take-back information, recycling options and/or refurbishment options. |
| Accessories | If the product is provided with or is intended for use with accessories, discuss as appropriate. Include a general warning advising users of problems that may occur if they use accessories other than those recommended. |
| Troubleshooting<br>• User<br>• Service Technician | Provide instructions detailing steps to take if a problem occurs. Anticipate any problems the user may have with the product's set-up, use, operation or maintenance.<br>Clearly describe each problem's symptom in as few words as possible, so the user can match the description to the problem observed easily. If the product displays error messages, list them and what they mean. Explain the necessary steps to correct the problem. Do not confuse the reader with technical reasons for problems unless the reasons are important to the corrective action.<br>If there are problems users cannot or should not try to solve themselves, include warnings or precautions and inform the user how to proceed. |

**Table 16-3. Labeling Risk Category Statements**

| Risk Acceptability Criteria | | | Severity | | | | |
|---|---|---|---|---|---|---|---|
| | | | Negligible | Minor | Moderate | Serious | Catastrophic |
| | | | 1 | 2 | 3 | 4 | 5 |
| Probability | Extremely unlikely | 1 | NOTE | NOTE | CAUTION | WARNING | WARNING |
| | Unlikely but possible | 2 | NOTE | NOTE | CAUTION | WARNING | WARNING |
| | Likely | 3 | NOTE | NOTE | CAUTION | WARNING | WARNING |
| | Very likely | 4 | NOTE | CAUTION | CAUTION | WARNING | WARNING |
| | Extremely likely | 5 | NOTE | CAUTION | CAUTION | WARNING | WARNING |
| | Almost certain | 6 | NOTE | CAUTION | WARNING | WARNING | WARNING |

a manner that conveys information of high importance with respect to user and/or patient safety. Appendix E of ANSI Z535.4 provides comprehensive guidance on the estimation of risk and selection of the appropriate category (aka signal words), symbols and colors.

## Identifying Labeling Risk Control Measures

Risk statements typically are identified during the product development process of the product. Once a certain condition of use is correlated to a potential harm that will include a risk statement as part of the mitigation, the next step is to determine whether the associated labeling risk control measure results in a warning, caution or note. The distinction between warnings and precautions is based on degree of likelihood and seriousness of the potential hazard or harm, as defined within the medical product's risk management file.

A potential risk of harm's acceptability should be a primary consideration when making decisions on the type of labeling risk control measure to apply, as it is important to categorize risk statements correctly to avoid user "warning fatigue." Warning fatigue is when users are exposed to so many warning statements they become likely to ignore the warnings. The secondary consideration, when several labeling risk control measure categories have been incorporated, is to prioritize the unacceptable risk associated with the highest severity, e.g., warning statements should be used for severity 4 and 5 harms.

An example of labeling risk statement categories correlated to the risk acceptability is shown in **Table 16-3**.

## Risk Statement Content and Layout

Risk statement content and layout described below are appropriate for most instances but can be altered as necessary to best communicate the information to the user. (Note, the risk statement category and/or symbol should appear first.)

### Signal Word

The risk statement's general category (e.g., WARNING, CAUTION) to alert the reader that what follows is important information. A symbol or icon also may be used to emphasize the effect of the various categories. Additional enhancement, such as bolding, larger type, underlining, italics or color may help the information stand out from the rest of the text.

### Hazard Description

This clearly states the nature of the hazard associated with the warning (e.g., allergic reaction to material, strong magnetic field) or caution (e.g., environmental effect, damage from re-sterilization), characterizing the hazard's severity and likelihood.

### Consequence

Specify the serious adverse events, potential safety hazards and limitations to product use that result if users do not follow instructions. The purpose is to give them a clear idea of the risk, which is likely to increase compliance. Hazard alert research has shown this element has a significant effect on readers. If the consequences are not included, the risk statement likely will be less effective.

## *Prevention*

Instruction to user in the form: "Do Not, Never, Avoid..." (or "Do," if more appropriate) followed by the action to avoid (or perform). This directive's objective is to give clear instructions to the user on how to avoid the hazard.

# Conclusion

At the very core, medical product labeling is intended to inform the user about the product's safe and effective use, which generally results in a multitude of information. However, many of the considerations outlined above can be incorporated into labeling processes and templates to ensure completeness and consistency and can be customized across various product types and families. Clear communication of labeling requirements throughout the entire product lifecycle is key to ensuring the appropriate types of labeling and associated content can be generated not only to ensure compliance, but to ensure the product continues to be used in its intended safe and effective manner.

### Recommended Reading
Publications

- Blicq R, et al. *Guidelines for Writing English Language Technical Documentation for an International Audience.* INTECOM International Language Project Group. http://www.tekom.de/upload/alg/INTECOM_Guidelines.pdf. Accessed 27 December 2016.
- Kohl JR. *The Global English Style Guide: Writing Clear, Translatable Documentation for a Global Market.* SAS Institute, 2008. ISBN 1599948427, 9781599948423.
- Safeer RS, Keenan J, Eds. "Health Literacy: The Gap Between Physicians and Patients," *Am Fam Physician.* 2005 Aug 1;72(3):463-468.
- Weiss EH. *The Elements Of International English Style: A Guide To Writing English Correspondence, Reports, Technical Documents, And Internet Pages For A Global Audience.* M.E. Sharpe Inc. 2005. ISBN 0-7656-1571-1.

### Regulatory References

- US FDA Guidance Documents for Drug, Biologic, and Medical Device Labeling. http://www.fda.gov/RegulatoryInformation/Guidances/default.htm.
- EU, European Commission Directorate General Health and Consumers. http://ec.europa.eu/dgs/health_food-safety/index_en.htm.
- EU, European Commission Directorate-General for Translation English Style Guide. https://ec.europa.eu/info/sites/info/files/styleguide_english_dgt_en_0.pdf
- Australia, Therapeutic Goods Administration http://www.tga.gov.au/
- Brazil, National Health Surveillance Agency (ANVISA) http://portal.anvisa.gov.br/contact-us
- Canada, Health Canada http://www.hc-sc.gc.ca/index-eng.php
- Japan, Pharmaceuticals and Medical Devices Agency http://www.pmda.go.jp/english/index.html
- Singapore, Health Sciences Authority http://www.hsa.gov.sg/
- IMDRF, Labeling for Medical Devices—Study Group 1 Final Document GHTF/SG1/N43:2005 http://www.imdrf.org/docs/ghtf/final/sg1/technical-docs/ghtf-sg1-n43-2005-labelling-medical-devices-050603.pdf

### Standards References

- BS EN 1041:2008 Information supplied by the manufacturer of medical devices
- EN ISO 639-1: 2002 Codes for the representation of names of languages—Part 1: Alpha-2 code
- EN ISO 3166-1 Codes for the representation of names of countries and their subdivisions—Part 1: Country codes
- ISO 15223-1:2012 Medical devices—Symbols to be used with medical device
- ISO 7000:2014 Graphical symbols for use on equipment—Registered symbols
- ANSI/AAMI/IEC TIR 60878:2003 Graphical symbols for electrical equipment in medical practice labels, labelling and information to be supplied—Part 1: General requirements
- ANSI Z535.4 Product Safety Signs and Labels
- IEC 60601-1 Edition 3.1 Medical electrical equipment—Part 1: General requirements for basic safety and essential performance

### Author

Tina O'Brien, MS, RAC (US) is Director of Regulatory Affairs at Aroa Biosurgery, Ltd. (Auckland, New Zealand). She started her regulatory career with Medtronic Navigation, subsequently working at Covidien and Terumo BCT. She then moved to New Zealand as Senior RA Specialist at Fisher & Paykel Healthcare. O'Brien has presented for AdvaMed and provides pro bono consultation services to new start-up device companies in the Auckland area. She earned the RAC (US) certification and holds an MS from Northeastern University.

# 17

# Background Packages

*By Jocelyn Jennings, MS, RAC*

## Overview

This chapter presents information pertinent to preparing background packages for submission to regulatory authorities in support of pharmaceutical, biologic or medical device products. Guidance regarding pharmaceutical and biologic meetings with the US Food and Drug Administration (FDA), European Medicines Agency (EMA) Scientific Advice meetings and medical device Presubmission meetings with FDA is presented. While the structure of these meetings differs, the preparation for them and information provided to regulators for review are very similar. Thus, most of the advice and information contained in this chapter can be applied to the preparation of background packages for any jurisdiction or country. The regulatory professional can assist the sponsor or applicant in focusing on the critical discussion issues for these meetings.

The key to successful writing is remembering the audience. The audience for any regulatory document is the regulator; therefore, regulatory documents should not be written for a supervisor, a corporate executive management team, the quality assurance department or any other corporate entity. If the audience of regulators who review the background package do not understand the data and information it contains, the battle is lost and any subsequent meetings or communication will be hampered. A lot of time will be wasted explaining and writing

responses to questions from the regulator. The regulator should be able to concentrate on the focused review of the pertinent documentation leading to meaningful and helpful feedback. Understanding the goal of the meeting and the ability to prepare focused, concise questions are key as well and are discussed further later in this chapter.

## US Pharmaceutical and Biologic Background Packages

### Introduction

It is important to understand why a sponsor or applicant is seeking guidance from FDA prior to compiling the documentation for the meeting request and subsequent briefing package. If the team preparing a background package does not understand its goals in seeking advice, it will be impossible for the regulators to provide useful guidance. Presenting a coherent, compelling and succinct story to the regulators with well-thought-out short questions, supported by the data or information included in the background package, is the key to receiving meaningful feedback.

Section 119(a) of the *Food and Drug Administration Modernization Act* of 1997[1] provided for a unified approach to all formal multidisciplinary meetings between sponsors and FDA. Additionally, FDA released a guidance in 2009, *Guidance for Industry: Formal Meetings Between*

**Table 17-1. FDA Meeting Types and Deadlines**

| Meeting Type | FDA Meeting Agreement or Denial | Meeting Deadline After Request Receipt | Deadline for Background Package Submission |
|---|---|---|---|
| Type A | 14 days | 30 days | 2 weeks prior to meeting date |
| Type B | 21 days | 60 days | 4 weeks prior to meeting date |
| Type C | 21 days | 75 days | 4 weeks prior to meeting date |

*the FDA and Sponsors or Applicants,*[2] describing the process for requesting a meeting with FDA via teleconference, video conference or face-to-face.

## Background

FDA offers three types of meetings (A, B and C) pharmaceutical and biologic sponsors can use to solicit feedback regarding their preclinical, chemistry, manufacturing and control (CMC) and clinical programs.

- A Type A meeting is used most often to help a stalled development program
- A Type B meeting generally is held at the beginning or end of a development phase or submission. Type B meetings usually are limited to one per submission stage.
- A Type C meeting is a meeting for any other purpose.

As discussed below, each of these meeting types has a different purpose; therefore, the information or data to be presented in the background package will vary. Nevertheless, teams should keep in mind some of the information or data from prior meetings or meeting requests can be leveraged for subsequent requests and background packages.

### Formal Meetings With FDA

Prior to requesting a meeting with FDA, the sponsor must determine what kind of feedback is needed. Often, the regulatory professional must identify, or guide a team in identifying, potential issues within existing or ongoing research plans, protocols or existing data. For example, if there is a specific guidance for the product or indication, but adherence to the guidance was hit or miss, FDA might be able to suggest a means of proceeding. Only after potential issues are identified clearly can a plan to frame the discussion with FDA be determined. Hopefully, this planning will lead to specific, focused questions for FDA. Additional advice on focusing questions can be found in the Content and Format of Meeting Request section.

Per the 2009 FDA guidance,[3] Type A meetings are intended to help an otherwise stalled product development program proceed. Reasons for a Type A meeting include: dispute resolution, discussion of clinical holds if a response has been submitted but FDA and the sponsor agree development is stalled and a new path forward should be discussed and special protocol assessment meetings requested by the sponsor after receiving an FDA evaluation of protocols under the special protocol assessment procedures. To request a Type A meeting, the sponsor should contact the review division in the Center for Drug Evaluation and Research (CDER) or Center for Biologic Evaluation and Research (CBER). Type A meetings should be scheduled to occur within 30 days of FDA receipt of the written meeting request.

Type B meetings can be one of the following:
- Pre-Investigational New Drug application (pre-IND) meetings[4]
- End-of-Phase 1 meetings[5]
- End-of-Phase 2 and Pre-Phase 3 meetings[6]
- Pre-New Drug Application (NDA) and Pre-Biologics License Application (BLA) meetings[7]

Type B meetings should be scheduled to occur within 60 days of FDA receipt of the written meeting request. FDA typically will not grant more than one of each of the Type B meetings for each potential application. Thus, it is advantageous for the sponsor to understand the meeting request goals and objectives thoroughly.

Type C meetings are any other meetings between CBER or CDER and a sponsor regarding product development and review. Type C meetings should be scheduled to occur within 75 days of FDA receipt of the written meeting request (see **Table 17-1**).

To prepare a meeting request and meeting briefing package, the sponsor or regulatory professional must be familiar with the information or data that will form the foundation for the questions needing FDA feedback. For example, if the sponsor needs feedback on appropriate animal species or the necessity for carcinogenicity studies, the regulatory professional should understand the preclinical plans or protocols. If the sponsor is making a manufacturing modification and is proposing an alternative clinical plan, the regulatory professional should know the clinical plan and understand the manufacturing changes. The regulatory professional will need to develop

**Table 17-2. Tips for Formulating Questions**

| | Examples |
|---|---|
| Address the audience | Good: "Does the Agency..." <br><br> Bad: "According to ABC corporate policy X..." |
| Be specific | Good: "Is the current clinical development plan, including two clinical trial sites in the US and one in the EU adequate to provide geographic diversity?" <br><br> Bad: "Do you have feedback on the development plan?" |
| Highlight knowledge | Good: "According to guidance document X, the following measures are required [specify]. Is the current plan adequate to fulfill these measures? If not, which additional measures are needed?" <br><br> Bad: "Does the plan cover enough measures?" |
| Refer to information in the briefing package | Good: "Based on the information regarding the nonclinical GLP study plan presented in Table B, does the agency anticipate the need for additional studies? Does Table B present any studies that appear superfluous?" <br><br> Bad: "What kinds of nonclinical studies could be done?" |

a timeline with other internal departments or groups to ensure the meeting request and briefing package are ready per the standard timeframes.

Effective questions are critical for ensuring the discussion is focused and the meeting is successful (see **Table 17-2**). The list of questions should be precise, optimize the time with FDA and provide the information needed to proceed with development. The questions should not be open to interpretation or about a topic not covered in the meeting request. For example, "what do you think of our clinical plan?" is too vague. A better question is, "Is our plan to conduct this trial at two large US centers, one on each coast, adequate to provide geographic diversity?" The sponsor should propose questions that will optimize its time with FDA and provide the information needed to proceed with development. Never present an open ended question such as "Do you agree with our preclinical plan?" but instead pick out specific issues or concerns and frame them as questions. For example, "Guidance document X states that X studies must be performed on two rodent species. Product X is a biologic therefore this study is not necessary. Does FDA agree we do not need to perform study X in two rodent species?" If the sponsor's questions are too broad, too vague or poorly written it is a wasted opportunity because FDA likely is not going to provide meaningful feedback.

## Meeting Request Content and Format

The meeting request should include:[8]
- product name
- application number (if applicable)
- chemical name and structure (for a biologic, provide a description of the product)
- proposed indications or product development context
- type of meeting requested (If a Type A meeting is being requested, a rationale should be included.)
- brief statement of the meeting's purpose and objectives (This statement should include a brief background of the issues underlying the agenda. It also can include a brief summary of completed or planned studies and clinical trials or data the sponsor intends to discuss at the meeting, the general nature of the critical questions to be asked, and where the meeting fits in the overall development plan.)
- proposed agenda, including the names and titles of the sponsor personnel who will speak, by section (Including a timeline (i.e., five minutes per section) will help keep the meeting on track as the meeting typically is an hour in length.)
- proposed list of questions, grouped by discipline (For each question, a brief explanation of context and purpose should be included.)
- list of all individuals from the sponsor, with titles and affiliations, who will attend the requested meeting
- list of FDA staff, if known or disciplines requested to participate in the meeting
- suggested meeting dates and times
- meeting format (i.e., face-to-face, video conference, or teleconference)

FDA decides whether to grant or deny the meeting and identify the meeting type granted, which may differ from the sponsor's request. For Type A meeting requests, FDA will respond within 14 days. For Type B or Type C requests, FDA will respond within 21 days.

## Meeting Briefing Package Content and Format

While the sponsor awaits a response from FDA, work on the meeting briefing package should continue. The regulatory professional can assist the sponsor in refining its questions, focus on describing the principal areas of interest and finalizing the attendee list. It is never a good idea to have too many personnel attending the meeting with FDA, so attendees must be able to discuss in detail the information cited in the meeting briefing package. Additionally, it is a good time to ensure pertinent FDA personnel were requested to attend, either by name or specialty area. Remember the meeting with FDA is for a finite time period; therefore, time must be used effectively.

To give FDA enough time to prepare, the briefing package must be submitted at least two weeks prior to a Type A meeting and at least four weeks prior to a Type B or C meeting. Briefing packages should provide summary information relevant to the product and supplementary information needed to develop responses to issues raised. Full study and trial reports or detailed data generally are not appropriate. As noted above, the meeting briefing package content must support the objectives detailed in the agenda and the questions. A rationale for any unusual request or deviation from an existing guidance should be provided.

For ease of review, the briefing package should be organized according to the proposed agenda, which should be organized in a logical order. For instance, preclinical background and questions should come before a clinical section and questions. The briefing package must be paginated with a table of contents, appropriate indices, appendices, cross references and tabs differentiating sections. The briefing package should contain:[9]

- product name and application number (if applicable)
- chemical name and structure
- proposed indication
- dosage form, route of administration and dosing regimen (frequency and duration)
- updated list of sponsor or applicant attendees, affiliations and titles
- background section including:
  - o brief history of the development program and the events leading to the meeting
  - o product development status (e.g., target indication for use)

- brief statement summarizing the meeting's purpose
- proposed agenda
- list of final questions for discussion grouped by discipline, with a brief summary for each question to explain its need or context
- data to support discussion organized by discipline and question

The last bullet point is critical for FDA to provide meaningful feedback. The regulatory professional should ensure the data in the briefing package are informative and relevant. For example, for a pre-IND meeting, a table presenting a synopsis of results of completed Good Laboratory Practice (GLP) animal studies is relevant if the sponsor has questions about the need for further animal studies. For an End-of-Phase 2 meeting, details of the planned Phase 3 trial(s) identifying the trial population, inclusion/exclusion, dose rationale and primary and secondary endpoints would be needed. If there are questions regarding statistical analysis for a Pre-IND or End-of-Phase 2 meeting, major analysis information or a preliminary statistical analysis plan with information on planned interim analysis or adaptive design features, they will go in the last section.

## Submission Process

The regulatory professional should create a slide presentation based on the agenda and submit it to FDA at least one week (Type A) or two weeks (Type B, C) prior to the formal meeting date. The slides should contain only information or data presented in the meeting briefing package. These slides work well to keep the meeting focused, to ensure all topics are covered and to track the time for each speaker. If the meeting is granted, FDA may provide preliminary feedback prior to the formal meeting. This feedback can be used as the basis for discussion during the meeting or if it provides the feedback needed it can be considered the final response from FDA upon agreement by both parties. The sponsor or applicant then would send a formal letter to FDA canceling the meeting. If the meeting moves forward, meeting minutes agreed upon by both parties will serve as the final formal written feedback from FDA.

# EU Medicinal Products

## *EU Scientific Advice Introduction*

Article 57-1 of Regulation (EC) No 726/2004 of the European Parliament and of the Council of 31 March 2004,[10] indicates EMA has a role in "advising undertakings on the conduct of the various tests and trials

**Table 17-3. Sponsor/Applicant-Areas That May Lead to Questions**

| | Examples |
|---|---|
| Animal Models | Does the applicant have questions related to preclinical studies such as the correct choice of animal model? |
| Toxicology Studies | Are more toxicology tests required for the specific drug? |
| CMC Information | Regarding CMC, is the characterization information sufficient to proceed? |
| Approved or Licensed Products | Are there comparability issues if this is a change in manufacturing process for a current marketed authorized product? |
| Clinical Trial Program | This is a First-in-Man study, but this is a different formulation strength and route of administration of a currently marketed product; is a Phase 2 study necessary? Can the applicant move directly to a Phase 3 study? |
| Marketing Authorization Application Strategy | If the applicant is close to submitting the MAA, is substituting some preclinical studies with literature references a good submission strategy? |

necessary to demonstrate the quality, safety and efficacy of medicinal products."

The Committee for Medicinal Products for Human Use (CHMP) established the Scientific Advice Working Party (SAWP) as a standing working party with the sole responsibility of providing applicants with scientific advice and protocol assistance, which is the name given to the scientific advice procedure for products with an Orphan Designation.[11] SAWP/CHMP meets this responsibility by answering questions based on documentation provided by the applicant based on a pre-specified calendar that can be found on its web site. While the scientific advice or protocol assistance received is not legally binding, it is taken into consideration during Marketing Authorization Application (MAA) review.

Questions may concern quality (manufacturing, chemical, pharmaceutical and biological testing), non-clinical (toxicological and pharmacologic tests) and clinical (studies in human subjects in either patients or healthy volunteers, including clinical pharmacological trials designed to determine the efficacy and safety of the product for pre or post-authorization activities, including pharmacovigilance plans and risk-management programs). Scientific advice may be given on issues relating to interpretation and implementation of draft EU guidelines. Scientific advice is prospective in nature and allows input on developments, which can be amended after SAWP/CHMP advice. Scientific advice also focuses on development strategies rather than pre-evaluation of data to support an MAA. Regulatory questions are out of the scope of scientific advice; these questions are handled by the agency secretariat.

Much like the briefing package for an FDA meeting, the information or data provided for scientific advice must be supportive and specific to the questions presented. Knowing what questions need to be asked is critical to ensuring a well-organized submission (see **Table 17-3**).

One difference between FDA and EU is that a fee is charged for scientific advice requests.

### Scientific Advice Draft and Final Briefing Packages

The scientific advice briefing package consists of the following:
- letter of intent
- briefing document with questions
    - o summary section
    - o questions and applicant's positions
    - o background information

The letter of intent is a five-page form that can be found on EMA's scientific advice website[12] and includes pages showing the required fields and notes for certain parts of the form. The form requires the sponsor or applicant to provide basic information such as substance name, product type, therapeutic field, contact name and address, type of request and area of advice, i.e., nonclinical, clinical, etc. The email address for submission of the letter of intent can be found in the scientific advice guidance or on the EMA website.

Prior to submitting the letter of intent or draft briefing package, the applicant must check EMA's website for the dates of SAWP meetings and submission deadlines to determine the timing. Sponsors should keep in mind the deadline is earlier if a presubmission meeting is being requested.

### Draft Briefing Package

For the draft briefing package, the applicant should refer to EMA's website for the CHMP scientific advice/protocol assistance briefing document template, which contains guidance in every section to assist the applicant in providing the required information. As stated previously, the applicant's questions are critical for a successful scientific advice draft briefing package. The questions should be followed by a standalone applicant's position statement, one- to three-pages long, that includes a comprehensive justification for the chosen approach.

### Final Briefing Package

A final briefing package, in MS Word format, is submitted electronically after all required changes received from PDCO have been made to the draft briefing package. It then is validated by a scientific advice officer. The final briefing package should contain the relevant publications included in the list of references in .pdf format. Annex documents providing information relevant to the questions should be provided in .pdf format; MS Word is permissible. Examples of annex documents are: protocols, Investigator's Brochure, study protocols or reports (final, draft, synopses) and previous scientific advice received.

### Submission Process

The final briefing package is submitted via Eudralink. SAWP assigns coordinators to shepherd the package through the review process. If SAWP decides no meeting is necessary, the CHMP-adopted final advice letter is sent to the sponsor or applicant by Day 40. If SAWP decides a discussion meeting is required, the coordinator will schedule the meeting with the sponsor or applicant around Day 60 and present the preliminary conclusion at the end of the meeting. The coordinators then must submit that preliminary conclusion to SAWP. The final advice letter is adopted by CHMP and forwarded to the sponsor or applicant by Day 70.

## Medical Device Meeting Background Packages

### Medical Device Pre-Submission Program

In 1995, FDA established the pre-Investigational Device Exemption (IDE) program as a resource for medical device applicants to obtain FDA feedback on future IDE applications prior to their submission.[13] However, over time, the pre-IDE program evolved to include FDA feedback on other medical device applications such as Premarket Approval applications (PMAs), de novo petitions and 510(k) submissions (Premarket Notifications). In 2014, FDA changed the name of the pre-IDE program to the pre-submission (Pre-Sub) program to broaden its scope to cover medical devices regulated by CBER, including those regulated as biologics.

A Pre-Sub is defined as a formal written request from an applicant or sponsor for feedback from FDA to be provided in the form of a formal written response or, if the manufacturer chooses, a meeting or teleconference in which feedback is documented in meeting minutes. The Pre-Sub's main purpose is for the manufacturer to gain FDA feedback on specific questions necessary for product development or application preparation. The Pre-Sub is voluntary and there is no user fee.

A Pre-Sub should be submitted to FDA early in the development process prior to conducting nonclinical, analytical or clinical studies or submitting an IDE, IND or marketing application when:

- The new device involves novel technology and it may be helpful to familiarize the FDA review team with the technology in advance of the submission.
- The sponsor is making a "first of a kind" indication or a new indication for an existing device.
- The new device does not fall clearly within an established regulatory pathway and informal input is required for a proposed regulatory strategy.
- The new device is a multiplex device capable of testing a large number of analytes simultaneously.
- The new device is an in vitro diagnostic (IVD) containing a new technology, has a new intended use, a new analyte, new clinical questions, complex data/statistical questions, or the predicate of or the reference method is unclear or uncertain.
- There are specific issues related to nonclinical study protocols or the planned clinical studies.
- Input is required to determine the extent to which existing data can be leveraged in preparing a PMA submission.

The Pre-Submission program is not meant to be iterative; however, it actually is good practice to submit another pre-submission if feedback was received from FDA more than six months prior to the initiation of performance testing or a clinical trial. The agency could have issued new draft guidance or its thinking on a subject could have changed.

### Pre-Submission Package Preparation

The manufacturer must assess the nonclinical, analytical and clinical testing program for its specific device type. What analytical testing is required for the device? Will the testing be completed internally or externally? What types of specimens are required? Will simulated specimens be used? Is the clinical program going to be conducted in the

**Table 17-4. 510(k) Submission Questions**

|  | Examples |
|---|---|
| Bench Testing or Preclinical | Is the justification for not conducting carcinogenicity studies adequate? |
| Software | Is the level of concern for the software appropriate? |
| Clinical Program | Fifty percent of the data was to come from the US, however, only 30% does, is this adequate? |
| Pediatric Program | The clinical plan was to enroll at least 20 pediatric subjects; however there were only 13 evaluable pediatric patients. Is this acceptable for a pediatric indication? |
| Statistical Analysis | Are the primary and secondary endpoints appropriate for the indication for use? Is the proposed sample size adequate? |

US only or will it be a multinational clinical program? Are animal studies required? Will human factors testing be required? What setting will be used for human factors? Who will participate in the human factors testing? Will a pilot instrument be used or production equivalent?

FDA prefers to review analytical testing or clinical protocols in Pre-Sub packages; however, detailed plans also are acceptable. For example, if five analytical tests will be performed, a master analytical plan with enough detail on each analytical test should be sufficient. An explanation of the sample size with information on the statistical methods used and results of any preliminary tests run should be provided.

If there are questions concerning the clinical program, clinical protocols or detailed plans should be provided and the plan must include the statistical analysis plan for each individual clinical trial. The manufacturer also should specify where the clinical study will be conducted and whether it will be prospective or retrospective as well as provide the study endpoints and study acceptance criteria information.

If the manufacturer is planning to submit a 510(k), predicate device information must be presented in the Pre-Sub package. A table showing the similarities and differences with rationale is a good mechanism for presenting this information. The 510(k) submission number of the predicate device should be provided as well. A comprehensive overview of the predicate device provided in the Pre-Sub will assist FDA in determining whether the appropriate predicate device was chosen.

### Content and Format of the Pre-Submission Package

- cover letter—clearly state the reason for the submission in the reference line and provide complete contact information (include the device name)
- CDRH Premarket Review Submission Cover Sheet[14]—can be used to submit to CDRH and CBER
- table of contents
- device description—can include engineering drawings, pictures, brief explanation of the manufacturing process, explanation of the user interface, explanation of materials and physical and biological characteristics of the device output (For an IVD, detailed technical description including instruments, reagents, components, software, principles of operation and accessories. For a device to be submitted in a 510(k), any anticipated predicate and a descriptive comparison of the device to the predicate device. This is best provided in tabular format for ease of review.)
- proposed intended use/indications for use
- previous discussions or submissions—provide a summary of any previous discussions with FDA or previous submissions (include the submission number, if applicable)
- product development overview—include an outline of nonclinical and clinical testing, planned or already completed
- specific questions—adjust based on application type (e.g., 510(k), IDE, PMA, etc.) (see more information below)
- feedback method—specify whether a face-to-face meeting, teleconference, facsimile or email is preferred (FDA will consider the manufacturers preference) (see more information below)

As discussed previously, the questions submitted are critical to ensure relevant FDA feedback.

If the submission will be a 510(k) the manufacturer may want to ask the questions presented in **Table 17-4**. Potential manufacturer questions for a PMA submission are listed in **Table 17-5**.

**Table 17-5. PMA Submission Questions**

|  | Examples |
|---|---|
| Clinical Study Report | Is the plan to address protocol deviations appropriate? |
| Statistical Analysis | The study did not meet its primary endpoint. Is it possible to proceed and, if so, how?<br>The statistical analysis has changed from that submitted in the IDE, does FDA agree the revised statistical analysis is appropriate? |

## Submission Process and Meeting Feedback

Before submitting the Pre-Sub package, the manufacturer should decide the meeting or feedback method desired. If the manufacturer wants a face-to-face meeting, three or more preferred dates and times should be presented in the Pre-Sub package cover letter and body. The planned attendees from the manufacturer should be listed as well as proposed personnel from FDA. The proposed meeting duration with a rationale if the request is for longer than one hour should be included in the package as well.

Once the Pre-Sub package has been submitted, FDA will send an acknowledgement email, letter or fax, which will contain the Q-Sub, a unique identification number to be used for all future correspondence, including requests for future meetings. If a face-to-face meeting or teleconference has been requested, the lead reviewer assigned will contact the manufacturer within seven days of receiving the Pre-Sub package to confirm the meeting date and time or to propose alternate meeting dates and times. Although FDA has 90 days from package receipt to respond with feedback, it typically will try and respond within 75 days, if possible.

If initial feedback is provided and addresses the manufacturer's concerns, the manufacturer can determine the written response serves as the final written feedback from FDA. It is worth noting if a subsequent Pre-Sub package is needed, any prior questions to and written feedback from FDA should be appended to the new Pre-Sub package, especially if the manufacturer is revisiting an issue on which FDA previously provided feedback. This gives the lead reviewer an opportunity to review the earlier feedback.

## Summary

A sponsor, applicant or manufacturer has many opportunities to receive feedback on its development programs. Background packages come in many forms and have different names but they all serve the same purpose, eliciting regulators' feedback. The sponsor, applicant or manufacturer must provide solid, well-thought-out plans or protocols for review. The questions posed to the regulator must be concise and relevant to the material presented in the background package. The questions are the most critical part of the background package because the regulators

look at the questions to put other data and information presented in context. If questions are too vague, the regulator's response likely will be just as vague or it will not provide feedback at all. A regulator's feedback is only as good as the data, information and questions submitted for review.

**References**

1. Food and Drug Administration Modernization Act of 1997, Section 119. FDA website. http://www.fda.gov/downloads/RegulatoryInformation/Legislation/SignificantAmendmentstotheFDCAct/FDAMA/FullTextofFDAMAlaw/UCM089145.pdf. Accessed 28 December 2016.
2. *Guidance for Industry: Formal Meetings Between the FDA and Sponsors or Applicants*, May 2009. FDA website. http://www.fda.gov/downloads/Drugs/.../Guidances/ucm153222.pdf. Accessed 28 December 2016.
3. Op cit. 2
4. 21 CFR Section 312.82 Pre-investigational new drug meetings. FDA website. http://www.accessdata.fda.gov/scripts/cdrh/cfdocs/cfcfr/cfrsearch.cfm?fr=312.82. Accessed 28 December 2016.
5. 21 CFR Section 312.82 End-of-Phase 1 meetings. FDA website. http://www.accessdata.fda.gov/scripts/cdrh/cfdocs/cfcfr/cfrsearch.cfm?fr=312.82. Accessed 28 December 2016.
6. 21 CFR Section 312.47 End-of-phase 2 meetings and meetings held before submission of a marketing application. FDA website, http://www.accessdata.fda.gov/SCRIPTs/cdrh/cfdocs/cfCFR/CFRSearch.cfm?fr=312.47. Accessed 28 December 2016.
7. 21 CFR Section 312.47 Pre-NDA and pre-BLA meetings. FDA website. http://www.accessdata.fda.gov/SCRIPTs/cdrh/cfdocs/cfCFR/CFRSearch.cfm?fr=312.47. Accessed 28 December 2016.
8. Op cit. 2.
9. Ibid.
10. Regulation (EC) No 726/2004 of the European Parliament and of the Council of 31 March 2004 laying down Community procedures for the authorisation and supervision of medicinal products for human and veterinary use and establishing a European Medicines Agency. Eur-Lex website. http://eur-lex.europa.eu/LexUriServ/LexUriServ.do?uri=OJ:L:2004:136:0001:0033:en:PDF. Accessed 28 December 2016.
11. *European Medicines Agency Guidance to applicants seeking scientific advice and protocol assistance*, EMA/691788/2010 Rev. 7, 19 September 2014. EMA website. http://www.ema.europa.eu/docs/en_GB/document_library/Regulatory_and_procedural_guideline/2009/10/WC500004089.pdf. Accessed 28 December 2016.
12. Scientific advice and protocol assistance. EMA website. http://www.ema.europa.eu/ema/index.jsp?curl=pages/regulation/general/general_content_000049.jsp. Accessed 28 December 2016.
13. *Request for Feedback on Medical Device Submissions: The Pre-Submission Program and Meetings with Food and Drug Administration Staff—Guidance for Industry and Food and Drug*

*Administration Staff*, 18 February 2014. FDA website. http://www.fda.gov/downloads/medicaldevices/deviceregulationandguidance/guidancedocuments/ucm311176.pdf. Accessed 28 December 2016.

14. CDRH Premarket Review Submission Cover Sheet. FDA website. http://www.fda.gov/downloads/AboutFDA/ReportsManualsForms/Forms/UCM080872.pdf. Accessed 28 December 2016.

**Author**

Jocelyn Jennings, MS, RAC is a regulatory professional working for a global healthcare company that manufactures therapeutic products using plasma proteins. She has more than 19 years of extensive global regulatory, quality assurance and global clinical trial experience in drugs, biologics and medical devices. Jennings is an adjunct professor at Northeastern University in the College of Professional Studies. She also is actively involved with local regulatory chapters in her area and with the Regulatory Affairs Professionals Society (RAPS). Jennings holds an MS in regulatory affairs from Northeastern University and has earned the RAC.

# 18

# Responses to Questions or Requests for Information

*Nathalie Innocent, MS, RAC*

## Introduction

Obtaining timely approval to market a drug, vaccine, biologic or medical device requires demonstrating the product's safety and efficacy (or effectiveness) adequately to the appropriate regulatory authority. One key to accomplishing this goal is communicating successfully with the regulatory agency in the initial submission to avoid questions. For example, when a sponsor submits an application or supplemental application to the US Food and Drug Administration (FDA), if the data were presented well, the outcome is no regulatory intervention or, more ideally, an explicit approval. However, it more often is the case that a health authority has questions about the application and the data contained therein, or requires additional information to evaluate the application properly. The more complex or novel the product, the more likely the regulatory authority is to have comments or questions.

Questions from regulatory agencies may come in many forms. For example, in the US, FDA may use formal information requests, take a regulatory action requiring the sponsor to prepare a written response or send an informal email to gain clarification on a minor question. The process of communicating deficiencies or comments is slightly different in the EU and involves a comment period for such communications and responses. This chapter examines the more formal requests for information or questions that may come from FDA or EU health authorities regarding an application for marketing authorization.

## FDA Questions or Requests for Information

In the US, FDA may communicate with sponsors in many ways. Some of the methods used by FDA include a discipline review letter, Information Request, complete response letter, additional information notification and a notification of clinical hold. These methods are described below.

### Discipline Review

Review of New Drug Application (NDA) or Biologics License Application (BLA) sections by FDA staff with expertise in that field (e.g., clinical; nonclinical pharmacology and toxicology; chemistry, manufacturing and controls (CMC); pharmacokinetics, etc.) is called discipline review.[1] Upon reauthorization of the *Prescription Drug User Fee Act* (*PDUFA*) in 1997, (*PDUFA II*), FDA began utilizing discipline review letters to provide early feedback to industry. FDA uses the discipline review letter to communicate initial thoughts on possible deficiencies found by the discipline review team in its portion of the pending application once it completes its review.[2] The discipline review letter is not considered an action letter and therefore has no impact on the review clock. It provides sponsors with an opportunity to begin preparing a response to any deficiencies, thereby reducing response time to the agency.[3]

### Information Request Letter

FDA uses information review letters to request further information or clarification required or that may aid in completing the discipline review.[4] Information review letters do not represent a complete review of the submission and, like the discipline review letter, do not stop the review clock.[5]

### Complete Response Letter (CRL)

The complete response letter indicates to the sponsor FDA has completed the application review, and it has not been approved. The complete response letter typically will list the deficiencies and provide the sponsor with a deadline to respond to them.[6] The complete response letter is an action letter, as it signifies complete submission review and the review cycle end. In the past, FDA would use several different action letter types, (not approvable, approvable or approval letter) for NDAs, Abbreviated New Drug Applications (ANDAs) and BLAs. The agency has discontinued the approvable and not approvable letters when taking action on these marketing applications.[7] It still utilizes approvable and not approvable letters when communicating action on medical device premarket approval applications (PMAs).

### Devices

Refuse to accept hold notifications and additional information requests are methods FDA uses to communicate with sponsors regarding medical device 510(k) clearance applications. When a sponsor submits a 510(k) application, FDA performs an acceptance review to determine whether the submission is administratively complete. If the agency finds the application to be incomplete, it is placed on refuse to accept hold, and the sponsor is issued a notification that lists the application's deficiencies.[8] The sponsor has 180 days to respond to the cited deficiencies. Notification of acceptance for review or notification of refuse to accept hold occurs within 15 days after the application is received.[9]

Once a 510(k) application is accepted for review, it proceeds to substantive review. Substantive review begins by Day 60 after the 510(k) submission is received. During the substantive review, the lead FDA reviewer will communicate with the sponsor through what is called a substantive interaction. This can be an email indicating FDA will proceed to resolve any outstanding deficiencies via interactive review or an additional information

request.[10] If the agency issues an additional information request, the application is placed on hold, and the sponsor has 180 calendar days from the date of the request to submit a complete response.

### Notification of Clinical Hold

FDA does not approve clinical trial applications (INDs) explicitly. Instead, the sponsor must wait 30 days before the trial can begin, which allows time for the agency to determine whether there are concerns about the trial. If concerns are identified, a clinical hold may be imposed, typically with notification by phone. Within 30 days of this phone call, the agency will issue a written notification describing the reasons for the clinical hold in detail.[11] Like other requests for information, the sponsor is required to submit a complete response to the issues cited in the clinical hold letter. It is important to note a clinical hold also can be imposed on investigations already in progress. As defined in 21 CFR 321.42, "A clinical hold is an order issued by FDA to the sponsor to delay a proposed clinical investigation or to suspend an ongoing investigation." Clinical investigations may proceed only after the agency has notified the sponsor the hold has been lifted.

## EU Health Authority Comments or Information Requests

EU marketing authorization regulations and procedures are quite different from those in the US. Consequently, EU regulatory authorities handle questions and requests for information differently. In the EU, communicating deficiencies or requests for information occur during the application review comment period.

The EU has several regulatory pathways. The Centralised Procedure, Mutual Recognition Procedure and Decentralised Procedure are discussed below.

### Centralised Procedure

The Centralised Procedure allows sponsors to submit a single application directly to the European Medicines Agency (EMA) to obtain marketing authorization valid throughout the EU. Sponsors utilizing this pathway apply directly to EMA, and the application is assessed by the Committee for Medicinal Products for Human Use (CHMP). A rapporteur, and if needed, a co-rapporteur, will be designated from among the CHMP members to coordinate the medicinal product assessment and prepare draft reports. Under this procedure, a list of questions is sent to the applicant by Day 120 after dossier submission. At this point, the review clock stops until the applicant submits responses to all of the questions. Under the

Centralised Procedure, the applicant also may have an opportunity to provide oral explanations.[12]

The Centralised Procedure is mandatory for certain products, such as those for serious illnesses like AIDS, cancer, neurodegenerative disorders or diabetes. Biotechnology-derived and orphan medicinal products also fall under the Centralised Procedure's scope.[13] Alternatively, most conventional medicinal products apply for marketing authorization using either the Mutual Recognition or Decentralised Procedure.[14]

### Mutual Recognition Procedure

The Mutual Recognition Procedure consists of recognition of an already existing marketing authorization by one or more Member States.[15] In this case, marketing authorization for the medicinal product exists in at least one Member State, and the applicant essentially is asking one or more additional Member States to recognize the existing authorization.

When an applicant wishes to obtain marketing authorization via the Mutual Recognition Procedure, the sponsor submits identical applications to one or more Member States. Once one Member State decides to evaluate the product, it becomes the Reference Member State and notifies the other Member States where the application was submitted, which become the Concerned Member States.[16] Within 90 days, the Reference Member State validates the application and submits an assessment report to the Concerned Member States. After the Concerned Member States validate the application and approve the assessment report, typically within 30 days of assessment approval, marketing authorization is granted in the Reference Member State and the Concerned Member States.[17]

### Decentralised Procedure

Under the Decentralised Procedure, a medicinal product marketing authorization application is submitted simultaneously in several Member States. One of the Member States is chosen as the Reference Member State. In contrast to the Mutual Recognition Procedure, no marketing authorization exists already in any Member State. At the procedure's end, national marketing authorizations are granted in the Reference Member State and Concerned Member States.[18,19]

Once the application is validated by the Reference Member State and Concerned Member States, the Reference Member State begins the assessment and sends a preliminary assessment report to the Concerned Member States and to the applicant; this occurs by Day 105 and stops the review clock. Within 15 days of receipt of the applicant's response, the Reference Member State will send a draft assessment report to the Concerned Member States and applicant. Upon Member States' approval of the assessment, the marketing authorization is granted.[20]

The key distinction between the Mutual Recognition Procedure and Decentralised Procedure is when it takes place relative to a product's initial EU marketing authorization. The Mutual Recognition Procedure involves obtaining marketing authorization in one or more Member States when the medicinal product has been approved by at least one EU Member State. In contrast, the Dentralised Procedure involves an application for marketing authorization for a product not approved already in any Member State.[21]

## Written Responses to Questions or Requests for Information

While this section primarily discusses responses to FDA questions or requests for information, the considerations for responding to EU regulatory authorities' questions are similar. Responses must be complete, well organized and address all the questions posed by the regulatory authority.

### Content and Organization

It is important to follow all instructions the agency provides. For example, an information request may require specific details in the response cover letter, such as a reference number or the review discipline to aid routing. Similarly, the response should not include information other than that the agency requested. An information request response is not an opportunity to present new data or propose additional indications, and incorporating unsolicited information in a response may extend review timelines. In other words, the agency may classify a response containing additional data as an unsolicited or major amendment to the submission and extend a target action date.

Responses must be complete. The information request is intended to obtain missing material or clarify something; therefore, it is important to address all the comments or deficiencies indicated in the agency communication. In fact, the agency likely will include a statement such as, "any partial response will not be reviewed" or "we will not process or review a partial response." It may be helpful to indicate specifically in the closing of the cover letter, "we are submitting a complete response" or "this resubmission is a complete response to the information requested received on…" to indicate the sponsor's understanding to the reviewer that all comments have been considered.

### Best Practices for Preparing Responses

When responding to an information request or other deficiency notification, the sponsor should provide a copy of the agency's communication to remind the reviewer of the information requested.[22] Submissions to FDA are in electronic form, which allows the sponsor to prepare and structure an easily navigable submission with links to reference documents.

**Figure 18-1** is an example of a possible FDA information request. In the example information request, the agency lists the supplemental application's deficiencies, provides a response deadline, provides specific details to include in the response (in this case, a reference number) and indicates the consequences of not providing the information requested by the due date.

In an information request response, it is advisable to list each deficiency statement and respond immediately below it.[23] In the first example below, the agency has requested the sponsor to establish specifications for the drug substance used in their product (see Example 1). Additionally, the sponsor may want to acknowledge agency comments not requiring a response, as in Example 2. This practice accounts for all requested information and is useful particularly when the information request or deficiency letter contains multiple items. In the second example, the sponsor merely is acknowledging the agency's comment. This kind of question and answer format will make it obvious all comments have been addressed.

## Example 1

Comment 1:
Please establish bulk and tapped density specifications for the drug substance, Questorequest USP.

Response:
We have established specifications for bulk and tapped density (NLT 0.123 g/cm³ and NLT 0.456 g/cm³, respectively) for the drug substance, Questorequest USP. The updated drug substance specification document is provided in Module 3.2.S.4

## Example 2

Facility Inspections
The Office of Compliance has no further questions at this time. The compliance status of each facility named in the application may be re-evaluated upon resubmission of your supplemental application.

Response:
We acknowledge the Office of Compliance has no further questions at this time, and the compliance status of each facility named in the application may be re-evaluated upon resubmission of our application.

In cases where the sponsor does not agree with the reviewer's comment, the sponsor should explain clearly why the issue is not relevant. The sponsor can use alternate data and applicable CFR or guidance references, where appropriate, to support its position. Example 3 demonstrates

how a sponsor can provide a thorough explanation for why a request cannot be fulfilled.[24]

## Example 3

Deficiency
In your submission, you state your device must stand during surgical placement.
Data were submitted to support stability; however, no data were presented to demonstrate the device has adequate strength to withstand bending in a clinical setting. To meet the criteria of reasonable assurance of safety, we believe additional data are needed to demonstrate the device will withstand bending during surgical placement. In a clinical setting, please evaluate the strength of the device to withstand bending during surgical placement.

Response:
FDA requested the strength of our investigational device to withstand bending during surgical placement to be evaluated through a clinical trial. The assessment of strength in a clinical trial is burdensome and difficult to assess quantitatively, as its measure may be confounded with other factors. We believe the strength of the device to withstand bending during surgical placement can be assessed adequately by bench testing. The maximum angle of bending during surgical placement is known. Therefore, testing device strength at this maximum angle is adequate to provide valid evidence of the device's safety. The methods, data and statistical analysis showing strength is adequate are attached.[25]

There is no doubt the response's format and organization are important elements in presenting a clear picture to the regulatory authority; however, it is equally important to provide appropriate, well-reasoned text supported by data, agency guidance and/or regulations. It is necessary to consider what is being requested and engage the appropriate subject matter experts or other stakeholders within the organization when preparing the response. For example, it may be necessary to reach out to an analytical method subject matter expert if the information request requires specific details on testing methodology. Additionally, the individual preparing the response should confer with appropriate stakeholders within the organization prior to including any commitments in the response.

### Timing

The amount of time a sponsor is given to respond to FDA can be anywhere from 10 days to a year, depending on the type of information request or deficiency letter. It is very important the sponsor respond within the timeframe the agency provides. Not responding to an information request may result in the issuance of a complete response letter or administrative withdrawal of the application. Typically, FDA will provide a date by which a response or action is needed and indicate the consequences for not meeting the indicated deadline. For example, a deficiency letter may indicate "please provide your response within 30 days of receipt of this letter" or, in the case of a more significant deficiency, the agency communication may indicate "please

**Figure 18-1. Example of Agency Deficiency Communication**

DEPARTMENT OF HEALTH AND HUMAN SERVICES

Food and Drug Administration
Silver Spring, MD 20993

ANDA 00321/S-001

**INFORMATION REQUEST**

Acme Pharmaceutical Corp
1234 Regulatory Way
Allentown, PA 18103

Attention: Jane Doe
Executive Director, Regulatory Affairs

Dear Madam:

Please refer to your supplemental Abbreviated New Drug Application (sANDA) dated and submitted on October 31, 2016 under section 505(j) of the Federal Food, Drug, and Cosmetic Act for Questorequest, 25 mg.

We have completed our review of this sANDA, and have the following comments.

<u>CMC</u>

1. Please establish bulk/tapped density specifications for the drug substance Questorequest USP.

2. Please provide lot numbers, COAs and any characterization information including expiry/retest date for any in-house standards used for related substances for the drug substance Questorequest USP.

Provide a complete response to this deficiency by January 22, 2017. We will not process or review a partial response. Facsimile or e-mail responses will not be accepted.

Send your submission through the Electronic Submission Gateway http://www.fda.gov/ForIndustry/ElectronicSubmissionsGateway/default.htm. Prominently identify the submission with the following wording in bold capital letters at the top of the first page of the submission:

**INFORMATION REQUEST
PRODUCT QUALITY
REFERENCE # 123456**

If you do not submit a complete response January 22, 2017, the review will be closed and the listed deficiencies will be incorporated in a COMPLETE RESPONSE correspondence. If you have any questions, contact John Smith, Regulatory Process Manager, at 240-555-1234.

Sincerely,
John Smith
Regulatory Process Manager

provide your response within six months of receipt of this letter." If the sponsor feels more time is needed to address the agency's comments fully, it is prudent to request an extension well in advance of the deadline.

## Summary

Health authority questions or information requests provide the sponsor an opportunity to clarify items in the application that may not have been clear to the reviewer.

In the US, questions may be presented at any time during the application review and may come in several different forms such as a complete response letter, formal information request or a regulatory action requiring sponsor follow-up. In the EU, health authority questions are presented during the application review comment period.

Although significant differences exist between how US and EU regulatory authorities communicate deficiencies or pose questions to sponsors, preparing responses to these inquiries include common elements. The sponsor should provide a complete response that addresses all the comments or deficiencies cited in the regulatory agency's communication. The sponsor should present all deficiencies clearly and provide the appropriate response with the supporting data and regulatory or guidance references. Sponsors also should avoid including new data in the response, unless there is a strategic decision to do so, with the understanding review timelines may be impacted.

### References

1. *Guidance for Industry: Information Request and Discipline Review Letters Under the Prescription Drug User Fee Act* (November 2001). FDA website. http://www.fda.gov/downloads/drugs/guidancecompliance regulatoryinformation/guidances/ucm172134.pdf. Accessed 9 January 2017.
2. Ibid.
3. Ibid.
4. Ibid.
5. Ibid.
6. Complete Response Letter Final Rule. FDA website. http://www.fda.gov/Drugs/GuidanceComplianceRegulatoryInformation/LawsActsandRules/ucm084138.htm. Accessed 9 January 2017.
7. Ibid.
8. *Refuse to Accept Policy for 510(k)s: Guidance for Industry and Food and Drug Administration Staff* (4 August 2015). FDA website. http://www.fda.gov/downloads/medicaldevices/deviceregulation-andguidance/guidancedocuments/ucm315014.pdf. Accessed 9 January 2017.
9. 510(k) Submission Process. FDA website. http://www.fda.gov/MedicalDevices/DeviceRegulationandGuidance/HowtoMarketYourDevice/PremarketSubmissions/PremarketNotification510k/ucm070201.htm. Accessed 9 January 2017.
10. Ibid.
11. IND Application Procedures: Clinical Hold. FDA website. http://www.fda.gov/Drugs/DevelopmentApprovalProcess/HowDrugsareDevelopedandApproved/ApprovalApplications/InvestigationalNewDrugINDApplication/ucm362971.htm. Accessed 9 January 2017.
12. Authorisation procedures—The Centralised Procedure. European Commission (EC) website. http://ec.europa.eu/health/authorisation-procedures-centralised_en. Accessed 9 January 2017.
13. Ibid.
14. Authorisation procedures for medicinal products. EC website. http://ec.europa.eu/health/authorisation-procedures_en.htm. Accessed 9 January 2017.
15. Authorisation procedures—The Mutual Recognition Procedure. EC website. http://ec.europa.eu/health/authorisation-procedures-mutual-recognition_en.htm. Accessed 9 January 2017.
16. Ibid.
17. Ibid.
18. Authorisation Procdures—The Decentralised Procedure. http://ec.europa.eu/health/authorisation-procedures-decentralised_en.htm. Accessed 9 January 2017.
19. Ghalamkarpour A. "Marketing Authorization Procedures in the European Union—Making the Right Choice." *Life Science Technical Bulletin* December 2009.
20. Ibid.
21. Op cit 18.
22. *Suggested Format for Developing and Responding to Deficiencies in Accordance with the Least Burdensome Provisions of FDAMA; Final Guidance for Industry and FDA Staff* (November 2000). FDA website. http://www.fda.gov/RegulatoryInformation/Guidances/ucm073679.htm. Accessed 9 January 2017.
23. Ibid.
24. Ibid.
25. Ibid.

# 19

## Interdisciplinary Document, Dossier Maintenance

*By Evelyn De La Vega*

## Introduction

When thinking of regulatory, it is easy to believe the work focus is simply developing submissions, product development strategies and communicating with regulators. However, regulatory includes the critical task of interdisciplinary document and dossier maintenance. Maintenance is required to ensure a marketed product remains in compliance with current standards and continues to fulfill the applicable quality system regulation requirements. This chapter discusses the different types of interdisciplinary documents common in US and EU dossiers, along with the concept of lifecycle management.

It is common for a number of dossier documents to remain unchanged; however, a few documents require routine updating due to the type of information they contain. This information is updated to reflect internal changes or improvements or ever-changing regulations and performance standards. In the US, Good Documentation Practices (GDPs) and Good Manufacturing Practices (GMPs) are revised and issued in a controlled and specifically documented system as part of the Code of Federal Regulations (CFR). These GDPs and GMPs then are subject to regular audits by the Food and Drug Administration (FDA). In contrast, the EU regulations enforce GDPs and GMPs in a less regimented manner. These also are subject to Notified Body or Competent Authority audits.

## Identifying Requirements

Different product types require different maintenance levels. In the US, device and drug submissions have to be maintained throughout the product lifecycle. Device requirements are based on the product's classification, with the exception of a few special devices that may require still higher classification requirements. Class I devices are not required to maintain a Design History File; however, the product must be made in accordance with GMPs. For this classification, Standard Operating Procedures (SOPs) and complaint files have to be kept and monitored. Class II and Class III devices require complete Design History Files under a full quality system, so data availability is significantly higher than for Class I devices. Both Class II and Class III devices require complaint records but also may need other postmarket surveillance documents (i.e., clinical and trending data).

In addition, submissions for most Class II devices include several types of documents that require routine lifecycle management, e.g., risk management information, stability data, sterilization validation, clinical data, product or engineering drawings, labeling, standard compliance and SOPs. For Class III devices, the same list applies, as well as patient brochures, requested safety data and applicable approvable promotional and marketing materials. A submission as a whole also requires its own maintenance in the form of annual reports, supplements or other types of submissions.

EU technical files and design dossiers contain a large amount of information and are not too different from each other in regard to content. Design dossiers may contain additional safety information reserved for specially classified or higher-risk devices. The EU classification system comprises Class I, IIa, IIb and III products. EU Class I devices are required to maintain technical files; however, they typically contain minimal information. Class IIa, IIb and III devices contain similar information to Class II and III US files but also include EU-specific documents such as clinical evaluation reports, Essential Requirements checklist, standards list, safety updates and a declaration of conformity that are revised on a routine basis. Postapproval changes are submitted through change notifications.

Pharmaceutical submissions, much like devices, also require document lifecycle management, based on the type of submission. Investigational drug applications contain a long list of documents to support labeling, chemistry, manufacturing and controls as well as pharmacology and toxicology information. This information is subject to change and is monitored throughout the clinical study. This information also is used in the drug application and requires monitoring throughout the review process. The application as a whole uses supplements throughout the product lifecycle. A similar process takes place in the EU, where drugs are subject to a clinical trial application and a Marketing Authorisation Application. All Marketing Authorisation Holders for medicines are legally bound to submit updated information. The agency uses this information to support data analysis, regulatory activities and communication. Changes to a device after approval are reviewed through a type variation submission process. A list of typical, routinely maintained documents seen in both device and drug submissions is included in the subsequent section.

Besides the US and EU, other countries also require dossier maintenance to market in that particular region. One notable submission is the Device Master File and Plant Master File information requested by India. The Device Master File contains an enormous amount of information regarding product design, development, verification and validation. It contains similar interdisciplinary documents as those required by the US and EU and, therefore, also requires routine maintenance. The Plant Master File contains information on company operations, procedures, personnel and environmental details. Using SOPs is common in that section of the file to maintain current information and minimize repeated

revisions. Routine dossier maintenance is becoming more and more common globally.

## Identifying Key Documents Requiring Maintenance

The US submissions (Investigational Device Exemption (IDE), 510(k) (Premarket Notification), Premarket Approval Application (PMA), Investigational New Drug Application (IND), New Drug Application (NDA), Abbreviated New Drug Application (ANDA)) and EU submissions (technical file, design dossier, Clinical Trial Application (CTA) and Market Authorisation Application (MAA)) for devices and drugs require maintenance of various document types to maintain product marketing compliance. These documents are updated constantly due to changes to the product, process or new data obtained.

The following list describes documents commonly maintained in various types of drug and device dossiers:

- Annual product review—documented evidence a drug product's quality standards have been evaluated to determine the need for adjustments in product specifications, manufacturing and control procedures. In the EU, this also requires a review of starting materials including packaging materials used; a review of marketing authorization variations submitted, granted or refused; and a review of postmarketing commitments.
- Drug Master Files—submission to FDA that may be used to provide confidential detailed information about facilities, processes or articles used in the manufacturing, processing, packaging and storing of one or more human drugs.
- Labeling—can be any part of the product or packaging labeling that is either immediately on the package or attached to it and the Instructions for Use. These are updated as needed.
- Risk Management—can be one or more documents required to fulfill quality system requirements regarding the assessment of a product's risks. Documentation includes a risk management plan, fault modes and effects analysis (FMEA), risk analysis or risk management reports. These are updated as needed and according to performance standards.
- SOPs—these contain all the basic operational instructions regarding the quality system and its various areas of focus such as quality control, quality assurance, quality monitoring and general quality system procedures. These are updated as needed.

- Shelf life/stability testing—testing that determines a given product's shelf life dating based on accelerated and/or real-time testing in product, package integrity and sterility tests. These are updated according to testing protocol requirements.
- Sterilization—testing that validates the parameters to be used for a particular product to confirm the required sterility assurance level. Depending on the sterilization process used, revalidation or routine audits must be completed and documented to ensure the original sterilization parameters remain valid. These are updated according to testing protocol requirements.
- Postmarket surveillance reports—the practice of monitoring and documenting a drug or medical device's safety after it has been released on the market; it is an important part of pharmacovigilance. These are updated according to internal procedures or specific FDA-mandated requirements.
- Standard assessments—evaluations completed against particular industry standards and documented with evidence of compliance with respect to an individual product or family of products. These are updated as needed and must remain up to date at all times.
- Essential Requirements checklist—required for EU device submissions; includes a number of requirements that need to be met according to the applicable medical device directive for a given product. These are updated as needed and correlate with current standards.
- Declaration of conformity—a sponsor's declaration stating compliance with the applicable medical device directive for a given product. These are updated as needed.
- Clinical evaluation report (CER)—a living document required for the EU market for all classes of new and existing devices, detailing a product's clinical evaluation throughout its lifecycle. These typically are updated annually.
- Literature search or monitoring—periodic published literature searches for peer-reviewed articles on similar devices or drug substances. These are updated as needed and must correlate with the CER, annual reports and safety updates.
- Safety update—periodic review of safety data such as complaints, postmarket surveillance, clinical and literature information. Can be in the form of a Periodic Safety Update Report (PSUR, periodic reporting on an approved medicinal product's safety) or a Drug Safety Update Report (DSUR, periodic reporting on the safety of medicinal products in clinical development) and the safety specification component that might be submitted with the marketing application.
- Periodic Benefit-Risk Evaluation Report (PBRER)—contains continuing analysis of relevant safety, efficacy and effectiveness information throughout a medicinal product's lifecycle—promptly (as important findings occur) and periodically—to allow an overall assessment of the accumulating data or additional safety signals. Typically includes safety-related, effectiveness, limitations of use or alternative treatments information pertinent to its benefit-risk assessment.
- Quality metrics—documented evidence that metrics calculated from data collected provide objective measures that, when used with additional internal data, will provide indicators of the pharmaceutical manufacturing quality system's effectiveness. These are updated as needed.
- Company Core Data Sheet (CCDS)—data sheet including sections related to safety, indications, dosing, pharmacology and other information concerning a medicinal product. A practical option is the use of the latest CCDS in effect at the end of the reporting interval as the reference product information for both the risk sections of the PBRER and the main approved indications for which a benefit is evaluated. These are updated as needed.
- Solicited reports—reports derived from organized data collection systems, including clinical trials, registries, postapproval, named patient use programs, other patient support and disease management programs, patient or healthcare provider surveys or information gathered on efficacy or patient compliance. These are updated as needed.

Maintaining routine and periodic updates in documents such as these is important because it aids in evaluating a drug or device's performance after it has been approved for marketing. The collection and use of new and additional information forces both the sponsor and the regulatory agency to ensure a product's safety to benefit the public health.

**Table 19-1. IDE Annual Report Contents**

| Basic elements |
| --- |
| Study progress includes clinical data from beginning of the study and summary of anticipated and unanticipated adverse effects, deviations |
| Risk analysis |
| Other changes, also may include summary of any changes in manufacturing practices and quality control |
| Future plans |

**Table 19-2. PMA Annual Report Contents**

| Basic elements |
| --- |
| Approved and pending supplements |
| Table of manufacturing, design and labeling changes that did not affect S&E |
| Literature search—published and unpublished |
| UDI information |
| Number of devices sold |

**Table 19-3. IND Annual Report Contents**

| Individual study information |
| --- |
| Summary information |
| Update to the general investigational plan |
| Investigator's Brochure updates |
| Significant protocol updates |
| Updates on foreign marketing developments |
| A log of outstanding business |

**Table 19-4. ANDA/NDA Annual Report Contents**

| Basic elements |
| --- |
| Manufactured batches, batch record, yield review |
| Change control review |
| Label and artwork change review |
| Analytical data review |
| Stability data review |
| Validation and qualification review |
| Nonconformances and LI review |
| Rejected/re-packaged batches review |
| Complaint review |
| Field alert and recall review |
| Retained sample review |
| GMP agreement |
| Previous APR review |
| Conclusions and recommendations |
| References |

## Specific Dossier Maintenance

Dossier maintenance also includes completing formulated and mandated annual reports containing specific information collected on a periodic basis. Both drug and device sponsors are required to submit this information. **Tables 19-1–19-4** contain a list of information typically found in an IDE, PMA, IND or NDA annual report.

In the EU, an annual product/quality review typically is completed. This consists of an evaluation of product materials, packaging materials and product changes that have been either submitted, approved or rejected. This also includes a review of any postmarketing commitments.

These are all special reports that must be completed annually, even if no changes have been made to a product's design, packaging or manufacturing process.

The EU also provides several databases for collecting, reporting, coding and evaluating data on medicines in a standardized and structured way.

## Cost to Business

Dossier and interdisciplinary document maintenance is an ever-consuming activity critical to business continuity. At times, and determined by the number of products in the market, several FTEs may be dedicated to these regulatory operational responsibilities. It has become the regulatory professional's role to be held accountable for adhering to current standards and regulatory filing obligations. However, it takes the efforts of an interdisciplinary team.

Failure to maintain dossiers and documents can result in several major issues, such as audit findings, disciplinary actions, loss of business continuity and an inability to prove a drug or device's safety and performance continuously throughout its lifecycle.

A regulatory professional can take several measures to navigate these potential issues successfully. The first is education and communication with key stakeholders and upper management. Their support will affect a team's ability to complete mandatory tasks in the proper timelines. Second, identifying subject matter experts early and obtaining their agreement on tasks are critical. Without interdisciplinary assistance, maintenance activities cannot be completed. Agree and place into practice data retrieval activities according to a schedule that coincides with key submission dates.

Additionally, identifying past nonconformances or audit observations that resulted from poor maintenance will help the regulatory professional understand where more effort is needed. It also will provide insight on why the regulatory agencies value particular documents and requirements. Sometimes, external experts can be utilized to help close gaps in such areas as labeling management or standard analysis, where specific expertise is needed. They also can help organize and maintain critical timelines in the event other personnel are temporarily unavailable.

With respect to internal documents and dossier management, electronic systems may be used. Validated systems allow elimination of manual or paper processes and are essential when dealing with a large number of files. They allow better organization and ensure critical deadlines are met.

## Conclusion

With such a large number of individual product or product family reports, documents and submissions requiring maintenance, it is necessary to maintain them in a controlled system. The ongoing introduction of new products makes maintenance a greater and greater task. The regulatory professional is an essential player in this role.

### References
- *The European regulatory system for medicines and the European Medicines Agency: A consistent approach to medicines regulation across the European Union.* European Parliament website. http://www.europarl.europa.eu/meetdocs/2014_2019/documents/envi/dv/ema_promo_/ema_promo_en.pdf. Accessed 28 December 2016.
- Kashyap UN, Gupta V, Raghunandin HV. "Comparison of Drug Approval Process in United States & Europe." *J. Pharm. Sci. & Res.* Vol.5(6), 2013, 131–136.
- Pazhayattil A. Annual Product Reviews: How to Conduct an Effective Annual Product Quality Review. 1 February 2012.
- IDE Application Reporting: Annual Reports. FDA website. http://www.fda.gov/MedicalDevices/ DeviceRegulationandGuidance/HowtoMarketYourDevice/InvestigationalDeviceExemptionIDE/ucm046717.htm#sugforforidepro. Accessed 28 December 2016.
- IND Application Reporting: Annual Reports. FDA website. http://www.fda.gov/Drugs/DevelopmentApprovalProcess/HowDrugsareDevelopedandApproved/ApprovalApplications/InvestigationalNewDrugINDApplication/ucm362663.htm. Accessed 28 December 2016.
- *Guidance for Industry and Food and Drug Administration Staff: Annual Reports for Approved Premarket Approval Applications (PMA)* February 2014. FDA website. http://www.fda.gov/downloads/medicaldevices/deviceregulation-andguidance/guidancedocuments/ucm089398.pdf. Accessed 28 December 2016.
- *Providing Regulatory Submissions in Electronic Format—General Considerations: Draft Guidance for Industry.* FDA website. http://www.fda.gov/RegulatoryInformation/Guidances/ucm124737.htm. Accessed 28 December 2016.
- *Guidance for Industry: Adaptive Design and Clinical Trials for Drugs and Biologics.* FDA website. http://www.fda.gov/downloads/Drugs/.../Guidances/ucm201790.pdf. Accessed 28 December 2016.

### Author

Evelyn De La Vega is a medical device industry consultant with more than 14 years of experience focusing on regulatory, quality systems and clinical affairs. Previously, she held positions with Abbott Laboratories Inc., Bausch + Lomb and B. Braun Medical. Her areas of expertise include regulatory strategy, US and global submissions, product development, company initiatives and due diligence. De La Vega is a member of the Board of Directors for the Orange Country Regulatory Affairs Discussion Group (OCRA), has earned the RAC (US) and holds an MS in regulatory science from the University of Southern California, Los Angeles.

# 20

# Value Dossiers

*By E. Mitchell Seymour, PhD, RAC and Kayla Ambroziak, PharmD*

## Introduction

In addition to health authority approval for marketing, drug companies seek reimbursement (drug coverage) for their products through payers such as insurance companies, both private and public (government). This chapter focuses on value dossiers (also known as health technology assessments (HTA)), which are used in the regulatory setting and often required as part of the reimbursement process. They are critical tools in Health Economics and Outcomes Research (HEOR), including Comparative Effectiveness Research (CER). In addition to reimbursement purposes, companies use these dossiers as guidance for upcoming studies and product lifecycle planning. They often are developed between product clinical testing Phase 3 and Phase 4, but can be revised later as the market changes, particularly in Phase 4.

As with other regulatory documents, clear and concise writing is imperative for value dossiers. These documents are read by many people with varied roles and educational backgrounds. In addition, their content varies widely from more-narrative socioeconomic arguments to detailed calculations and displays of cost-effectiveness. Visual information may be more important than in a typical regulatory document, as a picture "can be worth a thousand words" to the harried reviewer or medical professional. Illustrations and graphic data are very influential

additions to the value dossier and should be planned and executed thoughtfully.

## Value Dossier Purpose

Value dossiers are systematic, robust, transparent documents that:

- describe the product
- provide background on the relevant disease(s) indicated
- present the product's economic, humanistic and clinical value
- illustrate product safety and efficacy
- provide evidence to support product claims

## Primary Audiences for Value Dossiers

### Payers

Payers like insurance companies and government bodies are interested in professional guidelines and cost-effectiveness to determine coverage and product value. Payer team members may include clinical pharmacists, physicians and key opinion leaders (KOLs); health economists; managed care experts; regulatory professionals; and epidemiologists. Decisions to cover particular drugs are driven by both the unmet medical need and the cost, and these decisions may change over time as new information becomes available in both medical need and safety/effectiveness data.

**Table 20-1. AMCP Format**

| Section # | Section Title | Subsections[a,b] |
|---|---|---|
| 1 | Executive Summary | 1.1 Clinical Benefits |
| | | 1.2 Economic Benefits |
| | | 1.3 Conclusions |
| 2 | Product Information and Disease Description | 2.1 Product Description |
| | | 2.2 Place of the Product in Therapy |
| | | 2.3 Evidence for Companion Diagnostic Tests |
| 3 | Clinical Evidence | 3.1 Study Summaries |
| | | 3.2 Evidence Tables |
| 4 | Economic Value and Modeling Report | 4.1 Modeling Overview |
| | | 4.2 Cost Effectiveness Analysis |
| | | 4.3 Budget Impact Model |
| | | 4.4 Modeling Report and Interactive Model |
| 5 | Additional Supporting Evidence | 5.1 Clinical Practice Guidelines |
| | | 5.2 Health Technology Assessments and Systematic Reviews |
| | | 5.3 Compendia |
| | | 5.4 Other Economic or Outcomes Evidence |
| | | 5.5 Impact on Quality |
| | | 5.6 Other Evidence or Information |
| 6 | Dossier Appendices | 6.1 References Contained in Dossiers |
| | | 6.2 Economic Models |
| | | 6.3 Product Prescribing Information |
| | | 6.4 Patient Information |
| | | 6.5 Material Safety Data Sheet |

a. Additional subsections are present within these second-level headings.
b. Content descriptions are available at http://www.amcp.org/FormatV4/.

**Table 20-2. Comparison of AMCP Dossier and International HTA**

| AMCP Dossier | International HTA |
|---|---|
| • Summary | • Summary |
| • Background of disease | • Background of disease |
| • Product information | • Product information |
| • Clinical value | • Clinical value |
| • Economic value | • Economic value |
| • Supporting information | • Treatment options and guidelines |
| | • Unmet need |

## Healthcare Professionals

Healthcare professionals like pharmacists and physicians look for evidence pertinent to their patient population that supports the product value.

Pharmacists typically review these documents as part of formulary boards, helping to make decisions on coverage for new drugs. Their role is to confirm the information included will allow the audience to make informed decisions regarding use of the new health technology. Pharmacists ensure the document addresses safety, therapeutic value, disease burden and cost-effectiveness. This review helps decision makers overcome uncertainties and reach a decision more easily.

Physicians also may review these documents as part of formulary decisions, or even clinical care decisions if they are provided these documents by the company or its representatives. Therefore, the documents must remain current to the gold standards of clinical treatment and to the very latest prevalence data on a particular indication. Dated and/or inaccurate information will jeopardize the medical reviewer's impression of the entire value dossier, even if other information and value calculations in the dossier are accurate.

## Regional Differences in Value Dossiers

Value dossiers are used worldwide, especially with tightened regulations requiring companies to exhibit their products' value.

In the US, the Academy of Managed Care Pharmacy (AMCP) outlines evidence requirements in the AMCP Format (AMCP, 2016)[1] for use by manufacturers responding to unsolicited requests from healthcare decision makers (HCDMs) to support coverage, reimbursement and/or formulary placement of new and existing drugs, tests, devices or classes of drugs, tests or devices.

The AMCP Format supports the informed selection of drugs, tests and devices by:
- identifying the evidence required for evaluating the clinical and economic value of drugs, companion diagnostic tests and devices
- standardizing the synthesis and organization of the evidence in a concise document also known as the "AMCP dossier" or "product dossier"
- providing the manufacturer the opportunity to communicate a product's value that is grounded in evidence-based medicine principles
- supporting FDA's established unsolicited request process by which manufacturers must abide to

**Table 20-3. Team Members and Their Responsibilities**

| Role | Tasks |
|------|-------|
| Clinical Pharmacists/Physicians/Key Opinion Leaders (KOLs) | Healthcare professionals provide information to illustrate the treatment's importance and impact. Their opinions are critical for reimbursement. |
| Health Economists | Health economists leverage product insights, endorse strategy and align teams to optimize patient access and product reimbursement. |
| Managed Care Experts | Managed care experts provide the payers' perspective regarding pricing and reimbursement. |
| Regulatory | Regulatory professionals are a vital team component to ensure the information being communicated complies with all regulations (e.g., FDA, EMA). |
| Epidemiologists | Epidemiologists certify the messages illustrated in the dossier support reimbursement, according to outcomes and label claims. |
| Medical Writers, Editors | Medical writers translate health outcomes research into effective communications for both internal and external use. |

provide comprehensive information that goes beyond a product's FDA-approved label
- requiring economic models and projections of product impact on the organization and its enrolled population
- encouraging a clear, transparent and two-way communication process between manufacturers and HCDMs

The AMCP Format is designed to maintain a high standard of objectivity and credibility. Table 20-1 lists its sections and subsections.

Unfortunately, many countries do not have set templates to follow like the one provided by AMCP. Accordingly, there is much variation in dossiers written outside the US. However, all HTAs focus on evidence-based reports illustrating safety, efficacy, product value and the social, legal and economic impacts of use. This information is critical for guidance decisions regarding reimbursement.

There are variations among countries due to differences in healthcare coverage, culture and politics. In Japan, there has been limited HTA use.[2] Their use is expected to grow due to the need for increased healthcare access. Similarities and differences between the AMCP Dossier and HTA are described in Table 20-2. In Europe, HTAs often include background information on treatment options, professional guidelines and unmet medical need.[3,4] The AMCP may include these as part of supporting information, but their requirement is less proscribed.

## Compilation of Value Dossiers

The writing teams for these dossiers are very diverse, more so than those involved in drug marketing applications, making their compilation even more challenging. Some

roles and tasks are described in Table 20-3. While medical writers and editors are listed last, their role obviously is critical to harmonize the varied participants' messages. Artists and graphic designers also may be included as part of the writing and editing team to create effective visuals that summarize and enhance the narrative content.

## Sources of Education for Value Dossiers/HTA writing

Comprehensive HEOR and value dossier training resources include:
- ISPOR HTA Training Program: http://www.ispor.org/Education/HTATraining/Index
- HealthEcomonics.com: http://www.healtheconomics.com

**References**
1. The AMCP Format for Formulary Submissions Version 4.0 Copyright Academy of Managed Care Pharmacy April 2016. AMCP website. http://www.amcp.org/FormatV4/. Accessed 19 January 2017.
2. Kennedy-Martin T, Mitchell B, Boye K, et al. The health technology assessment environment in mainland China, Japan, South Korea, and Taiwan—implications for the evaluation of diabetes mellitus therapies. Value in Health Regional Issues 3C. 2014. 108-116.
3. Velasco-Garrido M, Busse R. Health technology assessment: An introduction to objectives, role of evidence, and structure in Europe. European Observatory on Health Systems and Policies. World Health Organization. 2005. WHO website. http://www.euro.who.int/__data/assets/pdf_file/0018/90432/E87866.pdf. Accessed 19 January 2017.
4. Velasco-Garriso M, Borlum-Kristensen F, Palmhoj-Nielsen C, Busse R. Health technology assessment and health policy-making in Europe: Current status, challenges and potential. European Observatory on Health Systems and Policies. World Health Organization. 2008. WHO website. http://www.euro.who.int/__data/assets/pdf_file/0003/90426/E91922.pdf. Accessed 19 January 2017.

**Authors**

E. Michell Seymour, PhD, RAC (US),  is the principal regulatory consultant for R&D Advisors, providing regulatory outsourcing services for industry and academia. His experience includes regulatory writing and regulatory submissions, FDA meeting preparation and engagement, regulatory strategy, regulatory intelligence and regulatory due diligence. Seymour also is an adjunct clinical professor at the University of Michigan College of Pharmacy and adjunct faculty in San Diego State University's graduate regulatory science program. He is an active member of the American Medical Writers Association. Seymour holds a PhD in biochemical and molecular nutrition from Michigan State University and the RAC (US).

Kayla Ambroziak is a Doctor of Pharmacy graduate from the University of Michigan College of Pharmacy. She has a strong interest in the pharmaceutical industry, as it allows her to assist in positively impacting millions of patients, indirectly, while working in cross-functional groups with team members from various backgrounds.

# 21

# Vaccines and Biologics

*By Lisa DeTora*

Biologics and vaccines can be considered subspecialty areas within the regulatory writing or medical writing communities.[1] However, as noted by writing experts, regulatory professionals within industry and regulators, specialty knowledge tends to stem not from differences in the types of documentation produced so much as scientific distinctions between biologics and chemically-derived small molecules.[2] For example, the definitions of biologics may vary depending on prior historic decisions, current scientific understanding and regulatory realities.[3] Thus, differences in regulatory writing for biologics are not related to document types. In other words, medical and regulatory writing for biologics generally requires the same basic documents required for small molecules, including:

- protocols
- informed consent forms
- Investigator's Brochures
- study reports
- background packages
- pediatric investigational plans
- Investigational New Drug applications (INDs)
- safety reporting

The general rules for producing and formatting such documents are the same for biologics and small molecules. Although differences may arise when writing US marketing applications, where biologics may be marketed under a New Drug Application (NDA) and/or a Biologics Licensing Application (BLA), as described by Robinett, the Common Technical Document (CTD) format may be used for both.[4] In short, regulatory writing about biologics requires a basic knowledge of regulatory writing in general as well as specialized knowledge about biologics, including regulatory definitions and applicable regulations.

This chapter reviews definitions of biologics, as well as key scientific and regulatory differences that can impact documentation, and provides high-level advice about effective writing in this complex scientific area.

## Defining Biologics

The history of the modern manufacture of biologics begins in the 19th century, but underwent a significant revolution in the 1980s when genomics became advanced enough to enable the manufacture of engineered proteins using cell cultures. Biologics and biomanufacturing are expected to increase in importance in the coming decades.[5]

Scientifically, the definition of biologics presents challenges because various groups express differing opinions, each of which is based on specific evidence.[6] Regulatory definitions are important because they help determine the appropriate methods for research and documentation to support marketing or registration.

**Table 21-1. Some Current US Biological Produce Definitions**

| 21 CFR 600.3 | The Public Health Service Act[a] | FDA Basics[b] |
|---|---|---|
| Any virus, therapeutic serum, toxin, antitoxin or analogous product applicable to the prevention, treatment or cure of diseases or injuries of man. | A virus, therapeutic serum, toxin, antitoxin, vaccine, blood, blood component or derivative, allergenic product or analogous product, or arsphenamine or derivative of arsphenamine (or any other trivalent organic arsenic compound), applicable to the prevention, treatment or cure of a disease or condition of human beings. | Biological products, or biologics, are medical products. Many biologics are made from a variety of natural sources (human, animal or microorganism). Like drugs, some biologics are intended to treat diseases and medical conditions. Others are used to prevent or diagnose diseases. Examples of biological products include: vaccines, blood and blood products for transfusion and/or manufacturing into other products, allergenic extracts, which are used for both diagnosis and treatment (for example, allergy shots), human cells and tissues used for transplantation (for example, tendons, ligaments and bone), gene therapies, cellular therapies and tests to screen potential blood donors for infectious agents such as HIV. |

a.   *Public Health Service Act (1944) Section 351 (a)(2)(C)(i)(I), updated under the Food and Drug Administration Modernization Act (FDAMA) in 1996.*
b.   *FDA Basics. What is a biological product? FDA website. http://www.fda.gov/AboutFDA/Transparency/Basics/ucm194516.htm. Accessed 17 January 2017.*

## Basic Definitions

Biologics, also known as biologically-derived or biological products, are medical products made from or containing substances derived from human or animal tissues, microorganisms or their cellular components.[7] Biologics can be derived directly from native sources or produced through genetic recombination. Some examples of biologics are vaccines, monoclonal antibodies and recombinant blood factor products. In general, biologics are much larger than chemically derived or small, molecules;[8–11] for example, aspirin is many orders of magnitude smaller than a monoclonal antibody. Epidermal growth factor receptor (EGFR) therapeutics in oncology (mAbs) tend to be around 150 kiloDaltons in size, compared with small molecules, which tend to be around 500 Daltons,[12] and even a nanobody, which is markedly smaller than a monoclonal antibody, remains orders of magnitude larger than a small molecule.[13] In the US, the broad biologics category includes all such products whether their intended mode of action is medicinal, therapeutic, diagnostic, curative or preventative[14,15] (**Table 21-1**, **Box 21-1**).

In the US and Europe, development, regulatory approval, postapproval surveillance and manufacturing processes and controls may all differ between biologics and chemically synthesized drug products; similarly, important regulatory differences exist between generics or 'follow on' biosimilar products. Regulatory definitions can have an important impact on product lifecycle management. For example, following the passage of the US *Patient Portability and Affordable Care Act* (*PPACA*),[16] certain novel biologics receive data protection for 12 years, compared to five years for new drug products, which reflects the costs of development and overcoming manufacturing challenges to enable large-scale production.[17,18]

Definitions of biologics vary between pages of the US Food and Drug Administration (FDA) website (**Table 21-1**).

As Kingham et al. note, distinctions between drug products and biologics in the US have been defined and adjusted on an *ad hoc* basis as a matter of policy, which has led to some inconsistencies.[19] While definitions in the US have changed over time, in the EU, current definitions are based on the identity of active substances and manufacturing methods (**Table 21-2**); of interest, several definitions provided by the European Medicines Agency (EMA) appear in biosimilars guidance.[20] In the US, some definitions of biologics also include proteins, especially in guidance written after after the passage of the *PPACA*.[21]

Of note, the International Council on Harmonisation (ICH) *Preclinical Safety Evaluation of Biotechnology-Derived Pharmaceuticals S6(R1)*, initially finalized in 1997, identifies the initial development of such products during the 1980's.[22]

In the US, 21 CFR 600 Biologics[23] also applies to trivalent organic arsenical compounds, defined as arsphenamine and its derivatives or any other trivalent organic arsenic compound applicable to the prevention, treatment or cure of diseases or injuries of man and included under the definition of biologics in the *Public Health Service Act* (*PHS Act*) of 1944.[24]

Therapeutic biologics, much like small molecule drug products, can be used to treat or cure disease in individual patients. In contrast, vaccines are intended to prevent disease whether for individuals, as with travel vaccines, or on a public health basis, as with routine childhood, adolescent and adult immunizations. Other biologic products are used in diagnosing diseases or other medical conditions.

## Therapeutic Biologics

In the US, biologics and drugs have been regulated by different offices and agencies over time (**Box 21-2**).[25] In 1991, an Intercenter Agreement between FDA's Center for Drug Evaluation and Research (CDER) and Center for Biologics Evaluation and Research (CBER) defined biologics versus drug products, largely on the basis of the active ingredient or manufacturing method (**Table 21-3**). The Intercenter Agreement left in place all products with approval pending under a BLA or NDA and allowed new products similar to already-approved products to continue to be assigned to CBER and CDER on an ad hoc basis by a jurisdiction committee. As of 30 June 2003, therapeutic biologics became the purview of CDER, while all other biologics and vaccines are handled by CBER.[26]

Thus, a definition of therapeutic biologics may be helpful for those preparing regulatory documentation (**Table 21-4**). Of note, these definitions and descriptions provide additional, helpful information regarding the agency's biologics' classifications. For example, monoclonal antibodies and gene therapy products are not mentioned in the definitions in **Table 21-1**, although such products are specified under 21 CFR 601.2. This shows not only the evolving nature of US definitions noted by Kingham et al.,[27] but also the results of a dynamic, innovative culture in biotechnology.[28]

As noted by Kingham and colleagues, regulatory definitions in the US have evolved over time.[29] Thus, the definitions and categories in **Box 21-2** do not fully overlap with those in **Table 21-1** or **Box 21-1**, each of which was provided by the FDA as guidance for industry, reviewers, and consumers. Furthermore, additional clarifications of the identity of biologics under the *PPACA*[30] now include proteins that are not grown in a biological source.[31]

## Specified Products Under 21 CFR 601.2

Most biologic products currently regulated by CDER fall into a one of four categories "specified" in 21 CFR 601.2,[32] to which certain regulations do not apply:[33]

- therapeutic DNA plasmid products
- therapeutic synthetic peptide products of 40 or fewer amino acids
- monoclonal antibody products for in vivo use
- therapeutic recombinant DNA-derived products

As indicated in 21 CFR 601.2, for the above product categories, 21 CFR sections 600.10(b) and (c), 600.11, 600.12, 600.13, 610.53 and 610.62 do not apply. Therefore, documentation for such products should reflect these requirements.

## Biotechnology-Derived Products

ICH S6 distinguishes between biotechnology-derived products and other biological products, marking the advent of such products in the 1980s.[34] The guidance's scope extends to:

- Products derived from characterized cells via a variety of expression systems including bacteria, yeast, insect, plant and mammalian cells.

**Box 21-1. Specific Biologic Product Definitions in 21 CFR 600.3**

A **virus** is interpreted to be a product containing the minute living cause of an infectious disease, including but not limited to filterable viruses, bacteria, rickettsia, fungi and protozoa.

A **therapeutic serum** is a product obtained from blood by removing the clot or clot components and the blood cells.

A **toxin** is a product containing a soluble substance poisonous to laboratory animals or man in product doses of one milliliter or less (or equivalent in weight) and having the property, following the injection of non-fatal doses into an animal, of causing to be produced therein another soluble substance that specifically neutralizes the poisonous substance and is demonstrable in the serum of the animal thus immunized.

An **antitoxin** is a product containing the soluble substance in serum or other body fluid of an immunized animal that specifically neutralizes the toxin against which the animal is immune.

A product is **analogous:**
To a virus if prepared from or with a virus or agent actually or potentially infectious, without regard to the degree of virulence or toxicogenicity of the specific strain used.

To a therapeutic serum, if composed of whole blood or plasma or containing some organic constituent or product other than a hormone or an amino acid, derived from whole blood, plasma or serum.

To a toxin or antitoxin, if intended, regardless of its source of origin, to be applicable to the prevention, treatment or cure of disease or injuries of man through a specific immune process.

**Box 21-2. US Biologics Regulation (1902–2003) Selected Important Developments[a]**

1902: The Public Health Service Hygenic Laboratory is established to regulate biologics under the *Biologics Control Act*

1906: The first *Pure Food and Drug Act* is passed; enforcement took place under the Bureau of Chemistry in the Department of Agriculture[b]

1927: Food Drug and Insecticide Administration added to the Bureau of Chemistry

1930: Biologics are regulated under the National Institutes of Health (NIH); Bureau of Chemistry becomes the Food and Drug Administration

1937: NIH creates the Division of Biologics Control

1938: The *Federal Food, Drug, and Cosmetic Act* (*FD&C Act*) is passed to update the 1906 *Pure Food and Drug Act* and requires product safety testing before marketing

1940: FDA transferred to the Federal Security Agency

1944: The *Public Health Service Act* (*PHS Act*) is passed, establishing rules for the licensure and regulation of biologics that remain current into the 21st century

1955: Division of Biological Control established as an independent entity in NIH

1968: FDA is moved to the Public Health Service

1972: FDA establishes a Bureau of Biologics; biologics regulation is transferred from NIH to FDA

1983: FDA Center for Drugs and Biologics established; *Orphan Drug Act* is passed

1986: *Childhood Vaccine Act* gives FDA authority to recall biologics and requires patient information regarding vaccines

1988: FDA Center for Biologics Evaluation and Research (CBER) and Center for Drug Evaluation and Research (CDER) established; *Food and Drug Administration Act* established FDA as a part of the Department of Health and Human Services

1991: CDER and CBER execute an Intercenter Agreement dividing products derived from living material between the two centers;[c] another Intercenter Agreement clarifies the centers responsible for various combination products[d]

1996: *Food and Drug Administration Modernization Act* (*FDAMA*) passes; among other developments, it amends the *PHS Act* to require stricter controls over certain potentially deadly biologics

2003: FDA transfer of therapeutic biologics to CDER

a.   FDA. About FDA. *Significant Dates in US Food and Drug Law History.* Available at: http://www.fda.gov/AboutFDA/WhatWeDo/History/Milestones/ucm128305.htm. Accessed 19 December 2016.

b.   Meadows M. Promoting Safe and Effective Drugs for 100 Years. *FDA Consumer magazine.* January-February 2006. Available at: http://www.fda.gov/AboutFDA/WhatWeDo/History/CentennialofFDA/CentennialEditionofFDAConsumer/ucm093787.htm. Accessed 19 December 2016.

c.   FDA. *Intercenter Agreement Between the Center for Drug Evaluation and Research and the Center for Biologics Evaluation and Research.* Available at: http://www.fda.gov/CombinationProducts/JurisdictionalInformation/ucm121179.htm. Accessed 19 December 2016.

d.   Kingham R, Klasa G, Carver KH. Key Regulatory Guidelines for the Development of Biologics in the United States and Europe. *Biological Drug Products: Development and Strategies. First Edition.* New York: Wiley, 2014.

o   These products active substances include proteins and peptides, their derivatives and products of which they are components.

o   The products may be derived from cell cultures or produced using recombinant DNA technology including production by transgenic plants and animals.

- Examples include but are not limited to: cytokines, plasminogen activators, recombinant plasma factors, growth factors, fusion proteins, enzymes, receptors, hormones and monoclonal antibodies.

The biotechnology-derived products described above and included within the scope of ICH S6 may cover intended indications such as in vivo diagnostic, therapeutic or prophylactic uses.[35] Excluded are: antibiotics, allergenic extracts, heparin, vitamins, cellular blood components, conventional bacterial or viral vaccines, DNA vaccines or cellular and gene therapies.[36] These biotechnology-derived

products correspond to what has been termed biomanufacturing 3.0 in a recent history.[37]

## Vaccines

Vaccines are an important subset of biological products. The US Department of Health and Human Services (HHS) defines vaccines as products that produce immunity from disease.[38] The World Health Organization (WHO) describes vaccines as a category of biologicals that improve immunity.[39] Vaccines are intended to prevent disease in an individual or, more commonly, a population basis, and, thus, often are considered as public health or military interventions. This circumstance affects clinical investigations of vaccines because vaccine efficacy studies require large-scale population-based evaluations of disease incidence.

Vaccines stimulate innate and/or acquired immunity in the host, generally through the administration of an inactivated form or component of a microbial pathogen (i.e., bacterium or virus). Thus, vaccines are intended to operate in advance of exposure to a disease-causing pathogen and to mobilize the body's own defenses to prevent disease. Vaccine clinical studies, therefore, often measure markers of immune response.

Vaccines can be divided into various types, depending on the population intended to be treated, the formulation, or the desired immune response. For example, routine childhood and adolescent immunization schedules are intended to protect the full population and therefore are considered public health measures. In contrast, travel vaccines should protect an individual who might be exposed to foreign pathogens. Vaccines for military recruits, elderly patients in group homes, pilgrims to the Hajj, healthcare workers and college freshmen are intended to protect individuals entering these new environments as well as those with whom they come into contact. Vaccines also can be categorized based on their content, as for whole-cell versus component-based pertussis vaccines, or on expected immune responses: anamnestic versus B-cell mediated.

## Regulation of Biologics

### Public Health Service Act (1944, amended 1996)

The history of formal regulation of biologics antedates the history of formal US drug regulation, and began in 1902 with passage of the *Biologics Control Act*, which was enacted in part to address the diphtheria epidemic of 1901.[40] The *Biologics Control Act* gave the Public Health Service and Marine Hospital Service's Hygienic Laboratory the ability to issue regulations. These regulations required annual licensure for manufacturers of vaccines, sera and antitoxins and gave inspectors the

ability to shut down facilities that violated regulations or posed public health dangers. Production was to be overseen by a qualified scientist. The *Biologics Control Act* also established standards for product labels, including clear presentation of the product name and expiration date.[41]

Subsequent laws governing the manufacture of many biologics include the *Food, Drug, and Cosmetics Act* (*FD&C Act*) and its amendments and the *PHS Act*, which provides a system of manufacturing controls and rapid interventions when these controls are not met, particularly in settings with a possible public health impact, such as the manufacture of seasonal influenza vaccines (**Box 21-2**). For example, vaccine manufacturers can be asked to cease production if an inspection reveals findings that my impact public health. The *PHS Act* also indicates that manufacturers must hold a license, which is to be obtained through a Biologics License Application (BLA).

In general, the history of biologics has been punctuated by public health problems such as epidemics or disease outbreaks caused by specific biological agents. For example, in 1955, inadequately inactivated polio virus was included in vaccines, which caused a disease outbreak, prompting the formation of the NIH Division of Biological Standards.[42] Various shifts of biologics regulation from one agency or division to another have been marked by disease outbreaks or other public health problems (**Box 21-2**).

Section 351 of the *PHS Act* includes specific examples of applicable biologics (**Table 21-1**). In addition, a 1996 amendment to the *PHS Act* under the *Food and Drug Administration Modernization Act* (*FDAMA*) states:

1. certain biological agents have the potential to pose a severe threat to public health and safety

**Table 21-2. European Medicines Agency (EMA) Biologics Definitions**

| EMA Glossary | Biosimilars | EMA Questions and Answers on Biosimilar Medicines |
|---|---|---|
| A medicine whose active substance is made by a living organism.[a] | Biological medicines are medicines that are made by or derived from a biological source, such as a bacterium or yeast. They can consist of relatively small molecules such as human insulin or erythropoietin, or complex molecules such as monoclonal antibodies.[b] | A biological medicine is a medicine that contains one or more active substances made by or derived from a biological source. Some of them may be already present in the human body, and examples include proteins such as insulin, growth hormone and erythropoietins. The active substances of biological medicines are larger and more complex than those of non-biological medicines. Only living organisms are able to reproduce such complexity. Their complexity as well as the way they are produced may result in a degree of variability in molecules of the same active substance, particularly in different batches of the medicine.[c] |

a.   *Glossary; Biological medicine. EMA website. http://www.ema.europa.eu/ema/index.jsp?curl=pages/document_library/landing/glossary.jsp&mid=&start-Letter=B. Accessed 17 January 2017.*

b.   *Biosimilar Medicines. EMA website. http://www.ema.europa.eu/ema/index.jsp?curl=pages/special_topics/document_listing/document_listing_000318.jsp. Accessed 17 January 2017.*

c.   *Questions and Answers on Biosimilar Medicines (EMA/837805/2011). EMA website. http://www.ema.europa.eu/docs/en_GB/document_library/Medicine_QA/2009/12/WC500020062.pdf. Accessed 17 January 2017.*

2. such biological agents can be used as weapons by individuals or organizations for the purpose of domestic or international terrorism or for other criminal purposes

3. the transfer and possession of potentially hazardous biological agents should be regulated to protect public health and safety

4. efforts to protect the public from exposure to such agents should ensure that individuals and groups with legitimate objectives continue to have access to such agents for clinical and research purposes

These measures were introduced to address possible terrorism, the use of biological weapons or accidents involving highly dangerous pathogens. Therefore, certain biological agents (such as anthrax or other highly communicable or deadly diseases) are subject to much stricter controls than others (such as recombinant Factor VIII products).

All biologics are subject to regulation under the *PHS Act* (See **Table 21-1**).[43] Biological products subject to the *PHS Act* also meet the definition of drugs under the current version of the *FD&C Act*.[44] However, some protein products, such as insulin, glucagon and human growth hormone, are regulated only under the *FD&C Act* and not the *PHS Act* due to historic precedent and the scientific principles the agency uses to classify biologics on an *ad hoc* basis.[45] Therefore, regulatory professionals and their research teams must consider the applicability of the *PHS Act* and other regulations to their products.

### Potency, Purity, Sterility

While chemically synthesized small molecular weight drugs, or "small molecules," generally have a well-defined structure that can be thoroughly characterized, this is not the case for many biological products. Often, large, complex molecules derived from living materials, such as whole cells used in vaccines and native proteins are heterogeneous and, consequently, cannot be characterized fully. Although recombinant biologics or products containing recombinant proteins may be less heterogeneous and better characterized than naturally occurring proteins, the manufacturing conditions for these proteins (e.g., cell culture) remain inherently more variable than those in large-scale chemical synthesis. Thus, biologic products must be evaluated for purity and potency, and the facilities in which they are manufactured must be able to ensure consistency. These evaluations, in some cases but not all, take the place of required safety and efficacy assessments that would be reported in an NDA.[46]

Potency assays are required because of the molecular complexity of biologics and can be understood as a surrogate for efficacy in some, but not all, circumstances.[47] For example, assessments of vaccine-induced antibodies against a target pathogen via an assay could be used to measure potency. However, vaccine efficacy may be assessed via population-based trials, which means that researchers and regulatory professionals must review current regulations and requirements.

Purity and safety assessments must consider the storage and testing of any cell substrates used in manufacture. Sterility, or freedom from contaminating microorganisms, must be assessed because source materials may transmit undesirable adventitious agents such as bacteria, fungi or viruses.[48]

The potency, sterility and purity assessment requirements are in 21 CFR 600[49] and the *PHS Act*.[50] See **Box 21-3** for the 21 CFR 600 definitions.

### Biosimilars or Follow-on Products

An additional important distinction between many biologic products and small molecules is the scientific and regulatory handling of generics. Whereas generic products generally must be identical in chemical composition to the original product, this is impossible for many biologic products.[51] Therefore, biologicals with similar properties, or biosimilars, may be developed following unique rules as described elsewhere in this book.[52]

## Scientific and Therapeutic Considerations

Therapeutic areas in which biologics have been identified as a means or possible means of addressing key targets include:

- anemia
- cancers
- cystic fibrosis
- diabetes
- growth deficiency
- hemophilia
- hepatitis
- inflammatory bowel disease
- rheumatoid arthritis
- some sexually transmitted diseases
- transplant rejection[53,54]

Each of these therapeutic areas is constrained by certain regulatory and research conventions that can affect documentation. For example, in oncology, unlike many other therapeutic areas, there often is a strong research justification for initiating Phase 1 trials in patients who have been unresponsive to other treatments instead of healthy adults.[55] This practice generally is undertaken because nonclinical toxicity findings indicate that risks to healthy volunteers may be unacceptable, not only because

**Table 21-3. Division of Products Between CDER and CBER Under the 1991 Intercenter Agreement[a]**

| CDER Responsibilities | CBER Responsibilities |
|---|---|
| Naturally occurring substances purified from mineral or plant source materials (excluding vaccines or allergenics):<br>• products produced from nonhuman animal or solid human tissue sources (excluding animalderived procoagulant products or antisera, venoms, red blood cell replacement products, vaccines, allergenic products, products composed of living cells, and certain other products)<br>• antibiotics as defined by Section 507(a) of the FD&C Act, regardless of the method of manufacture:<br>  o  certain agreedupon classes of substances constitutively produced by fungi or bacteria including: disaccharidase inhibitors and HMGCoA reductase inhibitors<br>• chemically synthesized molecules (excluding vaccines and allergenics) including: products produced by chemical synthesis that are intended to be analogies of cytokines, thrombolytics, or other biologic, or that function by binding to the receptors for biological products, chemically synthesized mononucleotide or polynucleotide products, including products complementary to RNA or DNA sequences<br>• hormone products, regardless of method of manufacturing, e.g., insulin, human growth hormone, pituitary hormones | **Biological products subject to licensure:**<br>• vaccines, regardless of method of manufacture, including those vaccines that at the effective date of this agreement are being studies under the active INDs administered by CDER (For the purpose of this agreement, a vaccine is defined as an agent administered for the purpose of eliciting an antigen-specific cellular or humoral immune response)<br>• in vivo diagnostic allergenic products, in vivo diagnostic tests for DTH, and allergens regardless of the method of manufacture intended for therapeutic use as "hyposensitization" agents<br>• human blood or human blooderived products including placental blood-derived products, animalderived procoagulant products and animal or cell culturederived hemoglobinbased products intended to act as red blood cell substitutes<br>• immunoglobulin products, whether monoclonal or polyclonal, produced in humans, animals or in cell culture<br>• products composed of or intended to contain intact cells or intact microorganisms including bacteria, fungi, viruses or virus pseudotypes, or viral vectors<br>• protein, peptide or carbohydrate products produced by cell culture excepting antibiotics, hormones, other products and products previously derived from human or animal tissue and regulated as approved drugs<br>• protein products produced in animal body fluids by genetic alteration of the animal, i.e., transgenic animals<br>• animal venoms or constituents of venoms<br><br>**Other product classes:**<br>• synthetically produced allergenic products that are intended to specifically alter the immune response to a specific antigen or allergen<br>• certain drugs used in conjunction with blood banking and/or transfusion |

a.   *Frequently Asked Questions About Therapeutic Biological Products. FDA website. http://www.fda.gov/Drugs/DevelopmentApprovalProcess/ HowDrugsareDevelopedandApproved/ApprovalApplications/TherapeuticBiologicApplications/ucm113522.htm. Accessed 15 January 2017.*

of adverse event profiles but also because the clinical data collected would not be helpful when considering the target patient population. In this therapeutic area, some biologics such as monoclonal antibodies, may impart fewer adverse events (such as hepatic or renal toxicity) because of differences in metabolism and excretion.[56]

## Specificity

Biologics, unlike small molecules, can be designed to target specific genetic mutations, replace particular proteins or bind at certain sites, which has implications for studies in many rare disease indications. Special studies are required to identify specific disease-causing mutation(s); when multiple mutations cause different types or subtypes of a disease, as in cystic fibrosis, multiple biologics would be required, and each new agent would be capable of treating only a subset of the rare disease population.[57] These considerations also are important in oncology, where treatments increasingly are being targeted to specific tumor types.[58]

Species specificity may affect nonclinical research.[59] For example, a biologic may not have the intended effects in nonhuman animals that lack specific receptors. In some cases, biologics may be more effective in animal models than in humans because of differences in immunogenicity, as when a biologic is recognized by the human immune system but not in murine models, leading to an overestimation of effects.[60] Differences in immunogenicity between species also can impact nonclinical safety evaluations.[61]

Orphan indication research generally is eligible for expedited review under the *Prescription Drug User Fee Act* (*PDUFA*), which presents additional logistical challenges and opportunities as discussed elsewhere in this book.[62] Rare disease settings often require adjustments to clinical studies to address one or more of the following potential challenges:

- small clinical trial sample sizes due to small patient populations and competing studies
- small number of potential investigators
- lack of verifiable or accepted endpoints for clinical trials

- lack of expert reviewers at the agency or health authority
- viability of scale-up and sustained, consistent manufacturing for small populations of patients[63]

### Nonclinical Science

As noted above, it may be impossible to characterize biologics fully, a circumstance that can affect nonclinical and clinical pharmacology studies.[64] For example, it may be difficult to characterize the absorption, distribution, metabolism, and elimination (ADME) pathways of protein products, especially those designed to replace naturally-occurring proteins.[65]

Thus, nonclinical and clinical programs often must be designed and evaluated on an *ad-hoc* basis, which presents challenges in regulatory documentation. Dossiers and documents should reflect program and study design rather than adhering too closely to guidance documents. ICH emphasizes the authors' responsibility to present nonclinical and clinical data to enhance reader understanding.[66] If direct study is impracticable, authors may need to rely on published information about similar products or proteins.

FDA has adopted ICH S6, which outlines the necessary steps to identify:

- an initial safe dose and subsequent dose escalation schemes in humans
- potential target organs for toxicity and whether this toxicity is reversible
- safety parameters for clinical monitoring[67]

These nonclinical research goals are similar to those for chemically derived pharmaceuticals as presented in the ICH *Guidance on Nonclinical Safety Studies for the Conduct of Human Clinical Trials and Marketing Authorization for Pharmaceuticals M3(R2).*[68] ICH S6 provides supplemental guidance for specific biotechnology products. As noted in this guidance[69] and by Kingham et al., nonclinical studies must be adjusted on a case-by-case basis to address problems of specificity and known side effects, such as developing immunogenicity against the product.[70]

Other types of studies, such as carcinogenicity and teratogenicity studies, may be less useful or inapplicable, depending on the specific biologic and intended clinical setting. These considerations have led to the need for careful design of biologics nonclinical programs on an individual basis.[71]

### Vaccines

Special considerations that may affect documentation stem largely from the need to evaluate vaccines as both a means of inducing immune responsiveness in individuals and a public health intervention. Vaccines against diseases with high incidence may be evaluated for immunogenicity—that is, antibodies formed in response to the vaccine's ability to kill the target organism—and also for their efficacy in reducing the expected disease incidence in a particular population. Thus, different types of studies may be performed to meet requirements demonstrating potency (as for all biologics) as well as expected benefits (as for any drug or vaccine product).

For some vaccines, it is difficult—for logistical or ethical reasons—to develop assays that measure immunogenicity directly.[72] Therefore, biological correlates of protection may be established and measured to support the product's immunogenicity and expected efficacy. Generally, these correlates are evaluated by specially designed assays (e.g., for evaluating meningococcal vaccines) that must be validated and accepted by regulatory agencies in addition to the clinical data they are used to evaluate. In some cases, development and acceptance of such protection correlates took place alongside pivotal clinical trials due to public health needs and the devastating characteristics of meningococcal disease.

Vaccines, which generally are administered to healthy persons, must support a benefit-risk balance that warrants their use in individuals.[73] The fact vaccines prevent rather than treat disease creates a much stronger safety burden for manufacturers. Very few unwanted side effects are considered tolerable, especially in vulnerable populations like infants and the elderly. Further, since expected benefits depend on widespread immunization, vaccines must be available and affordable. Also of note, since the route of administration generally is via injection (either intramuscular or subcutaneous), vaccine safety evaluations must account for reactions at, or proximal to, the injection site as well as systemic reactions, which can complicate documentation.

For childhood vaccines, safety and immunogenicity must be tested in accepted vaccination schedules to ensure concomitant administration of multiple products does not increase unwanted side effects unduly or cause antigen interference that might reduce protection. Similar considerations are important for evaluating combination vaccines—or vaccines containing antigens for several diseases or conditions. Clinical studies of such vaccines in infants pose challenges in areas such as assay development and evaluation; ethically, only limited amounts of blood may be collected from infants, and researchers, therefore, must plan assays carefully. Consistency across study centers and over time, while always important, is more critical in settings where it is unlikely repeat testing will be possible to interpret inconsistencies.

**Box 21-3. Sterility, Purity and Potency Definitions (21 CFR 600)**

The word **sterility** is interpreted to mean freedom from viable contaminating microorganisms, as determined by the tests conducted under 21 CFR 610.12.

**Purity** means relative freedom from extraneous matter in the finished product, whether or not harmful to the recipient or deleterious to the product. Purity includes but is not limited to relative freedom from residual moisture or other volatile substances and pyrogenic substances.

The word **potency** is interpreted to mean the specific ability or capacity of the product, as indicated by appropriate laboratory tests or by adequately controlled clinical data obtained through the administration of the product in the manner intended, to effect a given result.

## Regulatory Documentation

Regulatory documentation can be affected by many factors that remain uncertain for biologics and, to a lesser extent, vaccines. For example, given the urgency of developing treatments and vaccines against emerging deadly diseases, it is possible the research process can be accelerated in some cases.[74] In all cases, documentation must explain:

- the product development rationale
- how the research plan was designed
- studies undertaken to demonstrate potency and efficacy (if applicable)
- the safety profile, including side effects related to mode of administration and undesirable immune effects (if applicable)
- these studies' sufficiency to support benefits versus risks
- the manufacturing plan and how consistency, sterility and purity will be assured

As noted above, the history of biologics and vaccines has been informed by a need for case-by-case adaptations of studies, development programs and research considerations. Thus, documentation must be designed to reflect scientific and clinical decisions.

### Individual Study Reports

As noted elsewhere in this book, the ICH *Structure and Content of Clinical Study Reports E3* guidance recommends clinical research sponsors adapt the report format to accommodate special study design features and agency review.[75] It may be useful to add subheadings or rename headings, as ICH E3 suggests, to guide reviewers. For example, vaccine studies generally measure immunogenicity rather than efficacy and differentiate vaccine efficacy study results (in populations) from those of individuals' immunogenicity. Therefore, replacing the term "efficacy" with "immunogenicity" may be warranted in clinical study reports.

In addition, although injection or infusion site reactions might be included in Clinical Study Report Section 12.3, which includes deaths and significant adverse events, it may be more logical scientifically to break down the overall adverse event reporting in Section 12.2, which reports overall adverse events, into 'local' and 'systemic.' In studies where reactions at more than one injection site must be described and discussed, it may be helpful to develop a specific, consistent framework for reporting reactions at each injection site systematically to aid review. Similarly, the report sections describing methods should be adapted to parallel results sections, so reviewers more easily may find the specific measures and procedures used. If several similar studies are performed in a clinical program, consistency across reports can aid review.

In many organizations, clinical study report templates are mandated and may be embedded in dossier publishing systems. Organizations should consider their overall product pipeline's profiles when establishing templates. In some cases, it may be necessary to develop templates or guidelines for unique studies.

### Integrated Documentation

As noted elsewhere in this book,[76-78] integrated documentation must account for reviewers' needs and also accommodate collaboration across scientific specialty areas. For example, colleagues in serology or assay development may contribute to integrated discussions of clinical outcomes across vaccine studies. Input from genomics experts may enhance discussions of recombinant products. Therefore, as with all research in vaccines and biologics, teams should be constituted based on specific program needs, on a case-by-case basis. This may pose challenges in organizations where SOPs mandate document authors. As with report templates, organizations should consider the needs of all products or develop separate SOPs for biologics and vaccines.

Integrated documentation for BLAs and NDAs may follow the ICD format. Robinett has published a detailed

**Table 21-4. Division of Therapeutic Biological Products in CDER and Those Remaining in CBER as of 30 June 2003[a,b]**

| Biological Products Regulated by CDER (Under the *FD&C Act* and/or *PHS Act*, effective 30 June 2003) | Biological Products Regulated by CBER (Under the *FD&C Act* and/or *PHS Act*) |
|---|---|
| Monoclonal antibodies for in vivo use.<br><br>Most proteins intended for therapeutic use, including cytokines (e.g., interferons), enzymes (e.g., thrombolytics), and other novel proteins, except for those specifically assigned to CBER (e.g., vaccines and blood products). This category includes therapeutic proteins derived from plants, animals, humans or microorganisms and recombinant versions of these products. Exceptions to this rule are coagulation factors (both recombinant and human-plasma derived).<br><br>Immunomodulators (non-vaccine and non-allergenic products intended to treat disease by inhibiting or down-regulating a preexisting, pathological immune response).<br><br>Growth factors, cytokines and monoclonal antibodies intended to mobilize, stimulate, decrease or otherwise alter the production of hematopoietic cells *in vivo*. | Cellular products, including products composed of human, bacterial or animal cells (such as pancreatic islet cells for transplantation) or from physical parts of those cells (such as whole cells, cell fragments, or other components intended for use as preventative or therapeutic vaccines).<br><br>Gene therapy products. Human gene therapy/gene transfer is the administration of nucleic acids, viruses or genetically engineered microorganisms that mediate their effect by transcription and/or translation of the transferred genetic material, and/or by integrating into the host genome. Cells may be modified in these ways *ex vivo* for subsequent administration to the recipient or altered *in vivo* by gene therapy products administered directly to the recipient.<br><br>Vaccines (products intended to induce or increase an antigen-specific immune response for prophylactic or therapeutic immunization, regardless of the composition or method of manufacture).<br><br>Allergenic extracts used for the diagnosis and treatment of allergic diseases and allergen patch tests.<br><br>Antitoxins, antivenins and venoms<br><br>Blood, blood components, plasma-derived products (e.g., albumin, immunoglobulins, clotting factors, fibrin sealants, proteinase inhibitors), including recombinant and transgenic versions of plasma derivatives (e.g., clotting factors), blood substitutes, plasma volume expanders, human or animal polyclonal antibody preparations including radiolabeled or conjugated forms and certain fibrinolytics such as plasma-derived plasmin, and red cell reagents. |

a.  *These agreements do not supersede or alter the prior division of CDER and CBER regulated products under the Intercenter Agreement executed in 1991. FDA. Intercenter Agreement Between the Center for Drug Evaluation and Research and the Center for Biologics Evaluation and Research. Available at: http://www.fda.gov/CombinationProducts/JurisdictionalInformation/ucm121179.htm. Accessed 15 January 2017.*

b.  *Frequently Asked Questions About Therapeutic Biological Products. FDA website. http://www.fda.gov/Drugs/DevelopmentApprovalProcess/ HowDrugsareDevelopedandApproved/ApprovalApplications/TherapeuticBiologicApplications/ucm113522.htm. Accessed 15 January 2017.*

discussion on handling BLAs in the CTD format.[79] The discussion provides invaluable advice for handling chemistry, manufacturing and controls (CMC) documentation and offers high-level tips for avoiding annoyance factors (such as acronym and company jargon use) in the BLA. As noted above and in US guidances and regulations, documentation reflecting an understanding of the prior approval of similar products as well current practice in the therapeutic area can facilitate agency reviewers' work.

Unlike the ICH E3 guideline, CTD guidelines under ICH M4 do not recommend specifically that sponsors adapt the overall format to accommodate scientific discussion. Therefore, authoring teams must decide how to present sufficient information to allow regulators to evaluate their products and also handle the CTD structure. For example, in a program for a biologic product for which traditional nonclinical ADME studies were impracticable because of product characteristics, teams should include adequate information in the nonclinical written summary to justify the study choices and the expected product disposition profile. Similarly, in vaccine programs including both population efficacy studies and patient immunogenicity studies, care should be taken to ensure the clinical summary is clear and explains the relationships between the data collected and overall label claims.

In addition, especially for products eligible for expedited approvals, teams should review other regulatory requirements and *PDUFA* guidelines.[80] Of note, although many biologics and vaccines are developed to address acute, dangerous conditions or public health situations for which there are no current remedies, concerns also have been raised not only because of development programs that may skip phases, but also because these molecules may be characterized poorly.[81] Therefore, it is important to ensure regulatory documentation addresses these possible concerns.

Safety and manufacturing updates, as necessary, must follow appropriate guidelines. Regulatory professionals should ensure all integrated documentation can be easily adapted for downstream submissions.

## Conclusion

Biologics and vaccines are highly complex molecular entities. Although the regulatory documentation basics for these products are similar to those for chemically derived products, special considerations include adjustments to address scientific complexities, the history of case-by-case regulatory agency assessments of such products and the need to adapt standard documentation to address complex scientific realities.

### References

1. Swann P. Archived Document: Quality Review—Biologics. CDER Forum for International Regulators. FDA website. http://www.fda.gov/downloads/drugs/newsevents/ucm182539.pdf. Accessed 16 January 2017.
2. Van Etten A. What's Different About Regulatory Writing for Biologics? American Medical Writing Association National Meeting. San Antonio, TX. October 2015.
3. Morrow T, Felcone LH. "Defining the Difference: What Makes Biologics Unique." *Biotechnology Healthcare.* (2004) Sept: 24–30.
4. Robinett RSR. The Biologics License Application (BLA) in Common Technical Document (CTD) Format. *Vaccine Development and Manufacturing.* First edition. New York: Wiley, 2015.
5. Zhang YHP, Sun J, and Ma Y. Biomanufacturing: History and Perspective. J Ind Microbiol Biotechnol. 2016; DOI: 10.1007/s10295-016-1863-2.
6. Op cit 3.
7. FDA. Frequently Asked Questions About Therapeutic Biological Products. Available at: http://www.fda.gov/Drugs/DevelopmentApprovalProcess/HowDrugsareDevelopedandApproved/ApprovalApplications/TherapeuticBiologicApplications/ucm113522.htm. Accessed 16 January 2017.
8. Op cit 3.
9. Op cit 1.
10. Op cit 2.
11. Kingham R, Klasa G, Carver KH. Key Regulatory Guidelines for the Development of Biologics in the United States and Europe. *Biological Drug Products: Development and Strategies.* First Edition. New York: Wiley, 2014.
12. Imai K and Takaoka A. Comparing antibody and small-molecule therapies for cancer. *Nature Reviews Cancer.* (2006) 6:714–727.
13. Kijanka M et al. Nanobody-based Cancer Therapy of Solid Tumors. *Nanomedicine.* 2015; 10 (1): 161–174.
14. 21 CFR Part 600. Biologics. FDA website. https://www.accessdata.fda.gov/scripts/cdrh/cfdocs/cfCFR/CFRSearch.cfm?CFRPart=600. Accessed 16 January 2017.
15. Op cit 7.
16. *Patient Portability and Affordable Care Act.* US Department of Health and Human Services website. https://www.hhs.gov/healthcare/about-the-law/read-the-law/#. Accessed 16 January 2017.
17. Op cit 11.
18. *Federal Food, Drug, and Cosmetic Act*, Sections 505(b) and (d). Government Printing Office website. https://www.gpo.gov/fdsys/granule/USCODE-2011-title21/USCODE-2011-title21-chap9. Accessed 16 January 2017.
19. Op cit 11.
20. Ibid.
21. Op cit 16.
22. *Preclinical Safety Evaluation of Biotechnology-Derived Pharmaceuticals S6(R1)* 2011. ICH website. http://www.ich.org/fileadmin/Public_Web_Site/ICH_Products/Guidelines/Safety/S6_R1/Step4/S6_R1_Guideline.pdf. Accessed 16 January 2017.
23. Op cit 14.
24. *Public Health Service Act* (*PHS Act*) (1944). FDA website. http://www.fda.gov/regulatoryinformation/legislation/ucm148717.htm. Accessed 15 January 2017.
25. FDA History. FDA website. http://www.fda.gov/AboutFDA/WhatWeDo/History/. Accessed 16 January 2017.
26. Transfer of Therapeutic Products to the Center for Drug Evaluation and Research (CDER). FDA website. http://www.fda.gov/AboutFDA/CentersOffices/OfficeofMedicalProductsandTobacco/CBER/ucm133463.htm. Accessed 16 January 2017.
27. Op cit 11.
28. Op cit 3.
29. Op cit 11, page 76.
30. Op cit 16, Section 7002(b)(2) (2010).
31. Op cit 11.
32. 21 CFR 601.2 Licensing. FDA website. http://www.accessdata.fda.gov/scripts/cdrh/cfdocs/cfcfr/CFRSearch.cfm?fr=601.2. Accessed 16 January 2017.
33. Op cit 1.
34. Op cit 11.
35. Op cit 22.
36. Ibid.
37. Op cit 5.
38. Vaccines. US Department of Health and Human Services website. https://www.vaccines.gov/basics/. Accessed 16 January 2017.
39. Vaccines. WHO website. http://www.who.int/topics/vaccines/en/. Accessed 16 January 2017.
40. Op cit 1.
41. Bren L. The Road to the Biotech Revolution—Highlights of 100 Years of Biologics Regulation. *FDA Consumer Magazine.* January-February 2006. FDA website. http://www.fda.gov/AboutFDA/WhatWeDo/History/FOrgsHistory/CBER/ucm135758.htm. Accessed 16 January 2017.
42. Op cit 1.
43. Op cit 24.
44. Op cit 18.
45. Op cit 11.
46. Op cit 1.
47. Honig S. The Investigational New Drug (IND) and New Drug Application (NDA) Process. Johns Hopkins website. http://ocw.jhsph.edu/courses/drugdevelopment/PDFs/IND-NDA%20Lecture.pdf. Accessed 16 January 2017.
48. Op cit 1.
49. Op cit 14.
50. Op cit 24.
51. Stevenson JG, Green L. Biologics, Pharamcovigilance, and Patient Safety: It's All in the Name. *JMCP.* 2016; 22 (8): 927–30.
52. Ramchnadani M. Chapter 22 Biosimilars. *Regulatory Writing: An Overview.* Regulatory Affairs Professionals Society, Rockville, MD. ©2017.
53. Op cit 3.
54. Chan CH, Ng SC. Emerging Biologics in inflammatory bowel disease. J Gastroenterol. 2016. DOI 10.1007/s00535-016-1283-0; Richey EA
55. *Guideline on evaluation of anticancer medicinal products in man (Draft).* 25 February 2016. EMA/CHMP/205/95 Rev 5. EMA

163

website. http://www.ema.europa.eu/docs/en_GB/document_library/Scientific_guideline/2016/03/WC500203320.pdf. Accessed 16 January 2017.

56. Op cit 12.

57. Gulbakan B et al. Discovery of Biomarkers in Rare Diseases: Innovative Approaches by Predictive and Personalized Medicine. *EPMA Journal.* 2016;7:24. DOI 10.1186/s13167-106-0074-2. Available at: https://epmajournal.biomedcentral.com/articles/10.1186/s13167-016-0074-2. Accessed 16 January 2017.

58. Kijanka M et al. Nanobody-based Cancer Therapy of Solid Tumors. *Nanomedicine.* 2015; 10(1): 161–174.

59. Op cit 11.

60. *Guidance on Nonclinical Safety Studies for the Conduct of Human Clinical Trials and Marketing Authorization for Pharmaceuticals M3(R2)* (2009). ICH website. http://www.ich.org/fileadmin/Public_Web_Site/ICH_Products/Guidelines/Multidisciplinary/M3_R2/Step4/M3_R2__Guideline.pdf. Accessed 16 January 2017.

61. Op cit 22.

62. Rupprecht J. Chapter 26 Accelerated Filings. *Regulatory Writing: An Overview.* Regulatory Affairs Professionals Society, Rockville, MD. ©2017.

63. Ibid

64. Depla E. Development of ALX-0171, an inhaled nanobody for the treatment of respiratory syncytial virus in infants. Presented at: Human Antibodies and Hybridomas. 31 March to 2 April 2014. Vienna.

65. Op cit 11.

66. Op cit 22.

67. Ibid.

68. Op cit 60.

69. Op cit 22.

70. Op cit 11.

71. Ibid.

72. Plotkin S. Correlates of Protection Induced by Vaccination. *CVI.* 2010; July:1055–1065.

73. Op cit 11.

74. Frey JL. Overview of the IND Process. CBER 101. Gaithersburg, MD.

75. *Structure and Content of Clinical Study Reports E3* (1995). ICH website. http://www.ich.org/fileadmin/Public_Web_Site/ICH_Products/Guidelines/Efficacy/E3/E3_Guideline.pdf. Accessed 16 January 2017.

76. Aslam M. Chapter 12 CMC Documentation. *Regulatory Writing: An Overview.* Regulatory Affairs Professionals Society, Rockville, MD. ©2017.

77. DeTora L. Chapter 13 Integrated Nonclinical Documentation. *Regulatory Writing: An Overview.* Regulatory Affairs Professionals Society, Rockville, MD. ©2017.

78. De Tora L. Chapter 14 Integrated Clinical Documentation. *Regulatory Writing: An Overview.* Regulatory Affairs Professionals Society, Rockville, MD. ©2017.

79. Op cit 4.

80. *Guidance for Industry. Expedited Programs for Serious Conditions—Drugs and Biologics* (May 2014). FDA website. http://www.fda.gov/downloads/Drugs/Guidances/UCM358301.pdf. Accessed 16 January 2017.

81. Richey EA, et al. Accelerated Approval of Cancer Drugs: Improved Access to Therapeutics Breakthroughs or Early Release of Unsafe and Ineffective Drugs. *J Clin Oncol.* 2009; 27:4398–4405.

**Author**

Lisa DeTora is an assistant professor of writing studies at Hofstra University and a guest lecturer in humanities at the Hofstra Northwell School of Medicine. She began her career in medical writing at Merck and Co. Inc. and was a co-author of the company's internal guidances to comply with ICH E3 and M4. Her subsequent work experience has included regulatory writing and publication management in various therapeutic areas.

**Acknowledgements**

I am grateful to Monica Ramchandani for critical comments and advice on this chapter. I also thank Jenny Grodberg for her review of the outline.

# 22

# Biosimilars: Special Considerations

*By Monica Ramchandani, MS, PhD*

## Introduction

Biologics, including biosimilars, are biological medicines derived from genetically modified living organisms. Biologics represent a large proportion of approved therapies for several conditions, including cancer and chronic inflammatory diseases. These products represent a significant growing portion of the healthcare expenditure.[1]

A biosimilar is a biologic product that is very like an already approved biologic product (originator biologic/reference biologic). The US Food and Drug Administration (FDA) defines a biosimilar as a product that is 'highly similar' to the reference innovator product, notwithstanding minor differences in clinically inactive components, and with no clinically meaningful differences between the proposed biosimilar and the reference innovator product.[2–5]

To improve access to biologics, the US Congress passed the *Biologics Price Competition and Innovation Act* of 2009, which authorized FDA to oversee an abbreviated and expedited pathway (351(k) pathway) for biosimilar approvals.[6] A major milestone since this act was approved came with FDA's approval of its first biosimilar, Zarxio® (filgrastim-sndz), in March 2015. Since then, FDA has approved two monoclonal antibody (mAb) biosimilars, Inflectra™ (biosimilar infliximab) and Amjevita™ (biosimilar adalimumab), and first fusion protein, Erelzi™ (biosimilar etanercept), and additional approvals are expected in coming months. The EU also has created

guidelines for biosimilar development and approval of biosimilars, with its first biosimilar approval in 2006 for human growth hormone.[7]

### Biosimilars Versus Generics

To understand the distinction between biosimilars and generics, it is important to comprehend the science behind biosimilars. Biosimilars are not analogous to generics because, unlike generics, they are not "copies" of innovator agents. Small-molecule generic drugs have relatively simple and well-defined chemical structures and are manufactured by chemical synthesis, whereas biologics are large, complex molecules with manufacturing processes involving living systems such as microbial and animal cells, typically cultivated to adapt to unique growth environments. These living systems are highly sensitive to manufacturing processes, so each biosimilar is expected to differ from both the innovator and from other biosimilars.[8,9] **Table 22-1** depicts the key distinguishing features of the regulatory pathways for innovator products, generics and biosimilars.

The challenge of producing a biosimilar product is quite different from reproducing a small molecule for a generic drug product. The design and development of a successful biosimilar require an in-depth understanding of the reference product's structure and function and similarity to the reference product in both structure and

**Figure 22-1. Stepwise Process for Biosimilarity Demonstration**

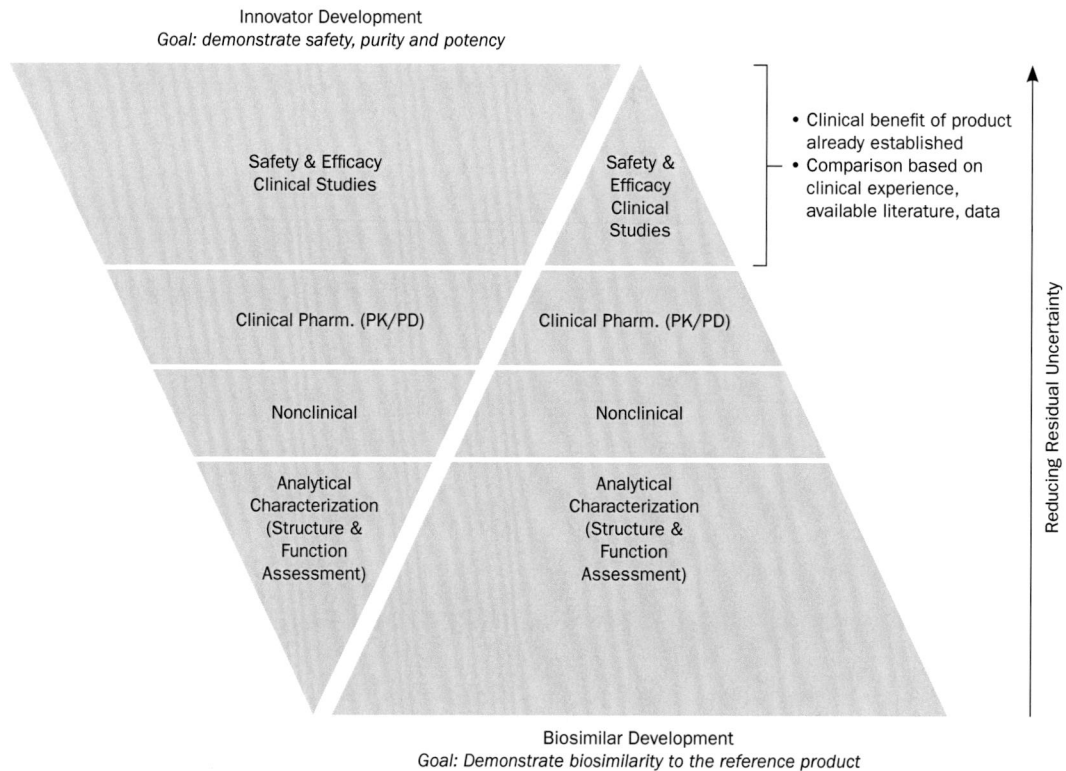

Innovator Development
*Goal: demonstrate safety, purity and potency*

Safety & Efficacy Clinical Studies

Safety & Efficacy Clinical Studies

- Clinical benefit of product already established
- Comparison based on clinical experience, available literature, data

Clinical Pharm. (PK/PD)

Clinical Pharm. (PK/PD)

Nonclinical

Nonclinical

Analytical Characterization (Structure & Function Assessment)

Analytical Characterization (Structure & Function Assessment)

Reducing Residual Uncertainty

Biosimilar Development
*Goal: Demonstrate biosimilarity to the reference product*

*Graphic adapted from Kozlowski S. Presented at: Biotechnology Technology Summit; June 13, 2014; Rockville, MD.*
*PD = pharmacodynamics; PK = pharmacokinetics.*

function, all with an eye to Quality-by-Design principles to ensure the biosimilar product's efficacy, safety and quality. A proposed biosimilar's target quality profile, therefore, is based largely on an understanding of the critical quality attributes used to evaluate potential analytical differences between the proposed biosimilar and the originator product, as well as their relationship to biological function.

## Biosimilars Development

To appreciate the challenges associated with biosimilars' development, it is important to understand the 351(k) regulatory pathway and how it differs from the originator or reference biologic product's pathway. **Figure 22-1** shows a schematic of the two regulatory pathways. The reference biologic's development pathway could be represented by an inverted triangle where analytical characterization (structural and functional) forms the bottom tip or vertex. This is followed by nonclinical characterization and clinical pharmacology assessments including Phase 1 studies and, finally, clinical investigations to

evaluate efficacy, safety and immunogenity. For innovator development, a clinical study has to be performed independently in each condition for which approval for use is sought. The program's goal is to establish safety and effectiveness of the new biologic agent.

As represented in the development triangle in **Figure 22-1**, the biosimilars' development pathway starts with analytical characterization, followed by nonclinical characterization, human pharmacology (pharmacokinetics (PK)/pharmacodynamics(PD)) and, finally, one comparative clinical study in a single representative indication to confirm similar efficacy, safety and immunogenicity with the innovator agent. The idea is to reduce residual uncertainty as the product moves up the development triangle. The goal of biosimilar development is not to demonstrate efficacy and safety *per se,* but to show the proposed biosimilar is similar to the innovator product.

FDA recommends a totality of evidence approach based on a stepwise biosimilar development process. The stepwise biosimilarity demonstration starts with analytical characterization, including structural and functional assessments, and, as noted above, is followed by nonclinical comparative pharmacology, PK and toxicology testing, and finally one or more clinical trials to confirm similar efficacy, safety and immunogenicity (**Figure 22-1**). The objective is to establish similarity assessment criteria based on the reference product profile, followed by a comparative assessment of the biosimilar candidate and the reference product. Thus, biosimilar development should begin with a comprehensive assessment of the reference product to understand its structural and functional characteristics. The knowledge and understanding gained from these studies then are used to develop a biosimilar product that matches the characterized reference product's structural and functional characteristics. A key feature of biosimilar development is a focused clinical development program in which the biosimilar's PK, efficacy, safety and immunogenicity are compared to those of the innovator product to confirm similarity. According to the guidelines, analytical studies form the cornerstone of biosimilarity demonstration. A high degree of analytical similarity and matching all biological functions provides justification for the reduced regulatory requirements for preclinical and clinical studies, which further justifies the overall abbreviated biosimilar approval process.

## Demonstrating Analytical Similarity

Extensive and robust comparative studies using state-of-the-art analytic techniques are required for a meaningful similarity assessment. Residual uncertainty is reduced if a comprehensive and well-designed analytical similarity assessment demonstrates the comparative results lie within prespecified assessment criteria based on reference product profiles. Physicochemical and biological properties should be shown to be highly similar between the proposed biosimilar and reference product. This assessment typically comprises a series of comparative studies of the proposed biosimilar and the reference product and examines product quality attributes in multiple analytical disciplines.

Analytical similarity assessment is a repetitive and iterative process conducted throughout biosimilar product development. The goal is to increase knowledge and confidence of the biosimilar candidate's analytical similarity with the reference product.[10,11] This includes determining the proposed biosimilar's biological activity with respect to the reference molecule's currently understood mechanism(s) of action. If the molecule, such as an mAb, contains multiple functional domains, the binding affinity and specificity at individual domains and the combined biological functions should be compared with those of the reference molecule.

It is important to understand the distinction between comparability and biosimilarity, as they pertain to

biosimilars' development. 'Comparability' refers to the comparative assessment of the biologic product's characteristics after a specific manufacturing process change, specifically implemented by the manufacturer for its product. Implementing such a change is supported by comprehensive knowledge and product development history. 'Biosimilarity,' on the other hand, is a relatively new concept where the sponsor develops a molecule to match in structure and function with the referece molecule using a new or different cell line and process. The biosimilarity demonstration is based on the comparative characterization of this new product produced by a different manufacturer with the innovator product.[12]

## Preclinical Considerations

During biosimilar development, animal studies for evaluating *in vivo* pharmacology (PK/PD), toxicology and immune response assays using suitable test species may serve to remove some residual uncertainty before human testing. Further, such *in vitro* assessments as cell-based bioactivity assays may be used as alternatives to *in vivo* studies.

## Clinical Considerations

The biosimilar clinical development program's goal is to demonstrate the absence of any clinically meaningful difference between the proposed biosimilar and the reference product. The clinical program's extent is determined by the residual uncertainty and the degree of similarity demonstrated in nonclinical and preclinical testing, including structural, functional and animal studies. According to FDA guidelines,[13] clinical efficacy studies may not be necessary if there is no residual uncertainty of biosimilarity between the proposed biosimilar product and the reference product, based on structural and functional characterization, animal testing and human PK and PD data (if there is a relevant PD efficacy marker). However, human safety and immunogenicity would need to be demonstrated through a clinical study in a sensitive population, with an appropriate duration of exposure and follow-up using sensitive assays to provide a totality of evidence and supplement the overall data, since these parameters otherwise cannot be predicted or determined indirectly. Comparative clinical efficacy and safety studies would be anticipated to be mandatory for large, structurally complex heterogeneous biologics such as fusion proteins and mAbs to confirm comparable efficacy and minimize the risk of adverse or undesirable outcomes.[14]

## Human Pharmacology (Pharmacokinetics and Pharmacodynamics)

Human PK and/or PD studies are fundamental to supporting biosimilarity and form a basis for product clinical evaluation. Proposed biosimilar clinical development begins with a Phase 1 study to demonstrate the candidate's PK similarity to the reference product.[15,16] This is central to the biosimilar abbreviated development program. When combined with the analytical and fuctional similarity demonstration, the pharmacological similarity demonstration allows the product to move forward to pivotal clinical studies directly after a Phase 1 study using the same therapeutic dose as the innovator product, without the need for Phase 2 studies. Human PD studies should be considered along with Phase 1 PK studies if a suitable marker relevant to the mechanism of action is available and provides information regarding clinical efficacy.

## Efficacy and Safety

Biosimilar clinical study design, including endpoints, assessment timing and trial duration, may be different from those in the innovator product safety and efficacy trial, because the intent is to detect clinically meaningful differences rather than *de novo* establishment of treatment effect.

Efficacy studies should be conducted in patient populations sensitive enough to detect clinically meaningful differences between the proposed biosimilar and the reference product.[17] The comparative clinical studies' goal is to demonstrate the biosimilar candidate has equivalent efficacy and has a comparable safety profile to that of the reference product. The most straightforward design is one in which the null hypothesis, based on a prespecified equivalence margin, is a two-sided test procedure demonstrating the proposed biosimilar is non- inferior and non-superior to the reference product.[18] The margins should be justified scientifically to enable detection of clinically meaningful differences between the proposed biosimilar and the reference product, if they exist. The primary efficacy endpoint may be a clinical benefit or meaningful surrogate. Ideally, safety is assessed in the same study as efficacy, but it is more important that safety be assessed in a sensitive population.

The use of surrogate endpoints is an important consideration during the development of biosimilars. For example, where overall survival is considered a gold standard for proving clinical benefit in oncology, it often is not a practical endpoint during biosimilar development; instead, the endpoints must be sensitive enough to detect any difference in activity. Overall response rate and complete response could be suitable endpoints.[19]

## Immunogenicity

FDA guidelines specifically emphasize that immunogenicity remains a critical factor when assessing biosimilarity, and that the agency will evaluate immunogenicity in a risk-based manner.[20] Most biopharmaceutical agents can induce immune responses, although in many cases these do not have clinically relevant consequences. The immune response may include development of antidrug antibodies (that could either bind to the drug with no consequence or reduce its effectiveness) or neutralizing antibodies (that eliminate activity). The most severe circumstance is the cross-reaction of antidrug antibodies with an endogenous protein, eliminating its critical function and potentially causing harm.

Of note, the extent of immunogenicity can vary due to manufacturing process changes for the same biosimilar product or differences among processes of different biosimilar and reference product manufacturers.

## Extrapolation

The concept of extrapolating indications is unique to biosimilars and creates the potential for a biosimilar product to be labeled for use in indications approved for the reference product that were not studied as part of the proposed biosimilar's clinical development program. This is an important consideration, because if clinical trials were needed for each indication, the breadth of biosimilar development programs effectively would negate the advantages of an abbreviated approval pathway.[21] The guidelines state extrapolation is allowable, provided scientific justification is available.[22] Scientific justification should address the mechanism of action, biodistribution, immunogenicity and expected patient population toxicities; these factors should be well-understood based on the proposed biosimilar's clinically evaluated indication(s) or should be justified scientifically based on the comprehensive similarity assessment. Additionally, any other factor that may affect the product's safety, effectiveness or immunogenicity in each condition of use should be addressed appropriately for each indication in the extrapolation justification. Supportive clinical data in a sensitive and representative population are critical to justifying extrapolation to other indications. Strong analytical and preclinical functional similarity, including matching all functions of the molecule and PK similarity, should provide support for extrapolation to additional indications.

## Other Regulatory Considerations

Implementing an abbreviated biologic product licensure pathway can pose challenges, given the scientific and technical complexities and hurdles that may be associated with larger and more complex biologic products.

### Geographic Jurisdiction

The law defines the innovator product as that approved in the local jurisdiction. Thus, for example, a proposed biosimilar must be shown to be similar to the US-approved reference product for US marketing authorization in the US, and shown to be similar to the EU-approved reference product for EU marketing authorization.[23] However, regulatory agencies acknowledge the complexity and expenses of biosimilar development and have taken steps to facilitate global development programs by implementing provisions to allow the use of foreign-sourced comparators in comparative clinical studies. From a regulatory and legislative perspective, acceptability of clinical data generated utilizing a foreign-sourced comparator is contingent upon successful establishment of a scientific bridge.[24] The scientific bridge between a local- and foreign-sourced reference product should include a comprehensive comparative analytical similarity assessment of the proposed biosimilar versus both comparators. Additionally, a three-arm PK similarity study in which bioequivalence is established among the proposed biosimilar and each respective comparator as well as two comparator arms should complete the bridge.

## Interchangeability

An additional regulatory consideration for biosimilars in the US is the determination of interchangeability. By law, an interchangeable biosimilar product is one in which the active drug substance has been shown to be biosimilar to the innovator product and is expected to produce the same clinical result as the reference product in any given patient.[25] For a biological product administered to an individual more than once, the safety or diminished efficacy risk due to alternating or switching between the biosimilar and reference products should not be greater than the risk of using the innovator product without such alternation or switch.[26] FDA now has issued draft guidance for demonstrating interchangeability.[27] This guidance also adopts the totality of evidence and stepwise approaches. According to this guidance, at least one switching study involving three or more switches between the biosimilar and its specific US-licensed reference product are required to support the expectation the biosimilar produces the same clinical result as the reference product in all indications of use. The sponsor may provide a scientific rationale to extrapolate data supporting interchangeability in one condition of use to the remaining conditions for which the reference product is licensed. It is recommended this study be conducted in appropriate patient populations in one or more indications of use with endpoints that assess the switch's impact on PK and PD (if a suitable PD marker is available). This is because PK and PD are expected to be more sensitive to changes in immunogenicity, if any, due to potential residual differences between the biosimilar and reference product that cause an immunogenic response stimulated by switching.

The request for interchangeability designation may be submitted as a supplement seeking approval for all the reference product's indications. Of note, the guidance states postmarketing data from products first licensed and marketed as biosimilar, without corresponding data derived from a prospective switching study or studies would not be sufficient to demonstrate interchangeability. The guidance further emphasizes the importance of adequate pharmacovigilance mechanisms for monitoring interchangeable products; postmarketing safety.[28]

## Naming and Pharmacovigilance

Some other considerations for successfully adopting biosimilars include naming criteria and safety monitoring or pharmacovigilance. FDA has issued guidance discussing the use of distinguishable names by adding a unique four-letter suffix to each biosimilar product's international nonproprietary name (INN).[29] It is important to remember approval for a particular biosimilar product's use in some indications will be based on evidence extrapolated from other indication(s), so each biosimilar agent may not be approved for all or even the same indications as the reference product. Therefore, distinguishable names for each biosimilar are vital to ensure the right medication has been dispensed to ensure optimal patient outcomes. This is an important consideration when deciding which product a patient should receive and avoiding inadvertent substitution by a pharmacist based on lack of a specific product name, particularly when products have not been approved as interchangeable. Distinguishable names also are important from a pharmacovigilance standpoint to ensure the appropriate attribution of adverse events. Thus, a robust risk management plan forms an integral part of the overall biosimilar program.

## Labeling

Appropriate, accurate labeling is an important consideration in biosimilar products' safe and effective use. A biosimilar product's label does not provide information regarding the clinical studies validating its biosimilarity or information about equivalent efficacy, safety or immunogenicity. Some countries like Canada and Japan have chosen to have transparent labels. However, the US and EU haven't elected to have biosimilar product labels nearly identical to those of the reference product. Labeling transparency could provide healthcare prescribers more confidence in these products with appropriate representation as biosimilars. This would be in contrast to generic drug labels, which essentially are replicas of those of their reference products and, therefore, are considered interchangeable upon approval. Since labeling is the primary source of information for practicing physicians,

**Table 22-1 Differences in Regulatory Requirements for Reference Products, Generics and Biosimilars**

| | **Reference Product** | **Generic** | **Biosimilar** |
|---|---|---|---|
| **Quality** | • Full process and product characterization | • Full process and product characterization<br>• Comparison with reference drug | • Full process and product characterization<br>• Comparison with reference biologic<br>• More involved than that for small molecules |
| **Preclinical** | • Full preclinical program | • N/A | • Abbreviated program based on complexity and residual uncertainty from quality |
| **Clinical** | • Phase 1 | • Bioequivalence only | • PK equivalence<br>• PD equivalence (dose-response) if marker available |
| | • Phase 2 | • N/A | • N/A |
| | • Phase 3 in all indications | • N/A | • Phase 3 in at least one representative indication[a] |
| | • Risk management plan[b] | • Yes | • Yes |
| | • Pharmacovigilance | • Yes | • Yes |

*N/A = not applicable; PK = pharmacokinetics; PD = pharmacodynamics.*
*a.   If the mechanism of action is the same.*
*b.   Requirement for the EU only.*

the current system does not allow transparency or provide physicians with information about the actual product being prescribed.[30,31] US biosimilar product labeling regulatory requirements currently are in development.

## Special Considerations

Confidence in using biosimilar products for human therapeutics will depend on robust quality, safety and efficacy standards. Meeting these standards begins with intentional science-based design, ensuring analytical and functional similarity followed by similar PK/PD characteristics and clinical efficacy, safety and immunogenicity profiles. Advances in cell culture engineering, state-of-the-art bioprocessing and high-resolution analytics have contributed to the ability to develop, design and manufacture molecules highly similar to originator or reference biologic products.

It is important to understand biosimilars are an independent new category of products calling for grassroots stakeholder education. Regulators, scientists, healthcare providers and payers all need to acquire in-depth knowledge regarding the science behind biosimilars. A major onus for providing appropriate educational venues falls on biosimilar manufacturers, medical writers and other content development experts. These individuals also need to acquire knowledge and understanding regarding biosimilars, their unique regulatory pathway and this pathway's implications for their approval and use.

There is considerable apprehension from both healthcare and patient communities regarding extrapolation,

interchangeability and substitution. Clinical study design for biosimilar evaluation is quite different from that for innovator products, in part because study populations and endpoints must be selected to ensure clinically meaningful differences between two very similar products can be detected. These aspects create the need for education regarding statistical considerations and clinical data interpretation. Further, the healthcare community is cautious about using new products approved for use without being clinically evaluated in those specific patient populations or conditions.

The stakeholder pool needing education about biosimilars includes not only the healthcare community of physicians, nurses, physician assistants and nurse practitioners, but also scientists, regulators, payers and patients. These stakeholders often use peer-reviewed publications as a source of information and education, which indicates a need to educate the publishing community. While considerable biosimilar analytical and biological aspect data are generated, only limited clinical data are generated during development, creating a unique challenge with limited opportunities for data dissemination to the clinical and healthcare communities. These data have to be well-synthesized for dissemination to a broad audience via appropriate channels. Further, scientists and content development experts, including medical writers developing regulatory and clinical documents and publications, must acquire an in-depth understanding of biosimilars' science and development. Medical writers generally focus on data synthesis from clinical studies; with biosimilars, there is greater need for disseminating the nonclinical, preclinical and Phase 1 data. Writers must develop an in-depth understanding of the analytical and functional characterization aspects to ensure well-synthesized data are available to educate stakeholders.

## Summary

Biosimilars are different from generics because a biosimilar molecule is not an exact replica of the reference molecule. Instead, a biosimilar product's quality attributes are expected to be highly similar to those of the reference product, with allowable minor differences that should not affect clinical activity. Therefore, the development and regulatory considerations for biosimilars necessarily differ from those for generic drugs (**Table 22-1**). Biologic products' development and regulation present considerable challenges due not only to their complexity and specialized production processes, but also to specific safety concerns linked to their immunological potential. A recommended stepwise approach for biosimilar product development involves comprehensive analytical characterization and demonstration of structural similarity and functional equivalence as the basis for biosimilarity. This approach forms the cornerstone of the rest of the development program, including decisions about the need for animal studies, followed by required human PK equivalence, PD equivalence (where a relevant marker exists) and, in most cases, the final step of at least one clinical study to confirm comparable immunogenicity or safety risk and similar efficacy to the innovator. Clinical study(ies) should be performed in sensitive populations to allow clinically meaningful differences to be detected. The biosimilar clinical development program's goal is not *de novo* demonstration of safety and efficacy or clinical benefit establishment, as is the case with a reference or originator product's development, but rather detecting and assessing potential differences between the proposed biosimilar and reference product. Considerable experience and expertise are required to develop a robust biosimilar that can be reproduced with predefined and established quality characteristics to ensure patients receive high-quality medicines. With so many unique challenges, there is a need for stakeholder education. Considering the field of biosimilars is new and evolving, educators, content development professionals and medical writers also need to develop expertise in this growing field. This will ensure appropriate educational content availability for key stakeholders, including healthcare providers, payers and patients, resulting in informed choices that lead to appropriate patient outcomes.

### References

1. The Global Use of Medicines: Outlook Through 2017 (2016). Quintiles IMS website. http://www.imshealth.com/en/thought-leadership/quintilesims-institute/reports/global-use-of-medicines-outlook-through-2017. Accessed 19 January 2017.
2. *Biosimilars: Questions and Answers Regarding Implementation of the Biologics Price Competition and Innovation Act of 2009: Guidance for Industry* (2015). FDA website. http://www.fda.gov/downloads/drugs/guidancecomplianceregulatoryinformation/guidances/ucm444661.pdf. Accessed 19 January 2017.
3. *Quality Considerations in Demonstrating Biosimilarity of a Therapeutic Protein Product to a Reference Product: Guidance for Industry* (2015). FDA website. http://www.fda.gov/downloads/drugs/guidances/ucm291134.pdf . Accessed 19 January 2017.
4. *Scientific Considerations in Demonstrating Biosimilarity to a Reference Product: Guidance for Industry* (2015). FDA website. http://www.fda.gov/downloads/DrugsGuidanceComplianceRegulatoryInformation/Guidances/UCM291128.pdf . Accessed 19 January 2017.
5. *Clinical Pharmacology Data to Support a Demonstration of Biosimilarity to a Reference Product: Guidance for Industry* (2014). FDA website. http://www.fda.gov/downloads/drugs/guidancecomplianceregulatoryinformation/guidances/ucm397017.pdf. Accessed 19 January 2017.
6. Kozlowski S, Woodcock J, Midthun K, Sherman RB. Developing the nation's biosimilars program. *N Engl J Med* 2011;365:385–8.
7. *Guideline on similar biological medicinal products containing biotechnology-derived proteins as active substance: non-clinical and clinical issues* (2015). EMA website. http://www.ema.europa.eu/docs/en_GB/document_library/Scientific_guideline/2015/01/WC500180219.pdf. Accessed 19 January 2017.
8. Op cit 4.
9. Op cit 5.
10. Op cit 3.
11. Op cit 4.
12. Declerck P, Farouk-Rezk M, Rudd PM. Biosimilarity Versus Manufacturing Change: Two Distinct Concepts. *Pharm Res* 2016;33:261–8.
13. Op cit 6.
14. Op cit 4
15. Ibid.
16. Op cit 5.
17. Ibid.
18. C.N. The US Biosimilars Act Challenges Facing Regulatory Approval. Pharm Med 2012;26:145–52.
19. Cortes J, Curigliano G, Dieras V. Expert perspectives on biosimilar monoclonal antibodies in breast cancer. *Breast Cancer Res Treat* 2014;144:233-9.
20. Op cit 6.
21. Op cit 18.
22. Op cit 4.
23. Op cit 3.
24. Ibid.
25. Biologics Price Competition and Innovation Act. Title VII—improving access to innovative medical therapies. Subtitle A—Biologics Price Competition and Innovation. Sec. 7002. Approval pathway for biosimilar biological products (2009). FDA website. http://www.fda.gov/downloads/Drugs/GuidanceComplianceRegulatoryInformation/UCM216146.pdf. Accessed 19 January 2017.
26. Ibid.
27. *Considerations in Demonstrating Interchangeability With a Reference Product: Guidance for Industry* (2017). FDA website. http://www.fda.gov/downloads/Drugs/GuidanceComplianceRegulatoryInformation/Guidances/UCM537135.pdf. Accessed 1 February 2017.
28. Ibid

29. *Nonproprietary Naming of Biological Products: Guidance for Industry* (2017). FDA website. http://www.fda.gov/downloads/drugs/guidances/ucm459987.pdf. Accessed 1 February 2017.
30. Op cit 19.
31. Mellstedt H, Niederwieser D, Ludwig H. The challenge of biosimilars. *Ann Oncol.* 2008;19:411–9.

**Author**

Monica Ramchandan, MS, PhD, leads publication and medical writing in Amgen's biosimilars division. Previously, she worked in pharmaceutical research focusing on formulation development, concentrating on novel drug delivery system design. Since then, she has focused on publication planning and development. In addition to her extensive experience within the pharmaceutical industry, Ramchandan has several publications to her credit. She holds an MS in pharmacy from Mumbai University. and a PhD in pharmaceutical sciences from the University of Nebraska Medical Center.

# 23

# Combination Product Design and Development

*By Jiyang Shen*

## Introduction

In recent years, the term "combination product" has become a buzz word in the pharmaceutical industry and a popular topic at such pharmaceutical conferences as Parenteral Drug Association Annual Meetings and Respiratory Drug Delivery conferences. New regulatory guidances and combination products' increasing popularity have been part of this increased interest. In addition, increasing numbers of US Food and Drug Administration (FDA) Warning Letters or requests for more information about the combination product development and manufacturing process have led many to seek new approaches.

A common theme in the combination product area is that formerly accepted truths no longer apply. For example, until 2013, in many cases, it was permissible to include a marketed device as a part of a combination product filing without much additional device design control work. However, recent guidance from the agency clarifies requirements for such work.

This chapter defines combination products, provides an overview of FDA's current Good Manufacturing Practice (CGMP) requirements and presents regulatory considerations for combination product design and development for the US market. It ends with some suggestions on combination product design, development and regulatory strategy planning.

## Combination Product Definition

According to 21 CFR Part 3, a combination product is composed of any combination of a drug, device and/or biological product. The drugs, devices and biological products included in combination products are referred to as "constituent parts."[1]

Detailed definitions the major combination product categories can be found in 21 CFR 3.2 (e), briefly summarized below for the purposes of this chapter:

- single entity combination product comprised of two or more regulated drug, device, and/or biologic components, such as a prefilled syringe or drug-eluting stent; these components may be physically or chemically combined
- "co-packaged" drug, biologic and/or device products, such as a surgical or first-aid kit
- "cross-labeled" product packaged separately intended for use only with an approved, individually specified drug, device or biological product if both are required to achieve the intended use, indication or effect

Combination products can be categorized roughly by the constituent part that provides the primary mode of action (PMOA); this also determines which FDA center will provide primary review.[2]

This chapter focuses only on those combination products whose PMOA is a drug or biological product (referred to as "drug-device combination product"). In most cases, the Center for Biologics Evaluation and Research (CBER) or the Center for Drug Evaluation and Research (CDER) reviews this type of combination product application. In this chapter, unless specifically noted, the term "drug" means one or more drug or biological constituent parts, and "device" means one or more device constituent parts. All discussion refers to FDA combination product regulations and guidance. For a combination product where the device provides the PMOA, the product is reviewed and approved by The Center for Devices and Radiological Health (CDRH) because the product's drug or biologic constituent part generally is intended to provide a secondary benefit (such as preventing infection) unrelated to the PMOA or its delivery.

## Overview of CGMP Requirements

The 2004 *Draft Guidance for Industry: Current Good Manufacturing Practices for Combination Products* was codified as the final rule in January 2013 in 21 CFR Part 4. The final rule clarified that CGMP requirements apply to each combination product constituent part because these components retain their regulatory status (such as device or drug) even after they are combined. This final rule also applies to combination products containing cross-labeled constituent parts manufactured separately and not co-packaged.

Since 2013, executing the final rule has been a challenge for both industry and the agency. Thus, FDA issued an additional draft guidance in 2015 in 21 CFR Part 4, which further clarifies two options to meet CGMP requirements:

- demonstrate compliance with all CGMP regulations applicable to each combination product constituent part
- (if the product contains both a drug and a device) implement a streamlined approach by meeting either the drug CGMPs (21 CFR Part 211) or the Quality System Regulation (QSR) (21 CFR Part 820), so long as certain additional conditions are met, including demonstrating compliance with specified provisions from the other CGMP requirement sets[3]

To reduce workload, most pharmaceutical companies adopt the streamlined approach. For combination products whose PMOA is a drug or biological product, this means product development and manufacture will follow drug CGMPs and then follow certain specified QSR

provisions in accordance with 21 CFR 4.4(b)(1). These are quoted from the regulation for convenience.[4]

(i) 21 CFR 820.20—Management responsibility: Management with executive responsibility shall ensure that the quality policy is understood, implemented, and maintained at all levels of the organization. Each manufacturer shall establish and maintain an adequate organizational structure to ensure that devices are designed and produced in accordance with the requirements of this part. Management with executive responsibility shall review the suitability and effectiveness of the quality system at defined intervals and with sufficient frequency according to established procedures to ensure that the quality system satisfies the requirements of this part and the manufacturer's established quality policy and objectives.

Each manufacturer shall establish a quality plan which defines the quality practices, resources, and activities relevant to devices that are designed and manufactured. The manufacturer shall establish how the requirements for quality will be met.

Each manufacturer shall establish quality system procedures and instructions. An outline of the structure of the documentation used in the quality system shall be established where appropriate.

(ii) 21 CFR 820.30. Design controls
Each manufacturer shall establish and maintain procedures to control the design of the device in order to ensure that specified design requirements are met.

(iii) 21 CFR 820.50. Purchasing controls
Each manufacturer shall establish and maintain procedures to ensure that all purchased or otherwise received product and services conform to specified requirements.

(iv) 21 CFR 820.100. Corrective and preventive action
Each manufacturer shall establish and maintain procedures for implementing corrective and preventive action, including:

(1) Analyzing processes, work operations, concessions, quality audit reports, quality records, service records, complaints, returned product, and other sources of quality data to identify existing and potential causes of nonconforming product, or other quality problems.

(2) Investigating the cause of nonconformities relating to product, processes, and the quality system;

(3) Identifying the action(s) needed to correct and prevent recurrence of nonconforming product and other quality problems;

(4) Verifying or validating the corrective and preventive action to ensure that such action is effective and does not adversely affect the finished device;

(5) Implementing and recording changes in methods and procedures needed to correct and prevent identified quality problems;

(6) Ensuring that information related to quality problems or nonconforming product is disseminated to those directly responsible for assuring the quality of such product or the prevention of such problems; and

(7) Submitting relevant information on identified quality problems, as well as corrective and preventive actions, for management review.

All activities required under this section, and their results, shall be documented.

(v) 21 CFR 820.170. Installation

Each manufacturer of a device requiring installation shall establish and maintain adequate installation and inspection instructions, and where appropriate test procedures. Instructions and procedures shall include directions for ensuring proper installation so that the device will perform as intended after installation. The manufacturer shall distribute the instructions and procedures with the device or otherwise make them available to the person(s) installing the device.

The person installing the device shall ensure that the installation, inspection, and any required testing are performed in accordance with the manufacturer's instructions and procedures and shall document the inspection and any test results to demonstrate proper installation.

(vi) 21 CFR 820.200. Servicing

Where servicing is a specified requirement, each manufacturer shall establish and maintain instructions and procedures for performing and verifying that the servicing meets the specified requirements.

Each manufacturer shall analyze service reports with appropriate statistical methodology in accordance with 820.100.

Each manufacturer who receives a service report that represents an event which must be reported to FDA under part 803 of this chapter shall automatically consider the report a complaint and shall process it in accordance with the requirements of 820.198.

## Special Combination Product Development Regulatory Considerations

Ostensibly, 21 CFR Part 4 does not introduce new requirements for combination product device constituent parts,[5] in part because the latest revision of the QSR (21 CFR Part 820) became effective in 1997. However, the final rule indicates an article that delivers a drug while containing and protecting it is considered a delivery device and may be subject to the QSR.[6] This conflicts with the May 1999 *Guidance for Industry: Container Closure Systems for Packaging Human Drugs and Biologics: Chemistry, Manufacturing, and Controls Documentation,*[7] which states the container closure systems can have drug delivery functions and follow 21 CFR Parts 210–211. Thus, 21 CFR Part 4 re-categorizes device constituent parts previously considered container closure systems (such as a piston syringe) as delivery devices.

As might be expected, this change impacted the pharmaceutical industry in two areas:

- Some device constituent parts previously developed as drug product container closure systems are out of compliance with current regulations because their development did not follow the QSR during development.
- Any new combination product device constituent part must comply with the QSR (21 CFR Part 820) rather than being treated as a drug product container closure system.

QSR compliance is new to many pharmaceutical companies, and how to retrospectively establishing combination product compliance approved under CFR 210–211 remains unclear. FDA currently is guiding pharmaceutical companies on how to backfill design control for inline products previously approved as drug products, but have been re-categorized as drug-device combination products, based on information in both the final rule and the 2015 draft guidance.

## Specific Considerations for Constituents With Prior Marketing Approval

### 510(K) Approval May Be Insufficient to Meet Final CGMP Rule Requirements

Imagine you are the regulatory representative on the product development team for a drug product or biologic filled into a cartridge for use with a reusable injection pen. This product contains both drug and device constituent parts and, therefore, is a combination product. The project lead has led the successful development of several similar products and is aware this product must follow the QSR for the device constituent part.

However, when asked how the injection pen will be selected, the team indicates that in the past, this selection was initiated when drug development was near completion. The intention was to select a commercially available injection pen platform with a 510(k) clearance which was used for other products that had been launched already. The project lead says the majority of the device constituent part's design control would be provided by the injection pen manufacturer since it is the 510(k) holder, and your company would not be required to do much additional device work.

This sounds very convincing; however, asking a few more questions about the 510(k) clearance could save the team a great deal of time and effort. For example, understanding the approved Instructions for Use (IFUs, such as clinical settings, target population and anatomical sites) might be helpful. Do the approved IFUs align with the combination product? Will the combination product adopt the same IFUs that were in the 510(k) cleared device?

Another key question is whether the plan is to repackage the 510(k) cleared injection pen with your product. This consideration is important because the "manufacture" definition in 21 CFR 4.2 includes, but is not limited to, designing, fabricating, assembling, filling, processing, testing, labeling, packaging, repackaging, holding and storage.[8] Therefore, the combination product application holder is responsible for complying with all CGMP requirements applicable to the entire manufacturing process across all facilities.[9] Although your company does not design or manufacture the reusable injection pen, it still is your responsibility to make sure the QSR for the device constituent parts are satisfied. Design control requirements in 21 CFR 820.30 can be troublesome and deserve special attention.

In 21 CFR 820.30(c) Design Input, it says each manufacturer shall establish and maintain procedures to ensure compliance and address the intended patient population.[10] If the 510(k) cleared injection pen's target population does not cover the intended user population specifically, the agency might argue the design inputs were collected inappropriately. If the intended user population's customer needs were not considered during the 510(k) cleared injection pen's design, additional measures may be needed for full QSR compliance.

According to 21 CFR 820.30(g) Design Validation, design validation includes testing "under actual or simulated use conditions."[11] Commonly, however, devices

like an injection pen may be developed as a platform with broad, general indications and target populations in mind. Therefore, the 510(k) cleared injection pen's IFU and packaging normally contain general information and, therefore, may be insufficient for a combination product with its specific indication and user population. If the IFU and packaging are redesigned after the injection pen is combined with a biologic or drug product, the new IFU and packaging designs must be validated with the intended user population. The IFU and/or packaging validation work provided by the injection pen supplier might not be enough for submission.

## Co-packaging

Co-packaging an independently marketed drug product with an independently marketed device product might not be as simple as it appears. The consideration of whether the drug and/or device will be repackaged, relabeled or modified plays a critical role in defining the regulatory and development strategy.

FDA has clarified the "convenience kit" definition as a kit including only products that are already marketed independently and packaged in the kit with the same labeling as for independent marketing.[12] If any product, label or IFU modifications are needed, all combination product CGMP requirements will apply.[13]

## Specific Rick Management Considerations
### Device Risk Management Is Not Just About Devices Anymore

Once a device and drug or biologic are combined, overall product risk assessment becomes complicated because risk management is required for all constituent parts. However, drug and device risk management activities may be performed by different functional groups, such as clinical safety and device engineering, whose members may have different educational backgrounds, work experience and, likely, mindsets about how to conduct risk analysis. Insufficient communication or a lack of understanding of the differences between clinical risk management and device risk management can cause problems.

ISO 14971 is a standard for the application of medical device risk management and is widely accepted by industry and regulatory agencies. It often is adopted to demonstrate conformity with the EU Medical Device Directive 93/42/EEC Essential Requirements. Risk management, as described in ISO 14971, is an ongoing process for identifying hazards, estimating and evaluating associated risks, controlling those risks and monitoring controls' effectiveness. This process contains risk analysis, risk evaluation, risk control and production and post-production elements.[14]

The core risk analysis concept is to identify hazards and estimate risks for associated hazardous situations. Risk is determined by the combination of the probability of occurrence of harm and that harm's severity.[15] Harm is defined as physical injury or damage to health, property or environmental hazard.[16] Well-trained device engineers can identify hazardous situations related to device use properly and estimate their probability accurately.

For combination products, ISO 14971 also is leveraged for combination product device constituent part risk management; however, combination product risks and hazards cannot be defined accurately without clinical, pharmacovigilance and drug development function inputs. For example, many combination product harm categories are not caused directly by device failures, but by adverse drug effects due to device failures, such as over- or under-dose. Thus, combination product device risk management must be navigated through multifunctional collaboration efforts among clinical or drug safety and device engineering.

### Device Risk Management Requires a Great Deal of Work

FDA has three device regulatory categories based on the control level needed to demonstrate device safety and effectiveness. The class applicable to the medical device largely determines the type of premarketing submission or application required for FDA market clearance, and developers can predict a medical device's development requirements and expectations accordingly. Unfortunately, a combination product's device constituent part cannot fit into these three regulatory classes because the combination effect of drug and device complicates the evaluation of product safety and effectiveness. As discussed above, combination product risk management must consider harms caused by each constituent part, following all appropriate regulations. In the past several years, CDER and CBER have treated the drug-device combination product cautiously and have required a level of device risk management similar to that needed for Class III devices, even when the device constituent alone would be considered Class I or II.

When applying ISO 14971 to device risk management for combination products, teams can employ a top down analysis approach such as Fault Tree Analysis (FTA) or Preliminary Hazard Analysis (PHA), or a bottom up analysis approach such as Failure Mode and Effects Analysis (FMEA) or Failure Mode, Effects and Criticality Analysis (FMECA). It also is possible to adopt a combination of approaches. In any case, it is necessary to analyze device risks from three perspectives: product use, design and manufacturing. A device supplier might be able to provide a thorough device design risk analysis, but combination product manufacturers also must assess the overall product use and manufacturing process, as well as effects in the clinic.

## Specific Human Factors Considerations

### Human Factors Testing Is Important Throughout Development

In 2011, FDA's Center for Devices and Radiological Health (CDRH) released draft guidance on how to apply human factors and usability engineering to optimize medical device design. In 2016, *Applying Human Factors and Usability Engineering to Medical Devices: Guidance for Industry and Food and Drug Administration Staff* was released, indicating systematic and iterative human factors (HF) engineering approaches, including HF analysis, HF testing and validation, should be included in medical device design and testing.[17] This systematic HF approach is part of a broader device and pharmaceutical development risk management application, and the final guidance's rules cover the device, its packaging and instructions for use. HF validation should be conducted with participants representing the device's intended users, and the device user interface tested should be the final design; all critical tasks should be tested and test conditions should be realistic enough to represent actual conditions of use.[18]

In early 2016, CDER issued *Human Factors Studies and Related Clinical Study Considerations in Combination Product Design and Development*, presenting a position on combination product HF requirements similar to CDRH's medical device HF approach.

In recent years, product approvals have been delayed due to insufficient HF validation results. Typical problems with HF validation include:

- device, packaging or instructions used in the HF study do not represent the final design
- lack of performance data on critical tasks
- finding user errors that can lead to unacceptable risks
- insufficient formative work resulting in use errors not controlled sufficiently and requiring additional mitigation and evaluation

For drug-device combination product design and development, a robust, systematic and iterative HF process is critical throughout the product lifecycle, starting during early stage design inputs and progressing throughout development into postmarketing surveillance. If HF work is treated only as the final validation step, review process delays likely will result. It can be costly and time consuming to fix issues detected in HF validation.

## Investigational New Drug Application (IND) Bar Might Be High

Traditionally, the investigational drug used in a Phase 1 study only follows the statutory requirements set forth in 21 U.S.C. 351(a)(2)(B) and is exempt from compliance with the regulations in Part 211.[19] Under the new 21 CFR Part 4, this exemption does not apply to combination products or constituents intended for use in Phase 2 or Phase 3 studies, or if the drug has been marketed previously. Further, investigational drug-device combination product development must follow the investigational rules for both drugs and devices, including design control. FDA clarified in its draft guidance on CGMP for combination products, even should CGMP exemptions apply, appropriate methods, facilities and manufacturing controls are needed, and hazards and risks must be considered.[20]

Supporting design control for an investigational drug-device combination product is new for much of the pharmaceutical industry. This is especially true if the device constituent part is in a special dosage form, as might be the case for an implantable device.

CDER's HF draft guidance states risk analysis should be a part of the combination product's investigational application. If the applicant decides not to conduct an HF study based on risk analysis results, the use-related risk analysis and justification for this conclusion should be provided to the agency.[21] If risk analysis indicates an HF study is necessary, FDA encourages applicants to obtain feedback prior to conducting this study.

To obtain this feedback, FDA requests:

- use-related risk analysis
- any updated risk analysis of design changes
- summary of HF formative study results and analysis
- summary of changes to the product user interface after the HF formative studies, including how the HF formative study results were used to update the user interface and use-related risk analysis
- draft HF validation study protocol
- intend-to-market labels and labeling (including any proposed instructions for use) to be tested in the HF validation study[22]

Assembling the above HF-related documents for an IND can be burdensome and delay development timelines. At the IND stage, the device design may not be sufficiently mature to conduct use-related risk analysis, and the prototypes may not be adequate for a formative study, especially if the device is commercially unavailable and needs to be designed or modified to accommodate the specific drug.

CDER's HF guidance is just a draft, and the final version might be more flexible. However, it is unlikely the agency will drop these expectations completely. Thus, the drug-device combination product developer should be prepared to provide a preliminary risk assessment of the device to be used in clinical studies.

## Use the Final Device in the Pivotal Clinical Study (if Possible)

CDER prefers for developers to complete the final finished combination product HF validation study before the pivotal clinical study, although, in some circumstances, this might not be necessary. In many cases, the device constituent must be customized to meet the drug formulation and intended users' requirements. Requiring the final combination product to be included in or run through HF validation studies prior to major clinical studies may cause significant delays.

Although the draft HF guidance may change, the need to bridge the HF validation results to the pivotal clinical study will not disappear. Therefore, the drug-device combination product developer should seek agency advice on clinical study device selection and include approaches to collect device use-related issues in the clinical study protocol. In the submission, it is important to explain how the device use-related issues observed in the clinical study were addressed in the product intended for market or submitted for review. A comparison should be performed between the clinical device and the final device, focusing on device features impacting drug delivery, drug efficacy and product use. Evidence should be provided to demonstrate the intended for market device's drug delivery performance meets the same performance measures as the clinical device, and its use-performance is equal to or better than the clinical device.

## General Recommendation

This chapter closes with three general recommendations in drug-device combination product design and development to help prevent review issues.

1. Get the device team involved early.

    In the past, for a drug-device combination project, device selection and/or development might start in a late stage. This makes sense, given the potential for failure in first-in-human studies and the risk of investing in device development before the drug is mature enough to move forward. However, making device selection a last stop to find a container to hold the drug could create a bigger issue. First, as discussed above, depending on the device and its associated risks, the regulation might not allow a clinical study to be conducted without providing risk assessment. Second, the proposed drug delivery approach may not work well with the target drug, or an HF evaluation may demonstrate intended users cannot use the product safely and effectively. In late development stages, it can be difficult and costly to modify device and/or instructions for use to address such issues. Changes could jeopardize clinical study results and require a new study.

2. Share the plan early with FDA.
   In several guidances discussed, FDA encourages the applicant to discuss combination product development plans with the agency. This type of discussion can be a part of a development meeting, such as pre-IND, IDE and EOP2 meetings.[23]

   It is good to share information with the agency, such as the device selection and development strategy, device risk management process, whether an HF validation will be conducted and what device will be used in early phase and pivotal clinical studies. This effort minimizes the chance of getting an unpleasant surprise at final submission.

3. Do not be afraid to discuss specifics and proposed strategy with FDA.
   Combination product design and development are relatively new for both industry and FDA. FDA admits it still is learning and sometimes adjusts regulations based on input from industry. Applicants should not hesitate to provide their proposed strategy specifics and rationale. Discussions can provide a learning opportunity for all and may lead to final regulations addressing everyone's needs better.

## References

1. *Guidance for Industry and FDA Staff: Current Good Manufacturing Practice Requirements for Combination Products* (January 2015). FDA website. http://www.fda.gov/downloads/RegulatoryInformation/Guidances/UCM429304.pdf. Accessed 20 January 2017.
2. Ibid.
3. Ibid.
4. 21 CFR 820.30 Quality System Regulation, Design control. FDA website. https://www.accessdata.fda.gov/scripts/cdrh/cfdocs/cfCFR/CFRSearch.cfm?fr=820.30. Accessed 20 January 2017.
5. 21 CFR Part 4, Current Good Manufacturing Practice Requirements for Combination Products. FDA website. http://www.fda.gov/downloads/CombinationProducts/UCM336194.pdf. Accessed 20 January 2017.
6. Op cit 1.
7. *Guidance for Industry: Container Closure Systems for Packaging Human Drugs and Biologics: Chemistry, Manufacturing, and Controls Documentation* (May 1999). FDA website. http://www.fda.gov/downloads/Drugs/.../Guidances/ucm070551.pdf. Accessed 20 January 2017.
8. Op cit 5.
9. Ibid.
10. Op cit 4.
11. Ibid.
12. Op cit 5.
13. Ibid.
14. ISO 14971:2007 Medical devices—Application of risk management to medical devices. ISO website. http://www.iso.org/iso/catalogue_detail?csnumber=38193. Accessed 20 January 2017.
15. Ibid.
16. Ibid.
17. *Applying Human Factors and Usability Engineering to Medical Devices: Guidance for Industry and Food and Drug Administration Staff* (February 2016). FDA website. http://www.fda.gov/downloads/MedicalDevices/.../UCM259760.pdf. Accessed 20 January 2017.
18. Ibid.
19. Op cit 5.
20. Op cit 1.
21. *Human Factors Studies and Related Clinical Study Considerations in Combination Product Design and Development: Draft Guidance for Industry and FDA Staff.* FDA website. http://www.fda.gov/downloads/RegulatoryInformation/Guidances/UCM484345.pdf. Accessed 20 January 2017.
22. Ibid.
23. Ibid.

## Author

Jiaying Shen is a director of engineering in device development at Merck. Her work primarily focuses on human factors, design control and risk management for drug delivery devices such as inhalers, injectors and implantable devices. Previously, she worked at Medtronic Neuromodulation R&D. Shen holds a PhD in industrial and system engineering from University the of Wisconsin—Madison.

# 24

# Rare Diseases—Special Considerations

*By Beth Silverstein, MS, RAC*

This chapter is intended to prepare the reader to draft and support an orphan drug designation request to the US Food and Drug Administration (FDA) Office of Orphan Products Development (OOPD). It is not intended to be a comprehensive review of orphan drug designation benefits or to compare in any great detail the similarities and differences between the US and other health authorities' orphan drug policies and procedures. The chapter touches briefly on other benefits FDA provides to sponsors developing medical devices intended to diagnose or treat patients with rare conditions, or drugs to treat rare pediatric diseases.

## Rare Disease Definition in a Regulatory Context

Many terms in the scientific, medical and regulatory community relate to diseases and conditions that affect a small number of individuals. Some of the more common are orphan disease, rare disease (or condition or disorder), neglected disease or some combination (such as rare and neglected disease).[1] Regulatory authorities' definitions of rare diseases differ as well.[2,3] For example, the European Medicines Agency (EMA) defines a rare disease or condition as a life-threatening or chronically debilitating condition that affects no more than five in 10,000 people in the EU. FDA defines a rare disease as a disease or condition affecting (a) less than 200,000 persons in

the US or affecting (b) 200,000 or more persons in the US and for which there is no reasonable expectation the cost of developing and making available a drug for such disease or condition will be recovered from sales in the US of such drug. In Japan, a rare disease is one affecting fewer than 50,000 Japanese people. In Australia, an orphan drug is used to treat a disease or condition affecting fewer than 2,000 individuals at any one time.[4] Canada is in the process of developing an orphan drug regulatory framework (the "Canadian Framework") in which an orphan drug is defined as one targeting a disease affecting fewer than five in 10,000.[5]

More recently, the terms ultrarare (or very rare or extremely rare), exceptionally rare or ultraorphan disease or condition have appeared,[6] but they have not been defined in the regulation. In the EU, for example, an ultraorphan disease has a prevalence of less than one case per 50,000 in the population.[7,8] Most ultrarare diseases affect far fewer patients. Some examples include Fabry's disease, which has a prevalence of less than 5,000 persons in the US, or Gaucher's disease, which has a prevalence of less than 2,500 persons in the US.

Similarly, different terminologies are used to describe a healthcare product developed to treat a rare disease. In the US, an orphan drug is a small molecule, biologic or a combination product regulated as a drug, intended to treat, diagnose or prevent a rare disease or condition.

FDA approves an orphan drug designation request for a drug intended to treat a disease or condition affecting fewer than 200,000; for a diagnostic drug, the number of patients subjected to diagnosis must be fewer than 200,000; and for a preventive drug, the number of people at risk of the disease must be fewer than 200,000.[9]

Orphan drug designation is granted for a rare disease or condition, not for an indication. FDA's website lists products and conditions for which orphan status had been designated (http://www.accessdata.fda.gov/scripts/opdlisting/oopd/). In the US, it is possible to obtain orphan designation for the same drug for more than one indication, although no single indication can exceed 200,000 patients. For example, the same drug may be granted orphan designation for two different rare cancers. If the same drug already is approved for the same indication, with or without orphan exclusivity, orphan designation is possible only if clinical superiority to the approved drug is demonstrated (for example, extended release versus immediate release drug). FDA considers treatment and prevention as separate orphan indications. Orphan designation may be revoked if the disease or condition's prevalence condition has been found to exceed 200,000 after designation was granted.

In the EU, an orphan indication requires, in addition to meeting the orphan medicinal product criteria, the disease or condition to be life-threatening or chronically debilitating, and there must be no authorized satisfactory method of diagnosis, treatment or prevention or evidence the drug promises a significant benefit to those with the disease or condition compared to existing methods.[10]

It is important to remember orphan designation does not affect the regulatory authority requirements for demonstrating safety and efficacy and for marketing application submission. However, sponsors may encounter some regulatory authority flexibility with regard to clinical investigation design, number or length.

## Why does a sponsor seek orphan drug designation?

A sponsor may find obtaining orphan drug/medicinal product designation offers several business benefits. Early in the drug development process, orphan drug designation demonstrates a potential for drug exclusivity to the investor community. In the US, an orphan drug may receive seven years of exclusivity upon marketing approval for a rare disease. During the exclusivity period, no other sponsor can receive marketing approval for the same drug and same indication unless it can demonstrate clinical superiority. In addition to exclusivity, orphan designation typically is accompanied by New Drug Application user fee waivers, eligibility for a priority review that reduces

marketing application review and approval time, research grant eligibility, clinical protocol design assistance and tax credits for costs associated with intended orphan drug designation clinical studies. In the EU, orphan medicinal product designation benefits include full or partial tax credits, protocol assistance and six or 10 years of marketing exclusivity.[11]

Many good reasons for requesting orphan drug designation exist, assuming the sponsor has preliminary information regarding the drug, biologic or combination product's potential to treat, prevent or diagnose the rare disease or condition effectively. No fee is imposed on the sponsor to have OOPD consider the request for designation. The designation request typically is not a lengthy document to prepare and generally includes approximately 20 pages of text with supportive data and literature as appendices.

## Obtaining US Orphan Drug Designation

An applicant may request orphan drug designation at any time during its drug development process prior to the time it submits a marketing application applicable to the same rare disease or condition. In the US, orphan drug designation is obtained by submitting an original and one copy of the request to FDA's OOPD. An electronic orphan designation application also can be submitted through FDA's Electronic Submission Gateway or on a CD-ROM disk with a signed cover letter. FDA guidance describes how to provide orphan drug designation requests and related submissions in electronic format.[12]

Sponsors wishing to apply for US and EU orphan medicinal product designation may utilize a common application form. A sponsor can use this form or the content and format specified in 21 CFR 316.20. A non-US sponsor must have a US resident agent to file an orphan drug designation application. In the EU, a resident agent also is required to file an orphan medicinal drug designation application.

Under 21 CFR 316.20, an orphan drug designation request to OOPD should contain:

- table of contents
- statement of orphan drug designation request
  - o statement the sponsor is requesting orphan drug designation for a rare disease or condition
- sponsor's contact person or resident agent's information
  - o name, address, title, telephone number, email address
- drug generic and trade name(s)
  - o name(s) owned by the company and used for marketing purposes, if available

- chemical name, including a description of the drug's molecular structure (if applicable)
- drug substance and drug product manufacturer's name and address
- rare disease or condition description
  - o disease pathogenesis, presentation, diagnosis, current treatment, prognosis and course
- drug description and rationale for use
  - o medically plausible basis to expect the drug will be effective in treating, preventing or diagnosing the rare disease or condition (typically includes a description of the drug, its proposed mechanism of action, nonclinical pharmacology but not toxicology data, and clinical data, if available)
- clinical superiority explanation (if applicable)
  - o only necessary if the sponsor is requesting orphan drug designation for a drug with the same active moiety as an already approved drug for the same indication
- drug for use in an orphan subset (if applicable)
  - o only if the sponsor intends to develop the drug for a medically relevant subset of patients
- drug regulatory status and marketing history summary
  - o list of US and foreign marketing approvals, and/or whether there is an active Investigational New Drug Application and/or any adverse regulatory actions
- drug's target population prevalence
  - o documentation to demonstrate the target disease or condition affects fewer than 200,000 people in the US or will be administered as a vaccine, diagnostic drug or preventative drug to fewer than 200,000 persons per year (If the orphan indication is based on the reasonable expectation the drug's research and development costs for the indication cannot be recovered by US sales, support should be provided.)
- statement of real party of interest
- references
  - o hard copies of references separated by tabbed dividers; however, orphan designation requests with references on a CD have been submitted successfully (Of note, when cited in the body of the designation, refer to references by author name.)
- product labeling
  - o for products approved outside the US, consider providing copies of the package insert

In addition, 21 CFR 316.20(b)(7) requires an orphan drug designation request sponsor to submit a summary of the drug's regulatory status and marketing history. This requires the applicant to self-certify that the company has not submitted a previous marketing application to FDA for the same active moiety and same rare disease or condition prior to submitting the orphan drug designation request. The self-certification statement can be added to the regulatory status and marketing history section or submitted as an amendment to the file.

Once the designation request is received, the sponsor receives a letter of acknowledgement with an orphan designation request number. Since 2014, the number of orphan designation requests received by OOPD has increased by as much as 30% in a single year. OOPD's current goal is to review, on average, 75% of designation requests within 120 days of receipt. An orphan designation request goes through two review cycles: original submission and review of supplemental information provided at OOPD's request. OOPD encourages applicants to ensure designation requests are complete and address all requirements fully.

At the completion of the review, OOPD will contact the sponsor with additional questions or a letter stating that orphan designation was granted or denied (and why). If OOPD provides guidance for additional information needed to reconsider the designation request, this information can be submitted. The sponsor then has the opportunity to provide OOPD with a response containing additional information or data, similarly to any response to the agency. When additional information is requested, FDA will hold the application in abeyance pending receipt of the requested information. The applicant should, within one year of the letter's date, submit either additional information to OOPD or a written request for an extension of time to respond. An extension request must include the reason for the extension and length of time requested. Failure to meet this one-year deadline may result in OOPD considering the designation request to be voluntarily withdrawn.

Recently, OOPD has offered sponsors the opportunity to meet with staff to discuss informally or formally questions or concerns about the orphan drug designation process or a specific submission.[13] Sponsors should send a meeting request to OOPD that includes: a brief statement of the meeting purpose, including product identification and any applicable designation request or grant application number; a preference as to an informal or formal meeting; suggested meeting dates; a preferred meeting format (teleconference or in person); and the email address to which OOPD should send the response. OOPD aims to respond within five working days of receipt and proposes a time for the meeting. At least two weeks before a formal meeting, the sponsor must provide a package to OOPD, which OOPD recommends be submitted electronically, usually in an email. The package contains information somewhat similar to that sent in a Pre-Investigational New Drug Application (IND) meeting request, specifically:

- meeting date, time and subject
- explanation of the meeting purpose
- basic product information (including product name or identifier, designation or application number, relevant rare disease or condition and brief background about the product including how it may be used for the rare disease or condition)
- proposed meeting agenda with a list of questions
- any data, information or presentation materials to support the discussion
- list of individuals who will be participating in the meeting

Once orphan designation has been granted, the sponsor is required to provide annual updates to OOPD. The first update should be submitted within 14 months of the date on which the orphan drug designation was granted, and subsequent updates should be sent annually thereafter until marketing approval. The annual report includes a short account of drug development progress, including a review of preclinical and clinical studies initiated, ongoing and completed during the reporting period and a short summary of such studies' status or results; a description of the investigational plan for the coming year, as well as any anticipated difficulties in development, testing and marketing; and a brief discussion of any changes that may affect the product's orphan drug status. Study reports or other very detailed data commonly provided in IND annual reports are not needed for orphan drug annual reports. Updates also are necessary when there is information about a change in population size and when the marketing application is submitted.

## Preparing a Persuasive Orphan Drug Designation Request

Unsuccessful orphan drug designation requests tend to result from several common missteps:

- they do not lead the reviewer through the information and consequently, the orphan designation justification is lost or misinterpreted
- they do not support the medical and scientific rationale with strong scientific and medical literature

- they include incidence rather than prevalence data to meet the orphan criteria
- they define a subset that is not medically relevant

By comparison, a successful orphan drug designation leaves little to no reason for OOPD to question the sponsor about its use of data and information to demonstrate the drug and condition meet the stated orphan designation criteria. The better-prepared orphan drug designation requests tell a story about the drug, about the disease or condition, about how the drug may play an important role in the disease or condition's diagnosis or treatment, about the disease or condition's rarity, and about the potential benefit to patients.[14]

Sometimes the orphan drug designation path is relatively straightforward. As an example, glioblastoma is well recognized as an orphan disease and, therefore, the story is relatively simple and readily supported by data. Glioblastoma is a serious condition with a high mortality rate. Methods for diagnosing glioblastoma are well established. The current US standard of care is surgical resection followed by chemotherapy and radiation therapy. Despite treatment advances, a cure for glioblastoma remains elusive. A proposed drug intended to treat glioblastoma would include data from clinical studies or nonclinical studies in an appropriate animal model that support a potential intervention that would provide significant patient benefit. Prevalence data from appropriate sources, such as peer-reviewed published articles and/or data from large patient databases, would be appropriate to support the contention that this is a rare condition affecting fewer than 200,000 persons in the US. FDA previously has granted orphan status to drugs to treat this disease. The sponsor should convey that orphan drug designation is an effective means to expedite the delivery of a promising therapy to patients who need it. Once the story is defined, the next step is to flesh out the body of the document, using the story synopsis and key messages.

Sometimes the path is more complicated. For very rare diseases, FDA reviewers may be unfamiliar with the disease, the patient population or the mechanisms by which drugs may be useful in diagnosing or treating it. In these circumstances, it is especially important to educate the reviewers on current knowledge about the disease and its diagnosis or treatment. Prevalence data for very rare diseases or an appropriate subset of disease populations may be more difficult to find, meaning the sponsor must be more creative regarding the prevalence information source or prevalence calculation from other estimates. For example, multi-year prevalence data, incidence data or information on a disease's duration can be used to estimate the number of US existing or ongoing cases at the time of submission.

## Tips for a Successful Orphan Drug Designation

### Support the Medical Rationale With Strong Scientific Data

The strongest evidence for the drug's use in treating the disease or condition comes from a clinical investigation of the proposed drug in patients with the stated indication. Such data often are not available for inclusion in the request, as sponsors frequently submit a designation request before clinical studies have been conducted. Strong support may come from a clinical investigation of the proposed drug in a similar relevant condition (for example, efficacy of the drug as a treatment for a similar tumor type). If no clinical data are available, data from *in vivo* studies in a relevant animal model are the next strongest support. The animal model chosen must be recognized by the scientific community as predictive of human response. Data from *in vitro* studies or information on a hypothetical basis for the drug's use for the disease or condition will be considered on a case-by-case basis but typically are not persuasive in the absence of other predictive data.

Data reports and publications should be provided with the designation request to support the medical rationale for the drug's use in treating, diagnosing or preventing the disease or condition. Study reports should be of sufficient quality to allow the agency to be confident in the conclusions, but animal studies do not have to be Good Laboratory Practice (GLP)-compliant nonclinical studies. Interim clinical study results also may be sufficient.

### Provide the Prevalence Calculation

Orphan drug designation requests should include information about the number of existing, ongoing cases in the target country or countries, or prevalence, at the time the request is submitted.

Prevalence is the number of people in a population with a diagnosis of a disease or condition, including those who were diagnosed in previous years and still may have the disease or condition. If a range exists for prevalence, the highest estimate should be used.[15] For many rare diseases, prevalence estimates are available from government websites, publications, patient advocacy organizations, etc. OOPD will not accept a disease as rare because it is so listed on a website as evidence of a prevalence in fewer than 200,000 persons.

"At the time of the submission of the request" is a key requirement not met readily. FDA's frequently asked questions regarding orphan drug designation requests states:

"A sponsor is expected to make a good faith effort in finding the most recent prevalence data that refers to the United States population. If any old and/or foreign data is available, the sponsor should explain this in the application. If data is old, the sponsor should explain why the data is still pertinent, and, if from a foreign source, why data with that country's population could be representative of US population."

The sponsor must identify the most defensible, recent prevalence estimate of the disease or condition, which may be three- to five-years old. Some sources may provide prevalence data estimating the prevalence in later years.

The sponsor and FDA must have confidence the estimates cited for prevalence are relevant at the time of the request. Consider the impact of disease prevention (which would lower prevalence) or better diagnostic tools (which may increase prevalence) on the prevalence point estimates. For example, the prevalence of gastric cancer is decreasing, potentially as a result of decreasing *H. pylori* prevalence due to the use of antibiotics, whereas the introduction of Prostate Specific Antigen (PSA) testing has led to an increase in the number of prostate cancers diagnosed, many of which previously might have gone undetected.

Often when searching for prevalence data, the sponsor will encounter disease incidence rather than prevalence rates. Incidence represents the number of new disease cases diagnosed in a given period (typically one year). Incidence rates may be classified by population subset, such as gender, race, age or diagnostic category. Only if the drug is intended for the treatment of an acute condition (i.e., it has a duration of one year or less, such as the acute treatment of severe traumatic brain injury), can incidence be used as an estimate of target population prevalence. For diseases or conditions with durations of greater than one year, prevalence can be calculated by multiplying incidence by median survival. Median survival data are not always available; therefore, a sponsor may need to utilize other statistics, such as survival statistics (the percentage of people with a disease alive after a particular amount of time) to compute and estimate prevalence.

If prevalence cannot be calculated from readily available sources, practicing physicians may be able to provide ballpark figures based on their own years of experience. FDA may accept three independent expert opinions of prevalence to support an orphan drug designation request.[16] If this type of supportive information is relied upon, the orphan designation request should include signed statements from experts detailing the nature of their practices and number of patients treated. If such data are available, prevalence might be estimated based on sales of specific medications to treat the disease or condition during a certain time period. Comprehensive marketing surveys also may provide information on the number of patients at risk.

### Support Subsets of Conditions and Avoid Salami Slicing

As defined in FDA's frequently asked questions about orphan designation requests, "an orphan subset means the use of the drug in a subset of persons with a non-rare disease or condition may be appropriate but use of the drug outside of that subset (in the remaining persons with the non-rare disease or condition) would be inappropriate owing to some property(ies) of the drug, for example drug toxicity, mechanism of action, or previous clinical experience with the drug." A medically relevant subset exists if the drug would be expected to treat only a subset of patients, for example, patients with a specific genotype or with later stages of cancer. Geriatric and pediatric patient populations also represent medically relevant subsets.

OOPD responds favorably to medically relevant subsets (also referred to as an orphan subset) but not to "salami slicing," or artificially defining a patient population of fewer than 200,000 patients to receive the seven-year orphan exclusivity. An example of salami slicing is a drug that will be tested only for patients who meet clinical trial inclusion criteria. If a sponsor seeks orphan drug designation for a drug for a subset of patients with a prevalence of fewer than 200,000, but the drug can be effective in the broader patient population, FDA is unlikely to grant the designation. In essence, there must be a drug feature or characteristic (e.g., mechanism of action or toxicity profile) that limits its use in that subset and precludes its use outside the subset.

### Demonstrate Clinical Superiority (if Appropriate)

Demonstrating clinical superiority is necessary if a sponsor wishes to obtain orphan drug exclusivity for the same drug for the same population as a drug that already has marketing approval. FDA provides "same drug" definitions in 21 CFR 316.3(b)(13). In general, a same drug has the same active moiety (the part of the drug that makes it work the way it does) or the same principal molecular structural features (e.g., amino acids, nucleotides). To demonstrate clinical superiority, the sponsor must provide clinical evidence that (a) its drug has greater efficacy than the approved drug; (b) its drug demonstrates greater safety in the target population than the approved drug; or (c) in unusual cases, its drug demonstrates a "major contribution to patient care." At the time of the

orphan request, the sponsor needs to provide only a medically plausible hypothesis the drug is clinically superior. However, to obtain orphan drug marketing exclusivity, the marketing application must contain evidence demonstrating clinical superiority.

## Helpful Resources

Many resources provide relevant information appropriate to include in an orphan drug designation request. These include peer-reviewed journal articles, medical and epidemiology textbooks, meeting conference abstracts, health-related databases, disease- or condition-specific organizations, national health surveys, etc. **Table 24-1** provides some examples of useful websites, but this list is by no means complete.

## A Word about Other Types of Orphan Designations

The potential availability of pediatric priority review vouchers has made rare pediatric disease designation a sought-after objective by sponsors.

A rare pediatric disease is "a disease that primarily affects individuals aged from birth to 18 years" (which FDA interprets as meaning more than 50% of the affected US population is aged 0 through 18 years and is "a rare disease or condition," which includes diseases and conditions affecting fewer than 200,000 persons in the US, and diseases and conditions affecting a larger number of persons but for which there is no reasonable expectation that the costs of developing and making the drug available in the US can be recovered from US sales of the drug. According to FDA guidance, a drug would qualify as a drug for a "rare pediatric disease" if the entire US prevalence of the disease or condition is below 200,000 and if more than 50% of patients with the disease are 0 through 18 years of age.[17] Another way a drug may qualify as a drug for a "rare pediatric disease" is if it is for an "orphan subset" of a disease or condition that otherwise affects 200,000 or more persons in the US, and if this subset is comprised primarily (i.e., more than 50%) of individuals aged 0 through 18 years.

A sponsor may choose to request rare pediatric disease designation. This designation process is entirely voluntary; requesting designation is not a prerequisite to requesting or receiving a priority review voucher. If sponsors choose to request such designation, Section 529(d)(2) of the *Food, Drug, and Cosmetic Act* (*FD&C Act*) states they shall do so "at the same time" they submit a request for orphan drug designation or a request for fast track designation. Note, while an orphan drug designation request may be submitted during any development stage, a request for fast track designation cannot be made prior to IND submission. While a request for rare pediatric disease designation may be submitted at the same time as a request for orphan drug designation, each should be separate.

The rare pediatric disease designation request contains the following information:

- sponsor, sponsor's primary contact person and/or resident agent's name and address, including title, address, telephone number and email address
- drug's nonproprietary and trade name, if any, or, if neither is available, the drug's chemical name or a meaningful descriptive name
- proposed dosage form and route of administration
- description of the rare pediatric disease for which the drug is being or will be investigated; the drug's proposed use; and IND number if previously assigned
- description of the drug to include (i) the active moiety's identity, if it is a drug composed of small molecules, or of the principal molecular structural features, if it is composed of macromolecules, or the active ingredient if it is a biological product; and (ii) its physical and chemical properties, if these characteristics can be determined
- explanation of the mechanism of action, with supportive data, suggesting the drug may be effective in the rare pediatric disease
- basis for concluding the drug is for a "rare disease or condition"
  - o FDA expects a lesser level of supportive data for rare pediatric disease designation than for orphan drug designation because of the differences between the two programs. *In vitro* data supporting the drug's mechanism of action in the disease or in a related disease may suffice for rare pediatric disease designation, whereas that level of data generally would not suffice for orphan drug designation. Such drug properties may include toxicity, mechanism of action or previous clinical experience.
- explanation as to whether, upon approval, the drug potentially may meet the voucher eligibility criterion of containing no previously approved active ingredient (including any ester or salt of the active ingredient) (If sponsors submit a rare pediatric disease designation request at the same time as or shortly after a request for orphan drug designation, any of the above information

contained already in their orphan drug designation requests can be cross-referenced.)

Sponsors should submit two copies, with at least one hard copy of the completed, dated and signed rare pediatric disease designation request.

The benefit of rare pediatric disease designation is a sponsor may be eligible for a rare pediatric disease priority review voucher if (a) it is seeking approval of a drug to treat a rare pediatric disease and (b) it requests the pediatric review voucher at the time of New Drug Application (NDA) submission for the rare pediatric disease. The voucher can be used to obtain priority review for a future NDA (reducing FDA review time from 10 to six months). The pediatric voucher is not used for the NDA to which it is attached. Rather, the sponsor can use the voucher for priority review of its next NDA or transfer it or sell it (for quite a bit of money; reported voucher sales have been more than $100 million). In essence, the voucher is the sponsor's reward for seeking approval for a drug useful in treating a rare pediatric disease. A rare pediatric voucher can be transferred (sold) an unlimited number of times. FDA guidance states, "Upon marketing approval, the sponsor for a rare pediatric drug may be issued a voucher redeemable for a priority review for a SUBSEQUENT marketing application that may otherwise not have qualified for a priority review." The Rare Pediatric Disease Priority Review Voucher program was set to sunset 1 October 2016. On 22 September 2016, the Senate passed the *Advancing Hope Act* of 2016, which amended the *FD&C Act* to revise the priority review voucher program for rare pediatric disease medications. Beginning 90 days after the bill's enactment, a sponsor who intends to request a voucher for a rare pediatric disease medication must notify FDA of that intent upon submitting the medication application. The bill applies to applications submitted to FDA before enactment of the bill that have not been approved. Applications submitted before 7 October 2012 are not eligible for a voucher. A voucher may not be issued for a rare pediatric disease product if a voucher was already issued for the medication under another program.

## Orphan Disease and Conditions and Humanitarian Use Devices

For medical devices, the comparable orphan designation is humanitarian use devices (HUDs) intended to benefit patients in the treatment or diagnosis of diseases or conditions occurring in fewer than 4,000 persons in the US per year.[18] As set forth in 21 CFR 814.102, an HUD request includes the following:

## Table 24-1. Available Resources

| Resource Type | Website | Information Available | Website Addresses |
|---|---|---|---|
| **General Information About Rare Diseases** | NIH Genetic and Rare Diseases Information Center (GARD) | Provides the public with access to current, reliable and easy-to-understand information about rare or genetic diseases | www.rarediseases.info.nih.gov |
| | Check Orphan | Information on rare diseases | www.checkorphan.org |
| | National Organization for Rare Disorders (NORD) | Information on rare diseases | www.rarediseases.org |
| | Orphanet | Information on rare diseases and inventory of orphan drugs | www.orpha.net |
| | Global Genes Allies in Rare Diseases | Rare disease patient advocacy organization | www.globalgenes.org |
| **Literature Citations** | Pubmed Embase Medline | Review articles on diseases/conditions, their etiology and treatment, including the standard of care. Publications with epidemiology and prevalence or incidence data | www.ncbi.nlm.nih.gov/pubmed |
| **Health Statistics** | Behavioral Risk Factor Surveillance System (BRFSS) | US system of health-related telephone surveys that collect state data about US residents regarding their health-related risk behaviors, chronic health conditions and use of preventive services | www.cdc.gov/brfss |
| | National Cancer Institute Surveillance, Epidemiology, and End Results Program (SEER) | Cancer statistics | www.seer.cancer.gov |
| | National Center for Health Statistics National Health and Nutrition Examination Survey (NHANES) | Estimates of selected diseases' prevalence | www.cdc.gov/nchs/nhanes |
| | Centers for Disease Control (CDC) National Center for Health Statistics | Estimates of selected diseases' prevalence | www.cdc.gov/nchs |
| | International Agency for Research on Cancer (WHO) | Cancer incidence statistics | http://gco.iarc.fr/today/home |
| | World Health Organization (WHO) | Disease and injury country estimates | www.who.int |
| | US Census | Population estimates | www.census.gov |
| **Disease-Specific Information** | NIH National Institute of Diabetes and Kidney Diseases (NIDDKD) | Health information on diabetes and digestive and kidney diseases | www.niddk.nih.gov |
| | NIH National Institute of Neurological Disorders and Stroke (NINDS) | Health information | www.ninds.nih.gov |
| | NIH National Cancer Institute (NCI) | Health information | www.cancer.gov |
| | NIH National Institute of Arthritis and Musculoskeletal and Skin Diseases (NIAMS) | Health information | www.niams.nih.gov |
| | American Heart Association | Health information on cardiovascular disease | www.heart.org |
| | American Cancer Society | Health information and statistics on cancer | www.cancer.org |
| | American Lung Association | Health information on lung diseases | www.lung.org |

| Resource Type | Website | Information Available | Website Addresses |
|---|---|---|---|
| **Drugs With Orphan Designation** | FDA orphan drug designations and approvals | List of drugs/indications that have received orphan designation and their exclusivity status | www.accessdata.fda.gov/scripts/opdlisting/oopd/index.cfm |
| **Patient Advocacy Websites** | National Brain Tumor Society | Health information on brain tumors/cancer | www.braintumor.org |
| | Muscular Dystrophy Association | Health information on muscular dystrophy | www.mda.org |
| | Cystic Fibrosis Foundation | Health information on cystic fibrosis | www.cff.org |
| **Other Useful Sites** | Agency for Healthcare Research and Quality (AHRQ) | Data on topics such as using healthcare, costs of care, trends in hospital care, health insurance coverage, out-of-pocket spending and patient satisfaction | www.ahrq.gov |
| | ClinicalTrials.gov | Registry and results database of publicly and privately supported clinical studies | www.clinicaltrials.gov |

- statement the applicant requests HUD designation for a rare disease or condition or a specifically identified orphan subset of a non-rare disease or condition
- applicant and primary contact person's title, name, address and telephone number
- description of the rare disease or condition the device treats or diagnoses, ideally with particular emphasis on the disease or condition's specific aspects relevant to the device's functionality, as well as the device's proposed indication(s) for use and the reasons such therapy is needed (If the device treats or diagnoses a non-rare disease or condition, the applicant must demonstrate an orphan subset for the device.)
- description of the device and discussion of the scientific rationale for the device's use for the rare disease or condition or orphan subset of a non-rare disease or condition
- documentation, with appended authoritative references, to demonstrate the device is designed to treat or diagnose a rare disease or condition affecting or manifested in fewer than 4,000 people in the US per year

A humanitarian device exemption (HDE) must be obtained before FDA will allow an HUD to be marketed. To obtain an HDE, a sponsor submits an HDE application to FDA. FDA provides an HDE checklist for filing decisions, describing the information to be included (http://www.fda.gov/downloads/MedicalDevices/DeviceRegulationandGuidance/HowtoMarketYourDevice/PremarketSubmissions/HumanitarianDeviceExemption/UCM056830.pdf). An HDE application contains similar data to those included in a premarket approval (PMA) application, but the sponsor is not required to demonstrate clinical effectiveness. The sponsor must demonstrate the device's effectiveness for its intended purpose and the absence of unreasonable or significant risk of illness or injury. The submission also must include information demonstrating that the probable health benefit outweighs the risk of injury or illness from its use (taking into account the probable risks and benefits of currently available devices or alternative forms of treatment), that no comparable are devices available to treat or diagnose the disease or condition, and that they could not otherwise bring the device to market. FDA provides a listing of CDRH humanitarian device exemptions on its website (http://www.fda.gov/MedicalDevices/ProductsandMedicalProcedures/DeviceApprovalsandClearances/HDEApprovals/ucm161827.htm). The application is similar to a PMA application but does not need to include information on the device's effectiveness; it must include sufficient information to demonstrate the device's safety.

## Conclusion

More and more pharmaceutical companies are seeking orphan drug designations for their drug products. In 2015, OOPD received 440 designation requests, which was a 22% increase over 2014. The benefits of designation are enticing: research and development tax credits, waiving the *Prescription Drug User Fee Act* filing fee, seven years of marketing exclusivity, increased access to FDA reviewers and more. For many rare conditions and diseases, the orphan drug designation prevalence criterion is met easily with a simple Internet search; but for some, it is more challenging and may require critical review of published data. Demonstrating the disease's rarity alone will not support designation. It is just as critical to provide evidence of a medical rationale for the drug's use in the intended patient population. This support typically comes from clinical investigations or studies in appropriate animal models. Together with an introduction to the disease or condition, its etiology and its current standard of diagnosis or care, this information can be included in a persuasive orphan drug designation request that will enable continued development of a promising medication.

## References

1. Richter T, Nestler-Parr S, Babela R, Khan ZM, Tesoro T, Molsen E, et al. 2015. "Rare disease terminology and definitions—A systematic global review: Report of the ISPOR rare disease special interest group." *Value in Health* 18, 906–914.
2. Aronson JK. 2006. Editor's view. Rare diseases and orphan drugs. *Br. J. Clin. Pharmacol.* 61, 243–245.
3. Op cit 1.
4. Sharma A, Jacob A, Tandon M and Kumar D. 2010. "Orphan drug: Development trends and strategies." *J. Pharm. Bioallied Sci.* 2, 290–299.
5. Lee DK and Wong B. 2014. "An orphan drug framework (ODF) for Canada." *J. Popul. Ther. Clin. Pharmacol.* 21 (1):342-e46.
6. Op cit 1.
7. Hughes DA, Tunnage B and Yeo ST. 2005. "Drugs for exceptionally rare diseases: Do they deserve special status for funding?" *QJ Med.* 98, 829–836.
8. Schuller Y, Hollak CEM and Biegstraaten M. 2015. "The quality of economic evaluations of ultra-orphan drugs in Europe—A systematic review." *Orphanet J Rare Dis.* 10, 92.
9. Reese JH. FDA Orphan Drug Designation 101. Worldwide Orphan Medicinal Designation Workshop, 10 March 2014.
10. Deneux M, Adetona T, Pailloux F, and Voisin E. 2015. "Orphan drug designation within the development strategy." *J. Rare Disord. Diag. Ther.* 1, 1–7.
11. Op cit 8.
12. *Draft Guidance for Industry. Providing Regulatory Submissions in Electronic Format—Orphan-Drug and Humanitarian Use Device Designation Requests and Related Submissions.* FDA website. http://www.fda.gov/downloads/ForIndustry/DevelopingProductsforRareDiseasesConditions/DesignatingHumanitarianUseDevicesHUDS/LegislationRelatingtoHUDsHDEs/UCM241281.pdf. Accessed 22 January 2017.
13. *Draft Guidance for Industry, Researchers, Patient Groups, and Food and Drug Administration Staff: Meeting with the Office of Orphan Products Development.* FDA website. http://www.fda.gov/downloads/ForIndustry/DevelopingProductsforRareDiseasesConditions/OOPDNewsArchive/UCM392593.pdf. Accessed 22 January 2017.
14. Silverstein B. *Tell me a story. Reg. Focus* Oct 2011. P. 35-37.
15. Op cit 9.
16. Ibid.
17. *Rare Pediatric Disease Priority Review Vouchers: Draft Guidance for Industry.* FDA website. http://www.fda.gov/downloads/RegulatoryInformation/Guidances/UCM423325.pdf. Accessed 22 January 2017.
18. *Guidance for Industry and FDA Staff: Humanitarian Use Device (HUD) Designations.* FDA website. http://www.fda.gov/ForIndustry/DevelopingProductsforRareDiseasesConditions/DesignatingHumanitarianUseDevicesHUDS/LegislationRelatingtoHUDsHDEs/ucm283517.htm. Accessed 22 January 2017.

## Recommended Reading

- Frequently Asked Questions (FAQ). FDA website. http://www.fda.gov/ForIndustry/DevelopingProductsforRareDiseasesConditions/HowtoapplyforOrphanProductDesignation/ucm240819.htm. Accessed 22 January 2017.
- Hall AK and Carlson MR. "The current status of orphan drug development in Europe and the U.S." 2014. *Intract. Rare Dis. Res.* 3, 1–7.
- Mildred M, Lee S. "The rise of orphan drugs in Europe vs the Unites States: Comparing orphan drug designations between the EMA and FDA." 2015. *Value Health* 18(7):A677.
- Mullard A. "FDA approves ultra-orphan on a 4-patient trial." 2015. *Nat. Rev. Drug Discov.* 14, 669.
- Tomita, N, Lee H, Korchagina D, Toumi, M, Remuzat, C & Falissard, B. 2015. Orphan drug regulation in the USA, European Union, Japan, and South Korea: A comparative analysis. *Value Health* 18(7):A678.

## Author

Beth Silverstein is a director of the scientific and regulatory consulting firm SciLucent LLC, where she currently manages the company's clinical and regulatory practice. She is an experienced regulatory affairs professional who routinely prepares and oversees the preparation of drug and medical device regulatory documentation for submission to FDA, including investigational new drug applications, new drug applications, investigators brochures, orphan drug designation requests, requests for expedited approvals, investigational device exemptions and premarket approval applications. Silverstein holds an MS in zoology (physiology) from The Ohio State University and has earned the RAC.

## 25

# Pediatric Investigational Plan (PIP)

*By Jocelyn Jennings, MS, RAC*

## Introduction

In 2006, the European Medicines Agency (EMA) mandated that pediatric studies be incorporated into clinical study plans for all pharmaceutical and biologic products to be marketed in the EU. The Pediatric Investigational Plan (PIP) is the mechanism for providing EMA with pediatric population data.

The PIP is a research and development program that ensures necessary data are generated determining the conditions in which a medicinal product may be authorized to treat the pediatric population. The PIP requirements are in Article 10 of Regulation (EC) No 1901/2006 of the European Parliament and of the Council of 12 December 2006 on medicinal products for pediatric use, the "*Pediatric Regulation.*"[1]

## The Pediatric Regulation

The *Pediatric Regulation* was a response to the absence of sufficient suitable, authorized medicinal products to treat conditions in children in the EU. Studies indicated most medicines used for children were not specifically tested for use in this population because manufacturers frequently did not carry out the necessary research and development to adapt medicinal products to children. Sponsors or applicants were reluctant to perform studies in this vulnerable population that usually require extensive informed consent forms and, sometimes, multiple assent forms. Additionally, sponsors or applicants typically did not have the in-house population expertise to design clinical studies for pediatric subjects. This left healthcare professionals to use products off-label or to use unauthorized products with the associated risks of inefficacy, adverse reactions and the possibility of incorrect dosage.

The *Pediatric Regulation* created a system of requirements, rewards and incentives together with horizontal measures to ensure medicinal products and vaccines are researched, developed and authorized based on data to support their effects and safety profile in children. The *Pediatric Regulation*'s key objectives are to ensure[2] high-quality research into the development of medicinal products for use in children and to guarantee that, over time, the majority of products used in children are authorized specifically for such use.

EMA's incentives or rewards to entice marketing authorization holders to develop PIPs are:[3]

- waivers for medicines unlikely to benefit children and timing deferrals to ensure medicines are tested in children only when it is safe to do so
- a six-month extension of the supplementary protection certificate (SPC)
  - o for orphan medicines, an additional two years of market exclusivity added to the

**Table 25-1. Pediatric Population**

| Pediatric Subgroup | Age |
|---|---|
| Pre-term and term neonates | 0 to 27 days |
| Infants (or toddlers) | 1 month to 23 months |
| Children | 2 years to 11 years |
| Adolescents | 12 years to 18 years |

existing 10 years awarded under the EU's *Orphan Regulation*
- a new type of marketing authorization, the pediatric use marketing authorization (PUMA), which allows 10 years of data protection for innovation (new studies) on off-patent products
- measures to maximize the impact of existing studies on medicines for children, including a public database of pediatric studies
  o an EU inventory of children's therapeutic needs to focus medicines' research, development and authorization
  o an EU network of investigators and trial centers to conduct the required research and development
  o a system of free EMA Scientific Advice for industry
- a provision on EU funding into research leading to the development and authorization of off-patent medicines for children

The *Pediatric Regulation* established the Pediatric Committee (PDCO), with members and alternates from the Committee for Medicinal Products for Human Use (CHMP), each EU Member State not represented on CHMP and health professionals and representatives from patient associations appointed by the European Parliament. PDCO assesses PIPs, applications for waivers and deferrals and forms opinions. PDCO also may assess Marketing Authorization applications' compliance at the request of the applicant, CHMP or a Competent Authority, or provide advice on other questions at the request of EMA's executive director or the European Commission.[4] Members and alternates are chosen to cover scientific areas relevant to pediatric medicinal products, pediatric research, pediatric medical practice, pharmacovigilance and bioethics.

## Pediatric Investigation Plan
### Developing the PIP

For all new products and indications, a sponsor or applicant must address how or whether its product would or should be used in children. For example, the sponsor or applicant must determine whether the mechanism of action is the same in children as it is in adults. The sponsor or applicant should, at minimum, consider the availability of and need for:
- disease or indication information
- preclinical data
- clinical study plan or protocol
- extrapolation study plan or protocol
- justification for age groups—this will be needed only if one or more pediatric subgroups is excluded
- postmarketing surveillance data
- publications
- modeling or simulation study plan or protocol
- request for waiver—provide justification for waiver of pediatric age groups
- request for deferral—provide justification for deferral
- appropriate pediatric subgroups

The application must cover all pediatric population subgroups (see **Table 25-1**) unless there are grounds for a waiver.

If pediatric subgroups other than these are more appropriate for the medicinal product, the choices must be explained and justified within the application.

Certain questions should be asked and answered during the planning. Does the indication affect all pediatric subgroups? Should the product target a specific pediatric subgroup? Will container closure size changes be needed? Will a different container closure system need to be developed? Will a different formulation need to be developed specifically for pediatric patients?

Before a sponsor or applicant can start preparing the PIP, it also must review already existing data for its product to determine a path forward. What testing will need to be done? Can modeling or simulation be used? Can existing adult data be extrapolated to the pediatric population? Will any waivers or deferrals need to be obtained? If the product has been marketed, does post-market surveillance data contain information pertaining to any pediatric subgroup? Is a therapy available providing a therapeutic benefit that may be lacking in the sponsor or applicant's medicinal product?

Once the sponsor or applicant has determined the appropriate plan, the pertinent PIP data and information must be compiled. PIP content and format are specified in *Guideline on the format and content of applications for agreement or modification of a paediatric investigation plan and requests for waivers or deferrals and concerning the operation of the compliance check and on criteria for assessing significant studies* (2014/C338/01).[5]

## PIP Contents

The PIP is comprised of six sections:
- Part A: administrative and product information
- Part B: overall development of the medicinal product
- Part C: application for a product-specific waiver
- Part D: proposed pediatric investigation plan
- Part E: Request for deferral
- Part F: Annexes

In addition, EMA's Application for Paediatric Investigation Plan/Waiver[6] form must be submitted. The application should be based on information relevant to the product's evaluation and development. This includes details of any incomplete or discontinued pharmacotoxicological tests or clinical trials or other studies relating to the medicinal product, or completed trials concerning indications not covered by the application.

A PIP for a PUMA may be limited to only relevant pediatric subgroups; it need not address them all. A template available on EMA's website can be used to satisfy Parts B–E.[7]

### Part A

Part A subsections must be completed unless information is unavailable:
- applicant and contact person's name or corporate name and address
- active substance name—should be stated by its recommended international non-proprietary name
- product type
- medicinal product details (all different pharmaceutical forms, formulations, strengths and routes of administration under development in adults and children) (For pediatric product development, information on the proposed strength, pharmaceutical form, route of administration and formulation including excipient details should be provided.)
- medicinal product's marketing authorization status (in tabular format)
- regulatory authority advice relevant to development in the pediatric population
- orphan medicine status in the EU and EU Register of Orphan Medicinal Products number (Indicate if orphan designation is being sought.)
- planned application for marketing authorization, extension of marketing authorization or variation

- application summary
- translations of the agency decision

An application form is provided on EMA's website. A checksum number is created when the form is downloaded and being completed.

### Part B

Part B should contain:
- discussion of condition similarities and differences between populations (adult and pediatric) and pharmacological rationale—address differences in etiology, severity, symptoms, evolution, prognosis and response to therapy
- current diagnosis, prevention or treatment methods in pediatric populations
- significant therapeutic benefit and/or fulfilment of therapeutic need—ultimately PDCO will perform this assessment based on available medicinal product data

The information in Part B is required for each indication and each pediatric population subgroup, with a description of how *Pediatric Regulation* requirements will be met. The sponsor or applicant should detail the methodology chosen to identify potential pediatric need conditions. If the medicinal product is being developed for children only, some of the Part B information may not be available. For those products being developed for PUMAs, only the concerned pediatric subgroup needs to be addressed in this section. If information is not available, the sponsor should indicate this rather than omitting a subsection.

### Part C

If a waiver is needed, Part C will include the required information and justifications. A waiver can be issued with reference to either one or more specified pediatric population subgroups, to one or more specified indications or conditions or to a combination of both.[8] Justification for a product-specific waiver could be due to lack of safety or efficacy data for all or part of the pediatric population, a disease or condition not occurring in the specified pediatric subgroup or a lack of therapeutic benefit, especially when compared to existing pediatric population treatments.

### Part D

Part D should contain:
- existing overall data strategy proposed for the pediatric development—the pediatric investigation plan and indication, selected population

**Table 25.2. PIP Submission Process**

| Time | Sponsor or Applicant | PDCO |
|---|---|---|
| Day 0 | Submits PIP via Eudralink and CD or DVD | Receives PIP |
| Day 30 | No action required | Provides draft summary report |
| Day 60 | Receives final opinion or respond to modification request | Adopts opinion or require modification |
| Day 90 (if modification required at Day 60) | No action required | Provides draft summary report on modification request |
| Day 120 (if modification required at Day 60) | Receives final opinion | Adopts final opinion |

subgroups and information on quality, nonclinical and clinical data

- pediatric formulation development, pharmaceutical form suitability (e.g., tablet, mini-tablet, etc.), strength, formulation and excipients
- nonclinical studies
- pediatric clinical studies:
  - o possible extrapolation from adult data to pediatric subjects and among pediatric subgroups (If extrapolation is a significant component, a description of the study with a defined protocol should be provided.)
  - o pharmacodynamic and pharmacokinetic studies, if relevant for the medicinal product
  - o dose finding studies, selected efficacy or safety primary and secondary endpoints and specific measures proposed to protect the pediatric population should be defined
- other studies—a tabular list of extrapolation or modeling and simulation studies should be provided (Any other studies deemed relevant should be in this section as well.)

The key elements form[9] is the PIP section that corresponds to Part D. This form captures the key elements (main features) of measures or studies proposed for PIP opinion or decision inclusion. The completed measures or studies will be verified against these key elements during compliance check. The whole study synopsis or protocol should not be inserted; these can be included elsewhere in the application (as part F). If information is not provided in a text field, provide appropriate justification.

## Part E

Part E is reserved for deferral requests. Deferrals allow the initiation or completion of PIP-specific pediatric studies or other measures after submission of the corresponding marketing authorization application in adults. Deferral requests must be justified on scientific and technical grounds or on grounds related to public health. A deferral

will be granted in accordance with the *Pediatric Regulation* when:

- it is appropriate to conduct studies in adults prior to initiating pediatric population studies
- pediatric population studies will take longer to conduct than adult studies

## Part F

Part F contains the annexes of supportive documents. Examples of information that could be provided in Part F are:

- Investigator's Brochure, approved summary of product characteristics and risk management plan reference number
- copy of any Scientific Advice relevant to the pediatric population from either EMA or a national Competent Authority
- copy of any US Food and Drug Administration written request
- any advice, opinion or decision relating to pediatric information from a regulatory agency outside the EU
- copy of any European Commission decision on orphan designation
- reference number or a copy of any previous agency decision on PIPs or negative PDCO opinion

Actual nonclinical or clinical study reports do not need to be submitted; a summary of the reports is sufficient. However, protocols should be submitted as an Annex to assist PDCO in its PIP review.

## PIP Submission Process

EMA's website includes documents containing PIP submission deadlines by year. The current or next year's schedule should be consulted to determine PIP submission timing (see **Table 25-2**). Once the sponsor or applicant has decided on a timeline, a letter of intent form[10] must be sent to EMA at least two months prior to starting the procedure. Once all the documents are ready for submission, the sponsor or applicant is required to submit everything via Eudralink and on CD or DVD to EMA and all PDCO members. At Day 30 after the initial PDCO discussion, a draft summary report will be sent to the sponsor or applicant. At Day 60, PDCO shall adopt an opinion on whether the proposed studies will ensure generation of data to support the medicinal product's use in the pediatric population. During this time, PDCO may have questions and could pose a request for PIP modification at Day 60. Therefore, the timeframe for adopting an opinion will extend another 60 days maximum. PDCO or the applicant could ask for a meeting at this time.

If the sponsor or applicant receives a request for PIP modifications from PDCO, it can contact the assigned pediatric coordinator to assist in clarifying PDCO comments or requests. The pediatric coordinator is a great resource for the sponsor or applicant and should be consulted as often as required.

## Modifying an Agreed PIP

As stated above, PDCO can come back to the sponsor or applicant to request PIP modifications. The modification process is the same as the initial PIP submission process. A modification to an agreed PIP usually occurs because one or more key elements become unworkable or no longer are appropriate. The sponsor or applicant should explain the lack of appropriateness or the feasibility issue underlying each key element for which modification is being requested. An application summary should accompany the modification application. For Parts B–F, only information relevant to the modification request should be provided; documents or information not relevant to the modification being proposed should not be submitted.

## Compliance Check

In order to guarantee the PIP is followed, national Competent Authorities or EMA perform compliance checks at various stages. The compliance check can occur as part of marketing authorization or extension or variation validation. PDCO may, on request, issue an opinion on compliance and clarify who can request an opinion and when. For example, the national Competent Authorities or EMA may request an opinion when validating an application. The compliance check determines whether:

- documents submitted cover all pediatric population subgroups
- documents cover existing and new indications, pharmaceutical forms and routes of administration
- all agreed PIP measures have been executed in accordance with its key approved, specified elements

If there is more than one PIP covering the application, all will be checked for compliance. Sponsors and applicants should submit the PDCO compliance report when submitting the marketing authorization application, extension or variation. A table cross-referencing the key PIP elements with the compliance position should be submitted in the marketing authorization, extension or variation application.

## Summary

The PIP is used to comply with EMA's requirement for pediatric population-relevant data for all new or currently marketed medicinal products. The PIP should contain well-thought-out plans or protocols that discuss how the sponsor or applicant will provide the necessary documentation for their medicinal product to be authorized for pediatric use. All pediatric subgroups must be taken into account when determining the needed study types and design. Justifications for waivers or deferrals must be grounded in science. If the medicinal product does not have therapeutic benefit for a particular subgroup, a waiver is justifiable. However, if a particular pediatric subgroup's recruitment is difficult, different recruitment methods should be employed. The PIP application is lengthy and detailed, with an annex that contains relevant supplementary information such as study reports, study protocols, Investigator's Brochure, etc. PDCO assesses the PIP and renders an opinion that must be provided in the sponsor or applicant's marketing authorization application, extension or variation. The application will not be authorized without the PDCO compliance check report. Therefore, it is extremely important for the sponsor or applicant to follow the agreed PIP and provide compliance evidence at the time of marketing authorization application submission. Submitting a marketing authorization application without thinking about the medicinal product's viability in the pediatric population is a practice of the past. Pediatric patients deserve breakthrough therapies tailored to their specific needs.

### References
1. Regulation (EC) No1901/2006 of the European Parliament and of the Council of 12 December 2006 on medicinal products for paediatric use and amending Regulation (EEC) No 1768/92, Directive 2001/20/EC, Directive 2001/83/EC and Regulation (EC) No 726/2004. Eur-Lex website. http://eur-lex.europa.eu/

legal-content/EN/TXT/?uri=celex:32006R1901. Accessed 23 January 2017.

2.  Ibid.

3.  Ibid.

4.  Ibid.

5.  *Guideline on the format and content of applications for agreement or modification of a paediatric investigation plan and requests for waivers or deferrals and concerning the operation of the compliance check and on criteria for assessing significant studies* (2014/C 338/01). EC website. http://ec.europa.eu/health//sites/health/files/files/eudralex/vol-1/2014_c338_01/2014_c338_01_en.pdf. Accessed 23 January 2017.

6.  Application for Paediatric Investigation Plan/Waiver. EMA website. http://www.ema.europa.eu/ema/index.jsp?curl=pages/regulation/document_listing/document_listing_000293.jsp. Accessed 23 January 2017.

7.  Template for scientific document (Part B-E). EMA website. http://www.ema.europa.eu/ema/index.jsp?curl=pages/regulation/document_listing/document_listing_000293.jsp#section1. Accessed 23 January 2017.

8.  Op cit 5.

9.  Key Elements Form. EMA website. http://www.ema.europa.eu/ema/index.jsp?curl=pages/regulation/document_listing/document_listing_000293.jsp#section1. Accessed 23 January 2017. www.ema.europa.eu

10. Template for letter of intent to submit an application. EMA website. http://www.ema.europa.eu/ema/index.jsp?curl=pages/regulation/document_listing/document_listing_000293.jsp#section1. Accessed 23 January 2017.

11. Op cit 5.

**Author**

Jocelyn Jennings, MS, RAC is a regulatory professional working for a global healthcare company that manufactures therapeutic products using plasma proteins. She has more than 19 years of extensive global regulatory, quality assurance and global clinical trial experience in drugs, biologics and medical devices. Jennings is an adjunct professor at Northeastern University in the College of Professional Studies. She also is actively involved with local regulatory chapters in her area and with the Regulatory Affairs Professionals Society (RAPS). Jennings holds an MS in regulatory affairs from Northeastern University and has earned the RAC.

# 26

## Accelerated Filings

*By Joanne Rupprecht, JD, RAC (US)*

## Food and Drug Administration (FDA) Initiatives

For more than 25 years, the US Food and Drug Administration (FDA) has been attempting to provide expedited pathways for product approvals to make promising therapies available to the public. The struggle then, as it is now, was "to speed the availability of new therapies to patients with serious conditions and/or rare diseases … especially when there are no satisfactory alternative therapies, while preserving appropriate standards for safety and effectiveness."[1]

The *Prescription Drug User Fee Act* (*PDUFA*) was passed in 1992 to promote the speedy evaluation of marketing applications by allowing sponsors to pay a fee to fund FDA staffing for expedited reviews. *PDUFA* mandated re-approval every five years. In 1997, the US Congress enacted the *Food and Drug Administration Modernization Act* (*FDAMA*), which amended the *Food, Drug, and Cosmetic Act* (*FD&C Act*; Title 21, Chapter 9 of the US Code) relating to the regulation of food, drugs, devices and biological products. Measures for expedited review were codified in 21 CFR Part 312, Subpart E.[2]

While the intended improvements to food, drug, device and biological products regulation can be subject to several interpretations, a common goal emerged: to get novel therapies, drugs and medical devices in consumers'

hands for disease prevention, management and cure. Prior to 1992, FDA began to recognize and lay the foundation for modernizing its systems, including those for drug, device and biological product submission reviews across its different divisions. As explained in more detail in Chapter 1, the frustrations of patients and manufacturers alike were apparent, and the public was vocal and active in the perceived need for FDA reformation.

FDA Advisory Committees also play an important role in reviewing data from clinical development programs for novel or improved therapies. For a product to proceed in the accelerated approval process, the proposed drug's safety and efficacy are reviewed for patients who had an inadequate therapeutic response to, or were unable to tolerate, other available products. If more data are required, additional and/or long-term outcomes trials may be required.

## The Importance of Communicating With FDA

Communication is key to all successful product development and approval programs, but accelerated processes require enhanced communication, in part because novel, necessary therapies for life-threatening or rare conditions may present more risk than normally tolerated in clinical studies, product submissions or clinical practice. One of the many FDA missions is to protect public health by ensuring devices, biologics, vaccines and drugs' safety and efficacy. Thus, FDA seeks to understand the benefits and risks of all therapies prior to approval. In the setting of rare diseases, the active participation of the public, especially patients, their caregivers and advocacy groups are encouraged. A final consideration is all development activities will be expected to occur at an accelerated pace to meet timelines.

A sponsor should be prepared to answer many questions in initial product development stages:

1. Is the condition and/or disease "serious," as defined by the expanded access regulations?
2. Is the product in question intended to treat the serious condition and/or disease?
3. Does the product have any effect on the serious condition and/or diseases?
4. Does a lack of treatment for the condition and/or disease qualify as an "unmet medical need"?
5. Are other therapies available? If so, does the product have an improved effect on the serious condition and/or disease compared to available therapies?

As discussed in more detail in the "rare diseases" section of this chapter, special designations may be discussed with FDA during pre-Investigational New Drug (IND) or pre-New Drug Application (NDA) communications, and if found to be appropriate, should be requested formally upon submission of the IND for Fast Track and Breakthrough Therapies, in the Biologics License Application (BLA) or NDA for Priority Review, and for Accelerated Approvals, as early as possible during development, so endpoints can be decided before clinical trials proceed or are concluded.

## Rolling Reviews

FDA allows "rolling reviews" for expanded access product approvals, which means the agency will review completed sections of the submission prior to the final assembly of the complete marketing application. Since a product IND will have been submitted, "rolling review" documents should be filed as amendments to the IND using Form FDA 1571 and identified as **REQUEST FOR SUBMISSION OF PORTIONS OF AN APPLICATION**, in bold, uppercase letters.[3]

Any document submitted on a rolling review basis should be complete and considered final, so FDA can provide meaningful review. If updates are required after the rolling submission, they are made via the formal amendment pathway. When in doubt, confer with the appropriate FDA point-of-contact for the product. Keep

in mind, Form FDA 3397 will be required each time information is submitted, and user fees will apply.[4]

Rolling review will not necessarily speed the complete submission review process. FDA review time is calculated only once the entire application package is submitted; therefore, the pre-submission sections ultimately may not accelerate approval.

## Expanded Access for Drugs and Biologics

In general, clinical trials are conducted in phases to ensure a product's safety and efficacy before it is introduced into commercial distribution. These phases often are broken down as:

- Phase 1—involves small groups of human subjects (both healthy volunteers and the target population) and covers first-in-human safety evaluations, clinical pharmacology, pharmacokinetics and pharmacodynamics, proof-of-concept and drug interaction studies
- Phase 2—involves larger groups of human subjects (usually in the target population) for dose selection, initial effectiveness evaluation and further safety evaluation
- Phase 3— involves large groups of human subjects in the target population to confirm effectiveness, further monitor side effects and conduct comparison studies with standards of care
- Phase 4—involves studies done after a product is approved to gather additional information about effects in various subpopulations, to answer questions raised during marketing application review or in the context of clinical use, or to continue monitoring side effects associated with long-term use

FDA and other health authorities recognize patients with acute heathcare needs exist and have launched various alternative pathways to approval. In the US, the following designations can be used for eligible products.

- Fast Track—for a drug intended to treat a serious condition, and nonclinical or clinical data demonstrate its potential to address an unmet medical need, or it has been qualified as an infectious disease product
- Breakthrough Therapy—for a drug intended to treat a serious condition if initial clinical data demonstrates the possibility for a substantial improvement to a clinically significant endpoint(s) over other available therapies
- Accelerated Approval—for a drug that treats a serious condition, provides an advantage over

other available therapies, demonstrates an effect on a surrogate endpoint intended to predict eventual clinical benefit, or a clinical endpoint or that can provide any other clinical benefit

- Priority Review
  - o for a drug that treats a serious condition and may provide a significant improvement in safety or effectiveness
  - o for any marketing application supplement proposing a labeling change based on a pediatric study under CFR §505
  - o for any marketing application for a drug qualified as an infectious disease product
  - o for any marketing application or supplement for a drug submitted accompanied by a Priority Review Voucher[5]

### Orphan Drug Designation

One of FDA's oldest accelerated review programs, Orphan Drug status is granted by FDA's Office of Orphan Products Development (OOPD) to support and advance the development of new therapies for rare diseases, defined as conditions affecting fewer than 200,000 people in the US, or therapies that can provide clinical benefit but will not generate adequate revenue to fund clinical research.[6] Since 1983, OOPD has helped make more than 400 drugs and biologic products available for rare diseases.[7] (For more information, see Chapter 24.)

Certain tax incentives for clinical trials and marketing application user fee exemptions are available to companies interested in participating in this program. For already existing treatments or drugs, an orphan designation will confer an additional seven years of US marketing exclusivity or patent protection. For orphan products, proof of clinical safety and effectiveness are required, and the regulatory requirements for approval are not accelerated. In addition, two grant programs are available for rare disease researchers: the Orphan Products Grants Program for drugs, biologics, medical devices and medical foods; and the Pediatric Device Consortia (PDC) Grant Program for pediatric medical devices.[8]

## Compassionate Use/Single Patient IND

Currently, the compassionate use process allows physicians to request FDA permission to use an investigational drug in the absence of a formalized clinical trial if no other treatment options exist, especially for a patient with a terminal illness. The request must be made jointly with the investigational drug manufacturer. The process is lengthy and complicated, which hinders FDA's goal of expanding access to investigational drugs.

Gaining access to investigational drugs through the compassionate use process is expected to get easier through the efforts of FDA's nonprofit arm, the Reagan-Udall Foundation (RUF). Assisting in this effort, Rep. Michael McCaul (R-TX) has proposed the *Andrea Sloan Compassionate Use Reform and Enhancement (CURE) Act*,[9] which would require manufacturers to make their compassionate use policies publicly available and create an "Expanded Use Task Force" to evaluate patient access to investigational drugs and improve the process for approving expanded access requests.[10]

This process is expected to be streamlined by the end of 2017, with the implementation of a "navigator" for non-emergency INDs; emergency INDs are requested over the phone or by email for a 24-hour turnaround by FDA. Hopefully, tracking these uses and their results will be incorporated into this process.[11]

## Special Considerations

When pursuing accelerated approval, manufacturers must consider all associated ancillary activities and the human resources required to perform them, including but not limited to protocol design, clinical site selection, Institutional Review Board (IRB) approvals, commercial production documentation (standard operating procedures, SOPs) and validation, stability studies, change control processes, regulatory filing preparation and postmarket study planning. Additionally, a robust pharmacovigilance process should be in place at the earliest possible development stage, given the increased risks associated with products approved through accelerated pathways.

Flexibility should be built into every process and procedure, and responsiveness to FDA communications, requests and requirements throughout the accelerated process is key as this very dynamic area continues to evolve.

## Humanitarian Use Device (HUD)/ Humanitarian Device Exemption (HDE)

The Humanitarian Use Device (HUD) program applies to medical devices intended to diagnose or treat diseases affecting fewer than 4,000 individuals in the US annually (21 CFR 814.3(n)).[12]

To obtain HUD approval from FDA, a sponsor must file a Humanitarian Device Exemption (HDE) application, which is similar to a Premarket Approval (PMA) application, but for effectiveness requirements.[13]

Although clinical investigations specifically demonstrating the device is effective for its intended purpose are not required,[14] the applicant must provide sufficient information to demonstrate the device does not pose an unreasonable risk of illness or injury, and the benefit of its use outweighs risks as demonstrated in clinical studies monitored by IRBs.[15] Labeling must indicate the device is for Humanitarian Use only, and the effectiveness of its indicated use has not been demonstrated.[16]

To date, more than 50 HDE products have received FDA approval through this program.[17]

## State Legislative Efforts to Address Unmet Medical Needs

Since 2014, at least 24 states have passed "Right to Try" laws, whereby patients with no other treatment options or who are terminally ill can gain access to investigational drugs that have completed certain Phase 1 clinical trials.[18,19] States that have passed "Right to Try" legislation include Alabama, Arkansas, Colorado, Florida, Georgia, Idaho, Indiana, Louisiana, Maine, Michigan, Minnesota, Mississippi, Missouri, Montana, Nevada, North Dakota, Oklahoma, South Carolina, South Dakota, Tennessee, Texas, Utah, Virginia and Wyoming.[20] Legislation has been introduced in Alaska, Arizona, Connecticut, Delaware, Hawaii, Illinois, Iowa, Kansas, Kentucky, Maryland, Massachusetts, Nebraska, New Hampshire, New Jersey, New York, North Carolina, Ohio, Oregon, Pennsylvania, Rhode Island, Vermont, West Virginia, Washington and Wisconsin.[21] In California, the governor vetoed the legislation.

Between 2009 and 2013, FDA received approximately 1,000 expanded-access applications each year; nearly all were approved.[22] FDA considers the severity of the patient's condition and whether other avenues of treatment have been exhausted. Patient advocates and policy experts support the agency's continued oversight because of its critical role in ensuring drug safety and effectiveness, despite the time such oversight takes. Nevertheless, FDA approving a request for an experimental drug does not compel the manufacturer to provide the drug to the patient.[23]

## Surrogate Endpoint Use and Validation and Biomarker Benefits

Since 1992, when accelerated approval regulations (21 CFR Part 314, Subpart H and 21 CFR Part 601, Subpart E) first were enacted, FDA has allowed additional endpoints to be used for drugs "intended to treat serious or life-threatening diseases and that either demonstrate an improvement over available therapy or provide therapy where none exists."[24] From 1992 through 2008, FDA approved more than 90 accelerated marketing applications for drugs based on surrogate endpoints.[25]

In 2012, the passage of the *Food and Drug Administration Safety and Innovation Act* (*FDASIA*)

officially permitted surrogate endpoints to be used for accelerated approvals of drugs for serious diseases that qualified as meeting an unmet medical need.[26]

In this setting, the time it normally would take to establish a clinically significant endpoint during clinical trials is not always available to a sponsor or, more importantly, patients. These circumstances may pave the way for FDA to accept a "surrogate" endpoint such as a laboratory measure, in place of clinical measures of benefits received from treatment.[27]

Scientific support still is required by FDA for the use of surrogate endpoints, which essentially serve as predictors of a given drug's benefit. Surrogate endpoints can benefit patients by easing access to therapies for life-threatening illnesses and serious diseases. Sponsors also benefit, since the time and expense normally associated with clinical trials is reduced.

Biological markers, or "biomarkers," can be very useful in identifying surrogate endpoints, especially when correlated with an accepted clinical efficacy endpoint.[28] Studies can establish whether a positive effect on the selected biomarker can predict clinical outcomes for a sufficient proportion of patients. In sum, the burden on the investigator is reduced, so treatment may be available to patients earlier than the traditional FDA approval process would allow.

## Challenges

The drawbacks raised by allowing patients access to these investigational and experimental drugs include the potential negative impact on the drug development process, and the product liability/personal injury risk to the manufacturers. Also, insurance coverage may be denied when special access is granted through the Right-to-Try laws, resulting in out-of-pocket expenses for patients or advocacy groups.

Public interest groups have expressed concern over FDA's ability to oversee accelerated pathway approvals and the studies associated with them properly. Thus, FDA has put certain initiatives in place to improve its oversight.[29] FDA also has discretion to withdraw any drug from the market if the manufacturer does not comply with required confirmatory studies, although it has not exercised its authority in this way for more than 13 years.[30]

Although critics allege these initiatives provide nothing other than false hope, when faced with the prospect of no hope, false hope is still a benefit for these patients.

**References**

1. *Guidance for Industry: Expedited Programs for Serious Conditions—Drugs and Biologics* (May 2014). FDA website. http://www.fda.gov/downloads/Drugs/Guidances/UCM358301.pdf. Accessed 23 January 2017.

2. Food and Drug Administration, Interim Rule, Investigational New Drug, Antibiotic, and Biological Drug Product Regulations; Procedures for Drugs Intended to Treat Life-Threatening and Severely Debilitating Illnesses (53 FR 41516, October 21, 1988). Federal Register. http://www.rsihata.com/updateguidance/usfda2/2006-1/append2. Accessed 23 January 2017.
3. Ibid.
4. Ibid.
5. Ibid.
6. Developing Products for Rare Diseases & Conditions. FDA website. www.fda.gov/ForIndustry/DevelopingProductsforRareDiseasesConditions/. Accessed 23 January 2017.
7. Ibid.
8. Ibid.
9. Gaffney A. Legislation Seeks to Overhaul FDA's Compassionate Use Program. Regulatory Focus. 9 December 2014. RAPS website. http://www.raps.org/Regulatory-Focus/News/2014/12/09/20946/Legislation-Seeks-to-Overhaul-FDAs-Compassionate-Use-Program/#sthash.lB38lXLU.dpuf. Accessed 23 January 2017.
10. Ibid.
11. Brennan Z. Expedited Compassionate Use for Investigational Drugs Coming Soon, FDA Says. Regulatory Focus. 16 May 2016. RAPS website. http://raps.org/Regulatory-Focus/News/2016/05/16/24951/Expedited-Compassionate-Use-for-Investigational-Drugs-Coming-Soon-FDA-Says/. Accessed 23 January 2017.
12. Op cit 6.
13. Humanitarian Device Exemption. FDA website. http://www.fda.gov/MedicalDevices/DeviceRegulationandGuidance/HowtoMarketYourDevice/PremarketSubmissions/HumanitarianDeviceExemption/default.htm. Accessed 23 January 2017.
14. Ibid.
15. Ibid.
16. Ibid.
17. Andrews M. Laws Spreading That Allow Terminal Patients Access to Experimental Drugs. Regulatory Focus. 19 November 2014. RAPS website. http://www.raps.org/Regulatory-Focus/News/2014/11/19/20787/Laws-Spreading-That-Allow-Terminal-Patients-Access-to-Experimental-Drugs/#sthash.D7R195XV.dpuf. Accessed 23 January 2017.
18. Ibid.
19. Op cit 17.
20. Gaffney A. "Right to Try" Legislation Tracker. Regulatory Focus. 24 June 2015. RAPS website. http://www.raps.org/Regulatory-Focus/News/Databases/2015/06/24/21133/Right-to-Try-Legislation-Tracker/#sthash.oMrk6IDf.dpuf. Accessed 23 January 2017.
21. Ibid.
22. Ibid.
23. Ibid.
24. *Guidance for Industry: Expedited Programs for Serious Conditions—Drugs and Biologics.* FDA website. http://www.fda.gov/downloads/Drugs/Guidances/UCM358301.pdf. Accessed 28 January 2017.
25. New Drug Approval: FDA Needs to Enhance Its Oversight of Drugs Approved on the Basis of Surrogate Endpoints (26 October 2009). GAO website. http://www.gao.gov/products/GAO-09-866. Accessed 23 January 2017.
26. Accelerated Approval. FDA website. http://www.fda.gov/ForPatients/Approvals/Fast/ucm405447.htm. Accessed 23 January 2017.
27. Fleming TR. Surrogate Endpoints and FDA's Accelerated Approval Process. HealthAffairs website. http://content.healthaffairs.org/content/24/1/67.full. Accessed 23 January 2017.
28. Ibid.
29. Op cit 25.
30. Ibid.

**Author**

Joanne Rupprecht, Esq., RAC (US, Global) is director of legal and regulatory affairs at Aytu BioScience Inc. responsible for the domestic and international regulatory compliance of pharmaceutical products (NDAs, BLAs, INDs), federal and state licensing and international import/export requirements. Previously, she worked for Abbott Laboratories in diagnostic medical device product development, regulatory affairs and medical writing, responsible for the clearance of eight 510(k)s for Class II medical devices and involved in PMA (Class III) and BLA product regulatory matters.

# 27

# Publications

*Eileen M. Girten, MS*

Medical writers help prepare a variety of regulatory documents comprising marketing applications and also develop documents to communicate periodic clinical trial result updates throughout the product's lifecycle. Publication writers help develop a variety of documents, such as manuscripts and abstracts, used to disseminate supporting product data to peer audiences. Disseminating clinical trial results in publications serves several purposes. The scientific community uses published clinical trial results to help expand knowledge of a disease, which may lead to future treatment option innovations.[1] Clinicians and healthcare providers make treatment decisions based on published scientific evidence. The scientific and medical communities make clinical practice guideline recommendations based on the results of systematic reviews or meta-analyses.[2-4] Policy makers use publications to make policy decisions.[5-7] Lastly, publishing clinical trial results is part of Good Clinical Practice (GCP),[8] which is important for demonstrating transparency[9] and minimizes duplicative research and unnecessary risk for clinical trial participants.[10]

Before publication work begins, a sponsor typically develops a plan for how data will be shared with the larger community. Publication planning involves such considerations as determining key scientific messages, selecting appropriate congresses, medical audiences, potential target journals, the number of primary and secondary manuscripts to be published, potential publication timing, authoring team makeup for these deliverables and resources needed to execute the publication plan.[11-15] Although publication planning typically begins sometime before late product development,[16,17] recent recommendations suggest planning begin early in development and before data become available.[18-21] The International Society of Medical Publication Professionals (ISMPP) provides information on publication planning in its GPP3 guidelines for communicating company-sponsored research, forming a publication steering committee, ethical considerations and adequate publication activity documentation.[22,23] Writing typically begins with a congress meeting abstract that, if accepted, becomes an oral presentation or poster and eventually forms the basis of a manuscript (**Table 27-1**). Other publication deliverables may include book chapters and symposium papers.

Regulatory and publication writing describe the data supporting the marketing application and approved label; however, there are differences between both types of writing (**Table 27-2**). For example, regulatory documents generally involve templates based on national and regional regulations and harmonized guidances, whereas publications deliverables are based on journal or congress meeting guidelines, including audience, reporting format (e.g., original article, brief report, case study, letter to editor) and stylistic considerations. Journals and congresses often set word, table, figure and even citation limits. They also

**Table 27-1. Common Publication Deliverables**

| Publication Deliverable | |
|---|---|
| Abstracts[a] | A summary that may follow a structured format (e.g., Objective, Methods, Results, Conclusion) or unstructured format (no section headers). Congress meetings will define format, including word or character limits. Depending on the congress meeting, may include tables or figures.<br><br>Also used as a summary for a manuscript. |
| Slide Sets | Used for oral presentations, poster presentations or for published manuscripts. |
| Posters[b] | Typically follows IMRAD (Introduction, Method, Results and Discussion) format. Uses more visual elements (e.g., figures and tables) and less text to communicate information. |
| Manuscripts | Used to summarize clinical trial results or methodology. Primary manuscripts describe primary/key outcomes, whereas secondary manuscripts describe secondary outcome measures.[c] |
| Encore Submissions (Abstracts, Slides, Posters) | Some congress meetings allow for encore presentations (e.g., EU meeting for attendees unable to attend a US meeting). Same abstract, oral presentation, or poster as in original submission, except for minor edits (e.g., spelling, units). |

a.    Lang TA. How to write an abstract. In: Lang TA. How to Write, Publish, & Present in the Health Sciences. A Guide for Clinicians & Laboratory Researchers. Philadelphia, PA, USA. American College of Physicians Press; 2010:105-9.
b.    Lang TA. How to prepare and present a scientific poster. In: Lang TA. How to Write, Publish, & Present in the Health Sciences. A Guide for Clinicians & Laboratory Researchers. Philadelphia, PA, USA. American College of Physicians Press; 2010:289.
c.    Graf C, Battisti WP, Bridges D., et al. Good publication practice for communicating company sponsored medical research: the GPP2 guidelines. BMJ. 2009; 339:b4330. doi: 10.1136/bmj.b4330.

**Table 27-2. Differences Between Regulatory and Publications Writing**

| | Regulatory Writing | Publications Writing |
|---|---|---|
| Reporting Guidelines and Initiatives | • Regulations<br>• Regulatory authority/health authority guidances<br>• International Council on Harmonisation (ICH)<br>• SPIRIT checklist<br>• Transcelerate (e.g., standard protocol format) | • Journal guidelines<br>• Congress meeting guidelines<br>• Region-specific requirements (e.g., SI vs conventional units, US vs UK English spelling)<br>• International Committee of Medical Journal Editors (ICMJE) Uniform Requirements<br>• Good Publication Practice 3 (GPP3)<br>• Other reporting guidelines (e.g., CONSORT) |
| Audience | • Regulators<br>• Ethics Committees<br>• Investigators | • Clinicians<br>• Scientific community<br>• Healthcare team<br>• Policy makers<br>• Patients and general public |
| Role of Investigator | • Design clinical trials<br>• Responsible for study conduct (e.g., patient enrollment, informed consent)<br>• Interpret clinical trial results | • Author, if authorship criteria are met<br>• Contributor<br>• Peer reviewer<br>• Publication steering committee |
| Data Sources | • Case report forms<br>• Validated data outputs (tables, figures and listings (TFLs))<br>• Regulatory source documents (e.g., protocol, clinical study reports)<br>• Regulatory style guides | • Validated data outputs (TFLs)<br>• Protocols (and protocol amendments)<br>• Clinical study reports<br>• Investigator's Brochure<br>• Statistical analysis reports<br>• Literature search results<br>• Company style guides<br>• Regulatory authority/health authority guidances<br>• ICH guidances |

typically describe the publication's submission formatting requirements. For example, a journal may require figures to be submitted in TIFF file format in a certain size and minimum resolution. Unlike regulations and guidances that help maintain consistency of information included in regulatory documents, content, style and formatting guidelines vary widely across journals and congress meetings. Therefore, the writer and authoring team should familiarize themselves with the author instructions before beginning a publication deliverable.

Another distinction between regulatory and publication writing is audience. Regulatory documents typically are written for investigators, regulatory authorities and Ethics Committees,[24] whereas publication deliverables are written primarily for the scientific community, clinicians and professionals involved in patient care. In addition, publications also may be written for policy makers and the general public. Therefore, the publication steering committee and potential authoring team need to consider the audience or readership when choosing a journal or congress.

An investigator's roles and responsibilities differ for regulatory and publication activities and deliverables. On the regulatory side, an investigator must possess relevant qualifications to conduct a clinical trial and comply with GCP guidelines, ensure data are accurate and provide written reports to Ethics Committees, the sponsor and regulatory authorities.[25] Moreover, an investigator may help design a clinical trial, contribute to protocol development, enroll clinical trial subjects and interpret study results.[26] However, an investigator's product development lifecycle responsibilities do not confer automatic authorship status in a subsequent publication.[27] Journals typically require authors to meet the International Committee of Medical Journal Editors (ICMJE) criteria defining authorship.[28] For investigators who do not meet ICMJE authorship criteria, a recommended practice is to acknowledge, with their written permission, their contributions.[29,30] Therefore, it is helpful to make decisions about potential authoring teams long before publication writing begins, such as before study start.[31–33] Increasing awareness of GPP3 and ICMJE guidelines on authorship can help address misconceptions and increase transparency related to authorship decisions.[34,35] Further, investigators may do more than author a publication deliverable. For example, they also may serve on publication steering committees[36–38] or apply their expertise as publication peer reviewers.[39]

Although regulatory and publication deliverables rely on validated data outputs (tables, figures and listings (TFLs)) and some regulatory documents, other publication deliverable sources also may include prior congress meeting abstracts, related presentation and literature search results. The publications writer also will want to review company policies, standard operating procedures and related resources governing publication writing, especially before each milestone. Reviewing the company style guide, if one exists, also is helpful. In addition, the writer should consult the congress meeting or journal's instructions to authors and related policies before beginning work. Some journals and congress websites include a helpful frequently asked questions section. Reporting guidelines (e.g., CONSORT) provide guidance on suggested publication content and may be required by some journals. The EQUATOR (Enhancing the QUAlity and Transparency of health Research) Network contains more than 300 reporting guidelines for different study types and other writing resources.[40]

The quality of regulatory documents may affect subsequent publications. For example, a regulatory document lacking essential information for a manuscript's methods section may result in additional work for the publication authors. Recent regulatory document reporting guidelines have included publication-related items intended to increase disclosure quality. For example, the SPIRIT checklist,[41] a collection of recommended items to include in a protocol, and its related explanation document,[42] were developed to improve protocol quality and increase transparency. Some recommended items are consistent with ICMJE and GPP3 guidelines, such as including the clinical trial registration number, describing the clinical trial funding sources, the authorship policy, whether a medical writer will be employed to write the publication, how and when the clinical trial results will be shared and whether the protocol and related documents will be made publicly available for secondary research.[43] Another checklist, the Template for Intervention Description and Replication (TIDieR), is meant to be used with the SPIRIT 2013 and CONSORT 2010 statements when describing study methods during manuscript preparation, but also may be used during protocol development.[44]

Several laws, regulations and guidelines dedicated to increasing responsible clinical trial data disclosures and improving clinical trial transparency[45–48] are changing publication writing (**Table 27-3**). Since 2004, when ICMJE first recommended clinical trials first be registered in a publicly accessible registry, such as clinicaltrials.gov, before submitting a manuscript to a journal,[49] other considerations have arisen, such as when disclosure should occur and how sponsors would provide supporting data to journals and the scientific community. For example, some guidelines are recommending manuscripts be submitted to a peer-reviewed journal no later than a year after the trial ends, although the timeframe may take up to two years with justification.[50,51] Other recommendations

**Table 27-3. Transparency Initiatives Affecting Publications Writing**

| Transparency Policies, Guidelines and Regulations | Description | Link |
|---|---|---|
| **Declaration of Helsinki** | • Register studies with humans in a publicly available registry before study begins<br>• Publish positive and negative study results | http://www.wma.net/en/30publications/10policies/b3/ |
| **World Health Organization Statement on Public Disclosure of Clinical Trial Results** | • Register studies in a primary registry<br>• Include clinical trial registration number in publication<br>• Submit primary manuscripts within one year of study completion | http://www.who.int/ictrp/results/reporting/en/ |
| **ICMJE** | • Publish results in a journal if the clinical trial was registered in a publicly available registry before the clinical trial begins<br>• Recommend clinical trial results be posted to a clinical trial registry | http://icmje.org/recommendations/ |
| **PhRMA/efpia Principles for Responsible Clinical Trial Data Sharing** | • Publish positive and negative clinical trial results<br>• Recommend publishing all company-sponsored clinical trials or at least all Phase 3 study results | http://phrma.org/sites/default/files/pdf/PhRMAPrinciplesForResponsibleClinicalTrialDataSharing.pdf |
| **Institute of Medicine (IOM) Sharing Clinical Trial Data** | • Build data-sharing into the clinical trial design<br>• Describe publication plan (which results will be shared and methods for disseminating the results) | http://nationalacademies.org/hmd/~/media/Files/Report%20Files/2015/SharingData/CompleteRecommendations.pdf |
| **Transcelerate Common Protocol Template** | • Standard clinical trial protocol template | http://www.transceleratebiopharmainc.com/initiatives/common-protocol-template/ |

include publishing all results, including negative results, for Phase 3 clinical trials.[52] Some journals may request supporting documentation, such as the protocol, statistical analysis plan (SAP) and related data sets for verification[53] to reduce the likelihood of selective reporting,[54,55] which may become mandatory for publication. The ICMJE has sought public comment on a proposed policy that will require de-identified individual patient data to be shared within six months as a condition of publication. In addition, ICMJE also would require a data-sharing plan in the manuscript.[56] Although ICMJE explains how the data-sharing plan may be disclosed, further guidance is needed on how individual patient data will be shared responsibly. Responsible clinical trial result dissemination is an ongoing challenge industry, and professional societies will continue to discuss and attempt to find solutions.

Medical writers preparing regulatory documents should consider the publications writer. For example, they may consider whether the protocol contains recommended information consistent with the CONSORT and SPIRIT guidelines. They can work with the protocol authoring team to recommend protocol content be consistent with ICMJE and GPP3 guidelines. The CONSORT flow diagram, for example, can be difficult to construct from the information typically included in a clinical study report (CSR) following ICH E3. Therefore, a regulatory writer could consult some of the publication reporting guidelines before developing a protocol, SAP or CSR. Shared learnings are another great opportunity for both regulatory and publications writers to educate one another on what content typically is included in the documents they develop. In addition, the American Medical Writers Association (AMWA), Drug Information Association (DIA) and ISMPP offer workshops and other educational sessions for regulatory and publications writers.

Building quality into regulatory documents is not limited to medical writers. Investigators could build quality into clinical trial disclosure during protocol development by incorporating data elements disclosed in publications.[57] Familiarizing investigators with different reporting guidelines can help them design study outputs and case report forms, so results can be shared in both regulatory documents and publications.[58]

In summary, publication writing is intended to share clinical trial results responsibly with the scientific community, clinicians, policy makers and the public. Publishing clinical trial results can help advance knowledge of a therapeutic area or disease. Because some differences exist between regulatory and publication writing, publications writers need to familiarize themselves with congress meeting or journal guidelines, ICMJE, GPP3 and reporting guidelines before beginning work on the publication. Likewise, regulatory writers may benefit from familiarizing themselves with reporting guidelines and good publication practices when developing regulatory documents. Last, both types of medical writers are encouraged to attend professional development workshops and meetings (e.g., AMWA, ISMPP, DIA, RAPS) to increase their understanding of these document types and their inter-relationships.

## References

1.  Institute of Medicine (IOM). *The Clinical Trial Life Cycle and When to Share Data.* National Academy of Sciences (2015). National Academies Press website. https://www.nap.edu/read/18998/chapter/4. Accessed 24 January 2017.
2.  Recommendations for drug therapies for relapsing-remitting multiple sclerosis. Ottawa (ON): Canadian Agency for Drugs and Technologies in Health (CADTH) (2013). CADTH website. https://www.cadth.ca/media/pdf/TR0004_RRMS_RecsReport_TR_e.pdf. Accessed 24 January 2017.
3.  Garvey TW, Mechanick JI, Brett EM, et al. American association of clinical endocrinologists and American college of endocrinology comprehensive clinical practice guidelines for medical care of patients with obesity. *Endocr Pract.* 2016; 22:842–84.
4.  Levine GN, Bates ER, Bittl JA, et al. 2016 ACC/AHA guideline focused update on duration of dual antiplatelet therapy in patients with coronary artery disease: a report of the American College of Cardiology/American Heart Association Task Force on clinical practice guidelines. *J Am Coll Cardiol.* 2016;68:1082–115.
5.  Ibid.
6.  Braun LT, Grady KL, Kutner JS, et al. Palliative care and cardiovascular disease and stroke: a policy statement from the American Heart Association/American Stroke Association. *Circulation.* 2016; ahead of print, DOI: 10.1161/CIR.0000000000000438.
7.  Totten AM, Womack DM, Eden KB, et al. Telehealth: Mapping the Evidence for Patient Outcomes From Systematic Reviews [Internet]. Rockville (MD): Agency for Healthcare Research and Quality (US); 2016 Jun. (Technical Briefs, No. 26.). University of Life Sciences website. http://www-ncbi-nlm-nih-gov.db.usciences.edu/books/NBK379320/. Accessed 1 February 2017.
8.  *Guideline for Good Clinical Practice E6(R1).* ICH website. http://www.ich.org/fileadmin/Public_Web_Site/ICH_Products/Guidelines/Efficacy/E6/E6_R1_Guideline.pdf. Accessed 24 January 2017.
9.  Moorthy VS, Karam G, Vannice KS, Kieny MP. Rationale for WHO's new position calling for prompt reporting and public disclosure of interventional clinical trial results. *PLoS Med.* 2015;12: e1001819. doi: 10.1371/journal.pmed.1001819.
10. Op cit 1.
11. Graf C, Battisti WP, Bridges D., et al. Good publication practice for communicating company sponsored medical research: the GPP2 guidelines. *BMJ.* 2009; 339:b4330. doi: 10.1136/bmj.b4330.
12. Sismondo S. Ghosts in the machine: publication planning in the medical sciences. *Social Studies of Science.* 2009;39:171–98.
13. Sismondo S, Nicholson SH. Publication planning 101: a report. *J Pharm Pharmaceut Sci.* 2009;12:273–279.
14. Charles L, Reidenbach F. Publication planners and medical writers: a natural alliance. *AMWA Journal.* 2011;26:8–11.
15. DeTora L, Foster C, Skobe C, Yarker YE, Crawley FP. Publication planning: promoting an ethics of transparency and integrity in biomedical research. *Int J Clin Pract.* 2015;69:915–21.
16. Fugh-Berman A, Dodgson SJ. Ethical considerations of publication planning in the pharmaceutical industry. *Open Med.* 2008;2:E33–6.
17. D'Angelo G, Baronikova S, Scheckner B. Publication planning at one pharmaceutical company: A guidance document creation to ensure compliance with industry best practices and laws. Poster presented at: the International Society for Medical Publications Professionals; 23–25 April 2012; Baltimore, MD, USA.
18. Op cit 13.
19. Op cit 15.
20. Battisti WP, et al. Good Publication Practice for communicating company-sponsored medical research: GPP3. *Ann Intern Med.* 2015;163:461–464. App 1, Aection 1.1, p. 1, Col. 2, Para 1-2, bulleted items 2–3.
21. Chipperfield L, Citrome L, Clark J, et al. Authors' Submission Toolkit: a practical guide to getting your research published. *Curr Med Res Opin.* 2010;26:1968–1980.
22. Op cit 11.
23. Op cit 20.
24. Op cit 8.
25. Ibid.
26. IOM. *The Roles and Responsibilities of Stakeholders in the Sharing of Clinical Trial Data.* National Academy of Sciences; 2015. Available at: https://www.nap.edu/read/18998/chapter/5. Accessed 24 January 2017.
27. Op cit 21.
28. International Committee of Medical Journal Editors. Recommendations for the Conduct, Reporting, Editing, and Publication of Scholarly Work in Medical Journals. National Academies Press website. http://icmje.org/icmje-recommendations.pdf. Accessed 24 January 2017.
29. Op cit 21.
30. Op cit 28. P.3, Col. 2, Para. 2.
31. Op cit 21.
32. Camby I, Delpire V, Rouxhet L, et al. Publication practices and standards: recommendations from GSK Vaccines' author survey. *Trials.* 2014;15. BioMed Central website. http://www.trialsjournal.com/content/15/1/446. Accessed 24 January 2017.
33. Marušić A, Hren D, Mansi B, et al. Five-step authorship framework to improve transparency in disclosing contributors to industry-sponsored clinical trial publications. *BMC Medicine.* 2014;12. BioMed Central website. http://www.biomedcentral.com/1741-7015/12/197. Accessed 24 January 2017.
34. Ibid.
35. Moher D. Along with the privilege of authorship come important responsibilities. *BMC Medicine.* 2014;12:214. doi: 10.1186/s12916-014-0214-2.
36. Op cit 20.
37. Op cit 32.
38. Op cit 33.
39. Op cit 21.
40. EQUATOR Network. Enahncing the QUAlity and Transparency of health research. Available at: http://www.equator-network.org/. Accessed September 13, 2016.
41. Chan A-W; Tetzlaff JM, Altman DG, et al. SPIRIT 2013 statement: defining standard protocol items for clinical trials. *Ann Intern Med.* 2013;158:200-7.
42. Chan AW, Tetzlaff JM, Gøtzsche PC, et al. SPIRIT 2013 explanation and elaboration: guidance for protocols of clinical trials. *BMJ.* 346:e7586. doi: 10.1136/bmj.e7586.
43. Ibid.

44. Hoffman TC, Glasziou PP, Boutron I, et al. Better reporting of interventions: template for intervention description and replication (TIDieR) checklist and guide. *BMJ*. 2014;348: g1687 doi: 10.1136/bmj.g1687.

45. Pansieri C, Pandolfini C, Bonati M. The evolution in registration of clinical trials: a chronicle of the historical calls and current initiatives promoting transparency. *Eur J Clin Pharmacol*. 2015;71:1159-64.

46. Simcoe D, Juneja R, Scott GN, Sridharan K, Williams-Hughes C; ISMPP 2013 Roundtable Committee. Proceedings from the 9th annual meeting of International Society for Medical Publication Professionals roundtable session: key insights. *Curr Med Res Opin*. 2014;30:407-13.

47. Koenig F, Slattery J, Groves T, et al. Sharing clinical trial data on patient level: opportunities and challenges. *Biom J*. 2015;57:8-26.

48. Bierer BE, Li R, Barnes M, Sim I. A global, neutral platform for sharing trial data. *N Engl J Med*. 2016;374:2411-3.

49. Clinical trial registration: a statement from the International Committee of Medical Journal Editors. ICMJE website. http://www.icmje.org/news-and-editorials/clin_trial_sep2004.pdf. Accessed 24 January 2017.

50. Sharing clinical trial data. Maximizing benefits, minimizing risk. Recommendations. IOM website. http://nationalacademies.org/hmd/~/media/Files/Report%20Files/2015/SharingData/CompleteRecommendations.pdf. Accessed 24 January 2017.

51. World Health Organization. 2015 WHO statement on public disclosure of clinical trial results. WHO website. http://www.who.int/ictrp/results/WHO_Statement_results_reporting_clinical_trials.pdf?ua=1. Accessed 24 January 2017.

52. PhRMA and efpia. 2014. Principles for responsible clinical trial data sharing. Our commitment to patients and researchers. PhRMA website. http://phrma-docs.phrma.org/sites/default/files/pdf/PhRMAPrinciplesForResponsibleClinicalTrialDataSharing.pdf. Accessed 24 January 2017.

53. Op cit 50. IOM Complete recommendations. IOM. 2015c. Sharing clinical trial data. Maximizing benefits, minimizing risk. Recommendation. National Academies website. http://nationalacademies.org/hmd/~/media/Files/Report%20Files/2015/SharingData/CompleteRecommendations.pdf. Accessed 1 February 2017.

54. Op cit 42.

55. Op cit 45.

56. Taichman DB, Backus J, Baethge C, et al. Sharing clinical trial data: a proposal from the International Committee of Medical Journal Editors. *Ann Intern Med*. 2016;164:505–6.

57. Op cit 26.

58. Simera I, Altman DG. Reporting medical research. *Int J Clin Pract*. 2013;67:710–716.

## Author

Eileen M. Girten, MS, is a principal medical writer with inVentiv Health Clinical, where she writes regulatory and publications deliverables. She is an adjunct assistant professor in biomedical rriting at the University of the Sciences, where she has taught regulatory documentation processes. Girten holds an MS in psychology from Saint Joseph's University and an MS in biomedical writing from the University of the Sciences in Philadelphia.

# 28

# Literature Reviews

*By Michelle Carey, PhD*

## Introduction

A literature review summarizes and provides an assessment of a specific topic's current state-of-the-art. A well-written and researched review should provide the reader with a comprehensive overview of the topic in question. The increasing need for literature reviews stems from the ever-increasing body of scientific and clinical literature. In MEDLINE alone, the total number of citations currently is more than 22 million (up from more than13 million in 2005).[1] Given the enormous amount of biomedical literature available and the exponential rate of increase, it is impractical for readers to search for and review all the primary material. Thus, reviews are important sources of synthesized evidence on a particular topic.

While the structure and approach to writing a literature review may vary by review type, the basic purposes invariably are the same and include:

- keeping up to date with the field
- providing a basis for developing clinical practice guidelines
- justifying further research
- presenting an overview of existing research
- assessing the current state of the field
- identifying key unanswered questions or knowledge gaps
- providing a context for original research

For the researcher or clinician, reviews can be valuable time savers, as they condense a large amount of information and often provide an expert opinion.

## Review Types

There are two main literature review types: narrative (or non-systematic) and systematic. Narrative reviews are a staple of medical literature and significantly outnumber systematic reviews.[2] **Table 28-1** summarizes some of the major differences between systematic and narrative reviews. Both have distinct qualities, goals and approaches.

Narrative reviews generally are descriptive and do not list the databases searched, the methods used or the selection criteria for including or excluding articles retrieved during a database search. A narrative review can be invaluable in many instances. For example, in an historic review tracking the development of a concept or field of research, the wider scope of a narrative review may be more beneficial than the restrictive nature of a systematic review.[3] However, narrative reviews are more prone to selection bias and to an author's personal bias compared to systematic reviews.

In contrast, systematic reviews are more rigorous and involve a more-detailed, well-defined approach. The literature search time frame and the methods used to search and evaluate the findings always are specified. Systematic reviews may include a meta-analysis, which

**Table 28-1. Narrative Versus Systematic Reviews**

| | Narrative Review | Systematic Review |
|---|---|---|
| **Research Question** | Broad | Specific and well defined |
| **Approach** | Non-exhaustive | Rigorous, pre-planned |
| **Reporting Standards and Methodological Guidelines** | None | Several (e.g., PRISMA, MOOSE, AMSTAR, QUADAS-2) |
| **Search Strategy** | Not usually described | Systematic and detailed |
| **Selection Criteria** | Not usually described | Specific inclusion and exclusion criteria |
| **Limitations** | Subject to bias | Scope may be limited |

uses statistical techniques to synthesize and summarize the results of multiple studies. The Cochrane Collaboration defines a systematic review as including "a clearly formulated question that uses systematic and explicit methods to identify, select, and critically appraise relevant research, and to collect and analyze data."[4] Of note, the Cochrane Collaboration[5] produces systematic reviews of primary research in human healthcare and health policy, and is globally recognized and respected. Their methods are considered a gold standard for medical evidence; however, many other guidelines for producing systematic reviews exist.

## Reporting and Methodological Guidelines

In 1999, to address standards for improving the quality of meta-analysis reporting from clinical randomized controlled trials, an international group developed a guidance called the QUOROM Statement (QUality Of Reporting Of Meta-analyses).[6,7] The guidance was updated in 2009 to address several conceptual and practical advances in systematic review science, and was renamed PRISMA (Preferred Reporting Items of Systematic reviews and Meta-Analyses).[8] PRISMA is an evidence-based minimum set of items for reporting systematic reviews and meta-analyses[9] and pertains to reporting reviews evaluating randomized trials, but also can be used to report systematic reviews of other types, particularly interventions.[10]

The PRISMA Statement consists of a 27-item checklist and a four-phase flow diagram and is intended to be used with the PRISMA Explanation and Elaboration document, which explains the meaning and rationale for each checklist item.[11,12] The checklist is intended to guide the content of a systematic review and meta-analysis, and includes items on the title, abstract, methods, results, discussion and funding sections of a manuscript.[13] The flow diagram depicts the information flow through the different systematic review phases and maps out the number of records identified, screened, included and excluded, and the reasons for exclusions.[14] The PRISMA statement now

is required or endorsed by many editorial organizations and medical journals publishing systematic reviews.[15]

The Meta-analysis Of Observational Studies in Epidemiology (MOOSE) guidelines cover reporting on meta-analyses of observational epidemiology studies.[16] The MOOSE checklist is for authors, editors and reviewers and contains sections on each review component, including background, search strategy, methods, results, discussion and conclusion.[17]

AMSTAR was developed in 2007 and is a measurement tool for assessing systematic reviews' methodological quality and can be used as a guide to performing a systematic review.[18] It consists of an 11-item checklist, including *a priori* design, duplicate study selection and data extraction, the use of "status of publication" as an inclusion criterion, and the assessment of publication bias likelihood.[19]

The Quality Assessment tool of Diagnostic Accuracy Studies (QUADAS),[20] and the revised version QUADAS-2,[21] were developed to aid methodological assessment in diagnostic reviews. The QUADAS-2 tool was designed to evaluate the risk of bias and applicability of primary diagnostic accuracy studies.[22]

## Information Sources

Although many reviews are based only on published information in peer-reviewed journals, information sources can include the following:

- patents
- books
- abstracts, oral presentations, posters and conference proceedings
- dissertations and theses
- white papers
- grey literature
- government documents
- blogs
- websites
- other sources, such as Cochrane Collaboration reviews

**Table 28-2. Examples of Electronic Information Sources**

| Database | Description | Web Address |
|---|---|---|
| MEDLINE | The National Library of Medicine® (NLM®) journal citation database, started in the 1960s, provides more than 23 million references to biomedical and life sciences journal articles back to 1946[a] | www.nlm.nih.gov/ |
| PubMed | Journal citation database, available since 1996, comprises more than 25 million citations for biomedical literature from MEDLINE, life science journals and online books[b] | www.ncbi.nlm.nih.gov/pubmed |
| EMBASE | Journal citation database of biomedical literature from 1947 to present day, with more than 31 million indexed records and more than 8,500 indexed peer-reviewed journals[c] | www.embase.com |
| The Cochrane Library | A collection of databases containing different types of independent healthcare information:<br>• Cochrane Database of Systematic Reviews (CDSR)<br>• Cochrane Central Register of Controlled Trials (CENTRAL)<br>• Cochrane Methodology Register (CMR)<br>• Database of Abstracts of Reviews of Effects (DARE)<br>• Health Technology Assessment Database (HTA)<br>• NHS Economic Evaluation Database (EED) | www.cochranelibrary.com |
| Google Scholar | A web-based search engine for searching across many disciplines and sources: articles, theses, books, abstracts and court opinions, from academic publishers, professional societies, online repositories, universities and other websites[d] | https://scholar.google.com/ |
| CINAHL (Current Index to Nursing and Allied Health Literature) | A database of nursing and allied health literature | health.ebsco.com/products/the-cinahl-database |
| PsycINFO® | A database of psychology, behavioral and social sciences literature | www.apa.org/pubs/databases/psycinfo/index.aspx |
| Scopus | An abstract and citation database of peer-reviewed literature: scientific journals, books and conference proceedings | https://www.scopus.com/ (log in required) |

a.  *Medline®. US National Library of Medicine (2016). NLM website. https://www.nlm.nih.gov/pubs/factsheets/medline.html. Accessed 24 January 2017.*
b.  *MEDLINE, PubMed, and PMC (PubMed Central): How are they different? US National Library of Medicine. (2014). NLM website. https://www.nlm.nih.gov/pubs/factsheets/dif_med_pub.html. Accessed 24 January 2017.*
c.  *Embase® Fact Sheet. Elsevier. (2016) Elsevier website. .https://www.elsevier.com/__data/assets/pdf_file/0016/59011/R_D_Solutions_Embase_Fact_Sheet-Web.pdf. Accessed 24 January 2017.*
d.  *About Google Scholar. Google Scholar (2016). Google website. https://scholar.google.com/intl/en/scholar/about.html. Accessed 24 January 2017.*

Journals are the most common information source. Databases are used to search for relevant journal articles; examples of the most common databases and search engines are given in **Table 28-2**.

Some research fields categorize literature sources as primary, secondary or tertiary. Primary sources refer to original work published primarily in peer-reviewed journals. Secondary sources rely on primary sources for information, e.g., review articles, textbooks. Tertiary sources rely on primary or secondary sources, e.g., dictionaries, encyclopedias or Wikipedia. Another category, known as "grey literature," refers to sources of information not published or distributed like the above categories. Examples of grey literature include dissertations or theses, white papers, conference proceedings, government documents and oral presentations. The most widely accepted definition is the "Luxembourg definition," which defines grey literature as "that which is produced on all levels of government, academics, business and industry in print and electronic formats, but which is not controlled by commercial publishers."[23] Grey literature can be an important source of information for review articles; however, acceptance of its inclusion in systematic reviews has varied.[24]

## Search Strategies

Databases can be searched using a controlled vocabulary or text words (keywords). Controlled vocabulary is used to establish common search terms or keywords, thereby ensuring a consistent way of retrieving information that may use different terminology for the same concept.[25]The controlled vocabulary or preferred list of search terms for the National Library of Medicine is called Medical Subject Headings (MeSH) terms. NLM has a MeSH browser and an online vocabulary look-up aid available for use with MeSH®. It is designed to help locate descriptors of possible interest quickly and show the hierarchy in which descriptors of interest appear.[26] Similar to NLM, Elsevier has its own list of subject headings for EMBASE called EMTREE.[27] EMTREE and MeSH have similar structures; both include broader and narrower terms and synonyms, but the search terms and indexing approach are not identical.[28]

Free-text, or keyword searching is less precise than controlled vocabulary searching; it will retrieve a greater number of hits, but they likely will be much less relevant. In addition, free-text searches retrieve the term in any record field. Although less precise than controlled vocabulary searching, free-text searching can present some advantages. For example, keyword searching may be useful for searches involving new concepts or terminology, since indexing terms can take many years to evolve.

Some databases allow truncation and wild card searches. This can be an effective method of finding plurals or variants of terms. For example, in PubMed, to search for all terms beginning with a word or part of a word, an asterisk (*) can be used as a wildcard character to retrieve all variants.[29] Another search technique is to combine search terms with Boolean operators (AND, OR, NOT). "AND" retrieves results that include all the search terms, "OR" retrieves results that include at least one of the search terms and "NOT" excludes terms from a search.[30] Some databases allow quotation marks to be used to restrict a search to an exact phrase. Most databases have online help sections with specific instructions for different search types.

An additional approach to supplement a search strategy is "hand searching." This involves searching bibliographies of retrieved articles to identify any additional useful articles that may have used other search strategies. Another supplementary search strategy is to search a citation index, which is a bibliographic index that allows searches for articles that cite a specific article. Citation index examples include Web of Science[31] and Scopus.[32] Google offers Google Scholar Citations, which also provide a simple way to search for article citations.[33]

Finally, when preparing any type of literature review, it is important to document the precise search strategy. The following items are important to include and consider:

- description of the research question or problem
- source names, e.g., electronic databases, grey literature
- dates on which the search was conducted and the time range searched
- any limits or filters, e.g., article type, publication dates, species, ages, languages
- keywords or subject headings, search terms and how they were combined (AND/OR)
- limits and filters
- inclusion and exclusion criteria
- number of hits

**References**

1. Detailed Indexing Statistics: 196 (2015). US National Library of Medicine website. https://www.nlm.nih.gov/bsd/index_stats_comp.html. Accessed 24 January 2017.
2. Bastian H, Glasziou P, Chalmers I. Seventy-five trials and eleven systematic reviews a day: how will we ever keep up? PLoS Med 2010; 7:e1000326.
3. Ferrari R. Writing narrative style literature reviews. *Medical Writing* (2015); 24:230-235.
4. What is a Systematic Review? (2016). Cochrane United States website. http://us.cochrane.org/frequently-asked-questions. Accessed 24 January 2017.
5. The Cochrane Collaboration. Cochrane United States website. http://us.cochrane.org/cochrane-collaboration. Accessed 24 January 2017.
6. Moher D, Cook DJ, Eastwood S, Olkin I, Rennie D, Stroup DF. Improving the quality of reports of meta-analyses of randomised controlled trials: the QUOROM statement. Quality of Reporting of Meta-analyses. Lancet 1999; 354:1896-1900.
7. History & Development of PRISMA (2015). PRISMA website. http://www.prisma-statement.org/PRISMAStatement/HistoryAndDevelopment.aspx. Accessed 24 January 2017.
8. Ibid.
9. Welcome to the Preferred Reporting Items for Systematic Reviews and Meta-Analyses (PRISMA) website! PRISMA website. http://www.prisma-statement.org/Default.aspx. Accessed 24 January 2017.
10. Ibid.
11. Who Should Use PRISMA? (2015). PRISMA website. http://www.prisma-statement.org/PRISMAStatement/PRISMAStatement.aspx. Accessed 24 January 2017.
12. Liberati A, Altman DG, Tetzlaff J et al. The PRISMA statement for reporting systematic reviews and meta-analyses of studies that evaluate health care interventions: explanation and elaboration. PLoS Med 2009; 6:e1000100.
13. Ibid.
14. Ibid.
15. PRISMA Endorsers. PRISMA website. http://www.prisma-statement.org/Endorsement/PRISMAEndorsers.aspx. Accessed 24 January 2017.
16. Stroup DF, Berlin JA, Morton SC et al. Meta-analysis of observational studies in epidemiology: a proposal for reporting. Meta-analysis Of Observational Studies in Epidemiology (MOOSE) group. *JAMA* 2000; 283:2008-2012.
17. Ibid.
18. Shea BJ, Grimshaw JM, Wells GA et al. Development of AMSTAR: a measurement tool to assess the methodological quality of systematic reviews. *BMC Med Res Methodol* 2007; 7:10.
19. Ibid.
20. Whiting P, Rutjes AW, Reitsma JB, Bossuyt PM, Kleijnen J. The development of QUADAS: a tool for the quality assessment of studies of diagnostic accuracy included in systematic reviews. *BMC Med Res Methodol* 2003; 3:25.

21. Whiting PF, Rutjes AW, Westwood ME et al. QUADAS-2: a revised tool for the quality assessment of diagnostic accuracy studies. *Ann Intern Med* 2011; 155:529–536.

22. Ibid.

23. Farace DJ and Frantzen J. Sixth international conference on grey literature: work on grey in progress. grey literature 2004 conference proceedings. 2005.

24. Saleh AA, Ratajeski MA, Bertolet M. Grey Literature Searching for Health Sciences Systematic Reviews: A Prospective Study of Time Spent and Resources Utilized. *Evid Based Libr Inf Pract* 2014; 9:28–50.

25. Bolderston A. Writing an Effective Literature Review. *J Med Imaging Radiat Sci* 2008; 39:8–92.

26. MeSH Browser Overview. NLM website. https://www.nlm.nih.gov/mesh/mbinfo.html. Accessed 24 January 2017.

27. EMBASE 103: Searching Using EMTREE. Elsevier website. http://supportcontent.elsevier.com/Support%20Hub/Embase/Files%20&%20Attachements/5415-Embase%20E103%20-%20Searching%20with%20Emtree%20-%20March%202015.pdf. Accessed 24 January 2017.

28. Comparison of Emtree® and MeSH®. Elsevier website. http://supportcontent.elsevier.com/Support%20Hub/Embase/Files%20&%20Attachements/4685-Embase_White%20Paper_Comparison%20of%20Emtree%20and%20MeSH_July%202015.pdf. Accessed 24 January 2017.

29. PubMed Help: Truncating search terms (2016). NCBI website. http://www.ncbi.nlm.nih.gov/books/NBK3827/#pubmedhelp.Truncating_search_terms. Accessed 24 January 2017.

23. PubMed Help: Combining search terms with Boolean operators (AND, OR, NOT) (2016). NCBI website. http://www.ncbi.nlm.nih.gov/books/NBK3827/#pubmedhelp.Combining_search_terms_with_B. Accessed 24 January 2017.

24. Web of Science (2016). Thomson Reuters website. http://ipscience.thomsonreuters.com/product/web-of-science/?utm_source=false&utm_medium=false&utm_campaign=false. Accessed 24 January 2017.

25. Scopus (2016). Elsevier website. https://www.elsevier.com/solutions/scopus. Accessed 24 January 2017.

26. Google Scholar Citations (2016). https://scholar.google.com/citations?view_op=new_profile&hl=en.

27. MEDLINE®. NLM website. https://www.nlm.nih.gov/pubs/factsheets/medline.html. Accessed 13 September 2016. Accessed 31 January 2017.

28. MEDLINE, PubMed, and PMC (PubMed Central): How are they different? NLM website. https://www.nlm.nih.gov/pubs/factsheets/dif_med_pub.html . Accessed January 2017..

29. Embase(R) Fact Sheet. Elsevier website. https://www.elsevier.com/__data/assets/pdf_file/0016/59011/R_D_Solutions_Embase_Fact_Sheet-Web.pdf. Accessed 31 January 2017.

30. Stand on the shoulders of giants. About Google Scholar. Google Scholar website. https://scholar.google.com/intl/en/scholar/about.html. Accessed 31 January 2017.

**Author**

Michelle Carey, PhD, is principal medical writer at inVentiv Health Clinical with more than 10 years industry experience, primarily in commercialization and publications documents. She has a background in biomedical research and spent more than 10 years working in academia in the fields of pharmacology, toxicology, immunology and pulmonology. She holds a PhD in pharmacology from University College Cork, Ireland.

# Index

Major discussions are indicated by page numbers in **bold** typeface. Figures, tables, and boxes are indicated by "f," "t" or "b" appended to the locator. Numbers are alphabetized as if spelled out.

Only laws, regulations or guidance documents explicitly discussed in the text are included in the index. Only the topic of tables, not the individual entries within the table, are included in the index.